Virginia's American Revolution

Virginia's American Revolution

From Dominion to Republic, 1776–1840

Kevin R. C. Gutzman

LEXINGTON BOOKS

A division of
ROWMAN & LITTLEFIELD PUBLISHERS, INC.
Lanham • Boulder • New York • Toronto • Plymouth, UK

LEXINGTON BOOKS

A division of Rowman & Littlefield Publishers, Inc.
A wholly owned subsidiary of The Rowman & Littlefield Publishing Group, Inc.
4501 Forbes Boulevard, Suite 200
Lanham, MD 20706

Estover Road
Plymouth PL6 7PY
United Kingdom

Copyright © 2007 by Lexington Books
First paperback edition 2007

All rights reserved. No part of this publication may be reproduced, stored in a retrieval system, or transmitted in any form or by any means, electronic, mechanical, photocopying, recording, or otherwise, without the prior permission of the publisher.

British Library Cataloguing in Publication Information Available

Library of Congress Cataloging-in-Publication Data

Gutzman, Kevin Raeder, 1963–
  Virginia's American Revolution : from dominion to republic, 1776–1840 / Kevin R.C. Gutzman.
    p. cm.
  ISBN-13: 978-0-7391-2131-3 (cloth : alk. paper)
  ISBN-10: 0-7391-2131-6 (cloth : alk. paper)
  ISBN-13: 978-0-7391-2132-0 (pbk. : alk. paper)
  ISBN-10: 0-7391-2132-4 (pbk. : alk. paper)
  1. Virginia—Politics and government—1775–1865. 2. Virginia—History—Revolution, 1775–1783. 3. Virginia—History—1775–1865. 4. Republicanism—Virginia—History—18th century. 5. Republicanism—Virginia—History—19th century. 6. State rights—History—19th century. 7. Republicanism—United States—History—18th century. 8. Republicanism—United States—History—19th century. I. Title.
  F230.G95 2007
  975.5'03—dc22
                                      2007024351

Printed in the United States of America

♾™ The paper used in this publication meets the minimum requirements of American National Standard for Information Sciences—Permanence of Paper for Printed Library Materials, ANSI/NISO Z39.48–1992.

*To Trianna, because there is no love like the first,
to Marika, whose smile could melt a glacier,
and to Cyril, the boy I always hoped for*

Contents

Preface ix
Acknowledgments xi

Introduction 1
1 Establishing a Republic 7
2 Implementing the Revolution, 1776–1788 45
3 The Virginia Ratification Convention of 1788 83
4 Defending Virginia's Revolution against the Federalists 113
5 "May All Your Dreams Come True" 135
6 "Like Dust and Ashes" 163
Conclusion: The Road from Southampton 207

Bibliography 209
Index 227
About the Author 235

PREFACE

My intention was to write a dissertation on John C. Calhoun. When I asked Peter Onuf, the Jefferson Professor at UVA, in the fall of 1992 where I might look for a master's thesis topic that would put Calhoun into perspective, he suggested that I take up the question of James Madison and the "Principles of '98." No one, he said, had thought much about Madison's role in formulating them.

I was hooked.

Research into the Principles of '98 soon had me interested in contextualizing them. What I discovered was that just as Calhoun's theory of nullification could not be understood apart from James Madison and 1798, so Madison's, and his fellow Virginians', position on their Old Dominion's place in the Union, on the relationship between their state and the federal government, had to be contextualized. This pushed me back to 1776 and beyond.

What you have in hand, then, is a study plumbing the nature of Virginians' understanding of "Virginia" in the early decades of republican self-government in America. The constitutional issues that led me to this topic run through the book, but that is not the only thing you will find in it. Instead, it considers all of the major social, political, economic, and racial questions that faced the Virginia revolutionaries as they established their independence beginning in May 1776.

Oddly, while there have been state-level studies of numerous other states during this period, historians interested in the most significant of states have tended to focus on Virginia's leading figures—Washington, Jefferson, Marshall, Madison—or on the causes they favored. Thus, for example, one relatively recent book takes the desirability of Jefferson's favorite state constitutional reform ideas as given, then chronicles Virginia's halting steps toward adopting them in the period 1776–1850.

My intention here was to do something different. When I got around to devising a dissertation topic, I told Onuf that I wanted to write about Virginia, but I did not think the world needed another Madison or Jefferson biography. Instead, I said, I wanted to consider Virginia from the state level, because my understanding of the politics (broadly understood) of the period was that state identity dominated people's consciousness in a way barely conceivable now.

The distinction between a great man-centered approach and the one I have taken is obvious in chapter 3, The Virginia Ratification Convention of 1788. The Richmond Convention met to consider whether Virginia should adopt the proposed federal constitution as its own, and accounts of that event typically start with Madison's role in writing the document, follow him through the Convention as he explains the document, and join him in celebrating the unconditional ratification of the document. As one historian put it, reading Madison's correspondence is a good entrée to the process, and one should not be surprised if Madison's understanding of things dominates the received wisdom.

My chapter takes matters up from a different angle: not what the Richmond Ratification Convention meant for the Union but what it meant for Virginia. In reading the record of the debates and the associated correspondence and publications (in newspapers, pamphlets, etc.), I saw that the chief theme of the discussion was not the kind of America ratification would make but what effect ratification would have on Virginia. In the course of the dispute, each side laid out its distinctive vision of what Virginia was (politically, economically, socially, religiously, in federal affairs, and so on) and what it might become (with a new federal constitution or without).

This same approach to things guided me through the whole era of the Revolution, through the life of the whole Founding generation. I am satisfied that it proved very fruitful.

ACKNOWLEDGMENTS

When I decided many, many moons ago that I would prefer to quit law and enter academia, I had only the vaguest idea of what this project would become. It would have been impossible to complete the task without the help of many people, some of whom I likely have forgotten along the way. To anyone who sees a debt unremarked here, please know that your omission is unintentional.

First, I must thank my parents for inculcating a love of books in me from the earliest point. Their support through thick and thin also got me through the tough times; no one could ask for more than that.

My honors government/economics teacher at Belton, Texas, High School, Wayne Carpenter, inspired a fascination with *The Federalist*, and politics generally, in me. This book is a long way from debating whether Reagan, Carter, or Anderson was best for the country—or is it?

To my teachers at the University of Texas, where I learned to love books and to agree with Sallust that an intellectual monument is far preferable to wealth or fame, thank you. Foremost among them must be George Forgie, whom I joined literally thousands of other Longhorns in judging the best teacher in Austin's megaversity and who took time to serve first as my undergraduate history mentor, then as author of innumerable letters of recommendation over the years.

An example of intellectual rectitude, of downright courage, was given me by Professor Lino Graglia of the University of Texas School of Law. Tenure is supposed to empower academics to speak truth to power, but few, alas, are willing to sacrifice as Lino has done in the name of truth. To top it off, he is usually right.

At the University of Virginia I encountered a remarkable cohort of fellow students, among whom Richard Samuelson, James Guba, Bob Guffin, Jack Morton, Matt Lassiter, and Marshall Shaw were by turns friends, interlocutors, and fellow sufferers. The faculty of the Corcoran Department of History went the extra mile on many occasions in support of my teaching apprenticeship and my scholarly endeavors, and I thank them—particularly Ed Ayers and Elizabeth Meyer—for it. Most importantly, of course, my dissertation advisor, Peter S. Onuf, put up with (or should I say "enjoyed"?) my cock-sure attitude at the commencement of our relationship and helped me on numerous occasions as I learned my way around a historian's task.

Numerous scholars at other schools have also encouraged me in this project. Among them are Lee Cheek, Clyde Wilson, Elizabeth Fox-Genovese, Don Livingston, R. Kent Newmyer, Forrest McDonald, and Tom Woods.

Several institutions supported me in graduate education and in producing the dissertation on which this manuscript is a substantial improvement. I thank the Institute for Humane Studies, the Intercollegiate Studies Institute, the International Center for Jefferson Studies, the Virginia Historical Society, and the University of Virginia for their financial and other support. Thank you, too, to the Heritage Foundation and the Liberty Fund for providing conferences at which many of the ideas in this study were fleshed out.

Thank you to *The Journal of Southern History* for permission to use the article that has now been reshaped into chapter 4.

Thank you, too, to Lance, Kathy, and their little guys for their encouragement and support. Similar thanks to numerous other friends in Connecticut.

Finally, and most importantly, I thank the three little people named in the dedication. Trianna and Marika were two and a half and not yet one, respectively, when I received my Ph.D., and Cyril was, as the saying goes, not yet a gleam in my eye; now they are ten, eight, and six. We have had some good and some hard times since then, but they have been my greatest encouragement. They will, I am sure, be happy to see that Daddy's book is finally done. Only when they are a bit older, I think, will they appreciate the dedication's full meaning.

INTRODUCTION

Virginia's revolutionary May Convention adopted its three resolutions of May 15, 1776. In doing so, it decided to craft a declaration of rights, a republican constitution, federal relations with other former British colonies in the New World, and foreign alliances for the fledgling Virginia republic. It did more than that, however: it also touched off a decades-long dispute about the meaning of republican self-government, about the shape the Virginians' new republic would take. On the mid-May day that it ran up a continental union flag atop the old colonial capitol at Williamsburg, James Madison said Virginia staked its claim to self-government. What proved more difficult was deciding what self-government would mean.

The American Revolution proceeded simultaneously on two levels: the state and the federal. The federal Constitution ratified in 1788 provided an international context in which the sparsely populated, weak new states could conduct the experiment in republicanism the Revolution was meant to inaugurate,[1] and the founding of the federal republic has naturally drawn the bulk of historians' attention. While federal reform was essential, and while Virginians took the lead in achieving it, the state-level activity of those years struck contemporaries as more important. As Thomas Jefferson noted in 1776, independence would have been for naught without success in state-level reforms of government and society.[2]

This study follows the Virginia revolutionaries through their revolutionary reforms from the beginning on May 15, 1776, with the adoption of the independence resolutions through the end of the Old Dominion's national political preeminence around 1830. In the Revolution's early days, a kind of euphoria swept the staid Virginia ruling elite. A new day, it seemed, had dawned. Within a federal context that left control of almost all internal matters to them, Virginians would argue about the contours of their new society and remake it along largely republican lines. This was the main activity of their revolution. By the story's end, to their surprise, virtually all of Virginia's republican leaders were disappointed with the postrevolutionary state of Virginia (to coin a phrase). The tale, oddly, has seldom been told.

Many old revolutionaries were disappointed that the old elite did not dominate the newly republican Old Dominion as it had the colonial one. This class-based disappointment was heightened by the old elite's discontentment with a new, less polished cohort's performance in office. Among other results, their unhappiness with unanticipated changes in their state's political culture and decline in their economic situation led the East's aristocratic leaders to shut the growing West out of political power, to treat western Virginia as a subordinate society—a colony. Ultimately, the East's attitude fostered a reciprocal sectionalism, a separate West Virginia consciousness. Analogous developments on the federal level would have even severer results.

Virginia's self-centeredness had extremely significant consequences, and its effects in the era of the Old Dominion's unchallenged dominance deserve to be chronicled. Colonial Virginia pamphleteer Richard Bland and his most illustrious acolyte, Thomas Jefferson, understood Virginia to be America. When they discussed colonial history in the documents at the center of chapter 1's discussion, the story they recounted was actually Virginia's. (It had little in common with, for example, Massachusetts's.) When Jefferson became president in 1801, he imagined—as other Virginia Republicans imagined—all Americans sharing a common understanding (the peculiar Virginian understanding) of the Revolutionary inheritance, including the United States Constitution. The question whether other states might have different traditions, valid alternative understandings, seldom occurred to them—seems never to have occurred to Jefferson. To be American was to be Republican, to be Republican was to understand things (for better or for worse) Virginia Republicans' way. When Jefferson said, hopefully, "We are all republicans, we are all federalists. We have called by different names, brethren of the same principle," he revealed not that he was simple-minded or that he had a Pollyanna hopefulness concerning human nature (and the likelihood that party contention would simply wither away) but that his horizons were limited.

Thus, when this study refers to Virginians' understanding of their revolution, when it says that they expected certain things for their new republic, it does not do so in order to slight other states or to insist on an imaginary homogeneity of the states. Rather, the point is that Virginians believed that other Americans agreed with them perforce, that all good men and true were (Virginia) Republicans, that this was the Revolution's promise.

Once they had adopted their declaration of rights and constitution in June 1776, republican Virginia's founders set out on a reforming career that changed the world. In the long decade 1776–1788, their new independence (for nearly all purposes) forced Virginians to adopt a number of monumental alterations to their legal, constitutional, and social structures. However, various factors combined to draw a large number of more plebeian men into the Virginia political system in the 1770s and 1780s, and the measures they adopted—especially in the economic field—gave rise to growing discontent among members of the old ruling class. One of the disgruntled, James Madison, hit upon a strategy calculated in part to undercut the power of the new republicans and their political leader, Patrick Henry: he would convene a sizable group of eminent men from all the colonies to adopt a new federal constitution. As he explained in *The Federalist* #10, Madison hoped that this constitution would be administered by a more select group of men than ran the state governments and thus would adopt more "continentally minded" policies. He and others succeeded in 1788 in securing ratification of the new federal Constitution they had taken the lead in drafting and defending, but only after Virginian opponents of this Constitution mounted the most persuasive of all state campaigns against it. Because of the strength of Virginian opposition, Virginia Federalists secured ratification only by promising Virginia's ratification convention that the new Constitution would have left Virginia's sovereignty essentially untouched. This momentous, though limited, accomplishment is chronicled in chapters 2 and 3.

Within months of the new federal government's inception, Virginia's political elite was almost unanimously displeased by the nationalizing program of the Washington Administration, which struck directly at Virginians' cherished control over their state's internal polity. Chapter 4 describes Virginia Republicans' ultimate response to the Federalist era in federal politics: the Virginia and Kentucky Resolutions. While these documents struck leading figures in other states as the height of particularist folly and constitutional sophistry, from the point of view of Virginians familiar with the vows made by Virginia Federalists in 1788, these touchstones of future state and southern sectionalism were merely "an appeal to the *real laws* of our country."[3] As at other points, so at this one, leading Virginians of the 1790s believed their opponents to be wrong-headed, dupes, or worse. Any honest patriot would agree with the Virginia Republicans.

Republicans, as most politically active Virginians called themselves, persuaded themselves in the 1790s that all would be well if only their man, Thomas Jefferson, were elected president, because a Jefferson administration would respect the rights of the states to rule themselves in all but a few specified areas; it would respect the federal government's limited role as guarantor of peace among the states and between America and foreign countries.[4] The final two chapters describe the growing unease with the Revolution's legacy among Virginia Republicans, including even Madison and Jefferson himself, in the first third of the nineteenth century. Seemingly, what Virginians had gained had come at a price. For example, John Tyler, Sr., and Jefferson agreed that the abolition of feudal land tenures chronicled in chapter 1 had left the Old Dominion bereft of a class of men fit to rule it. Republicanism was of no avail without such a class, they agreed, and Jefferson and Tyler's proposed solution, establishment of a three-tiered system of public schools, divided Republicans among themselves. Governor Tyler, in a melancholy missive to Jefferson, wondered whether the Revolution they had made had been worthwhile. Virginians perhaps had been more capable of governing themselves before they seized the prerogative.

The story here, then, cuts against the grain of traditional interpretations of the Revolution and Jeffersonian America. Central to it is the old reality of American political life that the state was the primary unit of political allegiance, the chief locus of political identity, and the level at which most significant political questions were decided in the Early Republic. It should be unsurprising that in the absence of television, radio, news magazines, national newspapers, air travel, interstate highways, the Internet, and even cheap postal service, and in a day when very few people went away to college, it was uncommon for anyone to "think continentally." When Virginians argued about what a republic should be, then, their concern was almost never some Platonic ideal republic, nor even the United States, but their own Old Dominion. The context of this dispute might be an American federation, but it was an American federation they understood as intended to be administered in a thoroughly Virginian way. The Virginians of Jefferson's day had very high hopes, and a good many of them had faith in legal and political reform as the solution to almost any social ill. There is a certain poignancy in the fact that by 1830 most had decided that America's—Virginia's—besetting problems were simply intractable.

The relative novelty of this approach to Virginia's history explains some of the unexpected omissions from the tale that follows. For example, George Washington and John Marshall, two of the most significant Virginians of the era, make fleeting appearances in this account. Instead of these epochal figures, the reader will encounter state-level politicians and intellectuals now far more obscure, such as Thomas Ritchie, William Branch Giles, John Tyler, Sr., George Nicholas, Francis Walker Gilmer, Spencer Roane, and the slightly more familiar John Taylor of Caroline and John Randolph of Roanoke.

This is a story whose repercussions radiated out beyond Virginia in the Early Republic and continue to be felt by all Americans even in our own day. Their state's decline in wealth and status led the East's ruling class into an increasingly defensive posture, both in federal politics and within the state. They opposed the American System of Henry Clay, and all similar proposals for an active federal government, and they defeated all hopes for an intrastate accommodation with the West Virginians from this defensive posture. The mode of constitutional interpretation concocted in Virginia in the days of the Imperial Crisis and Revolution, the accommodation between racial subordination and Lockean social compact theory chosen by the May Convention of 1776, the optimism about the potential of government-funded education and church-state separation that marked those days, the division over the relative attractions of republican and democratic government, and a number of other attitudes and postulates developed by Virginia's first republican leaders affected American politics and society markedly through the nineteenth century. Many are felt even now. If no one today would speak of "America" when he meant Virginia, in some sense, all Americans today really are Virginians—for better and for worse.

NOTES

1. David C. Hendrickson, *Peace Pact: The Lost World of the American Founding* (Lawrence: University Press of Kansas, 2003).
2. Jefferson, pining to leave Congress and return to Virginia to help draft the 1776 constitution, called the new state constitution "the whole object of the present controversy." As he explained the situation, "should a bad government be instituted for us in future it had been as well to have accepted the bad one offered to us from beyond the water without the risk and expense of contest." Thomas Jefferson to Thomas Nelson, 16 May 1776, *The Papers of Thomas Jefferson*, ed. Julian P. Boyd et al. (Princeton: Princeton University Press, 1950), 1: 292–93. He had to content himself, in the end, with writing the first draft of the Declaration of American Independence instead.
3. This characterization of them was offered by George Nicholas, whose "Antifederalist" explanation of ratification's significance had provided the margin of Federalist victory in 1788. For Nicholas in 1788, see Kevin R. C. Gutzman, "Edmund Randolph and Virginia Constitutionalism," *The Review of Politics* 66 (2004), 469–97.
4. David C. Hendrickson, *Peace Pact*.

1

ESTABLISHING A REPUBLIC

Adoption of the Virginia Constitution of 1776, the first of the world's written constitutions, was understood at the time and for decades thereafter to mark the moment of Virginia's independence.[1] The constitution itself, including its declaration of rights and preamble, marked the culmination of the preceding tradition—the colonial Virginia tradition—and the point of departure for Virginia's newly republican polity. In writing it, the members of Virginia's revolutionary May Convention of 1776 made several important ideological commitments on behalf of their compatriots. Rather than accept Parliament's claim to absolute control over Virginia, Virginia's indigenous elite opted to implement a constitution enshrining its own long-standing claims to self-determination. Complete self-government came to Virginia in precisely the form on which elite Virginians had insisted throughout the Imperial Crisis that began in the 1760s.

The May Convention both broke the tie that bound Virginia to Great Britain and established a new regime on the wreckage of the old one. The May Convention's work reinforced the powers of the state's "cousinocracy" in several significant ways. Most importantly, under the terms of the new Virginia constitution, the former colony's government would be dominated by the lower house of the General Assembly. Newly renamed the House of Delegates, it would have all of the power it had insisted on in its contests with the English and British kings' governors. The county courts, which concentrated the executive, legislative, and judicial powers of local government in the hands of county oligarchs, were entirely unreformed, despite the republican rhetoric surrounding the Revolution. Finally, the property qualification for voting remained in effect, insuring that half of white men in the Old Dominion would remain voteless. When coupled with the perpetuation of *viva voce* voting, this provision helped to insure the continuation of oligarchy in Virginia for decades to come. At least, that seems to have been what the assembled aristocracy of Britain's greatest former colony expected.

Yet, retaining the reins of power in their own hands was not the sole goal of the Virginia revolutionary elite. As a ruling class, it had become accustomed to seeing Virginia as its own collective enterprise. Since its members were men of the Whig tradition, they understood Virginia as a Whig society. Because theirs was the largest, most populous, wealthiest colony in British North America, they believed that their example would be copied by leading figures in other colonies. These conceptions helped to shape their behavior during the American Revolution.

From his seat in the Continental Congress at Philadelphia, Virginia's Richard Henry Lee wrote to his friend and political ally, Patrick Henry. Urging him to the utmost exertion, Lee told Henry that Virginia's Convention would shape the fate of "ages yet unborn."[2] Other Virginians shared this sense. The May Convention's work markedly stoked the fires of the American War for Independence. It was also a legal and philosophical milestone. Other colonies had drafted temporary ordinances to guide government until the row with the mother country ended, but Virginia's Constitution of 1776 was the first permanent constitution framed by the people's representatives in world history.[3] According to Thomas Jefferson, that constitution made Virginians "the first of the nations of the earth, which assembled its wise men peaceably together to form a fundamental constitution, to commit it to writing, and place it among their archives, where every one should be free to appeal to its text."[4]

Throughout the Imperial Crisis of the 1760s, Virginians had insisted on what they understood to be their colony's traditional place within the empire. The constitution's drafters understood themselves to be adhering to inherited ways, to "the constitution as it developed historically." In allowing George Mason of Gunston Hall primarily to compose it, they placed their reliance on a man avowedly committed to Virginia as a culturally British society.[5] In his draft constitution, he clearly captured the mood of revolutionary Virginia.[6]

As Virginia constitutional propagandist Richard Bland put it, he and his contemporaries were determined "to enjoy the Freedom, and other Benefits of the *British* Constitution, to the latest Page in History!" Unsurprisingly, therefore, the Virginia Constitution of 1776 emerged as a profoundly backward-looking document. Elite Virginians' motivations for revolution were mainly political at this stage. The document they drafted reflected this fact. Like the Glorious Revolution of 1688, Virginians' Revolution was glorious as much for what it left unchanged as for what it altered.[7]

Because it marked the beginning of Virginia's republican era, the Convention's 15 May 1776 declaration that it would write a new constitution and declaration of rights, as well as instruct its delegates to Congress to declare independence, seek foreign alliances, and confederate with the other newly independent colonies, constituted a de facto declaration of independence. That is how the members of the Convention understood the matter. As H. A. Washington, in a filiopietistic mode typical of the nineteenth century, put it, "By one and the same act of sublime valor and wisdom, did the men of '76 declare the ancient connection which had bound the Colony of Virginia to the mother country dissolved forever, and frame for themselves and their posterity an instrument of government."[8]

If the Virginia revolutionaries of 1776 were men of the dispensation of 1688, the "Glorious Revolution,"[9] they were also British patriots, especially since the French and Indian War. Those two events had left Virginians' political thought with three important strands: Virginians thought of theirs as the *most British* place in all of the king's dominions; they insisted on what they called their inherited rights; and they conceived of their rights as tied to those of the rest of "British America," from Georgia to Canada.

Unlike those of some other colonies, Virginia's population remained mostly of British extraction in 1776, and its elite (unlike its general population) remained predominantly Anglican. From the days of Charles II, the court had feared New England's republicanism, but Virginia always seemed loyal. Because it had been settled by orthodox Anglicans, and because of its abundant fertile soil, Virginia remained English in a way that a Congregationalist, seafaring colony such as Massachusetts could not. Virginia's leading men were proud of their mother country, and Britain's prestige in Virginia loomed large.[10] Thomas Jefferson noted that revolutionary Virginians' was the most British of aims, saying, "the purpose of opposing British imperial legislation was to rescue traditional British rights from the attacks undertaken by an omnipotent, and therefore revolutionary Parliament."[11] Their very insistence on their Britishness led Virginians to independence. The length of time involved in coming to the decision to assert that independence was precisely the time required for members of the Virginia gentry to recognize that the mother country intended to reduce them to an inferior status by depriving their colony of self-government.[12]

Even then, this was not a decision that leading Virginians made easily. Virginia's public life appeared tranquil in the mid-eighteenth century because it lacked "the disruptive forces—sectional hostility, religious conflict, factional strife, institutional rivalry between executive and legislature—that disturbed other colonies." Unlike other colonial elites, Virginia's traditionally conceded governors' rightful power. In fact, Virginia's loyalty—it recognized Charles II as its king, and thus the restoration of the monarchy, a year before his other dominions—led Charles II to call it the "Old Dominion." Virginians considered the title "Old Dominion" a badge of honor.[13]

Virginians in 1763, at the start of the Imperial Crisis, rested content with their colony's political system and its fortunate connection to Great Britain. Young Thomas Jefferson, on his first day in the House of Burgesses, drafted a resolution for presentation to Governor Lord Botetourt in which he characterized

Virginia's and Great Britain's interests as "inseparably the same." Five years later, in 1774, he justified Virginia's stance toward Parliament by reference to ongoing loyalty to the British Crown. Even in February of 1776, Edmund Pendleton, President of the Committee of Safety, still called the rift in the British Empire "this unnatural wound." Carter Braxton, a Virginian member of the Continental Congress, reminded Virginians that the British constitution had made Britain and Virginia wealthy and great. In the end, Virginians made their war partly out of the hope that their example would spur their countrymen in the homeland to insist on their own rights as Englishmen. This idea of their colony as a political "city on a hill" runs through the record of Virginia's dispute with Britain.[14]

The House of Burgesses responded to the Imperial Crisis by resting on its historic rights. "Our ancestors brought with them every Right and Privilege they could with Justice claim in their Mother Kingdom," they told the House of Lords in a message of 18 December 1764. Similar assertions peppered their proclamations, official and unofficial.[15]

In their Stamp Act Resolutions, Virginians insisted that the first Virginia colonists had taken all the rights of Britons, including the right to be taxed only by their representatives, to Virginia. According to the House of Burgesses,

> the first Adventurers and Settlers of this his Majesties Colony and Dominion brought with them and transmitted to their Posterity and all other his Majesties Subjects since inhabiting in this his Majestie's said Colony all the Priviledges, Franchises and Immunities that have at any Time been held, enjoyed, and possessed by the People of Great Britain.

The rest of the Stamp Act Resolves spelled out that Virginians' rights had been recognized by James I in two royal charters; called the right at issue, taxation only by representatives, "the distinguishing Characteristick of British Freedom"; noted that Virginians had always enjoyed the right to legislate for themselves in the areas of taxation and domestic police; and insisted that any infringement upon Virginians' rights threatened both British and American freedom.[16]

Virginians had always believed that they had full title to all the rights of Britons. As Pauline Maier noted, although Thomas Paine's *Common Sense* led many colonists to discuss the question of independence with a newfound freedom, their grievances remained rooted in historical controversies, not in any generalized argument against monarchy.[17] Men such as Thomas Jefferson based their arguments against British policy on the traditional ground of inheritance. In his *Summary View*, for example, Jefferson trotted out the entire history of Virginia, as elaborated over the preceding decade by his fellow Virginians, to show that Virginians' demands were not innovative and disloyal. Virginians wanted not to be disloyal, and they could only achieve that by relying on prescription.[18]

Virginians produced remarkably little in the way of political theory for a people so consumed with political life.[19] They were more concerned with the historical than with the speculative. Unlike their kindred on the home island, they had little political tumult to prompt them to philosophizing. The common law, that great bulwark against tyranny, took an entirely historical form: Edward Coke, author of one of the two legal texts Virginians were most likely to read, claimed the common law had existed "time out of mind before the [Norman] conquest."[20] Virginia's public declarations throughout the eighteenth century were sprinkled with assertions that its government rested on long-established rights. Sir John Randolph's speech on being reelected Speaker of the House of Burgesses, given on 6 August 1736, provides a good example. Sir John reminded his audience that the July 1621 charter underlay Virginia's constitution. He noted that James I and subsequent monarchs had confirmed Virginians' rights. His fellow burgesses undoubtedly approved of his performance, because all of them were familiar with the guarantee of English rights spelled out in Virginia's first charter.[21]

In 1766, Richard Henry Lee penned the Westmoreland Association for the freemen of his home county. He and his fellow subscribers began by pledging their loyalty to George III *insofar as it was consistent with "our Constitutional Rights and Liberty."* Their rights included jury trial and, of course, taxation only by representatives—in other words, effective self-government on virtually all matters. The Stamp Act, they insisted, violated the latter right, and so they would punish those who executed it. Among other things, the Westmorelanders pledged their "Lives & Fortunes" that they would protect their fellow signatories.[22] Westmoreland's model would be adopted all over Virginia.

Since Virginians based their argument for home rule on inherited forms, it is unsurprising that the Convention of 1776 left suffrage requirements "as at present," retained the Council, maintained geographic apportionment of the legislature, and did not abolish slavery. The changes the Virginians did make, such as explicitly recognizing the principle of separation of powers in the Declaration of Rights, were hemmed in by fealty to inherited ways.[23] Leading Virginians attached prime importance to their class's capacity to govern Virginia without interference, not to their form of government, the structure of their society, or the doctrines of the established religion—none of which were at issue.[24]

While political leaders in the home islands refused to concede that colonial precedents had any weight whatsoever, even the Virginians most hesitant to declare independence agreed with the argument that they had inherited certain latitude in governing themselves.[25] Landon Carter, for example, wrote in May 1776 that he had always "abominated this present contest which Great Britain certainly began with America by attempting to tax her out of the constitutional road."[26] As Jefferson wrote fifty years later, "with respect to our rights, and the acts of the British government contravening those rights, there was but one opinion on this side of the water."[27]

As the Imperial Crisis deepened, Virginians came into closer contact with other colonists, and increasing allegiance to what they called "British America" resulted. As Jefferson would recall in his *Notes*, there had never been much commerce among the North American mainland colonies.[28] Yet, the ministry's attempt in the wake of the Seven Years' War to render the colonies' constitutional system rational brought all of the old thirteen into the same type of friction with Great Britain that Virginia experienced. On considering the Townshend Revenue Act of 1767, Richard Henry Lee said, he became convinced that the ministry had arrived at a new strategy. He believed the ministers had determined that a wholesale attack on American liberties would fail, and that they had therefore turned to undermining the colonies' constitutional positions one colony at a time. Thus, all Americans must be vigilant in defense of the rights of all their fellows.

Predictably, Lee saw the Boston Port Act as "a most violent and dangerous attempt to destroy the constitutional liberty of and rights of all North America," and he moved for appointment of delegates to a continental congress to plan responses to "the systematic plan for" the destruction of Americans' "constitutional rights." Boston's cause, he told his friend Samuel Adams, was "the common cause of *British America* . . . all America will owe their political salvation, in great measure, to the present virtue of Massachusetts Bay." Lee succeeded in convening his congress, and his understanding eventually became that of American Whigs, and certainly of Virginia Whigs, generally. As Lee wrote to his brother William on 10 May 1775, "All the old Provinces not one excepted are directed by the same firmness of union and determination to resist by all ways and to every extremity." They insisted, he told the chairman of the Committee of Northumberland County, upon "securing the just constitutional rights and Liberty of North America."[29] When Virginians came to write their new constitution, the preamble justifying separation from their rightful king would not distinguish between his malefactions against Virginia and those he had committed against other colonies. Section 9 of that constitution recognized Virginia as one of the United States.[30] Their union stood for the colonies' right to rule themselves without British interference.

Virginians thought of their revolution as an opportunity to have a British polity without England's "corruption." Virginia would "prepare an asylum" for Britons fleeing Westminster's tyranny.[31] Mindful of seventeenth-century parallels, Arthur Lee said the ministry's attempts to rule some colonies without assemblies reminded him of Charles I's attempt to rule without Parliament.[32] The General Assembly stood in the same constitutional position within Virginia as Parliament held in Britain.

One cannot understand Virginians' revolution, particularly their new constitution, without first understanding their colonial constitution. Virginians' comparatively tranquil society had a calm relationship to the mother country. Anomalies in their form of government, if there were any, did not trouble them overmuch. Their government was rather more a mixed one than one typified by separation of powers. In this, as in most other things, it resembled that of the mother country. Over the course of their colonial history, the institutions of colonial government had come closer to the separated powers model (for example, with the ejection of the governor from the General Assembly and the separation of the meetings of the Council and the Burgesses), but Virginia's government still did not fit any philosopher's pattern.[33] As in England, the local gentry dominated Virginia's highly decentralized government.

The House of Burgesses' power grew in the eighteenth century, both vis-à-vis the governor and in relation to the Council. Its control over the colony's purse strings enabled it to pressure the governors into allowing it a significant voice in military matters, which traditionally had been considered "executive." Additionally, the House of Burgesses often flouted royal instructions, as in refusing for sixty-seven years to separate the offices of speaker of the House of Burgesses and treasurer of the colony.[34]

The Virginia General Assembly saw itself as a mirror image of the British Parliament from an early date, calling itself the "House of Commons" at least as early as 1645.[35] Prior to the Seven Years' War, the House of Burgesses did not display any calculated plan to accrue authority, but it did tend always to grasp at power, then to refuse to surrender it. In the heat of the Imperial Crisis, the House of Burgesses came to resent every dissimilarity between its own and the British House of Commons' constitutional position. By the end of that period, its members rejected "the suspending clause, the Crown's right of legislative review, the royal instructions, the governor's power to dissolve them, and the theoretical equality of the royal-appointed councils in matters of legislation[, which] served as constant reminders of their subordinate status." Only the House of Burgesses, they instructed Virginia's delegates to the first Continental Congress, could legislate for Virginia.[36]

Parliament saw the colonial assemblies as merely "so many Corporations at a distance, invested with an Ability to make Temporary By Laws for themselves," but Virginians understood Parliament's attack on the House of Burgesses' authority as an attack on the Virginia elite itself. As a matter of course, the colonial elite's resistance became a war for assembly rights in the manner of the English Civil War and 1688. Virginians, long accustomed to see the House of Burgesses as "the chief Support of the Liberty and Property of the Subject," felt those dear possessions threatened along with the House of Burgesses' prerogatives. Thomson Mason asserted that no statute of the British Parliament passed since 1607 (the year when Virginia, a dominion separate from those represented at Westminster, had been settled) bound Virginia. Since its settlement in 1607, he claimed, Virginia had been entitled to legislate for itself. The preamble to the Constitution of 1776 scored George III for his infringements of assemblies' rights.[37]

The Council declined and mutated across Virginia's colonial history. In terms of power and perhaps of prestige, the House of Burgesses eclipsed it. The Council theoretically served as Virginia's supreme court, as the upper house of its legislature, and as coexecutive with the governor, but the press of judicial and executive duties so overwhelmed it by 1763 that it ceased to play any legislative role other than through an occasional veto of the House of Burgesses' actions. It selected a president from among its number, and he served as governor in the sometimes lengthy periods between governors, but otherwise, the Council's executive functions were easily its most important and time-consuming. The Virginians on the Council served as a serious check on the king's governors during the eighteenth century.[38]

The Council and the House of Burgesses had occasional squabbles in the eighteenth century, but they were usually precipitated by what the Council saw as transgressions of the Council's prerogatives. In operation, the governors' supposed check upon the tendency of the lower house to overreach its legitimate privileges proved the merest shadow of a check when the principles of monarchy and local control came into conflict. With the rise of the House of Burgesses to constitutional supremacy in the eighteenth century, the Council ceased to monopolize the "best men," who no longer saw moving from the Burgesses to the Council as a promotion. This development accelerated the constitutional deterioration whose ultimate result was the constitution of 1776.[39]

Governors, on the other hand, needed the Council's cooperation immensely. As the preserve of leaders of Virginia's leading families, the Council sat at the top of Virginia society. Governors were outsiders with essentially no patronage powers. Their inherently weak position left them in need of the Council's support. In the eighteenth century, the governors whose administrations the Council opposed all failed.[40]

Virginians traditionally conceded what they took to be governors' legitimate, though circumscribed, power, and by 1763, Virginia possessed the strongest governorship in the mainland British colonies. Yet, the following decade made the link between the form of their chief magistracy and the monarchical principle clear, and they therefore rejected it in the end. First, they insisted on strict separation of powers, but when acts of legislation they took to be essential, or at least highly desirable, repeatedly suffered negation or were held in abeyance by the governor and his British superiors, Virginians became enraged. Finally, Lord Dunmore set their largest port city ablaze and called on their slaves to rebel, and that exceeded the bounds of their toleration.[41]

Governors had few options. The House of Burgesses' assumption of a number of executive powers gravely infringed upon governors' authority and impeded administration, but next to nothing could be done about it. The colonists insisted on their "control over supply," with the associated oversight authority, as their key protection against an inherently rapacious executive. Once elite Virginians decided that they stood in relation to England as the Saxon migrants to England had stood in relation to the Continent, imperial agents' position became simply untenable. Less than one year separated Jefferson's *Summary View* from Dunmore's political self-immolation.[42]

Local institutions—parishes with their vestries; county courts; and militia units—were far more important than the House of Burgesses, the Council, and the governor in the lives of common Virginians and members of the gentry alike. In those three sets of institutions, each dominated by the local gentry, the kin network whose apex was the House of Burgesses exercised its dominance over an almost entirely rural society. Each county's rulers constituted an oligarchy, and the leaders of the local oligarchies manned the colonial government. A small elite with power based in the county courts held the reins of political power, before the Revolution and after it. When a member of a county court died, before the Revolution and after, his successor was chosen by his surviving colleagues; thus, the institutions that engrossed all executive, legislative, and judicial authority in local government were entirely self-selecting, which resulted in decades-long dominance of many local courts by the same two or three kin networks. The ejection of the king's agents from Virginia's government was meant to insulate these county oligarchies from foreign control, and it succeeded.

Besides agreeing on the necessity of home rule, elite and common Virginians also agreed to a surprising degree on who should rule at home. The "Gentlemen Volunteers" of the Independent Company wrote to House of Burgesses Speaker Peyton Randolph on 1 June 1775, "May Heaven Grant You Long To Live The Father of Your Country, And The Friend To Freedom And Humanity!"[43] Language once reserved for the king was now applied to Virginia's foremost politician, the head of Virginia's leading kin network.

The great plantation owners, less than one percent of the colonial population, comprised the aristocracy of Virginia, and generation after generation of typical Virginians knew them as its rulers. Commoners evidently did not resent gentry domination of Virginia politics and society. As a blacksmith from Tidewater York County wrote:

> Who can but love the place that hath brought forth
> Such men of virtue, merit, honor, worth?
> The gentry of Virginia, I dare say,
> For honor vie with all America.
> Had I great Camden's skill, how freely I
> Would celebrate our worthy gentry.

Although the gentry dominated their fellows, the two groups' common participation in races, cockfights, court days, Anglican services, and militia musters, joined to their common economic interests and ideology, made the yoke of gentry domination light.[44] Virginians did not demand that their great men keep them "informed." Newspapers, filled with accounts of European courts and classically derived polemics, were not accessible even to those uneducated men who could afford them.[45]

Under its Constitution of 1776, Virginia's government would resemble England's in having a supreme lower house of legislature with the other organs of government much dependent on it. Their conscious elaboration of their theory of their own government began in Virginians' disputes with Britain in the 1750s and 1760s, which caused Virginian publicists to defend their assembly's powers on a wide front. By the time Virginians assembled in 1776 to create their republic, the political class generally agreed that the historical understanding of men such as Richard Bland, Landon Carter, and Thomson Mason was correct.[46]

Some historians have argued that economic factors led the great Tidewater planters to opt for revolution, while an excellent recent account credits the Virginia elite's fears concerning the places of slaves, Indians, and debtors in their society with precipitating their break with Great Britain.[47] If one takes the two decades of Virginia's constitutional dispute with Britain preceding the Revolution into account, however, it becomes clear that while economic incentives influenced the Virginians, it is impossible to say whether the constitutional disagreements or the economic and social interests that stood alongside them were more important. Virginians' economic and social problems became entangled with constitutional difficulties in virtually every phase of the prelude to the Revolution. Their main problem was that whatever accommodation to their circumstances their colonial government might make, the mother country could always intervene.[48] The "home" government's evident ignorance of conditions in North America and its inability to provide for Virginia's needs in a timely fashion led to recurrent friction.

From Virginia, it seemed to make perfect sense for Virginia's government to act for it in the same way the King-in-Parliament did for Great Britain. Each of the components of the British government had its analogue in Virginia, and English Whig arguments for the British government's theoretical perfection migrated easily. Virginia publicists adopted a slightly modified form of the Whig argument that England's was a Gothic constitution, which the Whigs had derived from Tacitus' description in *Germania* of ancient German governments.[49] In the end, their acceptance of the ideas behind Parliamentary supremacy led Virginians to reject the "foreign" Westminster parliament in favor of their own colonial version of it. They could, they insisted, legislate regarding their "internal Polity and Taxation" so long as they secured the king's consent.[50]

The first of the major constitutional arguments between Virginia and the mother country in the run-up to the Revolution came in the Pistole Fee Controversy. When Governor Robert Dinwiddie undertook the actions that sparked this controversy, he must have thought they were innocuous enough. Simply stated, he began to charge one pistole, or about 16 shillings sterling, enough money for "a good cow and calf," for all land patents.[51] Dinwiddie, the agent of the king, seems to have been within his rights in charging a nominal fee to people who essentially were being given the king's land. Virginia's political class, however, understood the matter differently. Richard Bland insisted that Dinwiddie had levied a tax without Virginians' consent, and thus degraded them from the position of Englishmen. Further, Bland, widely reputed to be the leading authority on Virginia's constitutional history, argued that no tax not established by law had been charged in Virginia since King William III's reign and that the people of

Virginia must now consent before any such fee could be established. Late in 1753, the House of Burgesses insisted Dinwiddie had contravened their charter rights and demanded that he revoke his fee. The governor relented.[52]

Later in the decade, the Parsons' Cause once again cast doubt upon the Virginia General Assembly's authority. Amidst irregular tobacco crops and a heavy burden from the Seven Years' War, the General Assembly enacted the two Two-Penny Acts, which authorized payment of Church of England clergymen in depreciated currency instead of tobacco. The Crown required the General Assembly to insert a suspending clause staying that act's enforcement pending royal approval into each statute it passed, but the Two-Penny Acts contained no such clauses. While the acts relieved Virginians of some of the taxes they might otherwise have had to pay, they also placed a great burden on the clergymen, who were used to accepting tobacco in support of their services in the event of poor tobacco markets and justly considered it only fair that they should have the same mode of pay in the opposite event.

The king's Privy Council disallowed the second Two-Penny Act. In a victory for Virginia, however, the form of the disallowal did not require Virginia to give the ministers back pay. The clergymen had won the theoretical point, but they never received their money. In response to the Privy Council's rejection of the second Two-Penny Act, the Burgesses pled necessity, thus laying the groundwork for future assertions of Virginia's autonomy.[53]

A year after the passage of the second Two-Penny Act, Landon Carter, in his 1759 *Letter to the Right Reverend Father in God*, asserted the constitutionality of any act passed by the General Assembly and signed by the governor. Richard Bland added in another pamphlet that the General Assembly could do what the people's welfare required.[54] Bland's 1764 pamphlet, *The Colonel Dismounted: Or the Rector Vindicated*, featured several arguments that loomed larger and had broader application as the 1760s went on. Virginia's external government—trade regulation, resolutions of questions of war and peace, and the like—was one thing, he said, and Parliament might have a large role there, but Virginia's internal government by right should and in fact could only be controlled by Virginians. If Virginia did not have plenary power over its own governance, that governance must be in the power of someone over whom Virginians had no control. Their government would then be government without consent, and Virginians would no longer be free Englishmen. When it came to Parliament's legislation, he held, "any Tax respecting our *internal* Polity . . . may be opposed."[55]

Opponents had objected to the Two-Penny Acts' form as evidence that they must be disallowed. Bland answered with the law Latin slogan, *salus populi est suprema lex* ("the good of the people is the supreme law"), which would justify virtually any emergency legislation. Virginians, Bland said, were Englishmen, so they had English rights, as Virginia's charters recognized. As only Parliament could legislate for the home islands, only the General Assembly could legislate for Virginia.[56]

Finally, in 1766, Richard Bland published his masterpiece, *An Inquiry into the Rights of the British Colonies.*[57] Following the latest Whig teaching and drawing upon the public pronouncements of the House of Burgesses,[58] Bland claimed that the Saxon constitution had been "founded upon Principles of the most perfect Liberty." Originally, all freemen had been members of the Saxon parliament, with only slaves and the landless excluded. It had been Henry VIII, a half-millennium after the Norman Conquest, who abridged the suffrage. Since all men had (and here he made a novel assertion destined to have lasting influence[59]) a natural right to emigrate, Britons who stayed in Britain were tacitly assenting to be governed by a government that deprived them of their rights. North America's colonists, said Bland, were unique among history's colonists in having established their colonies without expense to the mother country. Their emigration into an empty land at their own expense removed them from the ambit of English law, placing them under "the Law of Nature" and putting them at liberty to establish a mutually binding relationship with the Crown. James I's vow that Virginia's form of government would never be altered therefore bound his successors.

Virginia, Bland concluded, had only submitted to the English Commonwealth on the understanding that James I's pledge remained binding: Virginia would have the right to taxation via representatives and "such Freedoms and Privileges as belong to the free People of England." The Crown had repeatedly reiterated this understanding, Bland noted, in the commissions of Virginia's royal governors. In the absence of royal prerogative, Virginians had no claim to the rights of Englishmen and these avowals had been mere "Deceptions." Prerogative must extend at least this far. Charles II, Bland noted, had personally acted as the executive branch of Virginia's government in enacting a tax for Virginia to pay. He had also negated a British statute's operation in Virginia on the basis of Virginia's right to legislate for itself. In short, Virginians had always been immune to Parliamentary taxation.

Virginia's constitutional stance in the ongoing dispute with Great Britain changed little between the publication of Bland's *An Inquiry into the Rights of the British Colonies* and May 1776. Bland had encapsulated the Virginian position. The monarchs' recognition of English rights in Virginia, the General Assembly's exclusive power to legislate for Virginia, and the loyalty of Virginians to George III were all staples of Virginian proclamations, before *An Inquiry into the Rights of the British Colonies* and especially after. Virginians were so insistent on this last score that George III took them to be mocking him.[60] These arguments, betraying the influence of common law training in their almost exclusive reliance on history, were typical of the pragmatic, unphilosophical Virginians. Various British affronts to American "rights" would elicit reiterations of this position, which also would shape Virginia's revolutionary constitution.

Bland was not the last propagandist to stake out this ground prior to Jefferson's *Summary View*. Thomson Mason's letters of the "British American," which appeared in Virginia newspapers in June and July 1774, took a radical, even daring stance. In a summer of radicalized Virginia sentiment—when the denizens of Loudoun County, for example, characterized the Boston Port Act as "designedly calculated to enslave a free and loyal people"[61]—Mason, the brother of George Mason, went even further. The "British American" said America's goal should be to preserve British liberty and, failing that, to offer a refuge from tyranny to liberty-loving Britons. Virginians had had British rights from the beginning and had never submitted to Parliament. The Coercive Acts, which aimed not merely to stifle dissent in Boston but to subjugate all of America, clarified the British ruling clique's true nature. Still, he counseled against haste in either defending or condemning Parliament. Non-intercourse should be a last resort, for it would hurt British merchants who might otherwise sympathize with America. Loyalty to George III suggested forbearance. Yet, while he considered the theory of Britain's constitution excellent, the constitution itself had degenerated.[62]

In his final "British American" letter, Mason vented his full fury. Readers must confront "the British aristocracy" to show that Virginians "were determined to risk your lives and fortunes rather than submit." Virginia must insist (and here he broke new ground) that it would be bound by no act of the Westminster Parliament passed since 1607.[63] Acts of Parliament could not bind Americans, according to Mason, because Americans were not represented in Parliament. Thus, any judge who attempted to enforce a British statute in America should be considered a thief: those acts were "absolutely void, and m[ight] be legally resisted." Dozens of dead judges in each colony would be better than harming "twenty thousand of your innocent manufacturing fellow subjects in Britain." In other words, associations for non-importation of British goods did not affect only their intended targets, and Mason preferred reprisals directly against the guilty to retributive measures likely to cause "collateral damage."[64]

Submission to other subjects—for example, Parliament—seemed too humiliating to bear. Virginia should prosecute those who dared to enforce Parliament's illegal policies. If the British government responded with force, America should "recur to the first law of nature." Men from other colonies should be sent to fight for Boston.

Finally, in his passion, Mason reiterated his belief that America should be a refuge for liberty-loving Britons. God, the source of their liberty, would vindicate Americans who defended their rights. The "British American," a lover of Britain, "our mother country still," hoped none of these measures would be necessary. To show his good faith, he pulled back the mask of anonymity and signed his name, Thomson Mason.[65] The revelation of Mason's name must have been shocking, thrilling. His call for nullification, complete with its argument that Parliament had never had rightful authority in Virginia, marked the final stage of

Virginia's public argument. Anger had been added to self-righteousness, self-respect had taken the form of fiery insubordination.

Thomson Mason had company in lifting his face toward the revolutionary sun in July 1774. Thomas Jefferson, newly elected to the House of Burgesses, drafted instructions to Virginia's delegates in the upcoming Continental Congress. This pamphlet, soon dubbed "A Summary View of the Rights of British America," did what Jefferson is now famous for having done so well on another occasion: it put others' thoughts into memorable words. Jefferson captured the entire upswell of gentry anger and resentment, of colonial Virginia's climactic self-assertion, in a few pages.

There is virtually nothing in Jefferson's *Summary View* that Mason, Bland, Carter, or the Burgesses had not said before.[66] Yet, Jefferson had a far more direct, far more impertinent way of saying it. He dared to address the king personally and to upbraid him for dereliction of duty. The social distance traditionally separating a mere planter and the king of England gave way to simple instructions to a fellow officeholder.[67] Jefferson opened with the instruction that the delegates should seek George's permission to petition him "as chief magistrate of the British empire" concerning "complaints which are excited by many unwarrantable incroachments and usurpations, attempted to be made by the legislature of one part of the empire, upon those rights which god and the laws have given equally and independently to all." In thus asserting their claim to equality with Great Britain within George's empire, Jefferson added, Virginians would use language "divested of . . . expressions of servility. George was king solely for his subjects' good, and he had been elevated to that position by them.

In the spirit of Bland, Jefferson claimed that "our ancestors" had immigrated to Virginia from Britain by natural right, as the Saxons had left northern Europe before them. The Saxons had never bowed and scraped before their homeland, and neither would Virginians, in light of "the rights derived to them from their ancestors." Individuals acting on their own had conquered British North America, and Britain had given the Old Dominion monetary support only after the colony's establishment. British aid to Virginia in war had been of the same kind as that given, for example, to Portugal, and no one pretended Portugal had forfeited its sovereignty in accepting a British alliance.

Having settled in Virginia, Jefferson continued, the adventurers had adopted England's laws and sovereign as their own. They had done these things of their own free will, not under compulsion of either arms or morality. England conceded Virginia's right to free trade by treaty in the time of Cromwell, and Britain subsequently infringed on that freedom. "The true ground on which we declare these acts void," Jefferson summed up his argument, "is that the British parliament has no right to exercise authority over us."

Jefferson blamed the Imperial Crisis on a "deliberate, systematical plan of reducing us to slavery." New York's legislature had been suspended and the small electorate of Great Britain (Jefferson said 160,000 voters) had undertaken to legislate for four million Americans. Americans did not know and could not remove those who were to legislate for them. Through the Boston Port Act, all Boston was punished for the crime of a few. The king had been given the right to reopen two wharves at pleasure, which was a legislative power. Some Americans had even been denied their right to trial by a jury of the vicinage, which dated to Magna Carta. In sum, arbitrariness abounded.

There remained, Jefferson said, one possible cure for the imperial constitution's malady: George III could resume the monarchy's moribund role in legislation. The king possessed the sole "mediatory power between the several states of the British empire,"[68] and he should use his position to aid the innocent party in this dispute by seeking the unjust acts' revocation. When Parliament acted out of pure self-interest, he should veto its acts, and he should cease delaying legislative acts salutary for America.

Jefferson rebuked George III for delaying the General Assembly's legislation for reducing slave importation. His inaction had hurt "the lasting interests of the American states." George's dilatory attention to Virginia's legislation and his suspending clause requirement, Jefferson pointed out, were very inconvenient for Virginia, and so was his governors' repeated dissolution of the General Assembly, a tactic recognized as illegitimate in Britain since the Glorious Revolution. In Jefferson's account, George III must follow Virginian laws when acting as Virginia's chief executive exactly as he must follow British law in his British capacity. He must behave in a fashion that was consistent with home rule not only for Britain, but for Virginia.

George had no ministers drawn from among them, so Virginians had to speak forthrightly to him of their rights as to the people's servant. Virginia neither wanted nor stood to benefit from separation. George possessed "a great, *if a well-poised empire*," and Virginia supported "union on a generous plan." (These ideas would pepper Jefferson's writings for fifty years, with the substitution of the various federal governments for the Imperial government doing little to change them.) He closed his draft with a call to "fraternal love and harmony." In the end, Jefferson imagined Virginia as a co-equal state within the British Empire, one whose political and other traditions drew upon British traditions for inspiration. He wanted home rule within a redefined British Empire, but he hinted that the Virginians would put home rule first if it came to that.

Jefferson's admiration for the learning of Richard Bland is evident throughout the *Summary View*.[69] Having absorbed the teaching of his predecessor, Jefferson gave Bland's arguments greater force than their author ever had. Bland may have been the genius behind the Virginian argument for independence, but the Sage of Monticello's pen made it a fighting creed.

The *Summary View* caught the wave of anti-British anger and roused Jefferson's fellow Virginia politicians. Virginia's delegates were told that they were to insist that Americans had the same rights as Englishmen, so only American assemblies could legislate for them, and that Americans' obedience to British commercial regulations had been merely prudential, offered in exchange for the protection of British arms and not in response to a supposedly non-existent constitutional subordination.[70] Soon, Jefferson's idea of nullification, too, had its influence: on 4 February 1775, Richard Henry Lee wrote to Samuel Adams, Massachusetts's leading radical, of the latest rumored Parliamentary outrage, "Should such Acts pass, will it not be proper for all America to declare them essentially vile and void?"[71] Such acts would be "void" because they were contrary to the higher law: the colonies' inherited rights.

George III's speech in Parliament, made in late 1775 and published in America on 4 January 1776,[72] upset the Virginians greatly. Most importantly, George declared the colonies to be in rebellion and outside his protection. This speech convinced Jefferson, for one, of reconciliation's impossibility. George claimed that Britain was due the credit for the establishment and success of its American colonies, and thus threatened to remove the keystone of Jefferson's argument that Virginians had always had the right to govern themselves. As Richard Henry Lee wrote on 20 April, George and his Parliament had "to every legal intent and purpose dissolved our government, uncommissioned every magistrate, and placed us in the high road to Anarchy." All officers of Virginia's government had acted under the king's authority, he reasoned, so the proclamation that they were outside the law left them with no authority at all. Virginians had no choice but to take up self-government independently of the king's authority. Thus, a group of men who had on 26 August 1775 pledged "before *God* and the world, that we do bear true allegiance to His Majesty *George* the Third, our only lawful and rightful King" ordered its delegates to the Continental Congress to announce its independence less than a year later.[73]

One might dismiss Lee's view as unrepresentative, for he had favored independence for many months by April 1776. However, he was far from alone. John Page, Jefferson's lifelong friend, expressed a similar understanding. Since Dunmore's flight and constructive abdication, the governorship was vacant, Page noted, and Virginia's other institutions continued in their old paths only by inertia. "[T]o prevent Disorders," he concluded, "a Constitution should be formed as nearly resembling the old one as" practicable.[74]

Virginians expected the May Convention of 1776 to write a constitution. Page wrote Jefferson on 12 April that "almost every man here . . . is willing to declare for Independence." The only uncertainty concerned the question whether Virginia should proclaim its independence first or simply begin to act on it and leave the declaration to the Continental Congress, thereby hiding behind joint culpability.[75] Buckingham, James City, Cumberland, and Charlotte Counties all instructed their May Convention delegates to have Virginia's delegates to the Continental Congress declare independence, and the Convention received a petition from Augusta County East asking for a strong confederation and "an equal free and liberal Government that may bear the Test of all future Ages." The *Virginia Gazette* of 5 April 1776 said, "matters of the greatest importance are to come under immediate consideration." Independence was so dominant an issue that the drafting of a new constitution was simply taken for granted. The populace across the colony displayed great interest in the election of delegates with these momentous matters in mind.[76]

The chronicler of the Convention of 1776 described the scene as the May Convention met: "The crowd which filled the Capitol evinced the intensity of the public excitement. The most influential men from the neighboring counties, not then in office, had sought the city, and repaired early to the place of meeting." The Convention met on 6 May 1776 and the eminent Richard Bland straightway nominated Edmund Pendleton to preside, in his nominating speech pointing to Pendleton's esteemed service and his "abilities and integrity." From the May Convention's start, it, like the four before it, followed in the well-worn tracks of colonial procedure in the House of Burgesses.[77]

The Convention's actions reflected Patrick Henry's statement that "I have but one lamp by which my feet are guided, and that is the lamp of experience. I know of no way of judging the future but by the past." Henry and others found the touchstone of their statesmanship in English history. They also may have been affected by self-interest: their political and social advantage lay in the elevation of the House of Delegates and maintenance of the county courts' semi-autonomous position, and both occurred.[78]

Although it was known that the Convention would write a constitution and declaration of rights for a new commonwealth, one prominent delegate doubted that the time was right for Virginia to declare its independence. Written musings by Richard Henry Lee had planted the seed of an idea in Henry's mind, and it tormented him. What if Virginia declared its independence, then Britain agreed with France to partition North America? Virginia could end up far worse off. It could find itself transformed into a French province, or part of a French province.[79] The prudent Henry set his heart on an implicit, rather than an explicit, declaration of Virginia's changed status. On 20 May, five days after the Convention decided that a committee should draft a declaration of rights and a constitution and that confederation and foreign alliances would be sought, Henry wrote to Lee. He thought a French alliance essential to the success of the American effort, so he preferred to seek one before declaring independence. Otherwise, British offers of partition would arrive at Versailles in advance of American bids for friendship. Besides, did not the Americans need "a confederacy of our states previously?" That same day, Henry wrote John Adams that "an open declaration" must await those developments.[80]

In any event, the Convention adopted its resolutions on 15 May 1776, the same day Congress, at the instigation of Lee and Adams, recommended that states that had not yet done so adopt new systems of government. The Virginians did not know of Congress's recommendation. Virginia's congressmen received their instructions to act on their state's independence on 17 May 1776. In the Convention, Henry opposed both the forthright declaration of independence proposed by Edmund Pendleton and Meriwether Smith's formulation, which made it implicit. Henry proposed a simple resolution that the Virginia delegates in Congress move independence there. It fell to President Pendleton to reconcile his own, Smith's, and Henry's plans and achieve the "requisite" unanimity.[81]

Since the House of Burgesses had resolved unanimously on 6 May that "Great Britain had subverted the ancient constitution of the colony," independence was likely. With the lone exception of colonial Treasurer Robert Carter Nicholas, the delegates only disagreed as to how to implement it. In the end, they adopted Pendleton's poor pastiche of Henry's, Smith's, and his own proposals. In bowing to everyone's aims, it did nothing well. For example, it called for appointment of a committee to draft "a DECLARATION OF RIGHTS" and a constitution, but it instructed Virginians in Congress to declare independence. Thus, the Convention took actions that assumed independence without first forthrightly declaring it. Pendleton's biographer judged this "the most important document Pendleton ever wrote" and "one of the poorest pieces of composition of his career." Contemporaries agreed. Yet, the thing was finally done, and the way had been paved for Jefferson's Declaration. "The people" thought of Virginia as independent from 15 May 1776, "and a continental union flag was displayed on the capitol."[82]

Besides breaking the Old Dominion's legal tie to Britain, the resolutions of 15 May 1776 contemplated another fundamental innovation: establishment of a written constitution as the supreme law of Virginia. Pendleton appointed a committee to write a constitution that would "secure substantial and equal liberty to the people." The idea that removal of the theoretical ground of Virginia's government left the Old Dominion on the verge of anarchy was on the drafters' minds.[83]

Thomas Jefferson, in distant Philadelphia, was frantic to return to Virginia and participate in this process. After all, the new state constitution would be "the whole object of the present controversy; for should a bad government be instituted for us in future it had been as well to have accepted the bad one offered to us from beyond the water without the risk and expense of contest." He wrote three draft constitutions. He asked to be recalled from Congress. He contacted his agent in the May Convention, Edmund Randolph, to make a theoretical objection to the Convention's agenda. A constitution, Jefferson wrote, should be written by a body specially chosen for the purpose, and he denied the May Convention's qualification for the task.

Randolph presented Jefferson's qualms to George Mason, Pendleton, and Henry. All three noted that the May Convention had been chosen with the possibility of declaring independence in mind. If it could declare independence, and thus throw off the old government, they reasoned, it could adopt a new government to take the old one's place. The alternative was the anarchy Virginia's leading thinkers were so concerned to avert. Randolph noted that Henry, Mason, and

Pendleton feared that a declaration of independence without a new constitution would leave the relationship between Virginia and the Crown ambiguous. They insisted that all doubt must be removed. They therefore held Jefferson's reservations to be unfounded. In contradiction of his own argument, Jefferson submitted draft constitutions purporting to be permanent to the Convention.[84]

The process of writing the Virginia Constitution of 1776 (including the Declaration of Rights) consumed several weeks of the committee's time and a few days of debate in the Committee of the Whole. While the seven drafts known to have been before the committee spanned a relatively broad spectrum from more aristocratic (Carter Braxton's) to more democratic (Richard Henry Lee's "Government Scheme," patterned on his friend John Adams' "Thoughts on Government") to experimental/visionary (Thomas Jefferson's), George Mason's moderate, Whiggish draft became the working blueprint.

Thomas Jefferson, Thomas Ludwell Lee, and George Mason all wrote to Richard Henry Lee to ask that he serve as the May Convention's guiding hand, but he arrived only at the very end of the Convention. Matters were thus left to Mason, whom Patrick Henry, in complaining of the absence of worthy collaborators from the May Convention, had not known to be much of a Whig. Mason wrote to Richard Henry Lee on 18 May 1776, "We shall, in all probability, have a thousand ridiculous and impracticable proposals, and of course a plan formed of heterogeneous, jarring, and unintelligible ingredients." Then, in an implicit explanation of his unaccustomed willingness to bear this drudgery, he added, "This can be prevented only by a few men of integrity and abilities, whose country's interest lies next their hearts, undertaking this business and defending it ably through every stage of opposition."[85] True to his own protestations of devotion to the dispensation of 1688, Mason produced a constitution remarkably like Virginia's final colonial arrangement. Richard Henry Lee, John Page, and others had already arrived at supporting this prescription. Jefferson wrote the Preamble, which resembled the main body of the Declaration of Independence because it was drawn by the same author for the same purpose from the same materials.[86]

Among contemporary proposals that influenced the committee's drafting process were Lee's "Government Scheme" and Adams' "Thoughts on Government." Large portions of the structure and wording of the Constitution of 1776 came from those two sources. Some provisions, such as the retention of colonial suffrage requirements (which the House of Burgesses had tried to change in order to spur immigration, only to meet with London's rebuffs), evidently made their way into the final document as a result of pure inertia. (Decades later, Edmund Randolph judged that the colonial suffrage requirement "would have soon perished under a discussion.") The resulting constitution was more traditional than liberal or republican.[87]

The Convention changed apportionment slightly, in line with ambient complaints about "rotten boroughs" in England. Jamestown and the College of William & Mary each lost its delegate, and voting eligibility was limited to one county per citizen. However, a committee defeated Thomas Ludwell Lee's proposal to liberalize suffrage requirements, and George Mason had his way when the Convention perpetuated the traditional English notion that suffrage should be tied to "permanent common interest with, and attachment to the community" in the form of land ownership.[88]

Richard Henry Lee's "Government Scheme," published in the *Virginia Gazette* on 10 May 1776, unsurprisingly (Lee had both circulated his friend's sketch and trumpeted it in correspondence) hewed close to John Adams' line. Among changes Lee introduced were elimination of the Council's role as Virginia's supreme court and creation of a new upper legislative house. The state constitution ultimately incorporated both changes.[89]

Carter Braxton's "An Address to the Convention of the Colony and Ancient Dominion of Virginia" apparently had next to no positive influence, but it certainly did strengthen the resolve of some of the democratically inclined delegates. Braxton, like his namesake grandfather Landon Carter, was loath to see Virginia sever its links to Great Britain. Also like his grandfather, he feared that the impetus to radicalism latent in anti-British sentiment might yield a Virginia constitution marked by "the spirit of *Common Sense.*" He aimed in drafting this pamphlet to head off the Lee and Adams plans, which he thought calculated to foist an all-powerful assembly on Virginians.[90]

According to Braxton, Virginia should avoid both "blind attachment to ancient prejudices" and "a restless spirit of innovation." Since the English had lived under monarchy for centuries, Virginians were unsuited to its opposite, so they should beware unalloyed republicanism. He still preferred the old constitution, "its present imperfections remedied." The radical proposals of Lee and Adams, he said, were "never confirmed by . . . experience." Braxton favored triennial elections for the lower house, a governor who served "during his good behavior," a council for life, and giving Congress, newly apportioned by population, cognizance of interstate and international matters.[91]

The roof fell in on Braxton. Henry told Adams he suspected Braxton's Whiggism, and he called Braxton's "whole performance an affront and disgrace." Richard Henry Lee said that it displayed "aristocratic pride." William Fleming wrote Jefferson, "Mr. Braxton's address on government made him no friends in convention."[92] Some historians have joined Braxton's contemporary critics in judging his work simply that of a Tidewater aristocrat desirous of protecting his family's privilege and place. A more charitable historian described Braxton's proposal as "as close as any revolutionary tract to proposing a constitution faithful to English tradition," offering "an English Radical Whig diagnosis" of Great Britain's troubles and proposing a constitution for his newly independent country incorporating the "best" of England's constitution, coupled with protections against the "worst." In time, some of the radicals of '76 would adopt a few of Braxton's proposals.[93]

Less unpopular than Braxton's British approach was that of Edmund Pendleton, the president of the Committee of Safety and of the May Convention. To Braxton, he wrote on 12 May 1776,

> A democracy, considered as *referring determinations*, either legislative or executive, TO THE PEOPLE AT LARGE, is the worst form (of government) imaginable. Of all others, I own, I prefer the true English constitution, which consists of a proper combination of the principles of honor, virtue, and fear. I confess *there are some objections* EVEN TO THIS, which only proves that perfection is not in our power to attain.

His reference to "the true English constitution" was not an allusion to some fantasy of Gothic simplicity, as he made clear to Jefferson shortly after the Convention's close. In fact, just before the Convention met, Pendleton, as president of the Committee of Safety, had been assuring Dunmore's agents that the patriots would prefer to see the rift in the Empire papered over.[94]

Although one could not go so far as Braxton in avowing sympathy for the British Constitution and maintain his respectability among the patriots of 1776, several other delegates' views were similar to Pendleton's. After all, as disputes ranging back to the Pistole Fee Controversy had shown, Virginians insisted only on what they took to be their rights as Englishmen, chiefly their rightful share of self-government. Their attachment to the "pure" English constitution was consistent with this concept. Robert Carter Nicholas, for example, voted "no" on independence alone of all the delegates, then worked to insure that independence succeeded. Others also thought independence imprudent, but only he dared to say so. In Edmund Randolph's opinion, Nicholas's daring justified the high opinion universally held of him. Simply put, Nicholas had stood for the old ways in opposing independence, and he continued to do so in supporting Virginia's effort to make independence work.[95]

When the draft Declaration of Rights went to the floor, Robert Carter Nicholas objected to the first section, which asserted that men were naturally equal, "as being the forerunner or pretext of civil convulsion."[96] He was right, for a similar provision in Massachusetts would soon lead a court to declare slavery unconstitutional. Even if Virginia's traditionalist courts, sure to be headed by Pendleton, did not abolish slavery, the notion that the Declaration of Rights would serve by its very existence to instruct the people in republicanism gained wide acceptance. They must not be instructed that slavery was wrong. Nicholas said that if Mason's draft were true in saying that all men were by nature equally free and independent, he would have no trouble recognizing it. Of course, he continued, it was not true, for Virginia was filled with slaves, more of them all the time, and they were certainly not born free. Edmund Pendleton added a reference to Lockean contract theory, so that the revised first section of Virginia's Declaration of Rights said that men could not be divested of their rights "when they enter into a state of Society." Slaves, never having entered into society, did not fall under this declaration. Edmund Randolph testified that Nicholas' protest was initially met with insistence that a war for the "rights of man" seemed a poor setting for this objection, but this statement has the ring of the French Revolution about it, and we may wonder whether it is not an anachronistic interlineation. Randolph has been proven correct, however, in his assessment that Nicholas spoke "with too great an indifference to futurity." While the Virginia Declaration of Rights has been very influential, it is the draft version, not the final one, that has had such a looming impact.[97]

The unanimous vote to adopt the Declaration of Rights on 12 June 1776 was characteristic of the Virginia political culture, but securing that outcome required substantial compromise. Of special interest in this regard was the greatest achievement in the sixty-year political career of James Madison, the modification of the committee's religious toleration provision. George Mason's initial version had extended the "fullest toleration" "governed only by Reason and Conviction," "unpunished and unrestrained by the Magistrate." Madison, however, believed that multiplicity of religious beliefs constituted a good in itself, because it conduced to lack of confidence in government. Therefore, he found toleration of heresy inadequate and insisted that the Convention recognize "dictates of conscience" as the basis of a right. Madison's language reflected an accommodation of English religious institutions to the situation in religiously heterogeneous Virginia. In this sphere, perhaps more than any other, Virginia was notably distinct from England in 1776, and some recognition of the unsuitability of the Anglican Establishment to a country in which perhaps two-thirds of people were not Anglican had to be made.[98]

Virginia's Declaration of Rights won adoption as a preliminary to the body of the constitution on 12 June 1776. In adopting its declaration of rights before its constitution, the Convention once again showed itself to be heavily influenced by the British precedents of 1688–1689, when William and Mary had been required to accept an authoritative formulation of English rights and of the parameters of their own role before assuming the throne.[99]

The first article was the statement of men's equality—with the addition of the amendment on which Nicholas had insisted. The second article, perhaps equally fundamental to the Whig view of politics, was a simple statement of the sovereignty of "the People" and of the fiduciary nature of officers' power—an idea which had played a key role in such documents as Jefferson's *Summary View*. Article 3 laid claim to the right of revolution whenever the government should fail to inure to "the common benefit protection and Security of the People Nation or Community . . . [and] the greatest degree of happiness and Safety" or to be "most effectually secured against the danger of Mal-Administration." Virginians claimed all of these were prerequisite to a duty of obedience and loyalty. Implicitly, they were asserting that the government of George III had failed on all three scores—and justifying their war for independence. Their argument with the British presupposed the existence of a right of self-government which the king was bound to respect if he wanted to retain his post.

Article 4 banned "separate Emoluments or Privileges from the Community but in consideration of publick Services," and it declared that neither these, nor any office, should be hereditary. Once again, the Virginians insisted that their government must by right be under popular control. Article 5 took the principle of the need to share burdens even further, requiring executive and legislative officials to leave office at stated intervals so that they would "be restrained from oppression by feeling and participating the burthens of the People." Rotation in office rested on the notion that a representative could not be properly representative, as Bland had pointed out in deriding the concept of "virtual representation" a decade before, unless he had to bear his constituents' burdens. If rule by the British Parliament was not self-government, neither was rule by career politicians.

In Article 6, Mason's notion of "permanent common Interest" found its place. Only men sharing that tie, possession of a minimal amount of land, would have the right to vote. This article also asserted the right to be taxed only by, and to live only under laws made by, representatives. Article 7, a related article, said dissolving or proroguing the legislature was impermissible. This article followed logically from the assumptions underlying the earlier sections related to self-government, which soon led to the elevation of the House of Delegates to constitutional preeminence.

Article 8 contained several guarantees of rights in event of criminal prosecution. Among these were the right to confront one's accusers, the right to know the charge one faced, the right to speedy trial, the right to present one's own case, the right to jury trial (with its common-law incidents), the right against self-incrimination, and the right to due process of law, all of which were ancient British rights. Article 9, the companion article, said that in the event of arrest, "excessive Bail ought not to be required," and it added that in case of conviction, there should be no "excessive Fines imposed nor cruel and unusual Punishments inflicted." Mason took much of the language of these various provisions directly from ancient English documents. With these articles, the delegates once again demonstrated their intellectual debt to Great Britain and their desire to retain most elements of their British legal inheritance.

Article 10, a ban on general warrants, which the agents of the Crown infamously had used in New England to search various dwellings and other buildings without cause, was yet another direct response to a recent imbroglio with Great Britain. Article 11 protected "the antient Trial by Jury" in cases "between Man and Man," and Article 12 declared, "That the freedom of the Press is one of the great Bulwarks of liberty and can never be restrained but by despotic Government." Article 13 said free states should depend on "well regulated Militia composed of the Body of the People" for their defense, not upon standing armies. The latter were anathema in peacetime, for they were "dangerous to liberty," and the military should always be subordinate to civil officials. Each of these articles demonstrated the Convention's consciousness of the rights of Englishmen and the extent of British constitutional thought's influence on them.[100]

"Justice Moderation Temperance Frugality and Virtue" were essential to "free Government," and so was "frequent recurrence to fundamental Principles," according to Article 15. George Mason evidently first held that "frequent recurrence to the maxims on which [an institution] was formed" was necessary in a June 1775 speech advocating one-year terms for Fairfax County militia officers. The explanation offered by the expositor of Jefferson's constitutional thought, who said "frequent recurrence to republican principles" referred to "the personal consent of the people," is persuasive.[101]

Article 16, finally, was James Madison's and George Mason's compromise on religion. "Religion," it asserted, was "the Duty which we owe to our Creator," and therefore each man should be left to be pious or impious "according to the Dictates of Conscience." However, it concluded, all bore the "Duty . . . to practice Christian Forbearance Love and Charity towards each other." Here, as in Article I, the Virginians amended their inherited institutions to take account of New World reality.

Considering the Declaration of Rights as a whole, one can only conclude that the Virginians were true to their word: they wanted to retain the traditional British relationship between the individual and society, and they hoped to erect their new constitution on a broad base of popular participation in politics. There were to be no nobles in the new system, yet substantial ownership of real property was to be a condition of political participation. Government was to be responsive to "the people," defined as the white, landed people of Virginia.

After the Declaration of Rights, the May Convention wrote, adopted, and implemented Virginia's new republican constitution. Given that it had to justify Virginia's secession from the British Empire and establish a framework for the new government, the Constitution of 1776 is a model of brevity.[102] Its organization is simple, with the Preamble, a set of assertions justifying separation from Great Britain, consisting of charges and a conclusion. The form of Jefferson's Preamble assumed that, as he had claimed in his *Summary View* a dozen years before, George III was an officer entrusted by the people with performance of certain functions, the failure to perform which terminated his tenure in office. Thus, the first section of the Preamble said George III had been "intrusted with the exercise of the Kingly Office in this Government" and had "endeavoured to pervert the same." Then began the list of colonial grievances, which Jefferson transmogrified into George's "perversions" of his "Office." The items Jefferson listed in justification of his "country's" action all recall Virginia's constitutional complaints. Little was said about economics, nothing about religion. The chief issue was Virginia's self-government, which the British had unconstitutionally curtailed. George's suspending clause requirement came in for criticism, as did his vetoes of some laws "most wholesome and necessary" (that is, passed by the House of Burgesses). The Virginians were galled by royal governors' repeated dissolutions of the General Assembly, which on more than one occasion they did not replace by holding new elections "for a long period of time." Jefferson complained about the refusal of the Crown to approve naturalization laws, which were intended "for the population of our Country," about maintenance of standing armies and warships in Virginia in peacetime, and about superordination of the military over the civil power. Every policy that Virginians wanted to adopt, they should have been allowed to adopt.

The Preamble's longest section concerned George's actions "to subject us to a foreign Jurisdiction," that is, Parliament. Instead of defending Virginians' inherited right to home rule, in this account, George had done precisely the opposite. The Preamble itemized the trade restrictions, foreign soldiers, taxes, foreign trials, and suspensions of legislatures foisted on Virginia by Parliament. Turning to Lord Dunmore's conduct of the war, Jefferson asserted that George (in the person of Dunmore) had pillaged the coasts and set fire to the towns of Virginia, incited insurrections among other whites, and prompted "our Negroes to rise in Arms . . . those very negroes whom by an inhuman use of his Negative he hath refused us permission to exclude by Law." Finally, George had stirred up the Indians against Virginia, sent mercenaries to finish the job, and "abandon[ed] the Helm of Government and declar[ed] us out of his Allegiance and Protection." "By which several Acts of Misrule the Government of this Country as formerly exercised under the Crown of Great Britain," began the concluding paragraph, "is totally dissolved."

Here was the constructive abdication theory in all its glory. Here was insistence that only Virginia had a right to legislate for Virginia, and here was George III as usurper refusing to accept a position as head of a great commonwealth of dominions tied together by common loyalty to his dynasty. Here was the vindication of the Virginia constitutional tradition. Here was revolution as restoration of the mythical status quo.

The body of the constitution, like the Preamble, grew naturally out of the Virginia tradition of colonial protest. The transition from the Preamble to the Constitution's main body referred to the threat of imminent anarchy as spurring the Convention to establish a new government. First, the Constitution announced the separation of powers as the leading doctrine of its organization, exemption being extended to the county courts alone. This statement of abstract principle was unique among the provisions of the constitution. The treatment of the House of Delegates and the county courts, each of which combined legislative, executive, and judicial power, put the lie to the principle.

The Constitution established a bicameral legislature, requiring that it meet at least, as Mason and his colleagues put it, "once or oftener every Year." There were to be no Stuarts governing without legislatures in Virginia. The House of Delegates would include two representatives from each county and one each from Williamsburg, Norfolk, and any city the legislature might choose, but the legislature was required to discontinue representation of any city whose population fell below a certain level. Virginians would not tolerate the advent of "rotten boroughs" in their republic, but representation would be apportioned by community (the historic method of England and its colonies), not by population.

Members of the "Senate" (after the ancient Roman upper house) would be chosen from larger districts to serve four-year terms. Suffrage would remain "as exercised at present," and each house would choose its own speaker. Never again would a chief executive sit in the Virginia legislature. The Senate was to be a subordinate house of the legislature, for all laws would originate in the more representative, responsible House of Delegates, and the Senate was to have no power even to alter "Money Bills." Still, while the Virginia Senate was a weak body, Virginia's senators were the first such officers in British America to be given independent power bases: they were responsible to the electorate, not to other officials.[103]

The governor was to "be chosen annually by joint Ballot of both Houses" and to hold the office no more than three years in seven.[104] His exercise of executive powers was hedged by a remade "Council of State," and even the pardon power was to be inoperative in regard to statutes the legislature had exempted. The governor must "not under any pretence exercise any power or prerogative by virtue of any law statute or Custom of England." No claim of Norman power was to be raised to subvert Virginians' Saxon liberty. The governor was to have command of the militia "when embodied," and peacetime replacements of militia officers were to be made by the governor and Council on the advice of the county courts. The governor was explicitly disallowed from proroguing or dissolving the Assembly. He was liable to impeachment for misfeasance, but only after his term expired. In short, while their government obviously had to have an executive, Virginians had learned quite a lot from British history about the misuses to which executive power could be put.

The Council of State, composed of eight members, would be chosen by the two houses jointly, and it was to choose a president to govern in the event of the governor's incapacitation. Two members of the Council would be removed by joint ballot of the Assembly every three years, and those removed would be ineligible for reelection for three years thereafter. Councilmen were barred from sitting in the General Assembly.

Virginia's Continental Congress delegates were to be elected by joint ballot of the General Assembly and to be subject to removal by the same means. Judges of courts other than the county courts were to be selected by joint ballot of the General Assembly, to serve "during good behavior," and to "have fixed and adequate Salaries," which eliminated the possibility of governors' meddling in judicial decision making (an important factor in the Whig account of English history) and, supposedly, that of popular pressure on judges. Virginia's judges were thus made the first distinct judicial branch, in the modern sense of the term, in the world. Along with "ministers of the Gospel of every Denomination," judges were barred from concurrent service on the Council or in the General Assembly. They could be impeached.

The governor's power to replace justices of the peace was qualified by the requirement that he do so "upon the recommendation of the respective County Courts," which in effect meant that the county courts' de facto self-perpetuating status was formalized. Several local officers were to be appointed by the governor on the local courts' advice. These provisions served to maintain and formalize the dominance of the county oligarchies, the local branches of the Virginia aristocratic families.

Following a formula suggested by John Adams in "Thoughts on Government," the Constitution required that legal documents, such as commissions, grants, writs, and indictments, be issued "In the Name of the Common Wealth." Previously, they had run in the name of the king. Similar changes were made with regard to escheats and other payments. To avoid the troubles that had arisen as a result of the previous union of the offices of colonial treasurer and speaker of the House of Burgesses, the constitution required annual election of the treasurer by the General Assembly.[105]

Virginia's foreign concerns involved more than its relations with Great Britain and with potential allies such as France. Virginia had potential boundary disputes with several British colonies whose territory had been carved out of the original Virginia grant. The Constitution of 1776, at Jefferson's suggestion, headed off any such destructive disputes by explicitly recognizing the territorial claims of Pennsylvania, the Carolinas, and Maryland. Other than that, Virginia claimed the boundaries recognized by James I in 1609 and by France in 1763. It also rejected all private claims to having purchased land within Virginia from the Indians.[106]

The constitution provided finally that the Convention would choose republican Virginia's initial officeholders, which it immediately proceeded to do. As mentioned above, the Convention approved the constitution unanimously. The delegates had achieved their revolutionary purpose: they had put into law what had been brewing in Virginia's political life for decades. The new relationship among the various institutions of the government was not a break with tradition, but a continuation of it. The House of Delegates had its way, and the Council was reduced to a near nullity. The Senate was clearly subordinate to the House of Delegates. Governors had very tightly circumscribed power, and the mode of their selection made them, too, essentially subordinate. The appellate system erected to oversee the county courts was to be far more to Virginians' liking than the old system of sending Virginia's causes beyond the sea for eventual disposition. The county courts' organization went untouched, their dominance of local government formalized.

Finally, the existence of a written constitution leaving almost all important policy matters to the legislature marked a triumph for the way Virginians had imagined things should be, a revivification of the shrouded Saxon past. Bland stood triumphant. In combination, the Constitution of 1776 and the Virginia Declaration of Rights amounted to the establishment of the polity for which Virginia's elite radicals had contended all along. The freedoms of speech and from standing armies were secured, the protections offered by traditional British civil and criminal law procedures were perpetuated, appeals from courts' decisions were to be handled within Virginia (more specifically, within the Virginia gentry), and both the county courts and the House of Burgesses (rechristened the House of Delegates) were on firmer footing than ever before. In fact, none of the draft constitutions had elevated the House of Delegates at the expense of the other institutions to the extent that the final version did. The self-perpetuating nature of the county oligarchies had been written into Virginia's fundamental law, and the competing power centers—the Council and the Governorship (as agent for the Crown)—had been taken down a good two or three pegs. The whole edifice stood on the base provided by Bland's and Jefferson's notion of the significance of the nature of Virginia's first English settlement. Richard Bland's importunings had been heeded to an extent that must have exceeded his wildest dreams. Virginia's planter elite had only to win the Revolution to vindicate its claim to self-government.

Of course, while the impulse underlying Virginia's first republican constitution was essentially conservative, its implications were anything but. Gone was any link to the British Crown, which formerly had stood behind all Virginia law; gone was any tie to the Church of England, which once had validated even the Crown. In short order, Virginia's ruling elite would see the leveling implications of its revolution spin out of control. By the end of the revolutionary decade, Virginia law and society would have been extensively, though not thoroughly, remade.

NOTES

1. James Madison to William Bradford, c. 21 May 1776, *Papers of James Madison*, 1: 180; H[enry] A[ugustine] Washington, *The Virginia Constitution of 1776: A Discourse Delivered Before the Virginia Historical Society, at Their Annual Meeting, January 17th, 1852* (Richmond, Va.: Macfarlane & Ferguson, 1852), 5.

2. Richard Henry Lee to Patrick Henry, 20 April 1776, *The Letters of Richard Henry Lee*, ed. James Curtis Ballagh (New York: DaCapo Press, 1970), 1: 176.

3. John Carter Matthews, "Richard Henry Lee and the American Revolution" (Ph.D. dissertation, University of Virginia, 1939), 124; William Wirt Henry, *Patrick Henry: Life, Correspondence, and Speeches* (1891; reprinted Harrisonburg, Va.: Sprinkle Publications, 1993), 1: 407. Also see Hugh Blair Grigsby, *The Virginia Convention of 1776*, (1855; reprinted New York: DaCapo Press, 1969), 165.

4. Thomas Jefferson to Major John Cartwright, 5 June 1824, *The Writings of Thomas Jefferson*, ed. Albert Ellery Bergh (Washington, D.C.: The Thomas Jefferson Memorial Association, 1904), 16: 45–46.

5. H. Trevor Colbourn, *The Lamp of Experience: Whig History and the Intellectual Origins of the American Revolution* (Chapel Hill: The University of North Carolina Press, 1965), 150–51.

6. *Ibid.*, 151–52, vii.

7. *Ibid.*, 156–57; Albert Ogden Porter, *County Government in Virginia: A Legislative History, 1607–1904* (New York: Columbia University Press, 1947), 101–102; Elisha P. Douglas, *Rebels and Democrats: The Struggle for Equal Political Rights and Majority Rule during the American Revolution* (Chapel Hill: University of North Carolina Press, 1955), 7–8; *Revolutionary Virginia: The Road to Independence: A Documentary Record*, eds. Brent Tarter et al. (Charlottesville: University Press of Virginia, 1973–1983), 7: 627–28. An excellent biography of the underappreciated Bland is Robert Chester Daetweiler, "Richard Bland, Conservator of Self-Government in Eighteenth-Century Virginia" (Ph.D. dissertation, University of Washington, 1968).

8. H[enry] A[ugustine] Washington, *The Virginia Constitution of 1776: A Discourse Delivered Before the Virginia Historical Society, at Their Annual Meeting, January 17th, 1852*, 5. For a perceptive short sketch of Washington, see the introduction to "The Social System of Virginia" by Michael O'Brien in *All Clever Men, Who Make Their Way*, ed. Michael O'Brien (Athens: University of Georgia Press, 1992), 228–30.

9. See, for example, the reference to "The principles of the ever-glorious *revolution*" by "Brutus" in his letter "to the inhabitants of a certain county in this colony, assembled for the purpose of representing them in colony convention," 15 May 1775, *Revolutionary Virginia*, 3: 126–32, at 132.

10. Hugh Blair Grigsby, *The Virginia Convention of 1776*, 5, 6; Glenn Curtis Smith, "Pamphleteers and the American Revolution in Virginia, 1752–1776" (Ph.D. dissertation, University of Virginia, 1937), 2. Some Virginians of the Imperial Crisis period, at least, accepted James I's famous linkage of episcopacy and monarchy. *Revolutionary Virginia*, 189.

11. Elisha P. Douglas, *Rebels and Democrats*, 290.

12. See "A Va. Congressman to a friend in W'burg," 30 June 1775, *Letters of Members of the Continental Congress*, ed. Edmund C. Burnett (1921; reprinted Gloucester, Mass.: Peter Smith, 1963), 1: 148, wherein a leading Virginian holds out the certain hope that the Ministry will be punished for its unlawful behavior ere long; in the same vein, see Richard Henry Lee to William Lee, 20 September 1774, *Ibid.*, 37.

13. Jack P. Greene, "Society, Ideology, and Politics: An Analysis of the Political Culture of Mid-Eighteenth-Century Virginia," in *Negotiated Authorities: Essays in Colonial Political and Constitutional History* (Charlottesville and London: University Press of Virginia, 1994), 259–318, at 279, 285; Robert Leroy Hilldrup, "The Virginia Convention of 1776," 6; *Revolutionary Virginia*, 7: 722–23.

14. Jack P. Greene, "Society, Ideology, and Politics," 318; *Papers of Thomas Jefferson*, ed. Julian P. Boyd et al. (Princeton, N.J.: Princeton University Press, 1950–), 1: 26–27; "A Summary View of the Rights of British America," *Ibid.*, 1: 121–35, at 129; Edmund Pendleton to Richard Corbin, 19 February 1776, *Revolutionary Virginia*, 6: 112–13; *Ibid.*, 6: 518–26, at 521; "Stamp Act Resolutions," 29–30 May 1765, *Ibid.*, 1: 17–18. Also see the House of Burgesses's petition to the House of Commons, 18 December 1764, *Ibid.*, 1: 13–14.

15. These included Richard Bland's 1766 "An Inquiry into the Rights of the British Colonies, Intended as an Answer to the Regulations Lately Made concerning the Colonies, and the Taxes Imposed upon Them Considered in a Letter Addressed to the Author of That Pamphlet," *Revolutionary Virginia*, 1: 18–44; the General Assembly's petition to the House of Lords regarding the Quartering and Townshend Acts, 16 April 1768, *Ibid.*, 56–59; "The British American [Thomson Mason], No VI," *Ibid.*, 177–82; Thomas Jeffer-

son's draft Declaration of Rights, c. 26 July 1774, *Papers of Thomas Jefferson*, 1: 119–20; Thomas Jefferson, *Summary View*; *Ibid.*, 121–35; and Thomas Jefferson, "Notes on the State of Virginia," 23–232, at Query XIV, 177, *et seq.*, among others. For Bland's influence on Jefferson, see K[evin] R. Constantine Gutzman, "Jefferson's Draft Declaration of Independence, Richard Bland, and the Revolutionary Legacy: Giving Credit Where Credit Is Due," *The Journal of the Historical Society* 1 (2000–2001): 137–54.

16. *Ibid.*, 1: 17–18.

17. Pauline Maier, *American Scripture: Making the Declaration of Independence* (New York: Alfred A. Knopf, 1997), 90–91.

18. K[evin] R. Constantine Gutzman, "Jefferson's Draft Declaration of Independence, Richard Bland, and the Revolutionary Legacy: Giving Credit Where Credit Is Due."

19. Jack P. Greene, "Society, Ideology, and Politics," 287.

20. Thornton Miller, *Judges and Juries versus the Law: Virginia's Provincial Legal Perspective, 1783–1828* (Charlottesville and London: University Press of Virginia, 1994), 6; H. Trevor Colbourn, *The Lamp of Experience*, 8.

21. *English Historical Documents: American Colonial Documents to 1776*, ed. Merrill Jensen (New York: Oxford University Press, 1964), 268–71. That first Virginia charter said, in relevant part,

> Alsoe wee doe, for us, our heires and successors, declare by theise presentes that all and everie the persons being our subjects which shall dwell and inhabit within everie or anie of the saide severall Colonies and plantacions and everie of their children which shall happen to be borne within the limitts and precincts of the said severall Colonies and plantacions shall have and enjoy all liberties, franchises and immunities within anie of our other dominions to all intents and purposes as if they had been abiding and borne within this our realme of Englande or anie other of our saide dominions.

A. E. Dick Howard, *Commentaries*, 1.

22. *Revolutionary Virginia*, 1: 23–26.

23. M. J. C. Vile, *Constitutionalism and the Separation of Powers* (Oxford: Clarendon Press, 1967), 135.

24. Thad W. Tate, "The Coming of the Revolution in Virginia: Britain's Challenge to Virginia's Ruling Class, 1763–1776," *William and Mary Quarterly*, 3d series, vol. 19 (1962), 323–43, at 341–43.

25. Jack P. Greene, *The Quest for Power: The Lower Houses of Assembly in the Southern Royal Colonies, 1689–1776* (Chapel Hill: University of North Carolina Press, 1963), 16.

26. *The Diary of Landon Carter of Sabine Hall, 1752–1778*, ed. Jack P. Greene (2d edition, Richmond: The Virginia Historical Society, 1987), 1,045–46.

27. Thomas Jefferson to Henry Lee, 8 May 1825, *The Writings of Thomas Jefferson*, 16: 117–19, at 118.

28. Thomas Jefferson, "Notes on the State of Virginia," Query XIX, 216–17, at 216.

29. John Carter Matthews, "Richard Henry Lee and the American Revolution" (Ph.D. dissertation, University of Virginia, 1939), 38–40; Richard Henry Lee to Samuel Adams, 23 June 1774 [emphasis added], *Letters of Richard Henry Lee*, 1: 111–13; Richard Henry Lee to William Lee, 10 May 1775, *Letters of the Members of the Continental*

Congress, 1: 89–90. Richard Henry Lee to Chairman, Committee of Northumberland County, 5 December 1775, *Revolutionary Virginia*, 5: 54. Also see Richard Henry Lee to Arthur Lee, 26 June 1774, *Letters of Richard Henry Lee*, 1: 114–18 (wherein resentment of the ministry's behavior remains joined to protestations of the loyalty of George III's "truly loyal American subjects" at 117); Proclamation of a Day of Prayer and Fasting, 24 May 1774, *Revolutionary Virginia*, 1: 94–95; An Association of Late Burgesses, 27 May 1774, *Ibid.*, 1: 97–98, at 97; "The British American [Thomson Mason], No. VII," *Virginia Gazette*, 14 July 1774, *Ibid.*, 1: 182–87, at 184.

30. Thad W. Tate, "The Coming of the Revolution in Virginia: Britain's Challenge to Virginia's Ruling Class, 1763–1776," 323–43, at 324; *Revolutionary Virginia*, 7: 649–54; "Fifth Virginia Convention, Forty-Second Day (24 June 1776)," *Ibid.*, 592–99, at 597.

31. Jack P. Greene, *Landon Carter: An Inquiry into the Personal Values and Social Imperatives of the Eighteenth-Century Virginia Gentry* (Charlottesville: University Press of Virginia, 1967), 69–70; "The British American [Thomson Mason], No. IV," *Virginia Gazette*, 16 June 1774, *Revolutionary Virginia*, 1: 170–72, at 172.

32. Jack P. Greene, *The Quest for Power: The Lower Houses of Assembly in the Southern Royal Colonies, 1689–1776*, 442.

33. Evarts Boutell Greene, *The Provincial Governor in the English Colonies of North America* (Cambridge: Harvard University Press, 1898) 42, 202; M. J. C. Vile, *Constitutionalism and the Separation of Powers*, 126–27; Jack P. Greene, "Society, Ideology, and Politics," 279, 318.

34. Evarts Boutell Greene, *The Provincial Governor in the English Colonies of North America*, 203–4; Percy Scott Flippin, *The Royal Government in Virginia, 1624–1775* (New York: Columbia University, 1919), 369–70; M. J. C. Vile, *Constitutionalism and the Separation of Powers*, 127–28.

35. Benjamin F. Wright, Jr., "The Early History of Written Constitutions in America," in *Essays in History and Political Theory in Honor of Charles McIlwain* (Cambridge, Mass.: Harvard University Press, 1936), 348; Robert Leroy Hilldrup, "The Virginia Convention of 1776," 6.

36. Jack P. Greene, *The Quest for Power: The Lower Houses of Assembly in the Southern Royal Colonies*, 9, 438–39, 440–41; *Revolutionary Virginia*, 1: 237.

37. *Ibid.*, 13, 355, 450–51, 452–53; quotation from Jack P. Greene, "Society, Ideology, and Culture," 271; "The British American [Thomson Mason], No. IX," *Virginia Gazette*, 28 July 1774, *Revolutionary Virginia*, 1: 193–203, at 194.

38. James LaVerne Anderson, "The Governors' Councils of Colonial America, A Study of Pennsylvania and Virginia, 1660–1776" (Ph.D. dissertation, University of Virginia, 1967), 14, 15, 18, 22.

39. *Ibid.*, 27, 32, 33, 306; Jack P. Greene, "Society, Ideology, and Culture," 281; Percy Scott Flippin, *The Royal Government in Virginia, 1624–1775*, 364–65.

40. *Ibid.*, 362–65; Jack P. Greene, "Society, Ideology, and Politics," 282–85 (for an appraisal of the governorship of Governor Sir William Gooch, a "successful" governor whose tenure lasted from 1727 to 1749 and who "extirpated all factions" at the expense of effectively acquiescing in home rule).

41. Evarts Boutell Greene, *The Provincial Governor in the English Colonies of North America*, 196–97, 204–5; Jack P. Greene, "Society, Ideology, and Culture," 285, 287; Pauline Maier, *American Scripture*, 147. For Virginians' willingness to accept proper authority if it were properly delimited, see "The British American [Thomson Ma-

son], No. IX," *Virginia Gazette*, 28 July 1774, *Revolutionary Virginia*, 1: 193–203, at 200. There, Mason decried the shutting up of the port of Boston while he conceded that it was King George's prerogative to move the Massachusetts capitol.

42. M. J. C. Vile, *Constitutionalism and the Separation of Powers*, 127–28, 132; *Papers of Thomas Jefferson*, 1: 121–35, at 121–22.

43. "The Gentlemen Volunteers of the Independent Company to Peyton Randolph: An Open Letter," 1 June 1775, *Revolutionary Virginia*, 3: 178.

44. Jack P. Greene, "Society, Ideology, and Politics," 261–62, 264–65, 269; F. Thornton Miller, *Judges and Juries versus the Law*, 6; *Revolutionary Virginia*, 7: 627–29.

45. Albert Ogden Porter, *County Government in Virginia: A Legislative History, 1607–1904* (New York: Columbia University Press, 1947), 101; Willi Paul Adams, *The First American Constitutions: Republican Ideology and the Making of the State Constitutions in the Revolutionary Era*, 250; Rhys Isaac, *The Transformation of Virginia, 1740–1790* (New York and London: W. W. Norton & Company, 1982), 245. Virtually no one. George Mason, the leading author of the Declaration of Rights and the main body of the Constitution, had only one complaint about the May Convention's work: it had left too much authority in the hands of the gentry, acting through the county courts. Irving Brant, *James Madison: The Virginia Revolutionist* (Indianapolis and New York: The Bobbs-Merrill Company, 1941), 260.

46. See especially Glenn Curtis Smith, "Pamphleteers and the American Revolution in Virginia, 1752–1776"; and the convenient collection of many of the important pamphlets in *Revolutionary Virginia*, vol. 1.

47. T. H. Breen, *Tobacco Culture: The Mentality of the Great Tidewater Planters on the Eve of Revolution* (Princeton, N.J.: Princeton University Press, 1985); Bruce A. Ragsdale, *A Planters' Republic: The Search for Economic Independence in Revolutionary Virginia* (Madison, Wisc.: Madison House, 1996); Woody Holton, *Forced Founders: Indians, Debtors, Slaves, & the Making of the American Revolution in Virginia* (Chapel Hill: The University of North Carolina Press, 1999).

48. Jack P. Greene, "Society, Ideology, and Politics," 301–3.

49. After the Revolution, Thomas Jefferson encapsulated the constitutional thought of Bland, Thomson Mason, Carter, and other Virginians in Query XIII of his *Notes*. Thomas Jefferson, *Notes*, 153–76. Also see Francis D. Wormuth, *The Origins of Modern Constitutionalism* (New York: Harper & Brothers, 1949), 169–73.

50. Jack P. Greene, *Peripheries and Center: Constitutional Development in the Extended Polities of the British Empire and the United States, 1607–1788* (New York and London: W. W. Norton and Company, 1986); Petition of the General Assembly to King George III, 18 December 1764, *Revolutionary Virginia*, 1: 10–11.

51. Virginius Dabney, *Virginia, The New Dominion: A History From 1607 to the Present* (Charlottesville: University Press of Virginia, 1971), 100–101.

52. Glenn Curtis Smith, "Pamphleteers and the American Revolution in Virginia, 1752–1776," 9–10, 14–15, 18.

53. *Ibid.*, 30–31, 56–58.

54. *Ibid.*, 69–75.

55. *Ibid.*, 95–96.

56. *Ibid.*, 91–92; H. Trevor Colbourn, *The Lamp of Experience*, 144–45.

57. The following discussion is based on the text in *Revolutionary Virginia*, 1: 28–44.

58. For example, the 18 December 1764 communications to the House of Lords and the House of Commons each spelled out Virginia's claims that the right to taxation only by representatives was both essential to British liberty and one the first Virginia settlers had brought with them intact, that the Commons did not represent them, and that any other situation amounted to "slavery." "To the House of Lords," 18 December 1764, *Ibid.*, 1: 11–12; "To the House of Commons," 18 December 1764, *Ibid.*, 13–14. Also see *Ibid.*, *passim.*, which includes literally dozens of statements of these principles spanning the entire decade between 1763 and 1776 from individuals, local committees, local courts, the House of Burgesses, and the Committee of Safety. The most famous such statement is Thomas Jefferson's *Summary View*, which is a pithy digest of what his fellow gentry politicians had been saying for over a decade. As J. Derrida said of Jefferson in the case of the United States' Declaration of Independence, so he might well have said of him in this case, he "was not responsible for *writing*, in the productive or initiating sense of the term, only for drawing up, as one says of a secretary that he or she draws up a *letter* of which the spirit has been breathed into him or her, or even the content dictated." Pauline Maier, *American Scripture*, 267, n. 56.

59. K[evin] R. Constantine Gutzman, "Jefferson's Draft Declaration of Independence, Richard Bland, and the Revolutionary Legacy: Giving Credit Where Credit Is Due."

60. William Wirt Henry, *Patrick Henry*, 1: 358–59.

61. Also see Richard Henry Lee to Samuel Adams, 23 June 1774, *Letters of Richard Henry Lee,* 1: 111–13; Richard Henry Lee to Arthur Lee, 26 June 1774, *Ibid.*, 114–18.

62. "The British American, No. IV," *Virginia Gazette*, 16 June 1774, *Revolutionary Virginia*, 1: 170–72; "The British American, No. V," *Virginia Gazette*, 30 June 1774, *Ibid.*, 1: 172–77; "The British American, No. VI," *Virginia Gazette*, 7 July 1774, *Ibid.*, 177–82; "The British American, No. VII," *Virginia Gazette*, 14 July 1774, *Ibid.*, 182–87.

63. Thomas Jefferson picked up on this idea in his draft declaration of rights in 1774. Thomas Jefferson's Draft Declaration of Rights, c. 26 July 1774, *Papers of Thomas Jefferson*, 1: 119–20, at 119.

64. In the end, Virginia's political leaders would arrive at the conclusion regarding injury to innocent Britons due to American resistance that "charity must begin at home, and the liberties of North America be at all events secured." Richard Henry Lee to Catherine Macaulay, 29 November 1775, *Letters of Richard Henry Lee*, 1: 160–64, at 162.

65. "The British American, No. IX," *Virginia Gazette*, 28 July 1774, *Revolutionary Virginia*, 1: 193–203.

66. "Jefferson's Draft Declaration of Independence, Richard Bland, and the Revolutionary Legacy: Giving Credit Where Credit Is Due," *The Journal of the Historical Society* 1 (2001), 137–54.

67. For a similar composition written at the same time, see Jefferson's "Resolutions of the Freeholders of Albemarle County," 26 July 1774, *Papers of Thomas Jefferson*, 1: 117–18, n. at 118–19. Also see Pauline Maier, *American Scripture*, 112. For the *Summary View*, see *Papers of Thomas Jefferson*, 1: 121–35.

68. Jefferson would repeat this claim, and virtually the entirety of his *Summary View*, in his draft "Declaration of the Causes and Necessity of Taking up Arms," 6 July 1775, *Papers of Thomas Jefferson*, 1: 193–98.

69. K[evin] R. Constantine Gutzman, "Jefferson's Draft Declaration of Independence, Richard Bland, and the Revolutionary Legacy: Giving Credit Where Credit Is

Due." Jefferson characterized Bland as "the most learned authority on constitutional history in the colony" and as "the most learned and logical man of those who took prominent lead in public affairs." *Papers of Thomas Jefferson,* 1: 164, n. at 165. Also see Robert Chester Daetweiler, "Richard Bland: Conservator of Self-Government in Eighteenth-Century Virginia," 18.

70. "Virginia Instructs Her Delegates to the First Continental Congress," 6 August 1774, *Revolutionary Virginia,* 1: 236–39, at 237–38. While Jefferson's position here was consistent with that of the "British American," Thomson Mason, who had said that no act of Parliament passed since 1607 bound Virginia, was later contradicted by the July 1775 Fairfax County Resolves written by his brother George Mason, which conceded that Virginia had consented to Parliament's commercial regulations. Kate Mason Rowland, *The Life of George Mason, 1725–1792,* 1: 172–75.

71. Richard Henry Lee to Samuel Adams, 4 February 1775, *Letters of Richard Henry Lee,* 1: 127–30.

72. William Wirt Henry, *Patrick Henry,* 1: 363.

73. H. Trevor Colbourn, *The Lamp of Experience,* 165–66; Richard Henry Lee to Patrick Henry, 20 April 1776, *Letters of Richard Henry Lee,* 1: 176–80; Charles Ramsdell Lingley, *The Transition in Virginia from Colony to Commonwealth* (New York: Columbia University, 1910), 158.

74. John Carter Matthews, "Richard Henry Lee and the American Revolution," 42–43; Steven Harold Hochman, "Republicanism in Virginia and the Constitution of 1776" (M.A. thesis, University of Virginia, 1970), 8–9; Francis Lightfoot Lee to Landon Carter, 9 April 1776, *Letters of Members of the Continental Congress,* 1: 416–17; "Buckingham County Freeholders' Instructions to Their Delegates," 13 May 1776, *Revolutionary Virginia,* 7: 109–12.

75. Jack N. Rakove, *The Beginnings of National Politics* (New York: Alfred A. Knopf, 1979), 95; David John Mays, *Edmund Pendleton, 1721–1803: A Biography* (Cambridge, Mass.: Harvard University Press, 1952), 106.

76. William J. Van Schreeven, *The Conventions and Constitutions of Virginia, 1776–1966* (Richmond: Virginia State Library, 1967), 1; "Fifth Virginia Convention, Fifth Day (10 May 1776)," *Revolutionary Virginia,* 7: 87–89, at 87. Fletcher M. Green, *Constitutional Development in the South Atlantic States, 1776–1860: A Study in the Evolution of , Democracy* (Chapel Hill: University of North Carolina Press, 1930), 62–63; "Charlotte County Committee to Delegates Paul Carrington and Thomas Read: A Public Letter of Instructions, Fifth Virginia Convention (23 April 1776)," *Revolutionary Virginia,* 6: 447–48; "Buckingham County Freeholders' Instructions to Their Delegates (13 May 1776)," 7: 109–12; Irving Brant, *James Madison: The Virginia Revolutionist,* 197.

77. "Fifth Virginia Convention, First Day (6 May 1776)," *Revolutionary Virginia,* 7: 26–30, at 26–27; Hugh Blair Grigsby, *The Virginia Convention of 1776,* 9; David John Mays, *Edmund Pendleton, 1721–1803: A Biography,* 104. Of the many accounts of the May Convention, the best remains Kate Mason Rowland, *The Life of George Mason, 1725–1792,* 1: 228–66. Also see "introductory note," *Revolutionary Virginia,* 7: 1–15.

78. Hugh Blair Grigsby, *The Virginia Convention of 1776,* 71; H. Trevor Colbourn, *The Lamp of Experience,* xi; Steven Harold Hochman, *Republicanism in Virginia and the Constitution of 1776,* 28.

79. Richard Henry Lee to Patrick Henry, 20 April 1776, *Letters of Richard Henry Lee,* 1: 176–80, at 177–78; Irving Brant, *James Madison: The Virginia Revolutionist,* 221.

80. Patrick Henry to Richard Henry Lee, 20 May 1776, in William Wirt Henry, *Patrick Henry*, 1: 410–12; Patrick Henry to John Adams, 20 May 1776, in *Ibid.*, 412–13.

81. *Revolutionary Virginia*, 7: 140; Oliver Perry Chitwood, *Richard Henry Lee: Statesman of the Revolution*, 93; Hugh Blair Grigsby, *The Virginia Convention of 1776*, 18. Carter Braxton agreed with Lee and Adams regarding the significance of the Congress's advice. Carter Braxton to Landon Carter, 17 May 1776, *Letters of Members of the Continental Congress*, 1: 453–54; David John Mays, *Edmund Pendleton, 1721–1803: A Biography*, 2: 107, 108; *Revolutionary Virginia*, 7: 145–47, n. 8.

82. "Virginia Convention Instructs Congressmen to Move Independence, Form Foreign Alliances, Join A Confederation; Also Resolves to Write A Constitution," 15 May 1776, *English Historical Documents: American Colonial Documents to 1776*, ed. Merrill Jensen (New York: Oxford University Press, 1964), 866–67; David John Mays, *Edmund Pendleton, 1721–1803: A Biography*, 2: 108–10; Thomas Ludwell Lee to Richard Henry Lee, 18 May 1776, in Kate Mason Rowland, *The Life of George Mason, 1725–1792*, 1: 225; *Ibid.*, 1: 223; *Revolutionary Virginia*, 7: 147, n. 13; Charles Ramsdell Lingley, *The Transition in Virginia from Colony to Commonwealth*, 164; H. A. Washington, *The Virginia Constitution of 1776*, 5.

83. William J. Van Schreeven, *The Conventions and Constitutions of Virginia, 1776–1966*, 1–2.

84. Edmund Randolph, *History of Virginia*, ed. Arthur H. Shaffer (Charlottesville: University Press of Virginia, 1970), 251–52; Marc W. Kruman, *Between Authority & Liberty: State Constitution Making in Revolutionary America*, 18; Thomas Jefferson to Thomas Nelson, 16 May 1776, *Papers of Thomas Jefferson*, 1: 292–93; *Kamper v. Hawkins*, 1 Va. Cases 20 (1793).

85. Thomas Jefferson to Richard Henry Lee, 8 July 1776, *Papers of Thomas Jefferson*, 1: 455–56; Steven Harold Hochman, *Republicanism in Virginia and the Constitution of 1776*, 13; George Mason to Richard Henry Lee, 18 May 1776, in Kate Mason Rowland, *The Life of George Mason, 1725–1792*, 1: 226–27; Robert Leroy Hilldrup, "The Virginia Convention of 1776," 175–76.

86. John E. Selby, "Richard Henry Lee, John Adams, and the Virginia Constitution of 1776," *The Virginia Magazine of History and Biography*, 84 (1976), 387–400, at 396; Thomas Jefferson to Augustus B. Woodward, 3 April 1825, *The Writings of Thomas Jefferson*, 16: 116–17.

87. *Revolutionary Virginia*, n. 18 at 603–4; J. R. Pole, "Representation and Authority in Virginia From the Revolution to Reform," 21–22; Richard Henry Lee to Samuel Adams, 6 July 1776, *Letters of Richard Henry Lee*, 1: 207; Edmund Randolph, *History of Virginia*, 256.

88. Robert E. and B. Katherine Brown, *Virginia 1705–1786: Democracy or Aristocracy?* (East Lansing: Michigan State University, 1964), 290; J. R. Pole, "Representation and Authority in Virginia From the Revolution to Reform," 25. In England, suffrage had been tied to property since 1430. Chilton Williamson, *American Suffrage: From Property to Democracy, 1760–1860*, 5.

89. John E. Selby, "Richard Henry Lee, John Adams, and the Virginia Constitution of 1776," 397–98; Steven Harold Hochman, *Republicanism in Virginia and the Constitution of 1776*, 16; Richard Henry Lee to Robert Carter Nicholas, 30 April 1776, *Letters of Richard Henry Lee*, 1: 183–86; John Carter Matthews, "Richard Henry Lee and the American Revolution," 179.

90. *Revolutionary Virginia*, n. 18 at 604; Robert P. Sutton, *Revolution to Secession*, 40.

91. *Revolutionary Virginia*, 6: 518–26.

92. Patrick Henry to John Adams, 20 May 1776, in William Wirt Henry, *Patrick Henry*, 1: 412–15; Richard Henry Lee to Edmund Pendleton, 12 May 1776, *Letters of Richard Henry Lee*, 1: 190–91; William Fleming to Thomas Jefferson, 27 July 1776, *Papers of Thomas Jefferson*, 1: 474.

93. For the more perceptive view, Marc W. Kruman, *Between Authority & Liberty: State Constitution Making in Revolutionary America*, 2–3. Examples of later adoption of Braxton's views include the general abandonment of annual elections and the independence of the Executive Branch in the United States Constitution.

94. Edmund Pendleton to Carter Braxton, 12 May 1776, *Letters and Papers of Edmund Pendleton*, 1: 177; Edmund Pendleton to Thomas Jefferson, 26 August 1776, *Papers of Thomas Jefferson*, 1: 507–8.

95. Edmund Randolph, *History of Virginia*, 250–51.

96. As proposed, section 1 said, "THAT all men are born equally free and independent, and have certain inherent natural rights, of which they cannot, by any compact, deprive or divest their posterity," *Revolutionary Virginia*, 7: 271.

97. Edmund Randolph, *History of Virginia*, 253, 255; "A Declaration of Rights," *Revolutionary Virginia*, 7: 449–50; David John Mays, *Edmund Pendleton, 1721–1803: A Biography*, 2: 122. In June 1775, Mason pontificated that, "We came equal into this world, and equal shall we go out of it. All men are by nature born equally free and independent." Kate Mason Rowland, *The Life of George Mason, 1725–1792*, 1: 196–97.

98. A. E. Dick Howard, *Commentaries on the Constitution of Virginia*, 39; *Papers of James Madison*, 1: 104–6, 172–75; Irving Brant, *James Madison: The Virginia Revolutionist*, 247, 241; "Fifth Virginia Convention, Fifty-second Day (5 July 1776)," *Revolutionary Virginia*, 7: 706–9, at 708–9; Kate Mason Rowland, *The Life of George Mason, 1725–1792*, 1: 228–29. Mason's and Madison's drafts are at *Papers of James Madison*, 1: 172–75. As adopted, the religion provision of the Declaration of Rights said, "That Religion or the Duty which we owe to our Creator and the manner of discharging it can be directed only by reason and Conviction not by force or Violence and therefore all Men are equally intitled to the free exercise of Religion according to the Dictates of Conscience And that it is the mutual Duty of all to practice Christian Forbearance Love and Charity towards each other." *Revolutionary Virginia*, 7: 450.

99. This discussion is based on the final version of the Virginia Declaration of Rights, as found at *Ibid.*, 7: 449–50.

100. *The Eighteenth-Century Constitution, 1688–1815: Documents and Commentary*, ed. E. Neville Williams (Cambridge: Cambridge University Press, 1960), 27.

101. Irving Brant, *James Madison: The Virginia Revolutionist*, 196–97, 242; David N. Mayer, *The Constitutional Thought of Thomas Jefferson*, 300–301.

102. The following discussion is based on the final version of the Virginia Constitution of 1776, as found in *Revolutionary Virginia*, 7: 649–54.

103. Willi Paul Adams, *The First Constitutions: Republican Ideology and the Making of the State Constitutions in the Revolutionary Era*, 267–68. George Mason proposed a scheme similar to that which Jefferson discussed with Pendleton, in which electors would be chosen by the electorate of each Senate district to choose its senators. Mason failed to convince his May Convention colleagues of this idea's merit. Kate Mason Rowland, *The Life of George Mason, 1725–1792*, 1: 260.

104. None of the draft constitutions, including Jefferson's, incorporated a proposal that the governor be elected by popular vote. Charles Ramsdell Lingley, *The Transition in Virginia From Colony to Commonwealth*, 172–73.

105. Jack P. Greene, "The Attempt to Separate the Offices of Speaker and Treasurer in Virginia, 1758–1766: *An Incident in Imperial Conflict*," in Jack P. Greene, *Negotiated Authorities*, 319–27.

106. The constitution made no mention of the original Virginia grant so as not to impugn the notion of the original immigrants' "natural" right, trumpeted by Bland and Jefferson, to reach their own *modus vivendi* with the English Crown.

2

IMPLEMENTING THE REVOLUTION, 1776–1788

Implementation of the revolutionary constitution of 1776 was but the beginning. Having established their independence and vindicated their claim to self-government, Virginians had to replace the entire political, legal, and social system they had rejected. Convinced that provincial institutions were largely inconsistent with the principles that underlay their resistance to the government of George III, leading Virginians set out to reform them along republican lines. All of this had to be accomplished during a war pitting their ill-prepared commonwealth against the world's greatest military power. The long decade after the adoption of the Virginia constitution thus became a time of great military duress and of unprecedented political possibility.

Between the de facto declaration of independence of 15 May 1776 and the departure of a Virginia delegation for the federal convention in Philadelphia in 1787, Virginians subjected many of their basic social institutions to criticism, even outright rejection. In the press of war, the entire mass of reform projects could not be considered all at once. Some of the reformers' ideas met with stony rejection. Some were adopted, then never put into practice. Others sailed to easy adoption on a sea of consensus (not to say disinterest). This chapter describes the debates that marked the pivotal long decade of 1776 to 1788, the twelve-year period in which Virginians implemented republicanism.

Republicanization of the Virginia political system found the old colonial "cousinocracy," the network of notable families that had governed Virginia before independence, unable to supply adequate manpower to fill the attendant new offices. As a result, a new breed of leader followed Patrick Henry into the Assembly. More conservative Whigs grew restless with this new political reality. In addition, Virginians imagined themselves surrounded by rapacious neighbors bent on territorial expansion. Notables such as George Washington and Thomas Jefferson responded by proposing a web of internal improvements to bind the state together and extend its economic influence.[1]

Military vulnerability made the institutional situation more dire than it would have been in peacetime, and the neophyte status of its major institutions complicated Virginia's military task. Since the British deployed large forces in the South in the latter portion of the war, and since Congress could not or would not lend much aid, Virginians came to believe that they had borne others' burdens. High officials wrote to one another lamenting the difficulty of procuring recruits, but Virginia's failure to meet their ideal did not undercut their tendency to see the Old Dominion as far more patriotic than states apparently determined to shirk their responsibilities. Worse, Virginian civilians and even soldiers had to undergo privation as Virginia's contributions were showered on other states' soldiers. Herein lay the germ of Virginian politicians' subsequent certainty that the Old Dominion must instruct other states in political propriety. Other states' selfishness made them unreliable, Virginians agreed.[2]

A high estimation of their elite's relative merits marked Virginians' attitudes from the Revolution's earliest days. A resident of Williamsburg wrote to a kinsman in October 1774 to describe their country's delegation to the First Continental Congress: "Your countrymen" were of the highest quality. Peyton Randolph, the leading man in the delegation and in Virginia, had "a true Roman spirit," though he was no orator. George Washington "was bred a soldier." Patrick Henry was "moderate & mild, & in religious matters a Saint—but the very Devil in politicks—a Son of Thunder . . . He will shake a Senate, & some years ago had liked to have Talked treason in the house—in these times a very useful Man . . . very stern & steady in his Country's Cause, & at the same time such a Fool." Richard Bland, he offered, "has something of the look of musty old Parchments," while Edmund Pendleton outshone them all: he was as wise as Nestor, and "smooth tongued."[3]

The onset of the Revolution came at a time of crisis in the Virginia political system that had produced that delegation. Three of Virginia's leading men died as the war started. Richard Bland, whose air of "musty old Parchments" won him respect as the leading light in Virginia when it came to things constitutional, died in 1776, along with William Byrd III, heir to Westover and a seat on the Council. Even more importantly, Peyton Randolph, Speaker of the House of Burgesses, president of the First Continental Congress, and leader of the Randolph interest in Virginia politics, died that same year. Had there been nothing else to complicate the situation, these deaths would have created a precarious situation in Virginia political history.

The war drew a large slice of Virginia's political establishment into service in the army and Congress. The new republic also required new courts and new executive institutions, which occupied still more gentry personnel. In addition, the Constitution of 1776 established a new Virginia Senate, and several new counties, with the concomitant General Assembly seats and county offices, were created in this period. Finally, the legislature barred concurrent service in Congress and in the General Assembly, prohibited concurrent military and state service, and forbade simultaneous service in both city and county offices. Suitably qualified officials were in short supply, but the General Assembly intentionally created new demand. The House of Burgesses had once concentrated all the talents of a colony steeped in politics, but the House of Delegates of 1776–1788 came to be the home of second-rate men.

Virginia democrats saw developments differently. For them, the advent of self-government was a marvelous development, the elevation of men of less distinguished backgrounds a cause for celebration. As an observer of the first session of the republican General Assembly put it:

> [Our assembly is] now sitting—under the happy Auspices of the People only—I confess I am pleased—And tho' it is composed of Men—not quite to well Dressed—nor so politely educated—nor so highly born, as some Assemblies have formerly been—yet upon the whole—I like their Proceedings—& upon the whole, rather better than formerly—They are the People's Men (& the People in general are right)—plain & of consequence less [distinguished] but I believe to be full as honest—less intriguing—more sincere—I wish the People may always have Virtue enough, & Wisdom enough, to chuse such plain Men.[4]

Many leading politicians, on the other hand, found cause for alarm in the rise of a new cut of men to state office. Archibald Stuart told Thomas Jefferson that, "the people begin to feel their power and I am afraid have not wisdom enough to make a proper use of it." Public figures such as George Mason, Jefferson, and Thomas Adams were chastised by their acquaintances for abandoning the field of political activity to more plebeian Virginians. Mason counted public service a heavy burden when his fellow laborers were "Men in whom [he could]n't confide." Eventually, Jefferson's Albemarle County constituents elected him to the General Assembly despite his known wishes. They said that in Virginia's desperate plight, he must serve. Many others found themselves in the same situation as Jefferson. More than a matter of responsibility, the presence in the General Assembly of men such as Jefferson and Mason struck men like James Madison as a necessity. Perhaps surprisingly, many common Virginians did not resent the continued predominance of the former colonial elite.[5]

Madison became increasingly unhappy with Virginia's newly won self-government in this decade. The program of Patrick Henry, uncontested master of the House of Delegates, bothered Madison. Madison would have agreed with the advice Anne Cary Nicholas, the colonial treasurer's wife, gave to a son just stepping onto the political stage: "Your weight in the house will be much greater," this matriarch of the passing generation averred, "if you do not take up the attention of the assembly on trifling matters nor too often demand a hearing." While a rousing master of men's passions dominated Virginia politics, she told young Wilson that he should exhibit "temper & decorum" as "a public speaker" and "a modest diffidence" befitting "a young man." Patrick Henry had used his oratory to rouse ordinary Virginians to his support. Mrs. Nicholas's advice, which recalled the colonial system in which a fledgling politician was to be seen and not heard, was anachronistic. She and her ilk wanted to rally the gentry to restore the world of politics to its colonial tenor, for self-government must not beget democratization.[6]

Because of the people's favor, Henry spent five years as governor, a position of continental military responsibility and splendid domestic powerlessness. When he served in the General Assembly, however, political friend and foe alike conceded his preeminence. In the end, his frustrated opponents would look to reform of the federal constitution to offset Henry's dominance of Virginia politics.[7]

In Henry's absence, leadership in the General Assembly generally fell to sometime congressional president Richard Henry Lee. If Henry's localism and particularism chagrined those of "more enlarged & liberal principles," Lee pleased them more. He firmly opposed Madison's *bête noire*, paper money, which Henry often supported; he opposed Henry's laws delaying the collection of taxes; and, most importantly, he sprang from a long line of distinguished Virginians. Still, Madison had little admiration for either Henry or Lee, "the two great leaders of the House."[8]

State Treasurer Jacquelin Ambler lamented the enormous revenue shortfall the tax forbearance statute forced on him in 1783, but the newly democratic House majority cared more how the common farmers whose farms had been ravaged by British invaders and heavy taxation could pay their debts if the government did *not* "postpone" their collection. Discontented aristocrats, such as Thomas Jefferson and an anonymous *Virginia Gazette* columnist, insisted that any man could pay new taxes simply by giving up some superfluity, but Henry and his followers took a different position. They represented the drought-stricken farmers who burned down courthouses and clerks' offices in this decade rather than see their property seized for nonpayment of taxes.[9] To them, self-government meant responsiveness to the needs of common Virginia planters, whatever the effect on the few.

James Madison rued the elevation of what he understood as the majority's short-term pecuniary interest to the status of "the political standard of right and wrong." In answer to this systemic "problem," he and others wanted to rewrite Virginia's constitution to reduce the power of the House of Delegates. Yet, they realized that their cause was hopeless while Henry opposed it. In the meantime, one tactic adopted by some members of the elite was adoption of hidden taxes, such as tariffs. Governor Benjamin Harrison preferred the impost to property taxes because "the people at large do not see it and are therefore much better contented to pay money that way than in taxes on their landed and other property." Jefferson preferred a sales tax for the same reason, and Richard Henry Lee, who despite elite breeding was the reformers' opponent in most things, held imposts dangerous because imperceptible. In the new political environment, the gentry had to reckon with commoners' preferences even as it remained dominant.[10] Henry's opponents scored some successes when service as governor removed him from the House of Delegates.[11]

On his return to the Old Dominion from three years' service in Congress in 1783, James Madison became a leading figure in the General Assembly. In light of his youth, he might still have been on a low rung of the political ladder if not for the Revolution. Instead, with Henry governor and Lee in Congress, Madison played "a leading role on nearly every major issue." Critics decried the General Assembly's instability, a result of its newfound adherence to individual leaders, but the colonial House of Burgesses would have been less easily dominated by young men such as those who led it during parts of the Revolution.[12]

One prominent Virginian advanced a solution to the absence of the commonwealth's leading men from its most important governmental body: the General Assembly should cease choosing its leading members for nominally "higher" but actually far less important tasks. However prestigious a seat on the Council or on a court might be, leading roles in the House of Delegates and in the Congress, which did the work of governing Virginia and winning independence, should have prior claim on the best men.[13]

Reformers' perception that Henry systematically opposed them diverged from reality. Henry was a revolutionary, was widely seen as *the* democratic revolutionary, and therein lay the secret of their objections to his dominance. He seemed to Madison, particularly, to be too responsive to the immediate interest of the electorate and too devoted to popular government. When Jefferson heard complaints about tax burdens, he imagined prodigality lay behind them, but when Henry heard such complaints, he persuaded the General Assembly to delay, and eventually to cancel, collection of an entire year's taxes. His opponents said that a responsible fiscal policy could never be adopted, the Confederation could never be stable, so long as Henry prevailed. In the end, this reasoning drove Madison to plot erection of a new, more powerful federal government. If Madison could not win in the Virginia arena, he would see to the transfer of many of Virginia's most important governmental powers to a different government.[14]

However, before Virginia could cooperate more closely with the other twelve new states, all leading Virginians agreed, Congress had to reach some accommodation concerning Virginia's enormous extent of territory. The small states insisted that no confederation of equals could be formed of such disparate elements as Rhode Island, Delaware, and a Virginia including the whole Old Northwest, West Virginia, and Kentucky. Reasonably, Virginians agreed, insisting only that the western lands become new states entitled to enter the union on the same footing as the old. Virginia's west could not be ruled by Virginia in a republican manner, so the principle of self-government dictated creation of new states there. The principle of equality logically followed.[15]

Legalistic opposition to Virginia's western land claims led Virginians of all stripes, including Richard Henry Lee, Arthur Lee, Patrick Henry, Thomas Jefferson, James Madison, and Edmund Pendleton, to articulate a strict construction of the Articles of Confederation. From the earliest days, Virginians argued that their state had been "sovereign free and independent" prior to Congress's existence, thus laying the predicate for reserved powers arguments. With great ingenuity, they supported Bland's old history of the Virginia charter and Virginia's legal relations with the crown. If Virginia's charter claims were void, Virginian legalists said, the Old Northwest must belong to Canada. If Crown charters had no weight, by what right did Maryland claim *its* territory? If, as Patrick Henry had claimed in his famous "I am an American" speech (and as Richard Henry Lee had feared), George III's declaration putting the Americans *hors la loi* threw them into a state of nature, then Vermonters had legitimate claims against New York. Finally, if Congress, despite the clear language of the Articles of Confederation, claimed inherent authority, nothing limited the indignities to which the states might be subjected or the degree to which they might be subdivided. Eventually, Virginian congressmen, insisting that Congress had no right to entertain the topic, refused even to discuss the Old Dominion's western land claims. The principle of home rule dictated that only the powers the Virginians had voluntarily ceded to Congress inhered in Congress, so Congress had no right to discuss Virginia land claims.[16]

Ultimately, Virginia had its way. It ceded its western lands to Congress on the condition that the confederation carve equal states out of them. Since they had long looked upon even Kentucky as too distant to be governed from Williamsburg or from Richmond in the republican style, Virginians happily let their western territories go. Virginia would be small enough for self-government, and the Northwest would never become a field for congressional politicians to exploit or a severed limb of Virginia, outside the union and yet under its control. It would benefit from local self-government, too. The beginning of Virginia's long-running love affair with strict construction of federal constitutions and the notion that republicanism had a territorial limit thus each played a role in this interstate dispute.[17]

Many states had boundary problems in the period between independence and inauguration of the federal government. Virginia's case was paradigmatic. Besides contention with other states and with Great Britain over its claims in the Northwest, Virginia found itself involved in border disputes with North Carolina, Maryland, and Pennsylvania. The Carolina problem resulted from simple migration. As people moved farther west, they reached the limit of old boundary surveys. Resolution required simple extension of the old boundary line.[18]

The Pennsylvania border problem posed greater difficulty. As one prominent Virginian put it, the proprietary governor and Lord Dunmore "had contrived to raise" a boundary dispute between the two in late colonial days, and Virginia proposed a solution on 15 June 1776. Settlers in what are now northern West Virginia and southwestern Pennsylvania had moved to that area under the impression that they were still within their colonies of origin. Soon enough, jurisdictional disputes arose. Officials on each side employed violence, and a commission resolved the problem by extending the Mason-Dixon Line westward.[19]

The Articles of Confederation went unratified for years because of Maryland's objections to Virginia's western land claims. Virginians put their neighbors' hostility down to leading Marylanders' supposed speculation in land beyond the Ohio River. If Virginia had its way, Marylanders' purchases from the Indians would be for naught. The issue of navigation rights in the Potomac also set Virginia at loggerheads with its neighbor to the north. Delegations from Virginia and Maryland met at Mt. Vernon. Eventually, they made an arrangement. The road to the Philadelphia Convention of 1787 began there.[20]

Establishment of Kentucky as a separate state occupied Virginians' thoughts and demanded their legislative attention throughout the decade and beyond. Virginians early came to agree that Kentucky must be separate from Virginia. As John Marshall told his friend George Muter, representatives in distant Richmond could not "legislate wisely for you . . . and it is proper that you should legislate for yourselves"; distant government was not self-government. Kentucky statehood outside the Confederation could not please Virginia, however. Simple subtraction of population and territory from Virginia's promised only to reduce Virginia's influence to no good purpose. The Virginia constitution provided for Kentucky statehood as a matter of Virginian politics, not for Kentucky alone or for the Congress. Virginians insisted that Kentucky must accept a proportionate share of the state's debt as a condition of statehood. When Kentucky attained statehood on Virginia's conditions, Virginia's goal of establishing permanent boundaries had been achieved.[21] In light of the discussion of the western lands' governance, the distance between Williamsburg and the state's western counties made it seem unsuitable as a capital. Transferring the seat of government to Richmond resolved the issue.[22]

Resolution of the problem of state boundaries and the relocation of the capital helped to define Virginia's posture toward the rest of the American union and Virginians' relationship to their state government, but additional factors affected the prospects of Virginia republicanism. For example, farmers in western Virginia needed access to the Mississippi River to transport their produce to market. In the period 1776–1788, Thomas Jefferson and others dreamed of a continental commercial empire tied to a Virginia port. As Governor Patrick Henry explained, "I hope our country will ere long assume a new appearance from that attention which is given to our uncommon natural advantages." To that end, "Acts for clearing Potowmack and James Rivers, and opening a canal from the Carolina waters to those of Elizabeth, are passed without opposition."[23] If they succeeded, Virginia need no longer rely on the good will its neighbors.

In the wake of the Revolution, George Washington made himself the foremost lobbyist for connection of the great Virginia waterways to the rivers of the west, principally the Ohio. Virginia's waters promised to form a transportation route less than half the length of New York's, Jefferson explained, so even lackadaisical planning should funnel the lion's share of traffic through Virginia. Virginia would dominate the export trade of all the western states. Washington wrote that completion of the Elizabeth, James, and Potomac projects would "open channels of convenience and wealth to the citizens of this state that the imagination can hardly extend to, and render this [that is, Virginia] the most favoured country in the universe." Once the "ease" of these initial projects became manifest, similar projects must follow. An additional modicum of self-determination would come from the end of Virginia's need for its sister states' cooperation in wresting the Mississippi navigation from the European powers. Access to that river system would become superfluous, it was thought, once the inland territories were connected to Virginia's waters. The General and his abettors persuaded the General Assembly to charter companies in 1785 to clear the James and the Potomac for shipping well to the west of their falls, and they hoped for an eventual opening of Virginia's other two major rivers, canals among the minor rivers, and a web of water-borne commerce bringing North Carolina permanently under Virginia's economic domination.[24]

Also on an ad hoc basis, Virginia established road projects to open New Virginia and spur its development. During the war, George Mason sponsored and the General Assembly adopted a bill for construction of a road with the stated goals of "a free and easy Communication and Intercourse between th[e] Inhabitants in the Eastern and Western Parts" of Virginia, cementing common interests between the two sections, and facilitating "mutual Aid and Support." Like the water projects, roads were expected to keep the western lands within Virginia. Common ties of blood and the affection flowing from the benefits of regular government also promised to aid in the construction of Virginia's inland commercial empire.[25]

Yet, unforeseen events severely retarded such projects. The General Assembly ignored roads in this and the following decade. It did allow local tax levies to fund highway repairs, but county governments' efforts were perforce myopic. County courts' supervision of local roads broke down under the pressures of war, and the advent of toll roads failed to make up the shortfall. No successful turnpike appeared before 1802. Western counties lacked labor for road construction and maintenance. The mountainous terrain of present West Virginia and Kentucky added expense, as did scarcity of specie in the west. Rather than trumpeting the Kentucky road project, Virginians had reason to be frustrated over the pace of the backcountry's opening.[26]

Given the proximity of Spain and Britain, inland settlers' needs could not be ignored. Western communities might optimize their positions by playing the United States off against foreign suitors. Connection of Virginia's waterways, on the other hand, would truly unify the Old Dominion's economy. Transportation legislation and the creation of new counties constituted a grand endeavor to cement New Virginia into the commonwealth. In the end, legislative efforts failed and western resentment grew.[27]

Like the crisis of the shortage of gentry politicians to fill high offices, the questions of Virginia's boundaries, internal improvements, creation of new counties, and relocation of the capital all challenged, and unsettled, Virginia's domestic polity. The coming of a new breed of men, of a rougher, less finished type of politician, into the corridors of power had little to do with an upsurge of democracy. Uneducated men other than Tidewater bluebloods made their way into the General Assembly in this period because they were all their home counties had to offer. They cut their home towns off from the old county seats for reasons of simple convenience and republican equality.

While the war was pressing a new coterie of men into Virginia political life, Virginia for the first time found itself in a position to enact the policies it preferred. Fundamental issues such as the future of the established religion, the future of feudal land tenures, and the fate of African slavery drew serious attention, and a number of Virginians proposed radical solutions. Without the monarchy, the Church of England and feudal land tenures (the basis of English aristocracy) had little support in theory, and reforms soon swept them away. Slavery, which conflicted with many of the rationales offered in support of independence, fared better.

The classic political reform of this period was the Virginia Statute for Religious Freedom. When Thomas Jefferson first proposed a bill disestablishing the Church of England in 1776, it failed. Edmund Pendleton and Robert Carter Nicholas, two leaders of the old order who remained prominent during the Revolution, led the Establishment's defenders. Although James Madison had succeeded in replacing George Mason's toleration language with a guarantee of religious neutrality in the last article of the Declaration of Rights, Virginia retained several provisions favoring Anglicanism.[28]

In the wake of Jefferson's wartime disgrace, resuscitation of his "neutrality" proposal seemed unlikely. Besides the initial opposition of leading men such as Richard Henry Lee and Edmund Pendleton, many perceived a growing prevalence of immorality. The General Assembly repeatedly enacted statutes regulating gambling and tippling houses, and the seemingly common indulgence in luxurious imports caused consternation.[29]

The Virginia *General Gazette* of September 1783 called on the General Assembly to address "*public virtue, being the public care.*" Echoing Patrick Henry's proposal in the House of Delegates earlier that year, the paper hoped all Protestants might be united in this if the General Assembly were to "form a genuine system and mode of worship." In 1784, Henry resuscitated an old religious proposal, one that had been rejected in 1776 and again, when opponents of Jefferson's religious neutrality bill raised it as an alternative, in 1779. Virginia, Henry argued, should require all to pay a general assessment in support of the religion of their choice. In the first year of the Commonwealth, Governor Henry had written, "I am happy to find a catholick spirit prevailing in our country, and that those religious Distinctions, which formerly produced some heats, are now forgotten." Defense of common "religious and civil Liberties" united everyone. Henry could easily see the General Assessment proposal as consistent with long-standing Virginian goals.[30]

Henry evidently accepted the argument that the suspension of the Anglican levies had undermined Protestantism generally, thus undercutting popular morality. Rather than transferring the amounts of their old levies to religious leaders of their choice, Henry held, many Virginians had simply indulged themselves. Future governor John Page shared this view. Richard Henry Lee thought the resulting decline in popular morality perfectly predictable; religion, he insisted, was the only sure buttress of morality, and Lee said the Declaration of Rights did not ban Henry's proposal.[31]

Jefferson held the opposite view: that the Establishment amounted to "religious slavery." No polity needed popular religiosity. "It matters not whether my neighbor believes in twenty gods or no god. It neither picks my pocket nor breaks my leg." He looked to indoctrination in Jeffersonian principles ("education") to inculcate morals as religion traditionally had done. (James Madison, on the other hand, saw economic conditions as the determinants of public morality.) The General Assembly adopted Jefferson's proposal and permanently defeated Henry's because of the shortage of qualified political leadership and the happenstance timing of Henry's absence from the House of Delegates.[32]

The Church of England had occupied an uneasy place in Virginia society since the early days of the Imperial Crisis. The Bishop of London exercised jurisdiction over Virginia, but without canonical justification. Anglican Richard Bland, for one, argued that Virginia Anglicans should understand ecclesial authority in their colony to lie in the local courts, as he said the Saxons had. While he taught his fellow Virginians to think of their Burgesses as analogous to Parliament, then, he taught that the local courts served the functions of English bishops. In religion as in politics, Bland insisted on local control. The Parsons' Cause left the Burgesses with effective power over religion, as they had assumed the role of voice of Virginians and had faced down the church in Whitehall. The ministers had made the mistake of circumventing both the bishop's commissary and the General Assembly in their protest, so they had little recourse when their complaints fell on deaf ears in England. Petitions poured into the House of Burgesses, meanwhile, lamenting the Establishment's "probable" effect on immigration.[33]

In 1776, political neophyte James Madison encountered little difficulty in persuading the May Convention to opt for religious neutrality over toleration. Almost immediately upon declaring independence, the Virginians enacted a legal provision dealing with notoriously wanton ministers. In that same year, they also repealed statutes mandating church attendance, penalizing heretical opinions, and penalizing heterodox worship. Dissenters were no longer to be taxed to support the Establishment or its clergy. Besides its association with the threat to home rule, the Establishment also suffered from Virginians' growing religious heterogeneity.[34] In *The Transformation of Virginia, 1740–1790*, Rhys Isaac described the conflict between Evangelicals and Episcopalians as partially a struggle for social authority; besides home rule, it seems, Virginians were contending over who should rule at home. Some of the elite, however, held views quite congenial to the unlettered, emotional appeals of the Evangelicals. Like the Evangelicals, they found sober Episcopalian worship and ascetic teaching unnecessary or misleading. "God is love," as one put it, "and he that walketh in love, walketh in God and God in him." This left "forms of baptism and modes of faith" neither here nor there.[35]

Patrick Henry's stated motives for proposing a general assessment were mainly moral, not doctrinal or ecclesiological. His followers stated similar concerns, justifying the General Assessment on the ground that even the irreligious benefited from popular morality. Jefferson, by contrast, concerned himself mainly with these issues' political implications. So did James Madison, who guided Jefferson's proposal to enactment. In his youth, Madison had expressed the view that all of North America would groan under despotism if it had a common established religion. The young Virginian professed a preference for diversity of error over uniformity even of truth. Jefferson harbored similar sentiments.[36]

Henry often had his way in the General Assembly even when his fellow gentry luminaries opposed him. In one instance, for example, he lost a preliminary vote on a measure related to payment of British debts by thirty votes, only to win his bill's final passage "A few days afterwards" by fifty votes. A similar fate befell his General Assessment bill, but in reverse. At first, with Henry guiding the House of Delegates, the "commitment to organized religion" passed by a vote of forty-seven to thirty-two. Then Henry, possibly with Madison's connivance, won election as governor. From that moment, his plan's friends and foes alike foresaw his bill's defeat. As one participant explained, the Anglicans had miscalculated in 1776: they had accepted the Declaration of Rights' position on religion under the assumption that Henry would defend them—despite the inevitability of his one day not being in a position to do so.[37]

The interval between the forty-seven to thirty-two vote and the final vote witnessed an intensive effort by Madison and his supporters to drum up opposition to the General Assessment. Famously, many signatures were affixed to Madison's "Memorial and Remonstrance against Religious Assessments" and other anti-assessment petitions, and the clergy of all the Protestant sects save the Episcopalian settled into opposition to Henry's bill. Madison's "Memorial and Remonstrance" explained why self-government required church-state separation. Its first section stated clearly that a duty to "worship as they believe right" was paramount to civil obligations in the lives of all men. In its third section, Madison's screed opposed established religion on the theory that those who can establish "Christianity" can establish one "branch" of it, so they must be opposed from the beginning.[38]

In his fourth section, Madison held it unjust to exempt Quakers and Mennonites alone from various obligations of citizenship. This section did not, however, propose to subject conscientious objectors to military duties incumbent on all other Virginians; rather, its point was that no one should be made to pay to support religion in an increasingly egalitarian republic. Using the same kind of reasoning as that to which the General Assembly had pointed in its statute moving the capital from Williamsburg to Richmond, Madison implied that if any citizen of Virginia enjoyed a particular benefit, all must.

Section five objected to the idea of a general assessment on the ground that its implementation would necessarily involve the magistrates in guarding or manipulating religion: once the state decided to support "Protestantism," it necessarily would have to declare who was "Protestant" and who was not. This idea called to mind the popular English (thus Virginian) conception of the Inquisition. Republican Virginia must not go down that road.

The sixth section held the religious assessment bill objectionable insofar as it implied that Christianity needed such support. Madison appealed to the ego of the average Virginian Protestant by saying that of course Protestantism would fare well in republican Virginia. As the outcome of the general assessment controversy would demonstrate, Virginians seemingly wanted to believe that Madison was right about this: in their new republic, the sovereign was trustworthy. The seventh article ventured that establishment tended to corrupt and enervate religion, by which it meant to imply that Christianity would be harmed by state support. For the increasingly numerous Evangelical Virginians, in particular, this statement that their view concerning the proper relationship between church and state was "reasonable" would have been especially appealing; it contained the germ of later Virginia Evangelicals' happiness with Jefferson's metaphor of a "wall of separation between church and state." Section eight held meddling in religion to be unnecessary to the proper functioning of the civil government.

Turning from theoretical and religious to economic ramifications, Madison (echoing earlier anti-assessment petitions) forecast in sections nine and ten that an establishment would impede immigration and speed emigration, as Virginians unhappy with the new policy left the Old Dominion and potential immigrants opted to settle elsewhere. Both of these tendencies would inure to the remaining Virginians' detriment, Madison posited (and he obviously had an economic benefit in mind). He guessed in section eleven that an establishment would destroy Virginia's religious peace (which perhaps explains why no one proposed one); as he explained in section thirteen, dissenters were bound to flout the establishment.

As the pièce de résistance, Madison pointed to the Declaration of Rights' last article. The Declaration of Rights barred establishment, he said, and if he and his colleagues provided an example of clear disregard for this section of the Declaration, they would undermine all the other rights enumerated there. In order to establish lasting constitutionalism, in other words, Virginians must acquire the habit of obeying all of their societal charter's strictures.[39]

Patrick Henry's retirement from the legislature swung the contest of 1785. The margin for which Henry's advocacy accounted turned the other way on his elevation to the governorship, and the House of Delegates dealt the general assessment proposal a defeat.[40] Next, Virginia adopted Jefferson's bill, minus the

Jeffersonian preamble's homage to reason. This decision, like those related to the first and last sections of the Declaration of Rights, established that the Old Dominion's policy would subordinate the spiritual to other interests, particularly the economic—thus establishing Virginia's priorities for decades to come. Madison reported to Jefferson, "I flatter myself [we have] in this country [that is, Virginia] extinguished for ever the ambitious hope of making laws for the human mind." Virginia patriot Jefferson wrote from France to remark upon the favorable reaction to Virginia's policy among the *philosophes*.[41]

Reformers of the Revolutionary decade also attacked other key elements of the old order. Most importantly, they abolished the feudal land tenures, primogeniture and entail. Here, reformers gained a major victory, because as many as three-fourths of the acres in Tidewater Virginia and approximately one-half of those in the Commonwealth as a whole were freed up with this one bold stroke. Although the extent of the revision's effect on slaveholdings has not been measured, slave property, too, could be entailed before the reform.[42]

Jefferson recognized the importance of land tenures in cementing the domination of a small, ruling clique of proud, established families. His description of his ancestry in *Notes on the State of Virginia* showed that he did not ascribe particular merit to the old aristocracy (although one might read this as a pose). Through his other reforms, he also saw to it that not only subsequent sons, but daughters would inherit equally. Jefferson's intention was to create a republican Virginia in which success was somewhat dependent upon talent.

Then again, preference for talent over birth only went so far. While some members of the Virginia elite thought slavery inconsistent with their professed belief in the equality of man and their struggle for home rule, others seemingly restricted their profession to "white men" or "Anglo-Saxon men." Jefferson took up slavery's repugnance in the " Manners" chapter of *Notes on the State of Virginia*. Pondering slavery's effects on masters' fitness for republican citizenship, Jefferson concluded that slavery made whites tyrants from an early age. Ever hopeful, he noted that he looked forward to "a total emancipation" undertaken "with the consent of the masters, rather than by their extirpation." (The consent of the masters seemed a necessary alternative to the sacrifice of their economic interests, which the Virginia elite's consensus was fast coming to hold sacrosanct.) Jefferson *had* to reach this unlikely conclusion, for he believed that the continued employment of slave labor would undermine the popular notion that Virginians' "liberties are the gift of God," and then "the liberty of [the] nation [could not] be thought secure." Of *course* amelioration of the slaves' plight would come, and of *course* it would come relatively painlessly: things simply had to work out that way in order for self-government to succeed in Virginia.[43]

Leading Virginians disagreed about mastery's effects. Edmund Randolph answered Jefferson's assertion that ownership of slaves unfitted men for equal citizenship, making masters into despots virtually from birth, by saying that, "The existence of slavery, howsoever baneful to virtue, begat a pride which nourished a quick and acute sense of the rights of a freeman." Virginians "seemed to catch the full spirit" of theories of freedom, and Randolph explained this tendency by reference to their being masters of men. Randolph's reading made their mastery a key explanation of Virginians' habitual insistence on their rights—just as antebellum northerners would find southern slaveholders in general insistent upon their rights.[44]

In the first republican legislative session, their self-absolving argument held, Virginians had banned slave imports as they had long wanted to do, and they could be counted on to ameliorate slavery further. This prorepublican account overlooked the legislative history of the ban on slave importations, which included excision from the final bill of the draft's language concerning prevention of "the practice of holding persons in Slavery" and the provision for manumission.[45]

Virginians' willingness to consider slavery reform peaked in the flush of this first republican decade. Section 51 of the Revised Laws, adopted in the October 1785 session of the General Assembly, provided that only slaves in Virginia then, along with the "descendants of the females of them," would be slaves. Visiting slaves were to be freed after one year. However, it added that no black could be a witness in court unless all parties to the suit were black, instituted a pass system for travel outside the master's company, and banned gun wielding by slaves unless their masters had authorized it. This bill also included a Jeffersonian provision, perfectly consistent with Jefferson's proposal to extend Virginians' rights to "free white inhabitants" of other states, that all freedmen must leave Virginia and that any who failed to do so would be denied the laws' protection. Such proscription historically was reserved for the worst criminals. Ironically, Jefferson later pointed to this bill as having been slated to provide emancipation of afterborn children of slave women.[46]

In 1782, the General Assembly legalized private manumissions and provided for the support of aged and infirm slaves. Some Virginians, including Jefferson, portrayed this as a first step, but Edmund Randolph ascribed the manumission act to a fit of irresponsibility induced by euphoria over Yorktown. Others saw it as a moral imperative. Methodists began to agitate for emancipation. In April and May 1785, they circulated a petition. By the end of 1785, the House of Delegates rejected the Methodist plea for emancipation "without dissent but not without an avowed patronage of its principle by sundry respectable." Several anti-emancipation petitions, not to mention one "praying for a repeal of the law which licenses particular manumissions," came before the legislature in the same period.[47] As it turned out, repeal of the manumission law in 1805 after twenty years of petitions for its repeal marked the last step. Jeffersonian Virginia finally decided to retain slavery permanently. Virginians realized that the only alternative to slavery was incorporation of ex-slaves into the polity, and a society whose most egalitarian political leaders called slaves "boy" and looked for voluntary or forcible ways to resettle freed blacks abroad held racial equality impossible. Self-government was reserved to whites alone.[48]

It was not only in regard to slavery that the onset of the Revolution found Virginia law in flux. The colonial system of appeals to the governor's council, then to Whitehall came to an abrupt end with Lord Dunmore's flight. Instead, a legislative committee chaired by Jefferson proposed creation of an entirely new system of courts of statewide jurisdiction. Once they came into being, the extent of those courts' authority remained unclear. Before the end of the decade, in *Caton v. Commonwealth* and the Remonstrance of the Judges, the Virginia judiciary claimed the power to rule on statutes' constitutionality. Prominent men with judicial experience classified the move as "exaltation [of] the judiciary above the legislative," but the judges won in the end. Republican Virginia, through its constitutional provisions and its judges' self-assertion, had an independent judiciary with the power of judicial review. In theory, the state constitution was the supreme law of the state.[49]

Jefferson also sought to reform the county courts, which displeased him in several ways. First, vacancies were filled by the courts' remaining members, which seemed unrepublican. Second, like the House of Delegates, these courts combined executive, legislative, and judicial powers in the same hands. Jefferson and others wished to replace them with purely judicial courts elected at least indirectly, but his bill to create new county courts was never considered. It seems that inertia and economic interest partially explained the county courts' ability to survive the Revolution. As court reform proponent John Marshall noted, opponents of debt and contract enforcement formed a strong enough faction to thwart court reform. A third partial explanation of the county courts' survival lay in some politicians' concern to preserve the traditional local political hierarchies—which, after all, was the goal of the Revolution itself.[50]

Jefferson's court reorganization proposals formed part of the General Assembly's great initiative to republicanize Virginia law. That initiative, the Revision of the Laws, dwarfed all other reform programs in conception. The Revision's authors intended to rectify a situation in which "many [of the existing laws] are inapplicable to the powers of government as now organised, others are founded on principles heterogeneous to the republican spirit, others . . . could . . . never be repealed while the regal power continued, and others . . . are not so well adapted to our present circumstances." Virginians saw an opportunity to sweep away vestiges of monarchy and to enact other statutes the imperial government had long blocked.[51]

The Revisors' proposed 126 statutes spanned the gamut from religion to criminal law, from judicial reform to commercial matters, from education to immigration. The Revision's very length (353 pages in *The Papers of Thomas Jefferson*) soon became its greatest enemy. Although it passed in part by 1779, and in the main by 1786, some sections of the committee's proposal never won even a hearing in the General Assembly.[52]

The Committee agreed to Jefferson's suggestion that it should leave the common law unchanged except where change appeared necessary. No continental Civil Law code would be substituted for the English common-law inheritance. English statutes, too, would be retained except insofar as they appeared to jar with Virginia's new needs. In short, the English legal learning of the committee won out over ideological imperatives. Here again, Virginia's revolutionaries sought only republicanism, not to overthrow the social order of their state.[53]

The Revisors soon agreed to incorporate a leveling impulse into their final report. They proposed that males and females inherit equally in cases of intestacy, that the feudal quitrents still in effect in the Northern Neck be abolished, and that claims on unappropriated lands be limited to 400 acres per person per county (thus reinforcing the equalization of landholdings Jefferson and his colleagues had hoped to promote in abolishing primogeniture and entail). In sum, the Revisors proposed to republicanize property law by reducing artificial concentrations of ownership. The Commonwealth's law would be republican not only in name, but in effect if the Revisors had their way.[54]

They also proposed sweeping criminal law reform. They would reduce the sanguinary nature of British law. This could be accomplished by requiring more proof of a crime, as in the case of treason. It could also be done by simply reducing penalties. Crimes ranging from treason and murder to petty theft and pickpocketing were punishable by death under English law, and various others were punishable by sundry forms of maiming and dismemberment. Although Jefferson favored continued castration for rape and sodomy, his and the committee's proposals would have made Virginia's punishments far less bloody. Many of the punishments the Revision proposed to abolish had not been inflicted in decades, and their abolition flowed naturally from their lack of support in newly self-governing Virginia.[55]

One major portion of the Revision, Jefferson's education plan, would have provided basic education to all white males and a new-modeled college education to the cream of the cream. That plan was contested for the next half-century, and Jefferson finally succeeded only in establishing a state university on Enlightenment lines. His project for founding a new republicanism on republicanized laws, universal education, and equal landholdings failed on this score (among others).[56]

Besides rearranging their state's domestic institutions, Virginians of the Confederation years were in the vanguard of the effort to establish first a formal confederation, then a yet stronger confederation among the United States. Their desire to do so sprang from Virginia's military weakness and the proximity of the British and Spanish empires and various potentially hostile American Indian peoples. Virginians did not imagine their republic as an independent country able to defend itself against potential aggressors.[57]

The war's end did not slacken pressure on the Confederation for energetic governance. As Congressman James Monroe lamented in 1783, he had to concern himself with western troop postings, migration of Americans to the west, land policies for the unsettled lands, and relations with Indian and European neighbors, among other things. Congress also had to consider questions of foreign trade, assumption of state debts, apportionment of those debts, and coercion of states for their requisitions. The states consistently rejected requests for delegation of enhanced power. Their tendency to resist congressional initiatives hamstrung the Congress, leading to disgust with the state governments among congressmen and others. Richard Henry Lee denied that the center needed more power but insisted that the confederation's government should be remodeled along the lines of England's, so long as the "democratic influence" retained a role. He saw a "wonderful lassitude . . . in public affairs" by decade's end, and he espied hopes "beyond the water" of the Confederation's speedy collapse. It must be strengthened.[58]

James Madison grew terribly frustrated over the states' inability or unwillingness (he thought the latter) to comply with congressional requisitions. After several futile attempts to formulate amendments to the Articles of Confederation acceptable to all the states, he decided on a different course. Historical research led him to blame the failure of all previous confederations on lack of power at the center, so he sought a new, stronger American government. He saw no clear way to "mark the just boundary between the authority of Congress and that of the state," so he would err on the side of Congress. Madison not only held that Virginia must adhere to the strictures of international law in its dealings with other states, but he looked forward to the articulation of a Confederation common law "much more minute than that comprised in the foederal articles." He insisted that to avert reversion to monarchy, which could result either from perception of a need to strengthen the central government or from disgust with the states', the states must yield the Confederation so much power as was consistent with "fundamental principles." His efforts sometimes involved sleight of hand or subterfuge.[59]

The case of Edmund Randolph illustrates perspective's effect on appraisals of the United States' condition in the period 1776–1788. Eight months as a congressman under Madison's influence persuaded him that the center must be strengthened. Then he returned to Virginia, where he found the state government far more respectable than Madison had coached him to expect. In the end, Randolph became first a nonsigner of the constitution in the Philadelphia Convention, then the most tepid Federalist in the Richmond ratifying convention.[60]

Like Richard Henry Lee and Madison, George Washington grew in the war years to identify with America generally, not with Virginia specifically. In correspondence with Governor Henry, for example, he referred to Virginia as "your colony" and "your State," to the Americans as "a United people." As former commander of the American armies, Washington seemed the ideal leader of the nationalists, but advocates of federal constitutional reform had to husband his prestige wisely. His retirement at war's end and vow not to enter politics again made it necessary for the Federalists to preach up a jeremiad in their efforts to persuade Americans to adopt the constitution. Absent cataclysmic foreboding, Washington's return to the public stage would have been unjustified. (The General, for one, seems to have been sincerely distressed about the American confederation's prospects.)[61]

Patrick Henry favored delegation of more power to Congress through most of the decade. However, he grew to distrust Congress in light of the Jay-Gardoquí affair. Like other leading Virginians, including Madison, Henry held the right to navigate the Mississippi essential to the inland's economic future. John Jay's agreement with the Spaniard convinced Henry that there were worse things than a feeble confederation, and he had the House of Delegates warn Congress of this new understanding.[62]

Other Virginians conceded the risks of delegating further power to Congress and were willing to delegate it anyway. Jefferson, for one, decried "the pride of independence taking deep and dangerous hold on the hearts of individual states. . . . I know no remedy," he said, "so likely to prevent [internal contests] as the strengthening the band which connects us." Jefferson posited that Congress had power to coerce compliance with its legitimate mandates "by the law of nature," which he held applicable against noncompliant parties to all agreements. Another group, headed by sometime governor Benjamin Harrison, insisted Virginia not cooperate fully with Congress until Congress extracted compliance with certain treaty provisions from Great Britain. Finally, many Virginians joined George Mason in generalized skepticism of the motives of Congress. They tended to view each request for further concessions of power to Congress as power mongering on Congress's part. On the other hand, by 1786, Madison classed Mason's attitude as "Antifederal."[63]

A number of factors heightened dissatisfaction with the Confederation. Virginia really had borne the brunt of British military efforts in the last years of the war, and Virginians resented other states' unwillingness to meet even so much of their requisitions as they could. Virginia congressman John Francis Mercer noted that the chief financial officer of the Confederation attributed the Confederation's survival to Virginia's unexampled financial exertions. Like Richard Henry Lee, Mercer held that the tax burden associated with Virginia's exertions on behalf of the United States induced emigration from Virginia. As a historian described it, "Competition among the states to avoid tax burdens or to gain control of scarce resources . . . constituted the normal course of affairs under the Confederation; it was taken for granted that one state's gain was another's loss." To Virginians, it seemed that the loss was always theirs.[64]

Despite worries about other states' self-serving behavior, leading Virginia politicians recognized the need to finance the war. As Madison described it, the press of war and shortage of funds constituted a crisis from which it might be impossible to retrieve America's fortunes. The American army needed supplies so desperately that it had to depend on supply agents' private credit, leaving Congress and the people mutually disgusted and the army sick of both. Yet, the quality of men in Congress had declined so markedly by 1780 that state governments often ignored their requests. "[T]he same distrust of concurrent exertions that has damped the ardor of patriotic individuals," Madison wrote, "must produce the same effect among the states themselves." Still, even Madison would not go too far to finance the war: other states likely would never compensate Virginia for its great exertions, he warned.[65]

Another issue spurring Virginians to distrust the Confederation was access to the Mississippi River, which was essential to counties today in West Virginia and Kentucky. Patrick Henry's insistence on American access to the Mississippi River eventually drove him into an anti-Federalist position, and he made sure that he had followers. James Monroe tipped Jefferson off to the possibility that John Jay would barter America's claim to the Mississippi navigation for commercial advantages in Spanish colonies, and Jefferson wrote Madison late in 1787 to guess that the East's willingness to negotiate access to the Mississippi augured a future East-West separation. Madison agreed that "eastern" intentions regarding the Mississippi were apt to hamstring the entire effort for confederal reform, and Edmund Pendleton expressed the same fear. Henry Lee found himself excluded from Virginia's congressional delegation as a result of his partnership with the East on this issue; John Marshall's opinion that internal improvements projects would moot the question evidently garnered little support. Henry persuaded the General Assembly unanimously to adopt resolutions warning of the consequences if Jay's negotiations had the results Virginians feared, and Madison gauged that they captured Virginia's spirit.[66]

Most Virginians, analyzing their governments' performance, decided the center must be strengthened. John Harvie expressed the nub of the matter when he insisted that he loved state "sovereignty" and "civil rights" as much as anyone, but added that he thought Congress would be justified in doing what the war demanded. For its part, the General Assembly approved participation in a convention to consider revision of the Articles of Confederation (which ultimately became the Philadelphia Convention of 1787) by a unanimous vote.[67]

During the Revolution, Jefferson had held Virginia to be "one of thirteen nations, who have agreed to act and speak together." Now he believed that the United States should be "one nation as to foreign concerns" and "distinct in Domestic ones." He did not insist on the point, however. As he told Edward Carrington, "I confess I do not go as far in the reforms thought necessary as some of my correspondents in America; but if the Convention should adopt such propositions I shall suppose them necessary." Madison promised him from Philadelphia that the reconstructed federal government's new powers "will extend to taxation, trade and sundry other general [that is, national] matters," and Jefferson thought his wishes concerning the allocation of powers between state and federal governments had been fulfilled.[68]

While he looked forward to reform of the Articles of Confederation, Jefferson also hoped for reform of the Virginia constitution of 1776. He had disliked the constitution of 1776 even before seeing it, and he intended to obey his old mentor George Wythe's injunction to amend it at the earliest possible opportunity. He found reason to complain in the structures of the executive, the judiciary, and the legislative; in the apportionment system; in the suffrage provisions; and in other provisions that came to mind from time to time. Wartime proposals for establishment of a dictatorship sealed the matter, at least rhetorically, and his experience as governor early in the 1780s reinforced his sense of the constitution's inadequacy.[69]

In 1783, Jefferson sent Madison a draft state constitution. It would have conceded Jefferson's objection concerning the old constitution's impermanence. Jefferson based this argument on his erroneous assertion that the May Convention had not been elected with adoption of a new constitution in mind, so that the constitution rested on no firmer a bottom than any other ordinance. His proposal featured stricter separation of powers; three-year terms for delegates; extended suffrage; exclusion of executive officers from the General Assembly; a supremacy clause; limitations on the death penalty; bans on legislative pardons, ex post facto laws, torture, and attainders; a ban on slave importations; a gradual abolition provision; provisions strengthening the executive and the judiciary; an amendment procedure; and several other provisions such as Madison would later include in the Virginia Plan. Unlike the constitution of 1776, Jefferson's proposal represented a revolutionary break with Virginia's past.[70]

Jefferson remained unrealistically optimistic about the prospects for constitutional reform. Seeing that the people manifested no enthusiasm for constitutional change, other reformers hoped Henry might bring the Commonwealth's political class behind it. When Henry instead succeeded in placing a bar to future consideration of a constitutional convention on the House of Delegates' journal, Jefferson chose to pray for Henry's death, as he put it, and dream that the young would eventually change the constitution.[71]

Besides its institutional and political life, independence brought crisis to Virginia's economy. Many Virginians thought they had "a heavier taxation than prevails in any part of the world!" and they blamed the situation in part on the Confederation. The proximity of plentiful, cheap land joined with the Old Dominion's high rate of taxation, according to Virginians, to spur emigration from Old Virginia, and the General Assembly endured pressure to address the problem. Virginians also detected a tendency in Congress to exploit the Old Dominion's wealth for other states' benefit. Thus, Edmund Randolph notified James Madison in mid-1783 that the recent defeat of a proposal to empower Congress to levy an impost had been due in large part to the fear that Virginia, having suffered (so the General Assembly believed) more than other states in the way of despoliation, would face the necessity to import more than other states, and thus pay an abnormally high percentage of the Confederation's imposts, in the war's aftermath.[72]

Unavoidable economic conditions struck Virginia hard between 1776 and 1788. Many Virginians, captive to the new faith in government as a science, blamed their institutions; if they had a problem, there must be a political solution. In the wake of the war, specie outflow resulting from renewed foreign purchases, coupled with renewed competition from foreign concerns, pushed down prices. Government debt became more burdensome as Virginians had less money, and debtor class resentment of the income redistribution resulting from government debt service flared. Merchant profits fell, and trade slowed "in expectation of future price decreases." Per capita export growth declined by 1790 to a point far lower than the prewar rate, and expert growth recovery seemed very unlikely. A cyclical recession heightened dissatisfaction, and Americans tended to blame all of these basically intractable problems on the Confederation government, inheritor of the Crown's role as focus of discontent.[73]

In their exaggerated sense of their colony's importance, Virginians had expected that England would suffer severely from interruption of its trade with Virginia, and this led them to initiate a fateful tradition of economic coercion in the early years of the Imperial Crisis. Manifold disruptions in Virginia's economy flowed from severance of the colonial tie, and policymakers' response showed little evidence of system or forethought. Virginia depended on Great Britain for many things, among the most important of which was specie, the main circulating medium. Its absence from Virginia's economy in the war years caused severe economic problems. The legislature responded by printing paper money, which depreciated as the government printed more. Eventually, this process drove all the remaining specie out of circulation, causing more severe depreciation and additional resentment.[74]

At war's end, accumulation of specie in private hands artificially inflated British imports, which grated on the sensibilities of men who had just fought a war for independence. What good was self-government if British fashion still reigned and if British enterprises continued to dominate Virginia markets? Such concerns more acutely affected Virginia than some other states because Virginia had no great port to focus its entrepreneurial energies or great merchant houses to share in trade profits. Virginia's leading political thinkers believed imports also tended to the restoration of Virginians' dependence on "foreign" metropoles—whether they were in Britain, Pennsylvania, or elsewhere—and thus undermined home rule. Virginians were sure, despite the true prospects, that they could achieve more economic self-determination if only they took the right measures.[75]

One might have thought that one of those measures would be diversification of Virginia's economy, which surely would have strengthened the Old Dominion's position vis-à-vis Great Britain. Virginia's commitment to tobacco did wane in the Revolutionary period, but no one could mistake Virginia's economy for a diversified one. Once the Commonwealth's vacant lands were settled, thinkers such as James Madison believed, it might make sense to favor "manufactures & navigation." For the nonce, agriculture dominated Virginia's economy in fact and in policy; even private internal improvements projects the government supported were intended to grease the skids of inland agricultural trade, not to foster economic progress.[76]

Leading thinkers believed its status as a tobacco state guaranteed that Virginia would be in a minority position in Congress. Virginia's perceived need for free trade thus might well be thwarted. Manufacturing states would desire protection, this argument held, and they would have their way. Jefferson's friend Edward Carrington held that the Southern states had nothing to fear, for since they had far greater naval stores than New England, they could divert resources toward shipping if relative advantage shifted. Few accepted this rosy evaluation. Jefferson mused that it might have been better for the United States to abandon the sea altogether, and thereby avoid foreign embroilments. Richard Henry Lee, Meriwether Smith, and the *Virginia Independent Chronicle* displayed hostility to trade sometimes, with the last going so far as to concur in Jefferson's extremist utopian musings. Home rule had economic implications, too.[77]

Virginians' dependence on the North and on Great Britain simply galled them. Looking to British history, James Madison determined that the mother country had secured its economic independence by favoring its own trade. Virginia, he concluded, might want to do the same thing. Madison favored a general convention of the United States to see to the independence of American shipping, but some of his Virginian colleagues preferred to foster dependence on Great Britain in preference to New England, New York, and Philadelphia. Fear of Philadelphia's growing influence led Governor Harrison to insist that the new Confederation capitol be located in some other city. George Mason met with resistance propelled by the same notion when he endeavored to secure legislation restricting purchases of foreign superfluities.[78]

At war's end, Virginians found themselves in substantial debt, and who but the British and the great houses of Boston, New York, and Philadelphia stood ready to loan them money? Tobacco accounted for 85 percent of Virginia's exports in 1787, and more than 60 percent of that tobacco went to Great Britain. British products made up the majority of Virginia's imports, too. Virginia statesmen's hopes for ecumenical economic relations had been thwarted. Under the façade of self-government lurked the reality of continued dependence on the mother country.[79]

Casting about for some measure to promote economic self-sufficiency, James Madison hit upon the idea of fostering the development of one of Virginia's coastal cities into a great port. His vehicle was a bill to ban importation and exportation of goods through any port not designated by the General Assembly. Madison thought that by encouraging European shipping to come to Virginia, his bill would push prices down toward those paid in Philadelphia and Baltimore, but he told Jefferson that most of his colleagues feared the result would be increased transportation costs. Predictably, this policy failed to elevate any Virginia port into the ranks of Boston, Philadelphia, and New York. With the inauguration of the new federal government in 1789, the Ports Bill became a dead letter, and the idea of economic autarky died with it.[80]

Besides seeking economic self-determination in the context of revolutionary upheaval, Virginians also enforced Virginian political identity stringently in the first republican decade. Loyalists were proscribed, loyalty oaths enforced, expression of Loyalist sentiment banned. In the war's early days, Richard Henry Lee wrote Governor Henry to suggest Loyalists should be in "the same situation if we succeed in this war, that we undoubtedly shall be if the enemy prevail," by which he meant that Loyalists should be executed. At the end of the war, one bill would have excluded "natives who had borne arms against the state" alone among whites from immigration. Popular and official violence against the property of "British sympathizers" spread after Yorktown in 1781. Treason accusations flew freely, leading Governor Harrison and the Council to pardon treason convicts regularly. In time, however, the General Assembly repealed the requirement that all men take oaths of loyalty, effectively pardoning remaining Loyalists.[81]

Virginians remained Anglophobic for a generation after the Revolution, with enormous consequences. At the Revolution's close, Virginians were still prone to blame all their problems on British conspiracy. Arthur Campbell, for example, said the British planned to make independence useless to the Americans, and he pointed to their actions in "introducing luxury, draining our money, impairing public credit." Monarchies, Americans believed, tended to rely on "the *ultima ratio regum*," and that tendency justified two generations of Virginia's acting toward Great Britain as a petulant dog nipping at its heels. Britons would long remain "these wicked Invaders." Like an adolescent acting out against a same-sex parent, republican Virginia resented Britain at every turn.[82]

Virginia's adolescence extended to its felt need to impress older states. In keeping with the trend of the times, many Virginians hoped that theirs was an "Enlightened" "country." Jefferson intended to prove it was with his *Notes on the State of Virginia*, which at once demonstrated his own polish, touted Virginia, and laid out a program for state reform. Jefferson's influence in this regard affected Virginia markedly, for while men such as Edmund Pendleton and Richard Henry Lee possessed rather conventional Episcopalian views (as, for example, in Lee's scorn for "Mandevilles"), Edmund Randolph captured the influence of Jefferson's moral and religious teaching perfectly. One struggles to name a single prominent political leader in the period after 1800 who shared the religious convictions of the earlier days.[83]

For Jefferson, Enlightenment was not simply a philosophical disposition, it was a social necessity. A man should be embarrassed to represent a country not reputedly "Enlightened." His argument with the French naturalist Buffon, to which James Madison lent his efforts, constituted simply one manifestation of Jefferson's life-long desire to move his periphery to the center of the European world; his desire to see Virginia erect an estimable capitol and his pride in foreign response to the Virginia Statute for Religious Freedom were others. One could not avoid Enlightenment ideas in this period; they influenced everything, from religion to law to politics to education to sex roles to racial perceptions to aesthetics, and beyond. They affected the Virginians' foreign policy views, too. Thus, Madison called Spain, notorious among the British for its staunch (un-Enlightened) Roman Catholicism, "a nation . . . the genius of whose government religion & manners unfit them, of all the nations in Christendom for a coalition with this country."[84]

The desire to impress leading European thinkers provided the initial impetus behind the drive to adapt the Commonwealth's architecture to its new form of government. The cold beauty and republican meetness of some of the buildings he had seen in Europe impressed Jefferson, and when he learned that a new capitol was to be built in Virginia, he insisted it be designed in imitation of an ancient temple in the south of France. Other Virginia political leaders let him have his way, and his new capitol followed Roman lines. Jefferson held the opinion then, as he would later in designing the campus of the University of Virginia, that the organization of living space imbued people with political principles. His concern for Virginia's reputation abroad reinforced his preference for simple, beautiful public buildings.[85]

Virginia, in sentiment as well as name, was republican—despite the aristocratic desire to impress French intellectuals and despite the alliance with Europe's most prestigious monarch, Louis XVI. As George Mason and his fellow Prince William County petitioners put it in 1781, "the good People of Virginia took up Arms . . . with Great Britain, in Defence of their Liberty and Property, invaded by an arbitrary & tyrannical Government," and they would do it again if need arose. Edmund Pendleton stressed that in a "Free State" everyone, even the king, owed obedience to the law. (As Pendleton's exchange with Jefferson over the structure of the new Senate showed, their revolution had not been fought for democracy.) Virginia, now that Virginians ruled it, favored small farmers, the best material for republican citizenship—not to mention the largest voting constituency.[86]

Virginians, or at least some of them, believed that responsible, republican government would be incorrupt. The unique virtue Jefferson believed they had displayed in making their government responsible insured its purity. Statesmen in a republic would not deign to win elections by treating the electorate to alcohol, as in colonial times, but would willingly answer the public's spontaneous call to serve. Because their government rested on a solid foundation of virtue, it would be peace-loving and honest. Its people would love their liberty more than their lives, in the manner of their Revolutionary forebears.[87]

From the time of their break with the House of Hanover, Virginians assumed that only a country in which most had been born to freedom could remain free. Spain's unfitness to be an American ally meant that Spaniards were unfit to immigrate. Jefferson held that men immigrating from absolute monarchies tended to bring their principles with them. The same was true of Roman Catholics, whose religious views, he said, rendered them unfit for self-government. If immigrants from "benighted" lands came to Virginia, Jefferson wrote, and if they eschewed their former principles, they would substitute "an unbounded licentiousness" for them. Such a disposition, once passed on to a generation of children, would threaten the survival of the republic. Jefferson would allow immigration on the theory he borrowed from Richard Bland in *A Summary View*, but he certainly would not encourage it. The General Assembly agreed.[88]

Virginians had arrived at some understanding by the end of their first dozen years of independence concerning the true meaning of self-government. The record of their accomplishment in those dozen years included some truly stunning achievements. The Anglican Establishment, which had long since become an anachronism in the increasingly diverse religious environment of Virginia, had been abolished, and a clear statement of the principle of church-state separation sensibly adopted in its place. A thorough-going revision of Virginia's laws, aimed at making them consistent with Virginia's newfound commitment to republicanism, had included sweeping changes in the structure of Virginia's legal system and in important areas such as inheritance and land tenures; abolition of the feudal land tenures, for example, doomed the old landed aristocracy and insured that never again would land holdings in the Old Dominion be concentrated in a few families' hands.

Despite all of the important reforms that Virginia undertook between the adoption of its permanent republican constitution and 1788, however, many reformers found political conditions in their commonwealth completely unacceptable. The constitution of 1776 itself struck many as a pale shadow of a constitution, at once inconsistent with the latest theories of constitutional government and inappropriate to a truly republican society. These men, most conspicuous among whom were George Washington, Thomas Jefferson, and James Madison, also doubted that a General Assembly dominated by the new class of men who had entered the House of Delegates in the revolutionary decade ever could be swayed to forsake its allegiance to Patrick Henry in the name of fiscal prudence. What was perhaps even worse to the disenchanted was that the new men generally joined Henry in distrusting the Confederation government, in refusing to concede that it should have the power to perform the military and economic functions that they believed only the central government could.

Madison repeatedly met political defeat at the hands of Patrick Henry, whose mastery of the House of Delegates he simply could not overcome. For example, in 1784, Delegates Madison and Henry voted on eight recorded votes, disagreeing on four. Henry's side won all four.[89] Yes, Madison did maneuver the Virginia Statute for Religious Freedom past Henry, but only by supporting

Henry's election as governor. On the questions of the general vector of Virginia's taxation policy and of Virginia's attitude toward the Confederation, Henry's men in the House of Delegates seemed to form an unbreakable phalanx.

Madison's response was to circumvent Henry completely. If Henry controlled the Virginia legislature, Madison would help to create a new federal government with far stronger powers. In place of the undependable requisitions of donations from the states on which the Confederation government relied, he would struggle to win this new government an independent power to tax people directly; rather than have the federal legislators be elected by the state legislators (which meant, not only in Virginia but in other states, by people like Henry), Madison would endeavor to win delegation of these critical powers to a different breed of men. Ideally, the proposed new constitution would permanently deprive the states of power to adopt the economic measures that had so upset Madison and his fellows.

Finally, after several fits and starts, Madison and his collaborators won agreement from twelve of the thirteen states to send delegations to a convention to propose amendments to the Articles of Confederation. Actually, however, Madison intended all along to seek endorsement by a select body of the nation's leading men of an entirely new constitution giving the general government executive, legislative, and judicial powers, a bicameral legislature, and various other attributes of sovereignty—which would undercut the democratized home rule enjoyed by the states, not least Virginia, in the decade of the Revolution. His subterfuge in seeking Virginia's appointment of delegates to the Philadelphia Convention of 1787 was entirely in character: Madison believed that the Philadelphia Convention could be set up as a modern analogue of the ancient Lawgivers, such as Solon of Athens and Lycurgus of Sparta. The people, at large and in ratification conventions, were simply to be persuaded to acquiesce in the establishment of the new government their betters drafted for them. They would be left to oversee quotidian matters, but the constitution would be effectively elevated beyond their reach.[90]

Madison's gambit succeeded in the summer of 1787. The Philadelphia Convention, including leading figures such as Benjamin Franklin, George Washington, John Rutledge, Roger Sherman, Oliver Ellsworth, and Alexander Hamilton, drafted a constitution more or less in consonance with Madison's wishes. Eight states ratified. Then, in June of 1788, the Virginia Ratification Convention met in Richmond. Each side understood that the future of self-government was at stake.

NOTES

1. St. George Tucker to Theodorick Bland, 3 January 1781, Bland Family Papers, Virginia Historical Society; Richard Henry Lee to Benjamin Harrison, 9 July 1782, *Letters of Richard Henry Lee*, 2: 270–73.

2. Richard Henry Lee to George Washington, 12 June 1781, *Letters of Richard Henry Lee*, 2: 233–35; Patrick Henry to George Washington, 30 October 1777, William Wirt Henry, *Patrick Henry: Life, Correspondence, and Speeches* (3 vols.; reprinted Harrisonburg, Virginia: Sprinkle Publications, 1993), 3: 111–12; a leading politician noted that Virginia bore "almost the whole burden of the southern war" in Richard Henry Lee to Thomas McKean, 25 August 1781, *Letters of Richard Henry Lee*, 2: 246–48, at 247; Richard Henry Lee to Samuel Adams, c. 1 April 1781, *Ibid.*, 2: 218–20; and Richard Henry Lee to Arthur Lee, 4 June 1781, *Ibid.*, 2: 229–30. Governor Jefferson and the Council lamented other states' failure to appreciate and reciprocate Virginia's sacrifices in Thomas Jefferson to Samuel Huntington, 16 December 1779, *Papers of James Madison*, ed. William T. Hutchinson et al. (Chicago and Charlottesville: University of Chicago and University of Virginia Presses, 1962–), 1: 320–22; Prince William County Freeholders' Petition (by George Mason), 10 December 1781, *Papers of George Mason*, 2: 703–11, at 709.

3. Roger Atkinson to Samuel Pleasants, October 1774, Roger Atkinson Letterbook, University of Virginia.

4. Roger Atkinson to "Sammy," 20 November 1776, *Ibid.*

5. Archibald Stuart to Thomas Jefferson, 17 October 1785, *Papers of Thomas Jefferson*, 8: 644–46, at 645; Robert A. Rutland, *George Mason: Reluctant Statesman* (Baton Rouge and London: Louisiana State University Press, 1961); George Mason to Richard Henry Lee, 4 June 1779, *Papers of George Mason*, 2: 506–8; George Mason to ?, 2 October 1778, *Ibid.*, 1: 433–37, at 434; Richard Adams to Thomas Adams, July 1777, Virginia Historical Society ("It is really a melancholy reflection to find that we have not proper men of abilitys [that is, aristocrats] to fill the very important offices of the State."); James Madison to Edmund Randolph, 11 June 1782, *Papers of James Madison*, 4: 333–34, at 333; Foreword, *Papers of George Mason*, 2: vii–ix (Washington chastising Mason and Jefferson); James Monroe to Thomas Jefferson, 11 May 1782, *The Writings of James Monroe*, ed. Stanislaus M. Hamilton (7 vols., 1898–1903; reprinted, New York: AMS Press, 1969), 1: 14–15; Jack J. Reardon, *Edmund Randolph: A Biography* (New York: Macmillan, 1974), 56; Richard Henry Lee to John Adams, 8 October 1779, *Letters of Richard Henry Lee*, 2: 155–56, at 155.

6. Richard K. Matthews, *If Men Were Angels: James Madison & the Heartless Empire of Reason* (Lawrence: University Press of Kansas, 1995). Madison was terribly bothered by Henry's dominance of the all-powerful General Assembly, especially since he was no match for Henry in the House of Delegates. In 1784, for example, Delegates Madison and Henry voted on eight recorded votes, disagreeing on four. Henry's side won all four. Thomas Edwin Buckley, "Church and State in Virginia, 1776–1787" (Ph.D. dissertation, University of California, Santa Barbara, 1974), 152; Anne Cary Nicholas to Wilson Cary Nicholas, December 1784, Virginia Historical Society. (Mrs. Nicholas was the wife of colonial treasurer Robert Carter Nicholas.) Also see Jay Fliegelman, *Declaring Independence: Jefferson, Natural Language, & the Culture of Performance* (Stanford, Calif.: Stanford University Press, 1993), and "Extract of letter from Judge Spencer Roane to William Wirt," Henry Family Papers, Virginia Historical Society; George Mason to Martin Cockburn, 26 May 1774, *Papers of George Mason*, 1: 190–91. While Madison would maneuver at decade's end to reduce Henry's power and the power of the democratic leaders generally, Henry characteristically, solicited Madison's renewed participation in public life. Patrick Henry to James Madison, 17 April 1784, *Papers of James Madison*, 8: 18. Thomas Jefferson, "Notes on the State of Virginia," *The Portable*

Thomas Jefferson, ed. Merrill D. Peterson (New York: Penguin Books, 1975), "Query XVII: Religion," 208–13, at 213.

7. For Henry's dominance and one reason for unhappiness with it, Joseph Jones to James Madison, 14 June 1783, *Papers of James Madison*, 7: 143–45, at 144–45.

8. Joseph Jones to James Madison, 31 May 1783, *Ibid.*, 7: 99–101; Edmund Randolph to James Madison, 10 May 1782, *Ibid.*, 4: 225–27, at 225.

9. Jacquelin Ambler to James Madison, 1 June 1783, *Ibid.*, 7: 102; Thomas Jefferson to James Madison, 8 May 1784, *Papers of Thomas Jefferson*, 7: 231–34, at 233; "A Land-Holder" propounded the same argument about the ease of paying new taxes in the *Virginia Gazette* in May 1782; James Madison to Thomas Jefferson, 6 September 1787, *Papers of Thomas Jefferson*, 12: 102–4, at 103.

10. James Madison to James Monroe, 5 October 1786, *Papers of James Madison*, 9: 140–42, at 141; James Madison to Thomas Jefferson, 9 December 1787, *Papers of Thomas Jefferson*, 12: 408–12, at 410; Benjamin Harrison to Thomas Jefferson, 23 April 1784, *Ibid.*, 7: 114; Thomas Jefferson to James Madison, 8 December 1784, *Papers of James Madison*, 8: 177–80, at 177–78; Richard Henry Lee to Robert Wormley Carter, 3 June 1783, *Letters of Richard Henry Lee*, 2: 281–82, at 282.

11. Joseph Jones to James Madison, 14 June 1783, *Papers of James Madison*, 7: 143–45.

12. Edmund Randolph to Thomas Jefferson, 15 May 1784, *Papers of Thomas Jefferson*, 7: 259–61, at 260; William Short to Thomas Jefferson, 14 May 1784, *Ibid.*, 7: 256–58, at 257; James Madison to James Monroe, 13 May 1786, *Papers of James Madison*, 9: 54–55, at 55; Lance Banning, "James Madison, The Statute for Religious Freedom, and the Crisis of Republican Convictions," *The Virginia Statute for Religious Freedom: Its Evolution and Consequences in American History*, eds. Merrill Peterson and Robert C. Vaughan (Cambridge: Cambridge University Press, 1988), 109–38, at 124; Thomas Jefferson to Edmund Randolph, 15 February 1783, *Papers of Thomas Jefferson*, 6: 246–49, at 247; Thomas Jefferson to James Monroe, 5 October 1781, *Ibid.*, 6: 126–28, at 127.

13. Samuel Stanhope Smith to James Madison, c. November 1777–August 1778, *Papers of James Madison*, 1: 194–95; Edmund Pendleton to James Madison, 25 November 1782, *Pendleton Papers*, 2: 429–30; Edmund Pendleton to Thomas Jefferson, 22 July 1776, *Ibid.*, 1: 187–88 ; Edmund Pendleton to William Woodford, 31 January 1778, *Ibid.*, 1: 246–48, at 247; "Petition From Some Inhabitants of Albemarle County," 12 May 1777, *Papers of Thomas Jefferson*, 2: 14–15; *Hening's Statutes*, vol. 9, May 1777 Session, Chap. 25; Bill "for dividing the county of Cumberland," 20 May 1777, *Journal of the House of Delegates of the Commonwealth of Virginia, 1777–1778* (Richmond: Thomas W. White), 1777: 22; *Hening's Statutes*, vol. 9, October 1776 Session, Chap. 38, Chap. 40; *Ibid.*, vol. 9, October 1778 Session, Chap. 21.

14. *Ibid.*, vol. 11, October 1784 Session, Chap. 52.

15. Peter S. Onuf, *The Origins of the Federal Republic: Jurisdictional Controversies in the United States, 1775–1787* (Philadelphia: University of Pennsylvania Press, 1983), 101; Charles Thomson to Hannah Thomson, 25 July 1783, *Letters of Delegates to Congress, 1774–1789*, ed. Paul H. Smith (Washington, D.C.: Library of Congress, 1976–1996), 20: 452–54, at 454; Edmund Pendleton to James Madison, 25 September 1780, *Pendleton Papers*, 1: 308–10, at 309; George Mason to Joseph Jones, 27 July 1780, *Papers of George Mason*, 2: 655–62, at 656.

16. Peter S. Onuf, *Origins of the Federal Republic*, 150 and n. 11 at 257; Virginia's congressmen asked the Congress for that "page of the Confederation" in which

the power to determine states' boundaries "is delegated." Joseph Jones, James Madison, and Edmund Randolph to the Committee for Territorial Cessions, 10 October 1781, *Papers of George Mason*, 2: 722–23. Congressman Arthur Lee, supported by James Madison, made the same point in response to a petition for Kentucky statehood. "Charles Thomson's Notes of Debates," 27 August 1782, *Letters of Delegates to Congress*, 19: 96–99, at 96, 97. Congressman Benjamin Harrison in John Adams' Notes of Debates, 2 August 1776, *Ibid.*, 4: 603–4. For the Vermont analogy, see Thomas Jefferson to Edmund Randolph, 15 February 1783, *Papers of Thomas Jefferson*, 6: 246–49. The leading charter history was Thomas Jefferson, *Notes on the State of Virginia*, "Query XIII: Constitution," 153–76, at 153–62. Another example is that which George Mason wrote c. 20 May 1782. *Papers of George Mason*, 2: 727–31. George Mason to Samuel Purviance, 17 July 1782, *Ibid.*, 2: 738–41, quotations at 739, 741; Edmund Randolph to Thomas Nelson, 7 November 1781, *Letters of Delegates to Congress*, 18: 184–87. For Bland's legacy, see K. R. Constantine Gutzman, "Jefferson's Draft Declaration of Independence, Richard Bland, and the Revolutionary Legacy: Giving Credit Where Credit Is Due," *The Journal of the Historical Society* 1 (2001): 137–54.

17. Richard Henry Lee to James Madison, 30 May 1785, *Letters of Richard Henry Lee*, 2: 364–66, at 365; Peter S. Onuf, *Origins of the Federal Republic*, 75, 89; Edmund Randolph to James Madison, 27 June 1782, *Papers of James Madison*, 4: 375–76; Richard Henry Lee to Patrick Henry, 15 November 1778, *Letters of Richard Henry Lee*, 1: 451–53, at 452–53 (regarding government from Williamsburg).

18. Peter S. Onuf, *Origins of the Federal Republic, passim.*; Richard Henry Lee to George Washington, 26 December 1784, *Letters of Richard Henry Lee*, 2: 317–18. For related correspondence among the four states, see the appendix to *Hening's Statutes*, vol. 10.

19. Edmund Randolph, *History of Virginia* (Charlottesville: University Press of Virginia), 259; *Letters of Delegates to Congress*, n. 1 at 11, 171; Peter S. Onuf, *Origins of the Federal Republic*, 57.

20. Richard Henry Lee to Samuel Adams, 5 February 1781, *Letters of Richard Henry Lee*, 2: 213–15, at 215; *Hening's Statutes*, vol. 10, May 1779 Session, Chap 25.

21. John Marshall to George Muter, 7 January 1785, *Papers of John Marshall*, 1: 133–35; Richard Henry Lee to Thomas Jefferson, 29 October 1785, *Letters of Richard Henry Lee*, 2: 402–4, at 403; William Grayson to James Madison, 21 August 1785, *Papers of James Madison*, 8: 347–49, at 349; Speech of James Madison in Congress on Kentucky, 27 August 1782, *Ibid.*, 5: 83; James Madison to Richard Henry Lee, 7 July 1785, *Ibid.*, 8: 314–16, at 314; Richard Henry Lee to James Madison, 11 August 1785, *Letters of Richard Henry Lee*, 2: 382–84; Peter S. Onuf, *Origins of the Federal Republic*, 102, 159.

22. Edmund Randolph to James Madison, 9 May 1783, *Papers of James Madison*, 7: 32–34. The preamble to the statute moving the capital referred to both military and equitable concerns. *Hening's Statutes*, vol. 10, May 1779 Session, Chap. 21.

23. Thomas Jefferson, *Notes on the State of Virginia*, "Query XII: Counties and Towns," 151–52, at 152; Patrick Henry to Richard Henry Lee, 9 January 1785, William Wirt Henry, *Patrick Henry*, 3: 265–67, at 266–67; *Hening's Statutes*, vol. 11, October 1784 Session, Chap. 19, Chap. 43; *Ibid.*, vol. 11, October 1783 Session, Chap. 20.

24. Editorial Note, *The Papers of Thomas Jefferson*, 8: 191–92; James Madison to Thomas Jefferson, 9 January 1785, *Ibid.*, 7: 588–98, at 597; Thomas Jefferson to George Washington, 15 March 1784, *Ibid.*, 7: 25–27, at 26–27; George Washington to Patrick

Henry, 30 November 1785, William Wirt Henry, *Patrick Henry*, 3: 337–39; for the Mississippi Navigation, Richard Henry Lee to Henry Laurens, 1 August 1779, *Letters of Richard Henry Lee*, Richard Henry Lee to George Washington (the Jay-Gardoquí context) 2: 98–100, at 98; John Marshall to George Muter, 7 January 1785, *The Papers of John Marshall*, ed. Herbert A. Johnson et al. (Williamsburg, Va.: University of North Carolina Press, 1974–), 1: 133–35, at 134–35; Philip Morrison Rice, "Internal Improvements in Virginia, 1775–1860" (Ph.D. dissertation, University of North Carolina, 1948), 50. Also see Charles Royster, *The Fabulous History of the Dismal Swamp Company: A Story of George Washington's Times* (New York: Alfred A. Knopf, 1999); and John Lauritz Larson, "Jefferson's Union and the Problem of Internal Improvements," *Jeffersonian Legacies*, ed. Peter S. Onuf (Charlottesville: University Press of Virginia, 1993).

25. George Mason to Thomas Jefferson, 27 September 1781, *Papers of George Mason*, 2: 697–99; *Hening's Statutes*, vol. 12, October 1786 Session, Chap. 25; James Madison to Lafayette, 20 March 1785, *Papers of James Madison*, 8: 250–54, at 250–51; George Mason to Thomas Jefferson, 27 September 1781, *Papers of George Mason*, 2: 697–99, at 698.

26. Philip Morrison Rice, "Internal Improvements in Virginia," 41, 42, 50, 58–59.

27. Richard Henry Lee to Thomas Jefferson, 16 May 1785, *Letters of Richard Henry Lee*, 2: 357–59, at 358; James Madison to Edmund Pendleton, 2 October 1781, *Papers of James Madison*, 3: 273–74.

28. *Hening's Statutes*, vol. 12, October 1785 Session, Chap. 34; Rhys Isaac, *The Transformation of Virginia*, 282–83; *Documentary History of the Struggle for Religious Liberty in Virginia*, 80–81. Jefferson said that most "citizens" were then dissenters but most representatives were "churchmen." *Ibid.* In *Notes on the State of Virginia*, he estimated that "two-thirds of the people had become dissenters at the commencement of the present revolution." Thomas Jefferson, *Notes on the State of Virginia*, "Query XVII: Religion," 208–13, at 209.

29. Edmund Pendleton to Richard Henry Lee, 18 April 1785, *Pendleton Papers*, 2: 477–79, at 478; *Hening's Statutes*, vol. 11, May 1782 Session, Chap. 25; *Ibid.*, October 1779 Session, Chap 13; "A Bill to Amend the Act Regulating Ordinaries and Tippling-Houses," 19 October 1779," *Papers of George Mason*, 2: 541–42.

30. Thomas Edwin Buckley, "Church and State in Virginia, 1776–1787" (Ph.D. dissertation, University of California, Santa Barbara, 1974), 103–4; Edmund Randolph to James Madison, 15 May 1783, *Papers of James Madison*, 7: 44–46, at 46; Thomas Edwin Buckley, "Church and State in Virginia, 1776–1787," viii–ix; Governor Henry to the Delegates and Ministers of the Baptist Churches, 13 August 1776, *Official Letters of the Governors*, 3: 30.

31. John Page to Thomas Jefferson, 23 August 1785, *Papers of Thomas Jefferson*, 8: 428–50; Richard Henry Lee to James Madison, 26 November 1784, *Letters of Richard Henry Lee*, 2: 304–7 (quotation at 304).

32. Thomas Jefferson, *Notes on the State of Virginia*, "Query XVII: Religion," 208–13, at 210.

33. Thomas Edgar Gage, "The Established Church in Colonial Virginia, 1689–1785" (Ph.D. dissertation, University of Missouri, 1974), 99–100, 116, 128–29, 142; Editorial Note, *Papers of Thomas Jefferson*, 1: 525–29.

34. *Documentary History of the Struggle for Religious Liberty in Virginia*, ed. Charles F. James (reprinted 1971; Lynchburg: J. P. Bell, 1900), 28; House of Delegates

Resolutions concerning Religion, 1776, *Papers of Thomas Jefferson*, 1: 530–31; *Hening's Statutes*, vol. 9, October 1776 Session, Chap. 2.

35. Rhys Isaac, *The Transformation of Virginia, 1740–1790*; George Wythe, "The Late Chancellor Wythe's opinion respecting Religions, delivered by Himself," Virginia Historical Society. For elite deification of sentiment, see Andrew Burstein, *The Inner Jefferson: Portrait of a Grieving Optimist* (Charlottesville: University Press of Virginia, 1995).

36. Thomas Edwin Buckley, "Church and State in Virginia, 1776–1787," 134; Jefferson's aims perhaps were partly religious. David N. Mayer, *The Constitutional Thought of Thomas Jefferson* (Charlottesville and London: University Press of Virginia, 1994), 71; James Madison to William Bradford, 1 December 1773, *Papers of James Madison*, 1: 100–101, at 101; James Madison to William Bradford, 24 January 1774, *Ibid.*, 1: 104–6, especially at 105; Thomas Jefferson, *Notes on the State of Virginia*, "Query XVII: Religion," 208–13, at 211–12.

37. James Madison to Thomas Jefferson, 19 February 1788, *Papers of Thomas Jefferson*, 12: 607–10; Rhys Isaac, *The Transformation of Virginia*, 278; Thomas Edwin Buckley, "Church and State in Virginia, 1776–1787," 137; John Marshall to James Monroe, 2 December 1784, *Papers of John Marshall*, 1: 129–32; James Madison to James Monroe, 4 December 1784, *Papers of James Madison*, 8: 175; Edmund Randolph, *History of Virginia*, 263.

38. "Memorial and Remonstrance against Religious Assessments," c. 20 June 1785, *Papers of James Madison*, 8: 298–304; J. C. D. Clark, *The Language of Liberty, 1660–1832: Political Discourse and Social Dynamics in the Anglo-American World* (Cambridge: Cambridge University Press, 1994).

39. Also James Madison to James Monroe, 21 June 1785, *Papers of James Madison*, 8: 306–8, at 306.

40. For Mason's support of Madison against R.H. Lee and Henry, Note, "Madison's 'Memorial & Remonstrance' against the Assessment Bill," *Papers of George Mason*, 2: 834–35.

41. Bill 82, *Papers of Thomas Jefferson*, 2: 545–53, especially n. at 549–50; Rhys Isaac, *The Transformation of Virginia*, 293–95; James Madison to Thomas Jefferson, 22 January 1786, *Papers of Thomas Jefferson*, 9: 194–202, at 196; Thomas Jefferson to James Madison, 16 December 1786, *Ibid.*, 10: 602–6, at 603; Rhys Isaac, *The Transformation of Virginia*, 291–93.

42. This discussion is heavily reliant on Holly Brewer, "Entailing Aristocracy in Colonial Virginia: 'Ancient Feudal Restraints' and Revolutionary Reform," *William and Mary Quarterly*, 3d Series, vol. 54 (1997), 307–46; *Hening's Statutes*, vol. 9, October 1776 Session, Chap. 26; Thomas Jefferson, *Notes on the State of Virginia*, "Query XIV: Laws," 177–99, at 182.

43. Thomas Jefferson, *Notes on the State of Virginia*, "Query XVIII: Manners," 214–15, at 215; Andrew Burstein, *The Inner Jefferson: Portrait of a Grieving Optimist*, *passim.*, Jack P. Greene, "The Intellectual Reconstruction of Virginia in the Age of Jefferson," *Jeffersonian Legacies*, 225–53, at 230–32.

44. Edmund Randolph, *History of Virginia*, 193. Some Virginians disliked this trait. Richard Henry Lee to John Adams, 8 October 1789, *Letters of Richard Henry Lee*, 2: 155–56, at 155.

45. Quotations from Thomas Jefferson, *Notes on the State of Virginia*, "Query VIII: Population," 122–28, at 127–28; "Bill to Prevent the Importation of Slaves, &c.,"

16 June 1777, *Papers of Thomas Jefferson*, 2: 22–23, nn. at 23–24; *Hening's Statutes*, vol. 9, October 1778 Session, Chap. 1. A foreign visitor, H. K. van Hogendorp, thought that Virginia slaves' situation had improved markedly with the passing of the Revolution. "The master does not demand of the slave," he wrote in 1784, "the work of which a free man is capable." With the passing of the Association, he thought, slaves clearly worked less than formerly (with the predictable effect on Virginia's gross domestic product). H. K. van Hogendorp, "On Slavery," 1784 (author's translation), *Papers of Thomas Jefferson*, 7: 216–18.

46. *Hening's Statutes*, vol. 12, October 1785 Session, Chap. 77; "51. A Bill Concerning Slaves," *Papers of Thomas Jefferson*, 2: 470–42.

47. Edmund Randolph, *History of Virginia*, 329; *Papers of James Madison*, 8: 360, n. 1; James Madison to George Washington, 11 November 1785, *Ibid.*, 8: 403–4.

48. *Hening's Statutes*, vol. 11, May 1782 Session, Chap. 21; James Madison to Thomas Jefferson, 20 August 1784, *Papers of James Madison*, 8: 102–10, at 108; Paul Finkelman, "Treason Against the Hopes of the World," *Jeffersonian Legacies*, 218, n. 103; David Brion Davis, *The Problem of Slavery in the Age of Revolution, 1770–1823*, 232; James Madison to George Washington, 11 November 1785, *Papers of James Madison*, 8: 403–4, at 404; *Hening's Statutes*, vol. 11, May 1782 Session, Chap. 32; Richard Henry Lee to Mrs. Hannah Corbin, 17 March 1778, *Letters of Richard Henry Lee*, 1: 392–94, at 392 (no objection to women's suffrage); Richard Henry Lee to Landon Carter, 6 February 1778, *Ibid.*, 1: 385–86 ("boy"); Rhys Isaac, "The First Monticello," *Jeffersonian Legacies*, 77–108, at 99–100; George Mason, "Remarks on the Proposed Bill for Regulating the Elections of the Members of the General Assembly," c. 1 June 1780, *Papers of George Mason*, 2: 629–31, at 629.

49. Edmund Randolph, *History of Virginia*, 267, n. 24; Remonstrance of the Judges, 12 May 1788, *Pendleton Papers*, 2: 504–8; Joseph Jones to Edmund Pendleton, 12 November 1782, *Letters of Delegates to Congress*, 19: 371–73, at 372; James Madison to Edmund Pendleton, 2 October 1781, *Papers of James Madison*, 3: 273–74, at 274; *Hening's Statutes*, vol. 9, October 1776 Session, Chap. 15; *Ibid.*, vol. 9, October 1777 Session, Chap. 15, Chap. 17; *Ibid.*, vol. 9, October 1778 Session, Chap. 12; *Ibid.*, vol. 10, May 1779 Session, Chap. 22, Chap. 26; Editor's Note, "Drafts of Bills Establishing Courts of Justice," *Papers of Thomas Jefferson*, 1: 605–7, at 605; Thomas Jefferson to George Wythe, 1 March 1779, *Ibid.*, 2: 235; John Taylor of Caroline to E. Berkeley, 21 June 1785, Berkeley Family Papers, University of Virginia; Edmund Pendleton to James Madison, 8 November 1782, *Pendleton Papers*, 2: 427–28, at 428.

50. Edmund Randolph, *History of Virginia*, 267, n. 24; *Papers of Thomas Jefferson*, 605; John Marshall to Charles Simms, 16 June 1784, *Papers of John Marshall*, 1: 124–25, at 124; James Madison to James Monroe, 4 December 1784, *Papers of James Madison*, 8: 175; *Ibid.*, 8: 163–65; Joseph Jones to James Madison, 30 May 1786, *Ibid.*, 9: 66–68; Edmund Pendleton to William Woodford, 31 January 1778, *Pendleton Papers*, 1: 246–48.

51. "Bill for the Revision of the Laws," 15 October 1776, *Papers of Thomas Jefferson*, 1: 562–63; David N. Mayer, *The Constitutional Thought of Thomas Jefferson*, 66–67.

52. James Madison to George Washington, 11 November 1785, *Papers of James Madison*, 8: 403–4, at 403; "The Revisal of the Laws, 1776–1786," *Papers of Thomas Jefferson*, 2: 305–657; *Ibid.*, 2: ix–x.

53. David N. Mayer, *The Constitutional Thought of Thomas Jefferson*, 67.

54. "Plan Agreed upon by the Committee of Revisors at Fredericksburg," 13 January 1777, *Papers of Thomas Jefferson*, 2: 325–28; *Hening's Statutes*, vol. 12, October 1785 Session, Chap. 60, Chap. 61.

55. For capital punishment in England, see *Albion's Fatal Tree: Crime and Society in Eighteenth-Century England*, ed. Douglas Hay (London: Allen Lane, 1975). Edmund Randolph to James Madison, 5 October 1782, *Papers of James Madison*, 5: 183–84; Thomas Jefferson to Edmund Pendleton, 26 August 1776, *Papers of Thomas Jefferson*, 1: 503–6, at 505.

56. David N. Mayer, *The Constitutional Thought of Thomas Jefferson*, 69.

57. Richard Henry Lee to Samuel Adams, 10 September 1780, *Letters of Richard Henry Lee*, 2: 200–203; George Washington to George Mason, 22 October 1780, *Papers of George Mason*, 2: 677–78, at 678; Lance Banning, *The Sacred Fire of Liberty: James Madison & the Founding of the Federal Republic* (Ithaca, N.Y., and London: Cornell University Press, 1995); Woody Holton, *Forced Founders: Indians, Debtors, Slaves, and the Making of the American Revolution in Virginia* (Chapel Hill, N.C., and London: University of North Carolina Press, 1999), 3–38.

58. James Monroe to Richard Henry Lee, 16 December 1783, *The Writings of James Monroe*, 1: 22–24, at 23; Thomas Jefferson to James Madison, 1 July 1784, *Papers of Thomas Jefferson*, 7: 356–57, at 356; James Madison to Thomas Jefferson, 3 October 1785, *Ibid.*, 8: 579–82, at 580; Joseph Jones to James Madison, 14 June 1783, *Papers of James Madison*, 7: 143–45, at 143; Richard Henry Lee to George Mason, 15 May 1787, *Letters of Richard Henry Lee*, 3: 876–79; Richard Henry Lee to John Adams, 5 September 1787, *Ibid.*, 2: 433–36; Richard Henry Lee to Francis Lightfoot Lee, 14 July 1787, *Ibid.*, 2: 423–24; Richard Henry Lee to Samuel Adams, 18 November 1784, *Ibid.*, 2: 293–95, at 293, 294; Richard Henry Lee to ———, 22 August 1787, *Ibid.*, 2: 432–33, at 433.

59. James Madison to Edmund Pendleton, 7 November 1780, *Papers of James Madison*, 2: 165–66, at 166; James Madison to Edmund Randolph, 25 February 1787, *Ibid.*, 9: 299; James Madison to Edmund Pendleton, 29 May 1781, *Ibid.*, 3: 140–42, at 140–41; Editor's Note, *Ibid.*, 9: 4–22; James Madison to Edmund Pendleton, 28 July 1783, *Ibid.*, 7: 254–55, at 254; James Madison to Edmund Randolph, 10 March 1784, *Ibid.*, 8: 3–5, at 3–4; James Madison to Thomas Jefferson, 19 March 1787, *Papers of Thomas Jefferson*, 11: 219–23, at 219; K. R. Constantine Gutzman, "'Oh, What a Tangled Web We Weave': James Madison and the Compound Republic," *Continuity: A Journal of History* 22 (1998): 19–29.

60. John J. Reardon, *Edmund Randolph: A Biography*, 27.

61. Richard Henry Lee to John Adams, 8 October 1779, *Letters of Richard Henry Lee*, 2: 155–56, at 155; James Madison to Caleb Wallace, 23 August 1785, *Papers of James Madison*, 8: 350–57, at 350 ("Yet I have no local partialities which can keep me from any place which promises the greatest real advantages."); George Washington to Patrick Henry, 5 October 1776, William Wirt Henry, *Patrick Henry*, 3: 12–15, at 15; George Washington to James Madison, 5 November 1786, *Papers of James Madison*, 9: 161–62; George Washington to James Madison, 30 November 1785, *Ibid.*, 428–30, at 429.

62. Edmund Randolph to James Madison, 15 May 1783, *Ibid.*, 7: 44–46, at 44–45; James Madison to Thomas Jefferson, 25 April 1784, *Papers of Thomas Jefferson*, 7: 121–24, at 122; James Madison to James Monroe, 21 June 1786, *Papers of James Madison*, 9: 82–83, at 82; Resolutions Reaffirming American Rights to Navigate the Missis-

sippi, Virginia House of Delegates, 29 November 1786, *Ibid.*, 9: 182–83. Yankees supposedly plotted disunion if Jay's treaty were *not* ratified. James Monroe to James Madison, 3 September 1786, *Ibid.*, 9: 112–14.

63. Thomas Jefferson to John Adams, 16 May 1777, *Papers of Thomas Jefferson*, 2: 18–19, at 19; Thomas Jefferson to Edmund Randolph, 3 August 1787, *Ibid.*, 11: 672–73; Thomas Jefferson to Edmund Randolph, 15 February 1783, *Ibid.*, 6: 246–49, at 248; Benjamin Harrison to James Monroe, 27 February 1784, *Ibid.*, 6: 564–65; Benjamin Harrison to Virginia Delegates, 9 August 1783, *Papers of James Madison*, 7: 264; Richard Henry Lee to General William Whipple, 1 July 1783, *Letters of Richard Henry Lee*, 2: 283–85, at 284; James Madison to James Monroe, 13 May 1786, *Papers of James Madison*, 9: 54–55, at 55.

64. Joseph Jones to James Madison, 8 June 1783, *Papers of James Madison*, 7: 118–21; John Francis Mercer to James Madison, 12 November 1784, *Ibid.*, 8: 133–36, at 134–35; Richard Henry Lee to James Madison, 26 November 1784, *Letters of Richard Henry Lee*, 2: 304–7, at 305; Peter S. Onuf, *Origins of the Federal Republic*, 187.

65. Charles Royster, *A Revolutionary People at War: The Continental Army and American Character, 1775–1783* (New York and London: W. W. Norton, 1979); George Mason to Richard Henry Lee, 4 June 1779, *Papers of George Mason*, 2: 506–8; James Madison to Thomas Jefferson, 2 June 1780, *Papers of James Madison*, 2: 37–38; James Madison to Thomas Jefferson, 27 March 1780, *Papers of Thomas Jefferson*, 3: 335–36; James Madison to Edmund Pendleton, 30 October 1781, *Letters of Delegates to Congress*, 18: 168–70.

66. John Marshall to Arthur Lee, 5 March 1787, *Papers of John Marshall*, 1: 205–6, at 206 (Henry's preference for the Mississippi over the Confederation); Patrick Henry to Mrs. Annie Christian, 20 October 1786, William Wirt Henry, *Patrick Henry*, 3: 379–80, at 380; James Monroe to Thomas Jefferson, 16 July 1786, *Papers of Thomas Jefferson*, 10: 142–44, at 143; Thomas Jefferson to James Madison, 16 December 1786, *Ibid.*, 10: 602–6, at 603; Thomas Jefferson to Archibald Stuart, 25 January 1786, *Ibid.*, 9: 217–19; Edmund Pendleton to James Madison, 19 December 1786, *Pendleton Papers*, 2: 491–94, at 493; James Madison to Thomas Jefferson, 12 August 1786, *Papers of Thomas Jefferson*, 10: 229–36; James Madison to Thomas Jefferson, 4 December 1786, *Ibid.*, 10: 574–77, at 577; John Marshall to George Muter, 7 January 1785, *Papers of John Marshall*, 1: 133–34; James Madison to George Washington, 7 December 1786, *Papers of James Madison*, 9: 119–20, at 120 (Madison's assessment may have been aimed at spurring Washington back into the political arena); James Madison to Thomas Jefferson, 4 December 1786, *Papers of Thomas Jefferson*, 10: 574–77, at 575.

67. William Short to Thomas Jefferson, 14 May 1784, *Papers of Thomas Jefferson*, 7: 256–58, at 257; John Harvie to Thomas Jefferson, 29 December 1777, *Ibid.*, 2: 125; James Madison to Thomas Jefferson, 4 December 1786, *Ibid.*, 10: 574–77, at 574.

68. "Speech to Jean Baptiste Ducoigne," 1 [?] June 1781, *Ibid.*, 6: 60–63, at 61; Thomas Jefferson to James Madison, 16 December 1786, *Ibid.*, 10: 602–6, at 603; Thomas Jefferson to James Madison, 8 February 1786, *Ibid.*, 9: 264–67, at 264; Thomas Jefferson to Edward Carrington, 4 August 1787, *Ibid.*, 11: 678–80, at 678; James Madison to Thomas Jefferson, 6 September 1787, *Ibid.*, 12: 102–4, at 103.

69. George Wythe to Thomas Jefferson, 27 July 1776, *Ibid.*, 1: 476–77; *Ibid.*, n. at 6: 85–86; Henry Young to William Davies, 9 June 1781, *Ibid.*, 6: 84–85. See generally Robert P. Sutton, *Revolution to Secession: Constitution Making in the Old Dominion* (Charlottesville: University Press of Virginia, 1989).

70. Thomas Jefferson to James Madison, 17 June 1783, *Papers of Thomas Jefferson*, 6: 277–78; "Jefferson's Draft of a Constitution for Virginia," 1783, *Ibid.*, 6: 294–305.

71. James Madison to Thomas Jefferson, 16 March 1784, *Ibid.*, 7: 32–39, at 36; James Madison to Thomas Jefferson, 15 May 1784, *Ibid.*, 7: 258–59, at 258; George Mason to ?, 2 October 1778, *Papers of George Mason*, 1: 433–37, at 434–35; James Madison to Thomas Jefferson, 3 July 1784, *Papers of Thomas Jefferson*, 7: 359–62, at 360–61; Thomas Jefferson to Démeunier, 24 January 1786, *Ibid.*, 6: 280; Thomas Jefferson to James Madison, 8 December 1784, *Papers of James Madison*, 8: 177–80, at 178 ("pray"). Edmund Randolph responded to Jefferson's arguments for suffrage reform and popular ratification in *History of Virginia*, 252–53, 256–57.

72. Richard Henry Lee to James Madison, 20 November 1784, *Letters of Richard Henry Lee*, 2: 299–301; Edmund Randolph to James Madison, 14 June 1783, *Papers of James Madison*, 7: 147–48. Virgin land was far better suited to tobacco than fertilized land. Thomas Jefferson, "On Tobacco Culture," c. 4 May 1784, *Papers of Thomas Jefferson*, 7: 209–12, at 209–10; Edmund Randolph to James Madison, 9 May 1783, *Papers of James Madison*, 7: 32–34, at 33; Edmund Randolph to James Madison, 24 May 1783, *Ibid.*, 7: 72–74, at 73.

73. Gordon C. Bjork, "The Weaning of the American Economy: Independence, Market Changes, and Economic Development," *Journal of Economic History* 24 (1964), 541–60, at 559–60.

74. George Mason, Resolutions Against Paper Money, 3 November 1787, *Papers of George Mason*, 3: 1,008–9.

75. Gordon C. Bjork, "The Weaning of the American Economy: Independence, Market Changes, and Economic Development," 558–59; *Ibid.*, 543, 544, 554.

76. James Madison to Edmund Randolph, 20 May 1783, *Papers of James Madison*, 7: 59–62, at 60; Thomas Jefferson to James Madison, 20 December 1787, *Papers of Thomas Jefferson*, 12: 438–42, at 442; Drew R. McCoy, *The Elusive Republic: Political Economy in Jeffersonian America* (New York and London: W. W. Norton, 1980); Thomas Jefferson, *Notes on the State of Virginia*, "Query XIX: Manufactures," 216–17.

77. Edmund Pendleton to James Madison, 19 December 1786, *Pendleton Papers*, 2: 491–94, at 492–93; Richard Henry Lee to ?, 10 October 1785, *Letters of Richard Henry Lee*, 2: 387–90, at 389; Edward Carrington to Thomas Jefferson, 23 October 1787, *Papers of Thomas Jefferson*, 12: 252–57, at 254; Thomas Jefferson, *Notes on the State of Virginia*, "Query XXII: Public Revenue and Expences," 224–29, at 227; Bruce A. Ragsdale, *A Planters' Republic: The Search for Economic Independence in Revolutionary Virginia* (Madison, Wisc.: Madison House, 1996), 267.

78. James Madison to Edmund Randolph, 20 May 1783, *Ibid.*, 7: 59–62, at 61; James Madison to Thomas Jefferson, 22 January 1786, *Papers of Thomas Jefferson*, 9: 194–202, at 197–99; Edmund Randolph to James Madison, 30 August 1782, *Papers of James Madison*, 5: 91–92, at 92; *Papers of George Mason*, 3: 982; Bruce A. Ragsdale, *A Planters' Republic*, 264.

79. Bruce A. Ragsdale, *A Planters' Republic*, 260, 259.

80. *Hening's Statutes*, vol. 11, May 1784 Session, Chap. 32; *Ibid.*, vol. 12, October 1786 Session, Chap. 42; Thomas Jefferson, *Notes on the State of Virginia*, "Query XII: Counties and Towns," 151–52, at 152; George Mason to John Fitzgerald, 28 November 1786, *Papers of George Mason*, 2: 858; Philip Morrison Rice, "Internal Improvements in Virginia," 15–16; James Madison to James Monroe, 13 May 1786, *Papers of James*

Madison, 9: 54–55; James Madison to Thomas Jefferson, 20 August 1784, *Papers of Thomas Jefferson*, 7: 401–8, at 403; "Bill Restricting Foreign Vessels to Certain Virginia Ports," 8 June 1784, *Papers of James Madison*, 8: 64–65.

81. *Hening's Statutes*, vol. 9, October 1776 Session, Chap. 5; *Ibid.*, vol. 9, May 1777 Session, Chap. 3; *Ibid.*, vol. 10, May 1780 Session, Chap. 14; *Ibid.*, vol. 10, October 1779 Session, Chap. 33; Richard Henry Lee to Patrick Henry, 13 May 1777, *Letters of Delegates to Congress*, 7: 75–76; Richard Henry Lee to——, 15 January 1778, *Letters of Richard Henry Lee*, 1: 378–80, at 379; John Marshall to James Monroe, 12 December 1783, *Papers of John Marshall*, 1: 109–11, at 110; John J. Reardon, *Edmund Randolph: A Biography*, 59; Thomas Jefferson to Edmund Randolph, 15 February 1783, *Papers of Thomas Jefferson*, 6: 246–49, at 247. The act excluding natives who had borne arms against Virginia is *Hening's Statutes*, vol. 12, October 1786 Session, Chap. 10.

82. Arthur Campbell to James Madison, 28 October 1785, *Papers of James Madison*, 8: 381–84, at 383; Richard Henry Lee to Patrick Henry, 14 February 1785, *Letters of Richard Henry Lee*, 2: 331–36, at 333; Richard Henry Lee to Thomas Jefferson, 22 May 1779, *Ibid.*, 2: 56–57, at 57.

83. Richard Henry Lee to Henry Laurens, *Ibid.*, 2: 61–64, at 62–63.

84. Thomas Jefferson to James Madison, 8 May 1784, *Papers of Thomas Jefferson*, 7: 231–34, at 232–33; James Madison's notes on Buffon, completed c. May 1786, *Papers of James Madison*, 9: 29–46; James Madison to James Monroe, 21 June 1786, *Ibid.*, 9: 82–83, at 82. For Enlightenment influence on the everyday, Edmund Randolph to Thomas Jefferson, 30 January 1784, *Papers of Thomas Jefferson*, 6: 513–15, at 513–14. The image of Jefferson as a man of the periphery insistent on moving to the center is borrowed from Peter S. Onuf. Jefferson as man of the Enlightenment is the subject of Douglas L. Wilson, "Jefferson and the Republic of Letters," *Jeffersonian Legacies* (Charlottesville: University Press of Virginia, 1993), 50–76.

85. Thomas Jefferson to James Madison, 20 September 1785, *Papers of Thomas Jefferson*, 8: 534–35; Thomas Jefferson to James Madison, 8 February 1786, *Ibid.*, 9: 267.

86. *Papers of George Mason*, 2: 703–11, at 703; Edmund Pendleton to William Woodford, 25 October 1787, *Pendleton Papers*, 1: 230–231; Thomas Jefferson to Alexander Donald, 7 February 1788, *Papers of Thomas Jefferson*, 12: 570–72, at 571; Jack P. Greene, "The Intellectual Reconstruction of Virginia in the Age of Jefferson," 230–32; "Plan Agreed by the Committee of Revisors at Fredericksburg," 13 January 1777, *Papers of Thomas Jefferson*, 2: 325–28, at 327; Edmund Pendleton to Thomas Jefferson, 10 August 1776, *Pendleton Papers*, 1: 197–99, at 197–98 (Senate exchange).

87. George Mason, "Remarks on the Proposed Bill for Regulating the Elections of the Members of the General Assembly," c. 1 June 1780, *Papers of George Mason*, 2: 629–31, at 630; George Rogers Clark to George Mason, 19 November 1779, *Ibid.*, 2: 555–88, at 555; George Mason to ?, 2 October 1778, *Ibid.*, 1: 433–37, at 437; John Page to Thomas Jefferson, 7 March 1788, *Papers of Thomas Jefferson*, 12: 650–54; *Papers of James Madison*, 1: 193; Richard Henry Lee to Patrick Henry, 14 February 1785, *Letters of Richard Henry Lee*, 2: 331–36, at 333; George Mason to George Mason, Jr., 3 June 1781, *Papers of George Mason*, 2: 692–94, at 694.

88. Thomas Jefferson, *Notes on the State of Virginia*, "Query VIII: Population," 122–28, at 124–25; *Hening's Statutes*, vol. 11, October 1783 Session, Chap. 16. K[evin] R. Constantine Gutzman, "Thomas Jefferson's Draft Declaration of Independence, Richard Bland, and the Revolutionary Legacy: Giving Credit Where Credit Is Due."

89. Thomas Edwin Buckley, "Church and State in Virginia, 1776–1787" (Ph.D. dissertation, University of California, Santa Barbara, 1974), 152.

90. Gary Rosen, *American Compact: James Madison and the Problem of Founding* (Lawrence: University Press of Kansas, 1999); Alexander Hamilton, James Madison, and John Jay, *The Federalist*, (Middletown, Conn.: Wesleyan University Press, 1961), Essay #10 (written by Madison), 56–65.

3

THE VIRGINIA RATIFICATION CONVENTION OF 1788

After a decade of reform, many Virginians remained essentially dissatisfied with their newly republican society. Their solution was to enter into a firmer union with the other twelve states. According to the constitution drafted at Philadelphia in the summer of 1787, this could be done by ratifying that constitution.

By the time it assembled in June 1788, Virginia's ratification convention knew that several states already had approved the proposed federal constitution. When Virginia's delegates finally voted on ratification, the nine states required to put the new constitution into effect already had ratified. For Virginians, many of whom had been instrumental in bringing the Federal Convention about and in guiding it to a successful conclusion, 1787–1788 might have been expected to be a time of rejoicing. Instead, the contest over ratification developed into a hard-fought contest for the future of Virginia and the legacy of the Revolution.

The debate in Richmond that summer ranged from the geostrategic to the antiquarian, from popular appeals to learned disquisitions. The "Anti-Federalists," self-styled Republicans, set the terms of debate with their repeated claims that ratifying the constitution was tantamount to abandoning the self-government for which Virginians had only recently sacrificed so much. Federalists, confronted with the prospect of defeat, responded by portraying ratification as an option with few, if any, drawbacks. Their case joined a grim notion of the union's likely life span to an insistent and repeated appeal to class prejudice, then added a characterization of the revolutionary decade as one of crisis in which the failure of the idea that common Americans were capable of governing themselves had brought republicanism itself into disrepute.

Virginians' arguments equated Virginia with America and Virginia's experience in the Revolution with the American experience. In the end, Virginia's leading men voted to ratify the proposed constitution, but only by a vote of eighty-nine to seventy-nine. Delegates were closely divided on ratification because it implicated their sense of their Old Dominion, and of the American

Revolution, significantly. Federalists made a strong case for ratification while dealing forthrightly with the constitution's weaknesses. Republicans, on the other hand, made a myriad of predictions about negative effects the proposed constitution would have—most of which subsequently came true.[1]

When it came to the place of their state in the North American world, Virginians displayed little false modesty. Many assumed their verdict on the proposed constitution would be decisive.[2] After all, as its political leaders understood things, Virginia was the most populous state, it was easily the largest (as it then included what are now the states of West Virginia and Kentucky), its staple crop was the basis of New England's most profitable enterprise, and its record in the Revolution outstripped all others. From Virginians' perspective, the future likely would be theirs.[3]

Opponents of the unamended constitution's ratification found a rhetorical advantage in stressing Virginia's preeminence, its necessity to the success of any American federation. This tactic became notorious in other states. The following account of a speech by former Continental Congress acting president and future United States senator William Grayson is taken from a letter sent by one prominent North Carolina Federalist to another:

> Col. Graysons Trope of Rhetoric was more to the feelings of Virginians. He harangued the People at the Court House having in his Hand a snuff Box hardly so broad as a Moidore. The Point of finger and Thumb are inserted with difficulty. Perhaps said he you may think it of Consequence that some other States have accepted of the new Constitution, what are they? when compared to Virginia they are no more than this snuff Box is to the Size of a Man.[4]

Patrick Henry reputedly had said that Virginia could insist that the constitution be amended before Virginia would adopt it; he reportedly held that Virginia could hold out in the face of ratification by the nine states required to put the new government into effect, even after ratification by all twelve of the other states.[5] There is no reason to believe the Federalist propaganda, which Henry and his fellows always heatedly denied (and which would have been inconsistent with the balance of Henry's career[6]), that he and they were of the opinion that Virginia could "do much better without the Union than with it."[7] Rather, they simply disbelieved in the likelihood of disunion, because the whole continent loved the union.[8] It does seem plausible, however, that Republicans in Southside counties took their leader's position to mean, as the president of Hampden-Sydney College told Madison "many" took it to mean, that Virginia would be happy with a sectional confederation or a complete constitutional break with the other American states.[9] After all, Henry argued in Richmond that the other states would continue to act as if united with Virginia even in the event that they, but not Virginia, ratified. If Virginia levied its men and paid its taxes, the union could not resist the allure of Virginian resources. Virginia, in that case, would receive the benefits of the new union without its risks.[10] From a very early stage of the debate, Henry's fellow Republicans echoed his assertion that Virginia should put off ratification until given amendments.[11]

The Federalists' opponents carried statements of this type right into the Convention. "[T]he example of Virginia," Henry insisted soon after the Convention opened, "is a powerful thing."[12] Virginia would never have to go it alone. If it held out, other states would follow, and the constitutional amendments on which Henry and his fellows insisted would be adopted. Governor Edmund Randolph stood up to answer, and Federalists believed that he had "very well exposed" the weak ground on which Henry stood.[13] If the idea that Virginia could dictate to the other states struck many Federalists as implausible,[14] or if they felt compelled by their rhetorical imperatives to dispute the point, their overall argument shows that they shared their opponents' appraisal of the centrality of Virginia.

Randolph's behavior offers conclusive proof. With George Washington acting the part of the "patriot king," Randolph had been chosen by his fellow Virginia delegates to the Philadelphia Convention to serve as their floor leader.[15] Therefore, he had presented the famous "Virginia Plan" to the other states' delegations, despite the fact that its rough draft was the handiwork of James Madison. Randolph had gone on in Philadelphia to be one of the most active participants in the debates. Still, in the end, strong qualms about the Convention's product (or a desire to gauge political currents in Virginia before committing himself) kept him from signing it.

While George Mason, the other Virginian nonsigner in Philadelphia, left that Convention with well-known objections to the proposed constitution, Randolph's felt need to oppose the fruit of his years of effort clearly bothered the governor.[16] He hoped to spur the states to amend, thereby both salvaging the Philadelphia convention's product and allaying his own fears.[17]

Randolph's conduct displeased his constituents, who canceled the welcoming committee they had planned to send out to receive him on his return to Virginia.[18] Following his reelection as governor in October 1787, Randolph published a pamphlet outlining his objections to the constitution. He stressed the necessity of a union of all thirteen states along with security for Virginians' rights and Virginia's interests,[19] but he remained troubled by the document.

When the Richmond Convention opened, then, most of the delegates assumed that Governor Randolph would join the Republicans.[20] To their surprise, Randolph came out for ratification of the unamended constitution in his first speech to the convention.[21] Randolph agreed with the delegates who doubted that the eight states that had ratified before the Virginians met could be persuaded to amend as a condition of Virginia's ratification.[22] This left a choice between union and disunion, so Randolph decided he must vote to ratify the unamended constitution despite his misgivings.[23] He judged it unlikely that states that already had ratified would concede the superior wisdom of Virginia's position.[24] The governor insisted throughout the debate that while amendments remained necessary, the union must be preserved,[25] and he assumed that the union would collapse without Virginia.[26] Thus, while accepting their argument that the union required Virginia, Randolph turned the Republicans' conclusion on its head.

If the union needed Virginia absolutely, where did Virginia stand in relation to the other states? The majority of delegates in the Richmond Convention, Federalists and Republicans, agreed about the legal relationship of Virginia to the other American states.

Randolph and Mason had pressed in the Philadelphia Convention's last days for the addition of a bill of rights to the draft constitution. During the months between the constitution's signing on 17 September 1787 and the Richmond Convention's opening on 2 June 1788, the omission of a bill of rights became one of the chief bones of contention in all of the states where any contest over ratification occurred.[27] As the convention in Richmond wore on, the constitution's critics insisted on this protection for Virginians' individual rights.[28]

Toward the end of the Richmond Convention, Federalists believed they had found a solution. Would the concerns of the Republicans be allayed, they asked, if the form of ratification included a statement that the rights of conscience and of the press had been reserved[29] and a general statement of Virginia's right to reclaim its control over such questions in case of federal overreaching were affixed?[30] After all, the Federalists explained, when two parties made a contract, any conditions in the ratification were understood to operate as amendments, and this reservation would do the same here.[31] In the event of the violation of any of the reserved rights, the Federalists said, Virginians would only need to point to the conditions on which they had ratified, and their claim to exemption from the disputed statute would be recognized. As Federalist George Nicholas of Albemarle, Madison's lieutenant, explained it:

> If thirteen individuals are about to make a contract, and one agrees to it, but at the same time declares that he understands its meaning, signification and intent to be, what the words of the contract plainly and obviously denote; that it is not to be construed so as to impose any supplementary condition upon him, and that he is to be exonerated from it, whensoever any such imposition shall be attempted—I ask whether in this case, these conditions on which he assented to it, would not be binding on the other twelve? In like manner these conditions will be binding on Congress. They can exercise no power that is not expressly granted them.[32]

As James Madison described it, "The plan meditated by the friends [of] the Constitution is to preface the ratification with some plain & general truths that can not affect the validity of the Act," along with proposed subsequent amendments.[33] According to Randolph's private reckoning at the time the Federalists won five delegates' votes by his gambit, which makes it the decisive factor in securing ratification in Virginia.[34] (Even Madison conceded this.) Yet, Madison wrote to a friend between Randolph's offer to incorporate conditions into Virginia's instrument of ratification and the vote on ratification that the conditions would have no effect.[35] Whatever the merits of Madison's judgement concerning the legal effect of the statements contained in Virginia's instrument of ratification, Madison's political judgement failed him here. The instrument of ratification would soon be elevated by Virginia's moderate Federalists and Republicans alike to the position of the Rosetta Stone of American constitutionalism, the first article of the Jeffersonian Republican faith.

Only one conclusion can be drawn from the conversation concerning Randolph's conditions and its effect in changing delegates' votes: A sizable majority of the delegates understood Virginia to be a legally distinct entity from the other American states, and the American Revolution to have established its self-government.[36] Indeed, Randolph put the matter explicitly, saying that the federal government could never cede any portion of a state to a foreign country, for that would mean "that the creature can destroy the creator, which is the most absurd and ridiculous of all doctrines."[37] Virginians understood themselves to be entering into a compact/contract with the other parties: the other states.[38] The states were primary, the federal relationship a convenience.

George Mason had argued in the Philadelphia Convention that the South, as a minority economic interest in the union, must insist on an equal say in legislation regarding commerce. To this end, he had worked for a provision that enactment of any legislation regulating commerce require a supermajority. Otherwise, he had said, the "producing" states' interests would be sacrificed to the "carrying" states'.[39] Virginians' imperative to prevent northern dictation of tariff rates proved one of the most contentious issues in the Richmond Convention. One ingenious Federalist dealt with it by asserting that Virginia had both more manpower and more naval stores than New England, so Virginia's naval potential would check New England's ability to extort high shipping rates.[40]

If the delegates in Richmond had their doubts about Virginia's capacity to protect its economic interests, there was room in 1788 for disquietude regarding Virginia's physical integrity, as well. Where the Old Dominion's final boundaries would lie remained essentially an open question.[41] In a long speech on the necessity of ongoing union for Virginia, Edmund Randolph speculated on the results if Virginia refused to ratify in the face of ratification by its neighbors. "Are you weak? Go to history, it will tell you, you will be insulted."[42]

Republicans held, on the other hand, that Virginia faced no immediate military danger.[43] Federalist insistence that Virginia and its sister states faced an emergency situation requiring emergency measures such as adoption of a drastically centralizing constitution struck them as absurd.[44] For Richard Henry Lee, head of Virginia's delegation to Congress, it seemed that the Revolution immediately past would be the Americans' only war for the foreseeable future, and he pressed this case almost from the moment the Philadelphia Convention adjourned.[45] The Philadelphia Convention sent the constitution to the Confederation Congress for referral to the states, and Lee appraised the situation there in a letter to George Mason:

> It was with us, as with you, this or nothing; & this urged with a most extreme intemperance—The greatness of the powers given & the multitude of Places to be created, produces a coalition of Monarchy men, Military Men, Aristocrats, and Drones whose noise, impudence & zeal exceeds all belief—Whilst the commercial plunder of the South stimulates the rapacious Trader. In this state of things, the Patriot voice is raised in vain for such changes and securities as Reason and Experience prove to be necessary against the encroachments of power upon the indispensable rights of human nature.

Virginia should forebear ratifying, he said, until the constitution had been amended to secure the great rights of the states and of the individual citizen; he lamented that self-government should be diluted in such a rush: "It is certainly the most rash and violent proceeding in the world to cram thus suddenly into Men a business of such infinite Moment to the happiness of Millions."[46] Lee thought that "a temporary insanity" lay behind public support for the constitution.[47]

Lee found the Federalist argument that the proposed constitution's shortcomings should be remedied *after* ratification especially galling. "[T]o say (as many do) that a bad government must be established for fear of anarchy," he told Randolph, "is really saying that we must kill ourselves for fear of dying." Forebodings of doom seemed to be "generated by design upon weakness." The government would be far easier to change before it went into operation than after.[48]

Some Federalists insisted on the Confederation Congress's "imbecility" as a matter of dogma.[49] For James Madison, the period of the 1780s marked the "crisis of republican government," a time when the inability or refusal of the extremely responsive governments devised in the first flush of independence to perform what he conceived to be their essential functions disgusted all the friends of liberty—and threatened to ruin self-government's good name.[50] What were the "critical" issues? Constitutional reformers, for whom one Virginia newspaper spoke in the Philadelphia Convention's wake, saw several:

> [T]he pressing requisitions of Congress were treated with haughty contempt; . . . the continental treasury was exhausted; . . . the national character was rapidly depreciating in the opinions of foreign nations; . . . our commerce was decaying, from the want of a sufficient power to protect it; . . . civil insurrections had disturbed the tranquility of some of the states; and . . . all were liable to be invaded.[51]

Francis Corbin, the Federalist delegate from Middlesex County, told his fellow delegates that if the mere fact that twelve states had sent delegations to the Philadelphia Convention did not prove the Articles of Confederation inadequate, the sorry economic condition of Virginia farmers and ports, the breakdown of Virginia's former West Indies trade, Great Britain's noncompliance with the Treaty of Paris, and the horrible state of the public credit should do the job.[52]

As Madison conceived of it (and other Federalists echoed Madison's description of the "crisis"[53]), several "vices," each a function of weakness at the center, afflicted the American political system.[54] States had often, in Madison's view, infringed on each other's rights, transgressed the boundary between their own and the Confederation's authority, and violated the United States' treaties with foreign nations and Indians. These infractions contained the seeds of disaster. Indian depredations in western Virginia and the continued British presence in forts they were supposed to relinquish under the Treaty of Paris led to resentment not of the state governments Madison held responsible, but of the United States for not forcibly evicting the British forces.[55] Great Britain obviously would never leave the Midwest until British creditors received justice in state courts, and it seemed unlikely that state legislators would ever undertake to adopt the measures Madison thought necessary.

Madison's experience in the Virginia General Assembly, where he served for three years in the 1780s, reinforced his desire to see the federal government strengthened. In an evaluation redolent with class prejudice, Madison judged that most of his fellow legislators lacked the education and experience necessary to their posts.[56] The perspective needed to legislate with proper attention to American affairs required continental experience the typical state legislator simply did not have, Madison believed.[57] He also judged state legislators harshly as a result of their tendency to follow Patrick Henry's lead in opposing the reforms of, among others, James Madison.[58] This group of complaints was to be remedied by the famous "extension of the sphere" spelled out in *The Federalist* # 10. By delegating responsibility for formulating policy in important areas to an elite group of men elected in far larger districts than those represented in state legislatures, Madison hoped both to elicit more conservative decisions from the political system and to retain a significant tincture of republicanism in a system he thought fast bound toward anarchy.

While the General Assembly's emergency actions of the war years may have followed in the tradition established by the old House of Burgesses in support of the Seven Years' War, which was to make frequent appeals to the English legal maxim *salus populi est suprema lex*,[59] Madison could not bear the various paper money, stay, and other populist measures that state governments continued to enact long after the war's end. By 1787, he thought the bad odor in which such statutes had put republicanism itself constituted a serious crisis. The General Assembly took action between the Philadelphia and Richmond conventions: spurred by George Mason and with the support of Patrick Henry, the House of

Delegates unanimously adopted a resolution against issuance of paper money.[60] However, one such measure did not strike Federalists as a trend. The federal constitution would take these questions forever out of the Henry supporters' hands by banning state laws impairing the obligation of contracts and reposing sole authority to coin money in the federal legislature.

Finally, Madison decried the "mutability" and "multiplicity" of state laws.[61] These, he wrote, were the fruit of a legislature consisting of men a cut below him in education and background, fellows who myopically represented only their small, local interests. Many other Federalists agreed. "A True Friend," writing in the *Virginia Independent Chronicle* of 14 November 1787, noted that credit was only available at high rates, and he blamed Virginia courts' and statutes' capriciousness. In the old days, the Crown's veto had protected the interests of English creditors, but now prodebtor laws and mutual recriminations stifled credit.[62] In Madison's view, only replacement of the run of state legislators with men who could "think continentally," who were not beholden to contracted, local interests (that is, who were financially independent), would remedy the problem.[63] Thus, while his "great desideratum in Government" was to prevent both minority rule and majority tyranny, his "auxiliary desideratum for the melioration of the Republican form" was to "extract from the mass of society the purest and noblest characters which it contains." Government must be taken out of the hands of the common men who took their cue from Patrick Henry and given over to "continental thinkers," to the best men, to men like James Madison—and soon.

Republicans, for their part, rejected the idea of a Critical Period threatening republicanism in Virginia. From Congress, Richard Henry Lee wrote that he would not be persuaded by references to a fictitious crisis. The United States had war debt, true, but Americans would not again encounter problems such as those that had led them to incur that debt anytime soon. They had only to live frugally and pay off their debt to enjoy a prosperous republican future. The future president James Monroe made a similar argument in the Richmond Convention, where he said that the need for an enhanced Confederation taxing power soon would decline precipitously and then would continue to decline.[64]

Still, Patrick Henry made the most powerful case against the Critical Period notion. He claimed that the Philadelphia Convention had transformed "a general peace, and an universal tranquility" into unease. In his estimation, Virginia's transition to republicanism was a great success. "I conceive the republic to be in extreme danger. . . . [W]hence has arisen this fearful jeopardy?" From the proposal to substitute the Philadelphia convention's proposal for Virginia's present happy constitution.[65] He conceded that there had been disorder elsewhere (as in Massachusetts), but then added that there had been no problems in Virginia. Why had Virginia's esteemed delegates to the Philadelphia Convention hazarded so much? Later in the convention, he noted that this initial request for proof that Virginia faced a domestic crisis had "received no answer."[66] "[T]hose dangers," he said, "cannot be demonstrated."[67]

At the first mention in the Richmond Convention of the notion that Virginia faced a crisis, Henry denied that he had ever heard of it before. That Virginia suffered from the absence of peace and commerce, from a decline of wealth and population, "These things, Sir, are new to me," he proclaimed.[68] So far as he had known, Virginia's history in the period since 1775 had been marked by an unparalleled absence of civil strife. Its laws were respected, its people were comfortable and happy, and all was well. Only this sudden agitation for a complete centralization of the government (as he consistently characterized it) had roused the people from their pastoral idyll. "The great question between us, is, does [a crisis] exist?" If not, the Convention would have no warrant to ratify, for the people wanted no change. There was, Henry insisted, no ground in their affections for a new government.[69]

William Grayson summed up his response to the Federalist blandishments by noting that the Confederation *was* defective, but that its defects were in the nature of confederacies, in which the general good characteristically yielded to the particular. Virginia's problems, which had been overstated, were not the Confederation's fault. "We have been told of phantoms and ideal dangers. . . . If the existence of those dangers cannot be proved—if there be no . . . rumours of wars, . . . there cannot be any reason for adopting measures which we apprehend to be ruinous and destructive." The Confederation had sent 1,500 men to help suppress Shays's Rebellion, the Dutch were "willing that we should owe them more," and, as his service in Congress had made clear to him, American trade flourished. If the Confederation had credit problems, Grayson concluded, they resulted from the failure to use sales of public lands in the Northwest Territory to pay America's debts. In short, he insisted, there was no crisis. Virginians did not need to settle for an extremely attenuated form of self-government.[70]

Grayson's forecast of the American future stood almost at the opposite pole from Madison's. While the Federalist generalissimo foresaw dissolution, moral and political, if things were left in their old traces, Grayson expected exactly the opposite. The apparent incapacity of the Confederation and the states ever to pay the debt they had incurred in winning their independence troubled Madison, but Grayson joined Richard Henry Lee in doubting that another such extraordinary expense would arise in the near future. He expected even the burden of that debt to decline. The United States should not pay off today a debt they could put off until tomorrow, because population growth would continue indefinitely, so the per capita debt burden would continue to decline. In time, it would be both prudent and easy to pay the cost of independence. America's short-term policy should be to pay only the interest. Grayson did not blame those who had not paid their requisitions overmuch: embargo and want had been the main causes of noncompliance. Issuance of paper money had flowed from the same source, and he would not apologize for that, either. Grayson did not expect Virginia to resort to those contingencies again, ratification or no ratification.[71]

Mason took Federalists to task for ignoring the incapacity of the states to bear the load of Congress's requisitions. He agreed that the Confederation had suffered from "inefficacy," as his participation in the constitutional reform movement showed, but Congress had made requisitions "impossible to be complied with." In fact, he computed, they had requisitioned more gold and silver than the total amount in the United States. Of course the states had not complied.[72]

Mason also drew the convention's attention to another matter: "This Government does not attend to our domestic safety. It authorises the importation of slaves for twenty odd years, and thus continues upon us that nefarious trade. Instead of securing and protecting us, the continuation of this detested trade, adds daily to our weakness." Rather than aiding the Virginian experiment in self-government by halting importation of slaves, in other words, the new constitution promised to undermine Virginians' safety by continuing the dastardly trade. Mason's complaints to the same effect in Philadelphia had been vociferous, and he had decried the arrangement between New England and the Deep South that had written it into the constitution. Rather than the result of Virginia's newfound surfeit of slaves, this complaint was consistent with Mason's position through a quarter-century-long career.[73] Not only did the new constitution promise to make slaves more numerous in Virginia, Mason noted, but it did nothing whatever about security for slave property Virginians already held. Nothing could keep the North and East "from meddling with our whole property of that kind." While the clause banning prohibition of slave importations prior to 1808 should not have been included in the constitution, to be deprived of slaves they already had "would bring ruin on a great many people"—thus, perhaps, spurring them to adopt measures of exactly the type Federalists decried.[74]

Edmund Pendleton's unanimous election as president of the Convention on its opening day highlighted the fact that in the Old Dominion's heavily stratified society, Virginia's few great families still played a predominant role in politics.[75] They articulated a certain pattern of political practices and expectations, and, as in the ancient Roman Republic, a politician who hoped to reach a given rung on the political ladder had a set of well-understood lower rungs to climb. Men knew their place, and they generally stayed in it. A Revolutionary anecdote involving Benjamin Harrison provides a good illustration of this tendency. As Harrison prepared to leave for Philadelphia in 1774 to attend the first Continental Congress, a delegation of his neighbors came to see him off. They told him that they had detected "a fixed intention to invade our rights and privileges." They lacked the information necessary to come to informed conclusions of their own, they said, "but since you assure us that it is so, we believe it. We are about to take a very dangerous step, but we have confidence in you and will do anything you think proper."[76]

As the Commonwealth's senior politician, Edmund Pendleton could reasonably expect to win the presidency of the Convention. The speeches he made on the occasion of his election and, at the convention's close, in answer to his fellow delegates' expression of thanks for a job well done constitute a veritable primer on old school expectations regarding political comportment. A long-running dispute in the Convention between Edmund Randolph and Patrick Henry provided a glimpse of the ways of Virginia-future.

As in the May Convention of 1776, Pendleton told his fellow delegates that he was unfit for the high honor they had voted to bestow upon him. Surely the crush of years, he said, had made it impossible for him to serve: his mental faculties, which he judged never to have been too great, had dimmed with the passage of decades, and he could not even stand (as the president customarily did). Yet, he would endeavor to preside.[77]

Pendleton admonished his fellow delegates to maintain the proper spirit. They must remember, he said, that they were all brothers, and they should work to see that their reason, not their passions, carried the day. In addition, they should remember that they had been delegated by a great people, the people of Virginia, to consider a very solemn question, and on their decision rested the hopes of their country (meaning Virginia).

At the end of the Convention, Pendleton told the delegates that election as president had capped his political career. He rejoiced to see that all his life's political labors had been appreciated by his countrymen, and he appreciated the Convention's indulgence.[78] Pendleton had always been an even-tempered, conservative figure.[79] He had been among the Virginian political leaders who had opposed firebrands such as Richard Henry Lee and Patrick Henry in their agitation for separation from the British Empire over a decade before.[80] The fealty to the House of Hanover and the easy acceptance of hierarchy that had long been strong elements of Virginians' mental makeup died hard in him. Also typically of Virginians of his time, Pendleton hesitated to change anything about his country's political structure.[81] His reputation for even-handedness and legal learning, coupled with his immense wealth, had earned him high judicial office. In the old fashion of Virginia politics, his fellow delegates *intended* his unanimous election to the presidency of the Convention as his crowning glory. He, in turn, implored them in his opening address to comply with the traditional code of conduct of Virginia politicians.[82]

Not only the men at the top of the pyramid recognized the continuing power of the old social structure. Rather, one of the most notable speeches of the Richmond Convention came from a relatively unknown delegate, Spotsylvania County's John Dawson.[83] After sitting mutely through several days' debates, he finally rose to say that he had held his tongue until then because of the rarefied company. It seemed inappropriate for so obscure a man to take the Convention's time, he continued, when his society's great men were holding forth so ably. He did not presume to be on the level, as a thinker, a speaker, or a statesman, of the many distinguished men who had already addressed the Convention. Still, the freeholders of his home district had deputized him to speak for them, and no one else could. On this pressing occasion, they simply must be heard.

Deferential attitudes such as these, the mirror image of Federalists' desire to cut commoners out of the political process, made their appearance regularly in the Convention, but new notions about the way Virginia's politics should be conducted also impinged upon that assemblage. In the weeks and months before and during the Richmond Convention, Federalists repeatedly complained to one another and in the press about their opponents' manipulation of what we would call "public opinion."[84] Mason, his partisan opponents said, had taken to frightening the "herd," presenting them with "unreasonable" objections to the constitution. Apparently, he would "stoop" to anything.[85] Men such as George Washington and James Madison had grown accustomed through Mason's long career to numbering him among the "old-fashioned" political leaders, those least interested in cultivating popularity. They found his new mode of behavior (the novelty of which they doubtless exaggerated) distasteful.[86] Federalist writers found William Grayson a particularly blustery public speaker, which earned him much obloquy.[87] (Hugh Blair Grigsby, the nineteenth-century historian of the Richmond Convention, said that contemporaries generally accounted Grayson the ablest debater in Virginia.[88]) The set of assumptions behind these complaints—including that Virginia's politics were, and should be, hierarchical; that those politics were, and should be, conducted among the leading men in the lower house of the legislature; that politicians were, and should be, dependent on length of tenure for advancement; and that politicians were, and should be, dependent on family networks for advancement—were precisely the Federalist, pre-Revolutionary notions that Pendleton captured in his opening and closing orations.

The one Republican whose political tactics came in for the most complaints and criticism, predictably, was Patrick Henry. He and Pendleton had bumped heads repeatedly in the twenty-three years since Henry introduced the epochal Stamp Act Resolves in 1765.[89] Henry's refusal to accept the assumptions of "the system," as for example in propounding his brash Resolves in his very first days in the Burgesses, grated on the "Gentlemen of Ability and Fortune."[90] His preeminence in Virginia politics in the 1780s and the uses to which he put it were the main factors underlying Madison's unhappiness with Virginia politics. Henry rejected the idea that the politics of the Old Dominion should continue to be run by the landed elite in the old way, and he refused to accept policies of continental "reformers" as proper for Virginia.[91] His Federalist opponents resolved that if the people would not vote to reject Henry's politics, Federalists would take the choice from them.[92]

Famously, Henry explained on the hustings that he had rejected an appointment to attend the Philadelphia Convention because he "smelt a rat."[93] Although Henry did not snipe at political opponents, we may reasonably guess that he considered the deceit displayed by Federalists in calling for the Philadelphia Convention "to amend the Articles of Confederation" when they intended to scrap them all along a violation of the republican ethos.[94] Indeed, it seems that Madison's decision to call for ratification by special conventions sprang in part from a felt need to circumvent the General Assembly, where Henry reigned supreme. Henry saw to the root of these tactics, but Federalists shut off debate on this question when Henry raised it in the Convention.[95]

Edmund Randolph urged Henry to sway the average Virginian to support the constitution. If only he would throw his weight into the Federalist scale, Virginians' hostility to Federalism virtually would cease. Another Federalist wrote that the constitution would have faced no notable popular opposition in Virginia if Lee, Randolph, Mason, and Henry had supported it.[96] Obviously, the Federalist view of the nature of Virginia's polity hearkened back to the prerevolutionary relationship between Benjamin Harrison and his neighbors. For them, the revolutionary establishment of self-government meant the assumption of full power within Virginia by the native elite; the average Virginian's proper role was to endorse what his betters did on his behalf.

Henry rejected this view. In his opinion, common Virginians elected and re-elected him to high office because he spoke as they would. If he were to endeavor to persuade them to come around to the Federalist view, he insisted, they would reject *him*.[97] He did not sit atop a social hierarchy, in his conception, but spoke as a revolutionary, a representative Virginian. The people at large, good republicans, opposed the constitution on the grounds Randolph had offered in his public explanation of his refusal to sign it on 17 September 1787. Henry himself, having learned from Randolph (as he told the Convention), opposed it, too.[98]

While Randolph encouraged the Republicans, and particularly Henry, to attempt to manipulate public opinion, most Federalists seem to have thought it entirely improper for the Republicans to persist in making their case outside the hall. They repeatedly besought them to eschew democratic politics, which they labeled "demagoguery."[99] Consistently with their hierarchical view of Virginia society, Federalists insisted that all the arguments on either side should be kept within the elite fraternity and clearly stated only in the Convention itself.[100]

Federalist insistence that the Commonwealth's political system remained, and should remain, essentially unaffected by the Revolution had a firm basis in reality. Federalist John Marshall, for example, told his correspondents that he had been elected a delegate from heavily Republican Henrico County despite his constituents' knowledge of his staunch support for ratification.[101] He was simply the best man in his county, and, as in the days of old, that had translated into election.[102] Yet, perhaps the most spectacular account we have of an effect of the old-fashioned relationship between electorate and delegate concerns the election in Tidewater York County.[103] On election day, the sheriff, the four candidates, and some of the voters arrived at the polling place. Virginians voted *viva voce*, so voters conversed with candidates.[104] An old gentleman appeared and began to speak with one of the candidates, noting that he had always supported him for office, yet could not do so now. He would happily let him exercise his judgment on his behalf once again, he said, but the candidate had made up his mind before the argument had begun. The voter thus favored George Wythe and John Blair, for they were uncommitted. The other Federalist candidate agreed, both of them announced that they hoped all would support Wythe and Blair, and the two non-candidates were elected unanimously. The voters trouped *en masse* to Wythe's house, where they informed him of his election.

Some Federalists found it necessary to make concessions to the republican spirit Henry espied in the citizenry, however. James Madison, for example, received word from his Piedmont home county, Orange, that he would lose the election if he did not appear at the polls in person.[105] He therefore hurried home from New York to do so. While his correspondence is full of complaints about the "low arts"[106] of Henry and the willingness of Mason to stoop to electioneering, Madison had to admit that "for the first time," he had had to "harangue" the electorate to secure his own election.[107] Self-government was downright degrading if it involved solicitation of common Virginians' approval, in the opinion of this leading Federalist. Under his proposed system, such behavior would be required of members of the elite far less often.[108]

The changing nature of Virginia politics, then, had varied effects. Some of the leading men, whose names were redolent of power and influence, could still be elected on the basis of their merit. Edmund Randolph was one of these people. Some, such as Henry, made no pretense of *hauteur*—but perhaps had mastered the opposite affectation. A third class, those who were eminent on their own but not of great families, had to stoop to practices they found distasteful—yet did so with protestations of political virginity. This group included James Madison. The delegates met in Richmond as a new political society was aborning.

The clash of perceptions that flowed from this change most famously manifested itself in a prolonged exchange between Randolph and Henry. Randolph let slip the word "herd" in relation to the run of Virginians. This usage had been a common one in pre-Revolutionary days, when it reflected elite Virginians' social pretensions and the social distance they had succeeded in creating between themselves and the lower echelons of society.[109] Randolph evidently thought nothing of the word, which encapsulated his acceptance of the old notion that the "best" men would accept the burdens of all public offices, high and low, and "that all good men should concern themselves with the welfare of their country."[110] This aristocratic ethic suffused Randolph's entire performance in Richmond, from his many protestations of disinterestedness and his sense of obligation through his continuing criticism of the constitution he had endorsed[111] to his resignation of the governorship in the gathering's wake. Still, he seems to have been quite annoyed when the word "herd" came back to haunt him.[112]

Henry made much of Randolph's use of "the h word." He called Randolph's the spirit of the new constitution. The aristocrats hoped to put the "herd" back in its place; they hoped to leave the people at large very little say in Virginia's affairs.[113] As Henry put it, the Federalists wanted the federal government to take responsibility from Virginia and its "180 Representatives, the choice of the people of Virginia" because "They [we]re a mobbish, suspected *herd*."[114] "To suppose that ten Gentlemen have more real substantial merit, than 170 is humiliating to the last degree. If, Sir, the diminution of numbers be an augmentation of merit, perfection must centre in one."[115] Mason, speaking on the same topic, made reference to "the spirit of aristocracy, which had lately been imported from England."[116] Perhaps he had read the letters of Publius.[117]

Virginians, in sum, disagreed on the questions what self-government had come to mean in Virginia and what it ought to mean. Patrick Henry believed that Virginia politics were broadly participatory, but his opponents told one another that Henry's political power rested on demagoguery.[118] This conception made Henry a corrupter, a man who seduced average people away from their proper deferential role and into opposition to the constitution[119] (as he had previously led them in secessionism and in opposition to the Statute for Religious Freedom and in opposition to revision of the constitution of 1776 and . . .). Recent scholarship has exposed a certain jealously in this appraisal of Henry.[120] Some Federalists also bore him a grudging respect. One Federalist observer of the Convention wrote home to tell his family that Randolph, Madison, Marshall, and other Federalists were acquitting themselves well, but that Henry's oratory struck more powerfully than he could have imagined; it had to be witnessed to be believed.[121] On the other hand, Randolph wrote in his history of Virginia that Henry's achievement had its root in his "discovery" of the fact that "a pronunciation which might disgust in a drawing room may yet find access to the hearts of a popular assembly."[122] His ascendancy in politics, in this view, had a coarsening—democratizing—effect. Henry would have agreed.

In the eyes of a man of Henry's convictions, the Federalists were scheming to undercut the Revolution itself. Federalism, in its attempt to wrest control of Virginia's politics from the General Assembly and give it to a Congress in which Virginians would have only ten representatives and two senators, and those almost exclusively of the "better sort," threatened to degrade the citizenry into a "herd" again. Better to suffer the threatened privations as free Virginians, in this view, than to live as fattened cattle of a far-off farmer. Better ordinary Virginians should rule at home than be ruled by aristocrats ensconced in the "ten miles square." Henry believed that Virginians ruled themselves well in June 1788. The Federalists held that the many had botched things almost irretrievably.

The argument about the kind of internal polity Virginia should have consisted of more than a simple disagreement over whether it remained essentially an ancien régime society or dispersed social and political influence more broadly. Leading Virginians also disagreed regarding the proper relationship between citizens and their state. George Mason had urged toward the end of the Philadelphia Convention that the assemblage take up the issue of a bill of rights.[123] Mason's Virginia Declaration of Rights included a few general statements, such as that all men enter into society free and equal, that we would associate with thinkers like John Locke. Its bulk, however, guaranteed Virginians "the rights of Englishmen."[124] To Republicans' dismay, the proposed constitution included no protection for several of the latter type of rights. Mason stressed this point, and Henry joined him.[125] Federalists responded that they had not explicitly guaranteed each of these things either because they were implicitly guaranteed or because it would have been impossible to do so.[126]

All this is well known. What are most interesting for our purposes, however, are the terms of the debate. One side repeatedly appealed to reason and representation; the other couched its argument in the language of fealty to inherited ways. An undercurrent of the main argument between Federalists and Republicans, the question who should rule in Virginia, ran through it all.[127] Henry stressed the idea that the cabal of aristocrats plotted to undermine Virginians' liberty, which he understood as British liberty. Repeatedly, Henry referred to the rights Virginians' ancestors had won through warfare and suffering, rights their sons would be ingrates to surrender so easily.[128] You have the rights you have inherited, and you will never lose them, he insisted—so long as you do not ratify this constitution unamended.

Federalists, eager to establish their republican bona fides, responded that the people would never allow their representatives to establish a system of tyranny over them.[129] (Federal) elections would form an adequate safeguard against the abuses Henry and the Republicans feared. While representation may have been an inadequate check upon usurping executives in England long ago, the principle of representation had been perfected here, and now it had only to be applied properly.[130] (This argument clashed with the private views of, for example, James Madison, for whom the ratification campaign formed the culmination of a long, desperate campaign to reduce the influence of "demagogues."[131])

Republicans rejected this argument. They did not want to hear about principles that had not been verified by history. Unlike the Federalists, Republicans bore an emotional as well as an intellectual attachment to inherited forms. Henry persistently referred to the English practice as Virginians' proper benchmark, holding that liberty had only arisen in England. England's constitution, he said, was easily the best in the world, and American practice should not deviate from the practice of many centuries in "the mother country" without good reason.[132]

For some Federalists, the Republicans' emotional tie to Britain, their inherited insistence on being more British than the British,[133] was matched by an insistence on an independent identity, on forming a society owing no more than necessary to British ways, on seeking a new dispensation—a *novus ordo seclo-*

rum.[134] If Henry thought of England as his mother country, some Federalists viewed it as their bête noire.[135] Henry Lee, for one, insisted that Virginia was not under the tutelage of England. Unlike some others he saw around him (one imagines him glaring at Henry), he had come under the fire of troops sent by the king Henry loved so well, and he did not admire their master. To his mind, Americans had learned a thing or two about government, and England might do well to copy them.[136]

The provisions in the proposed constitution relating to the militia also exercised the Republicans. Self-defense was the most basic attribute of self-government, yet it was endangered by this new constitution. If the federal government had authority to train the militia, might it not as easily neglect to train them, thereby leaving Virginia without a native force to defend it against federal tyranny?[137] What other reason could there be for giving the federal government this power than to strip the states of their capacity for self-defense? After all, an Imperial governor had once privately instructed Westminster that omission to provide for training their militia promised to bring the Americans to heel.[138] Virginia's militia made the Old Dominion a self-sufficient polity, in Republican eyes, and Republicans asked what good the constitution's reservation of the choice of militia officers to the states would do if "they were sworn to obey the superior power of Congress."[139] How would militia members react to being called into militia service, then sent many miles to put down a rebellion? In the end, no one would be willing to serve in the militia, and the whole institution would collapse—exactly, Republicans divined, as some of the Federalists intended.[140] Once again, Republicans found Federalists to be too quick to surrender state institutions, and they concluded that the Federalists wanted to substitute government by a national elite for local self-determination.

Federalists found these accusations very difficult to answer. While we see in these arguments the attitudes responsible for the American Revolution, Federalists must (like generations of historians) have judged them wild, unreasonable, even demagogic. Henry Lee responded by falsely accusing the militia of performing badly in the Battle of Guilford Courthouse, in which he and his regulars had played a prominent part.[141] He had seen militia in action, and they had not made a favorable impression.[142] The federal government must regulate militiamen's training. For the Federalists, pragmatism was the operative attitude, and, as Lee said, there was no reason not to think of America generally as their "country."[143] Republicans consistently meant Virginians when they spoke of "us" and Americans at large by "them."

Repeatedly, Federalists answered Republican complaints about the delegation of certain powers to the proposed federal government by reference to the representative nature of the new federal institutions. All the officers of that government, they noted, would be chosen either mediately or immediately by the people.[144] England, even Virginia, could not say as much. Federalists saw no threat to freedom of speech from the federal government, because Congress would represent the people. Federal control of the militia did not trouble the Federalists, because neither the president nor the Congress would dare to offend the people. The first Congress under the new constitution would have ten representatives and two senators from Virginia, which would make Virginia's the largest delegation from any state.[145] Republicans considered this only a shell of representation and warned that most of the decision making in federal councils would be done by "others."[146] While Federalists lamented that the Continental Congress was both in form and in function an assemblage of ambassadors, Republicans preferred a Congress of that type.

Repeatedly, Mason and Henry saw Congress as "them." "You," they would say, are to be a pitiful minority;[147] you will have no control over levels of taxation, war and peace, even abolition of slavery.[148] Under the cover of the necessary and proper clause, people from other states might exploit Virginia for their own purposes.[149] The representatives from the other states would have no "fellow feeling" for Virginians.[150] They would not experience Virginia's natural calamities, they would not share its inherited religion, they would not have known its burdens in the Revolution, different varieties of taxation would not affect them in the same way,[151] they would not have the same interest in preservation of chattel slavery,[152] and they simply would be unequipped—besides disinclined—to represent Virginia.

In order to serve its function, representation must be "ample," Mason lectured, as it was in the Virginia government. While ten representatives and two senators could not speak for every region of Virginia and every interest in Virginia society, the Republican position ran, the General Assembly of 180 included representatives of all Virginian interests. Each Virginian had an actual voice in his legislature, not a theoretical one. A geographic area must be assured of a say, not of mere nominal power.[153] The representatives must actually come from among the people, not from among their "betters." Additionally, in order to be truly representative, they must not be insulated from the misfortunes of the common man. For that reason, they should have far shorter terms than the two and six years of the proposed congressional terms. The Continental Congress, with its one-year terms and three-term limit, was far "superior" in this regard to the proposed Congress, and in Virginia's state government, officials all served short terms. Federalists, who believed that the attributes of Virginia's political system the Republicans approved had led to the "crisis of republican government," answered with references to the ultimate responsibility of federal officeholders and with assertions that the Congress need not reflect the fortunes of average citizens as closely as the General Assembly because it would not have cognizance over local questions.[154]

Republicans said that even if Virginia's representatives in the new federal Congress proved responsive, which seemed unlikely, Virginia would join a permanent minority. If Virginia was not ostracized itself, surely the South in general would be. The result for Virginia would be betrayal of the Revolution. If Virginia would submit to taxation by a less apt institution than its General Assembly, why had it fought the Revolution in the first place?[155]

Federalists claimed to owe their liberties to septennial elections (those to the House of Commons), so the biennial ones provided by the new constitution would be perfectly adequate.[156] As they were more numerous than congressmen would be, Federalists assured their opponents, state legislators must always have more weight with the people—and thus an effective check on Congress.[157] Federalists intended to make Virginia less like the state the Republicans were describing; they did not dispute the description. The disagreement between Federalists and Republicans on the issue of representation masked a debate over the question whether Virginia republicanism itself had succeeded.

From the Federalists' point of view, the events of the 1780s showed that the union would soon break down. If the Confederation collapsed, there would follow a long series of wars, regional confederacies would spring up, and Americans would have to arm themselves against one another forevermore. Fraternal feeling could not overcome geostrategic reality. In the Federalists' estimation, then, the American union was essentially a legal entity. This notion never persuaded Republicans, who responded with incredulity to Federalists' prognostications of wars with neighboring states.[158] Republicans viewed the American union not as a mere legal fiction, but as a hard fact. It was based on ties of consanguinity,[159] of experience, and of language. It had survived the travails of war, and it could survive the collapse of the Confederation. Asked how the Confederation could finance a war without radical constitutional changes, Henry referred to "the American spirit," a mystical bond of patriotism, in asserting that Americans did not need a war-like form of government to provide for their defense.[160]

Sentiment toward the union may appear to be irrelevant to Virginians' conception of Virginia, but it actually helps us to distinguish between two different approaches to the matter of identity. In respect to Virginia, as in respect to America, there were two markedly different ways to approach the issue. Some delegates, such as Patrick Henry, knew Virginia through an emotional identification. They had no doubt about Virginia's continued existence, for they felt (and I use that word advisedly) their own ties to it. They believed that their countrymen, including Federalists, shared their sentiments. For a second group of delegates, military experience shaped bonds of affection. These veterans told fellow delegates that their feelings of kinship extended to non-Virginians, by whose sides they had fought, as to Virginians.[161] Although Virginian identity purportedly was secondary to these men, they approached the question of their own identity, of their primary allegiance, in the same emotional, visceral way Henry did.

The other group clustered around James Madison. The delegate from Orange County, like his friend, fellow delegate, and spokesman, George Nicholas of Albemarle County, saw the "crisis of republican government" as an intellectual challenge. Nicholas and Madison may have felt most like Virginians, but their rhetoric might as easily have come from James Wilson of Pennsylvania, Oliver Ellsworth of Connecticut, or another non-Virginian. For this group, the Revolution had made a sort of republican experiment.[162] Perhaps historians have been mistaken, then, in their ascription of stronger patriotic feelings to the Federalists. Maybe Republicans were less prone to see danger to the union because they had a *stronger* attachment to it.[163]

George Mason asked all the delegates who had voted "nay" to assemble the evening after their defeat in the final vote for ratification. When they did so, they gave Patrick Henry an opportunity to demonstrate that, whatever ungracious opponents had speculated he might have in mind, he had spoken forthrightly throughout the ratification debate. Called to the chair, he told the assemblage that he would have no part of resistance. The Republicans must give the Federalists' handiwork a fair trial. He had fought a good fight, he said, but he had been defeated; Republican Virginians knew how to behave in the wake of a fair defeat.[164] Yet, Henry vowed that as leader of the General Assembly, he would keep a close eye on the new federal government.

NOTES

1. George Mason referred to "Federalists, as they improperly style themselves." Opponents of Federalism called themselves "Republicans," while Federalists called them "Antifederalists." George Mason to John Francis Mercer, 1 May 1788, *Documentary History*, 9: 779. For Federalists' Orwellian use of language, see Gordon S. Wood, *The Creation of the American Republic, 1776–1787* (1969; reprinted New York and London: W. W. Norton, 1972), 562–64.

2. So, evidently, did men in other states. See Cyrus Griffin to James Madison, 26 May 1788 (New York), *Documentary History*, 9: 877; George Washington to Thomas Johnson, 20 April 1788, *Ibid.*, 9: 743 (New Hampshire's postponement struck many as an act of deference); *Baltimore Maryland Gazette*, 3 June 1788, *Ibid.*, 10: 1784 ("North-Carolina will doubtless follow the example"); Hugh Williamson to James Iredell, 11 June 1788 ("N Carolina will follow Virginia in adopting or rejecting"); William R. Davie to James Iredell, 22 January 1788 ("The great deference this State [North Carolina] has been accustom'd to pay to the political opinions of the Old Dominion will have an ill effect"); George Washington to Tobias Lear, 29 June 1788 ("little or no question is made of North Carolina treading in the steps of Virginia"); Comte de Moustier to Comte de Montmorin, 25 June 1788, *Ibid.*, 10: 1,679 (the new government exists "in name," but it

cannot "in fact" absent Virginia); William Bingham to Tench Coxe, 12 June 1788, *Ibid.*, 10: 1,613 (Virginia's ratification essential to the constitution's success); "Extract of a letter from a gentleman in Virginia, to his friend in this town," *Massachusetts Gazette,* 10 June 1788 ("North-Carolina generally follows this state, and it is probable she will join us in the decision of this great . . . question"). But see Edward Carrington to Thomas Jefferson, 14 May 1788, *Ibid.,* 9: 795 (Virginia can only decide whether there will be "convulsion"); George Washington to Benjamin Lincoln, 2 May 1788, *Ibid.,* 9: 780 (Maryland's ratification will be decisive in Virginia).

3. For Virginia as America's *entrepôt,* see Thomas Jefferson, "Notes on the State of Virginia," *The Portable Thomas Jefferson,* ed. Merrill Peterson (New York: Penguin Books, 1975), 25–232.

4. Hugh Williamson to John Blount, 3 June 1788, *Documentary History,* 9: 608–9.

5. Edward Carrington to Henry Knox, 13 March 1788, *Ibid.,* 8: 492. Also see Speech of Patrick Henry, *Ibid.,* 8: 951.

6. Henry had long favored more power in the federal government. *Cf. Ibid.,* 8: 490–91, n. 10.

7. *Pennsylvania Gazette,* 18 June 1788, *Ibid.,* 10: 1650. Madison divided Richmond delegates into three classes: those who would ratify the constitution without amendments, those who would ratify it with amendments, and those who would reject it. This classification has often been taken, despite the protestations of those putatively in the third group, as an accurate description of the situation. Madison made the special meaning of the third classification clear in the same letter, though, where he described people who fell into it as those whose proposed amendments "strike at the essence of the System." In other words, people who wanted a less national government than he did— say, in that they favored incorporation of a supermajority requirement for tariff legislation—became "disunionist" (or "antifederal"); their preferred mode of proceeding, he said, would end in "several Confederacies." James Madison to Thomas Jefferson, 9 December 1787, *Ibid.,* 8: 226–27. Republican George Mason held that union was a good thing only "on terms of security." J. Thomas Wren, "The Ideology of Court and Country in the Virginia Ratifying Convention of 1788," *The Virginia Magazine of History and Biography* 93 (1985), 389–408, at 402.

8. Speech of Patrick Henry, 24 June 1788, *Documentary History,* 10: 1,480.

9. John Blair Smith to James Madison, 12 June 1788, *Ibid.,* 9: 608.

10. Speech of Patrick Henry, 5 June 1788, *Ibid.,* 9: 966–67.

11. Edward Carrington to Henry Knox, 10 February 1788, *Ibid.,* 9: 606 (Carrington said that Henry had persuaded the people in Manchester, Virginia, and that "his demagogues are loud in their clamours," even calling for Virginia to hold out alone until certain amendments were granted.)

12. John Kukla, "A Spectrum of Sentiments: Virginia's Federalists, Antifederalists, and 'Federalists Who Are For Amendments,' 1787–1788," *The Virginia Magazine of History and Biography* 96 (1988), 277–96, 296.

13. Bushrod Washington to George Washington, 7 June 1788, *Documentary History,* 10: 1,581.

14. Edward Carrington to James Madison, 10 February 1788, *Ibid.,* 8: 577–78.

15. Ralph Ketcham, *Presidents Above Party: The First American Presidency, 1789–1829* (Chapel Hill: University of North Carolina Press, 1984); Isaac Kramnick,

Bolingbroke and His Circle: The Politics of Nostalgia in the Age of Walpole (Cambridge, Mass.: Harvard University Press, 1968).

16. George Mason to Thomas Jefferson, 22 May 1788, *Documentary History*, 9: 882. For Madison on Mason's "humor," see James Madison to George Washington, 18 October 1788, *Ibid.*, 8: 76; Speech of Edmund Randolph, 15 September 1787, *Notes of Debates in the Federal Convention, reported by James Madison*, ed. Adrienne Koch (1966; reprinted New York: W. W. Norton, 1987), 650–51.

17. Edmund Randolph to James Madison, 30 September 1788, *Ibid.*, 8: 25. He first called for a second convention during the Philadelphia Convention. *Ibid.*, 8: 10, 8: 260.

18. *Carlisle Gazette*, 24 October 1787, *Ibid.*, 8: 19–20, n. 1. For Virginians' pride in him before learning of his refusal to sign, see *Virginia Independent Chronicle*, 26 September 1787, *Ibid.*, 8: 19.

19. *Documentary History*, 8: 260–74.

20. *Ibid.*, 8: 630, n. 4; "Extract of a Letter from a Gentleman in Fredericksburg, (Virginia) to His Friend in This Town, dated March 30, 1788," *Maryland Journal*, 11 April 1788, *Ibid.*, 9: 736; "Extract of a letter from a gentleman of character in the state of Virginia, to his friend in this city, dated 30th March 1788," *Philadelphia Independent Gazetteer*, 16 April 1788, *Ibid.*, 9: 739. His decision was made before the Richmond Convention. St. George Tucker to Frances Bland Tucker, 3 October 1787, *Ibid.*, 8: 35; Tobias Lear to John Langdon, 25 January 1788, *Ibid.*, 8: 321–22.

21. One unsurprised delegate was James Madison, who had waged a remorseless campaign to convince Randolph that Henry was aiming at disunion, that Mason was denigrating the characters of Federalists (even moderate ones), and that the union depended on immediate ratification. See James Madison to Edmund Randolph, 10 January 1788, *Ibid.*, 8: 288–91; James Madison to Edmund Randolph, 10 April 1788, *Ibid.*, 9: 731.

22. Speech of Edmund Randolph, 6 June 1788, *Ibid.*, 9: 971.

23. Speech of Edmund Randolph, 24 June 1788, *Ibid.*, 10: 1,482.

24. "C. D.," *Virginia Independent Chronicle, Ibid.*, 8: 259.

25. *Ibid.*, 9: 932–33. He was not alone in holding this view. Petersburg Town Meeting, 24 October 1787, *Petersburg Virginia Gazette*, 25 October 1787, *Ibid.*, 8: 97.

26. That the choice was ratification of a bad constitution or disunion was also the view of Virginia's Chief Justice Paul Carrington and of Federalist delegate George Nicholas. Edward Carrington to James Madison, 8 April 1788, *Ibid.*, 9: 706; George Nicholas to David Stuart, 9 April 1788, *Ibid.*, 9: 712.

27. Herbert J. Storing, *What the Anti-Federalists Were For*, 64–70; Robert A. Rutland, *The Ordeal of the Constitution: The Antifederalists and the Ratification Struggle of 1787–1788* (1966; reprinted Boston: Northeastern University Press, 1983); *The Constitution and the States: The Role of the Original Thirteen in the Framing and Adoption of the Federal Constitution*, ed. Patrick T. Conley and John P. Kaminski (Madison, Wisc.: Madison House, 1988); Jack N. Rakove, *Original Meanings: Politics and Ideas in the Making of the Constitution*, 288–338.

28. George Mason, for example, had said that the Philadelphia Convention should add one to the instrument it was drafting. Speech of George Mason, 12 September 1787, *Notes of Debates in the Federal Convention, reported by James Madison*, 630. He made omission of a bill of rights the first item in his "Objections to the Constitution of Government formed by the Convention," *Documentary History*, 8: 43. Also see Speech of Patrick Henry, 7 June 1788, *Ibid.*, 9: 1,046–47; Richard Henry Lee to Edmund Pendle-

ton, 26 May 1788, *Ibid.*, 9: 878–79; Speech of James Monroe, 10 June 1788, *Ibid.*, 9: 1,111–12; Speech of Patrick Henry, 12 June 1788, *Ibid.*, 10: 1,212–14; and Speech of William Grayson, 16 June 1788, *Ibid.*, 10: 1332; among others.

29. Report of the Committee appointed for the purpose of drawing up an instrument of ratification, 25 June 1788, *Ibid.*, 10: 1,537–38.

30. Speech of Edmund Randolph, 21 June 1788, *Ibid.*, 10: 1,455–56.

31. Speech of George Nicholas, 24 June 1788, *Ibid.*, 10: 1,506–7. Thus, Jack N. Rakove's repeated claims that Federalists secured an unconditional ratification are erroneous. Jack N. Rakove, *Original Meanings: Politics and Ideas in the Making of the Constitution.*

32. *Documentary History,* 10: 1,507.

33. James Madison to Alexander Hamilton, 22 June 1788, *Documentary History,* 10: 1,665. Madison wrote a similar letter to Rufus King on the same day. *Ibid.*, 10: 1,665, n. 1.

34. Samuel Smith to Tench Coxe, 22 June 1788, quoting Randolph as saying, "the scruples of some have been quieted by a peculiar form of Ratification which will be offer'd." *Ibid.*, 10: 1,666.

35. James Madison to Alexander Hamilton, 22 June 1788, *Ibid.*, 10: 1,665. Madison wrote to Rufus King to similar effect on the same day. *Ibid.*, 10: 1,665, n. 1.

36. Speech of Edmund Randolph, 13 June 1788, *Documentary History,* 10: 1,254; "Cato Uticensis," *Virginia Independent Chronicle,* 17 October 1787, *Ibid.*, 8: 71. For corroboration, consider the argument about the question whether the constitution would create a "consolidated" government. See, for example, Speech of Patrick Henry, 5 June 1788, *Ibid.*, 9: 959.

37. Speech of Edmund Randolph, 13 June 1788, *Ibid.*, 10: 1,254.

38. Speech of Patrick Henry, 24 June 1788, *Ibid.*, 10: 1477. James Madison famously said as much in *The Federalist* 39, where he called ratification a "federal" act. Alexander Hamilton, James Madison, and John Jay, *The Federalist,* 254. King George III recognized the individual states' independence and sovereignty in the Treaty of Paris. Treaty of Paris, Article I, *Colonies to Nation, 1763–1789,* 419.

39. For his continued assertions to this effect in the days leading up to the convention, see "George Mason's Objections to the Constitution of Government Formed by the Convention," *Ibid.*, 8: 45. Also see William Grayson to William Short, 10 November 1787, *Ibid.*, 8: 151.

40. "The State Soldier V," *Virginia Independent Chronicle,* 2 April 1788, *Ibid.*, 9: 651.

41. "A Native of Virginia: Observations on the Proposed Plan of Federal Government," 2 April 1788, *Documentary History,* 9: 693; Speech of Edmund Randolph, 6 June 1788, *Ibid.*, 9: 979.

42. Speech of Edmund Randolph, 10 June 1788, *Ibid.*, 9: 1,093–94.

43. Richard Henry Lee to Samuel Adams, 5 October 1787, *Ibid.*, 8: 38; Richard Henry Lee to George Washington, 11 October 1787, *Ibid.*, 8: 51; Richard Henry Lee to Edmund Randolph, 16 October 1787, *Ibid.*, 8: 61.

44. Speech of Patrick Henry, 24 June 1788, *Ibid.*, 10: 1,479.

45. He wrote that

> It is a mere begging the question to suppose, as some do, that only this Moment and this Measure will do—But why so, there being no war external or internal

to prevent *due* deliberation on this most momentous business—The public papers will inform you what violence has been practiced by the Agitators of this new System in Philadelphia to drive on its immediate adoption—As if the subject of Government were a business of passion, instead of cool, sober, and intense consideration.

Richard Henry Lee to Samuel Adams, 5 October 1787, *Ibid.*, 8: 38.

46. Richard Henry Lee to George Mason, 1 October 1787, *Ibid.*, 8: 28–30. Lee had earlier iterated his position that amendments could make the proposed constitution acceptable in Richard Henry Lee to Elbridge Gerry, 29 September 1787, *Ibid.*, 8: 25.

47. Richard Henry Lee to William Shippen, Jr., 2 October 1787, *Ibid.*, 8: 33.

48. Richard Henry Lee to Edmund Randolph, 16 October 1787, *Ibid.*, 8: 61; James Monroe echoed the point in "James Monroe's Observations on the Constitution," *Ibid.*, 9: 875; the "design upon weakness" quotation is from Richard Henry Lee to Samuel Adams, 28 April 1788, *Ibid.*, 9: 765.

49. For example, see the 20 October 1787 call of the Fredericksburg Town Meeting for that town's delegates to the General Assembly to support the call for a ratification convention. *Ibid.*, 8: 85–86; John Brown to James Breckenridge, 16 December 1787, *Ibid.*, 8: 243, n.3; From John Brown, 5 June 1788, *Ibid.*, 10: 1,579–80.

50. Madison's thinking in this regard is treated in Lance Banning, *The Sacred Fire of Liberty: James Madison & the Founding of the Federal Republic*, Part I, 13–107. One can see the effect of this period on Madison's political thought in, for example, *The Federalist* 10. Alexander Hamilton, James Madison, and John Jay, *The Federalist*, ed. Jacob E. Cooke (Middletown, Conn.: Wesleyan University Press, 1961), 56–65.

51. "Americanus I," *Virginia Independent Chronicle*, 5 December 1787, *Documentary History*, 8: 201, 204. Edmund Pendleton listed a similar set of concerns in his Richmond Convention speech of 5 June 1788, *Ibid.*, 9: 944. Also see Speech of Henry Lee, 5 June 1788, *Ibid.*, 9: 951.

52. Speech of Francis Corbin, 7 June 1788, *Ibid.*, 9: 1,008.

53. See Speech of Edmund Randolph, 6 June 1788, *Ibid.*, 9: 971–72. Compare Rev. James Madison to James Madison, 1 October 1787, *Ibid.*, 8: 31–32 to the latter's "Vices of the Political System of the United States," April 1787, *infra*.

54. "Vices of the Political System of the United States," April 1787, *The Papers of James Madison*, ed. William T. Hutchinson et al. (Chicago and Charlottesville: University of Chicago Press and University Press of Virginia, 1962–), 9: 348–57. The following discussion draws heavily on this document.

55. "A True Friend," *Virginia Independent Chronicle*, 14 November 1787, *Documentary History*, 8: 159–61.

56. Madison contrasted the expected "stability & repose" under the proposed system to the "injustice and follies" of the state legislatures and Confederation Congress. James Madison to Thomas Jefferson, 9 December 1787, *Ibid.*, 8: 227–28.

57. There is a good discussion of the two sides' views regarding representation in Jack N. Rakove, *Original Meanings: Politics and Ideas in the Making of the Constitution*, 203–43.

58. "Service in Congress or abroad constituted an honorable refuge for gentry leaders who found themselves thwarted at home by popular politics in general and by Patrick Henry in particular." Herbert Sloan and Peter Onuf, "Politics, Culture, and the

Revolution in Virginia," *The Virginia Magazine of History and Biography* 91 (1983), 281.

59. Jack P. Greene, "Society, Ideology, and Politics: An Analysis of the Political Culture of Mid-Eighteenth-Century Virginia," 293. The law Latin translates, "The welfare of the people is the supreme law."

60. Bushrod Washington to Robert Carter, 4 November 1787, *Documentary History*, 8: 144. *Ibid.*, 8: xxviii. In the Richmond Convention, Henry noted that, "We are at peace on this subject." Speech of Patrick Henry, 9 June 1788, *Ibid.*, 9: 1,055.

61. He often repeated the point, as in James Madison to Archibald Stuart, 14 December 1787, *Documentary History,* 8: 237; James Madison to George Washington, 14 December 1787, *Ibid.*, 8: 239. Thomas Jefferson called "the instability of our [Virginia's] laws . . . really an immense evil." Thomas Jefferson to James Madison, 20 December 1787, *Ibid.*, 8: 252.

62. "A True Friend," *Virginia Independent Chronicle*, 14 November 1787, *Ibid.*, 8: 159–62. On the paucity of available credit, also see Adam Stephen to Horatio Gates, 19 December 1787, *Ibid.*, 8: 244; "Extract of a letter from a gentleman at Williamsburgh," *Boston Independent Chronicle*, 6 January 1788. Apparently, the political appeal of debtors' cause was overwhelming. How else can one explain James Madison's statement that Republicans should vote to ratify because to "establish uniformity of justice" would benefit *debtors* by raising their property values? Speech of James Madison, 20 June 1788, *Ibid.*, 10: 1,419.

63. Again, this is the (only half-explicit) argument of Publius/Madison's *The Federalist* 10. Alexander Hamilton, James Madison, and John Jay, *The Federalist*, 56–65.

64. Speech of James Monroe, 10 June 1788, *Ibid.*, 9: 1,109.

65. Speech of Patrick Henry, 4 June 1788, *Ibid.*, 9: 929.

66. Speech of Patrick Henry, 5 June 1788, *Ibid.*, 9: 954.

67. Speech of Patrick Henry, 5 June 1788, *Ibid.*, 9: 955.

68. Speech of Patrick Henry, 7 June 1788, *Ibid.*, 9: 1,037–38.

69. Speech of Patrick Henry, 9 June 1788, *Ibid.*, 9: 1,050–51.

70. Speech of William Grayson, 11 June 1788, *Ibid.*, 9: 1,165–67. Henry also played upon the notion that the "crisis" was imaginary in his speech of 12 June 1788. *Ibid.*, 10: 1,209.

71. Speech of William Grayson, 12 June 1788, *Ibid.*, 10: 1,187–90.

72. Speech of George Mason, 4 June 1788, *Ibid.*, 9: 938.

73. For example, Mason had noted in 1765 that "the most flourishing Government that ever existed" (Rome's) owed its decay, "perhaps" its ruin, to "the Introduction of great Numbers of Slaves—an Evil very pathetically described by the Roman historians." Jack P. Greene, "Society, Ideology, and Politics: An Analysis of the Political Culture of Mid-Eighteenth-Century Virginia," 311.

74. Speech of George Mason, 11 June 1788, *Documentary History,* 9: 1161.

75. Jack P. Greene, "Society, Ideology, and Politics: An Analysis of the Political Culture of Mid-Eighteenth-Century Virginia"; Jack P. Greene, "The Hopefullest Plantation, 1584–1660," *Douglas Southall Freeman Historical Review* (Spring 1996), 3–36; Jack P. Greene, "Unjustly Neglected by Its Own Inhabitants, 1660–1720," *Ibid.*, 37–71; Jack P. Greene, "The Happy Retreat of True Britons, 1720–1775," *Ibid.*, 72–101. For the political system, see Charles S. Sydnor, *Gentlemen Freeholders*.

76. Jack P. Greene, "Society, Ideology, and Politics: An Analysis of the Political Culture of Mid-Eighteenth-Century Virginia," 279. Virginia's great men expected this

type of deference. "A Freeholder," *Virginia Independent Chronicle*, 9 April 1788, *Documentary History*, 9: 719; Jack P. Greene, "Society, Ideology, and Politics: An Analysis of the Political Culture of Mid-Eighteenth-Century Virginia," 264. They did not always receive it. "Senex," *Virginia Independent Chronicle*, 19 March 1788, *Documentary History*, 8: 505–7; "Cassius I: To Richard Henry Lee, Esquire," *Virginia Independent Chronicle*, 2 April 1788, *Ibid.*, 9: 642–47; "Cassius II: To Richard Henry Lee, Esq.," *Virginia Independent Chronicle*, 9 April 1788, *Ibid.*, 9: 713–18; "A Native of Virginia: Observations Upon the Proposed Plan of Federal Government," 2 April 1788, *Ibid.*, 9: 693; "The State Soldier III," *Virginia Independent Chronicle*, 12 March 1788, *Ibid.*, 8: 485–87.

77. Richard Brookhiser, *Founding Father: Rediscovering George Washington* (New York: Free Press, 1996), 24. Also see Douglas Southall Freeman, *Washington* (1968; abridgement New York: Macmillan, 1992), 220. Speech of Edmund Pendleton, 2 June 1788, *Documentary History*, 9: 910–11. For Pendleton's inability to stand, Hugh Blair Grigsby, *The History of the Virginia Federal Convention of 1788*, 1: 65, text and n. 76.

78. Elite men took their peers' omission to reward them with high office as a negative judgment on a whole career. Jack P. Greene, *Landon Carter: An Inquiry into the Personal Values and Social Imperatives of the Eighteenth-Century Virginia Gentry* (Charlottesville: University Press of Virginia, 1967).

79. David John Mays, *Edmund Pendleton, 1721–1803: A Biography*, (2 vols.; Cambridge, Mass.: Harvard University Press, 1952).

80. A parvenu himself, Pendleton had come to love the old ways. Henry Mayer, *A Son of Thunder: Patrick Henry and the American Republic*, 74–75 and *passim*; James Monroe to Thomas Jefferson, 12 July 1788, *Documentary History*, 10: 1,704.

81. Holly Brewer, "Entailing Aristocracy in Colonial Virginia: 'Ancient Feudal Restraints' and Revolutionary Reform," *The William and Mary Quarterly*, 3d series, vol. 54 (1997), 341.

82. Charles S. Sydnor, *Gentlemen Freeholders: Political Practices in Washington's Virginia*, *passim*.

83. The following is from Speech of John Dawson, 24 June 1788, *Documentary History*, 10: 1,488.

84. John Blair Smith wrote from his Southside county that "Before the Constitution appeared, the minds of the people here were artfully prejudiced against it so that all opposition at the election for delegates to consider it (against Mr. Henry) was in vain." John Blair Smith to James Madison, 12 June 1788, *Documentary History*, 9: 607.

85. James Duncanson to James Maury, 7, 13 June 1788, *Ibid.*, 10: 1,582–83 (speculating that Mason and Henry will incite mob violence).

86. These old-fashioned politicians, commonly called the "responsibles," included Mason, Richard Henry Lee, Landon Carter, and George Washington, among others. Jack P. Greene, "Society, Ideology, and Politics: An Analysis of the Political Culture of Mid-Eighteenth-Century Virginia," 298.

87. Cyrus Griffin to James Madison, 14 April 1788, *Documentary History*, 9: 737.

88. Hugh Blair Grigsby, *The History of the Virginia Federal Convention of 1788*, 1: 199.

89. Edmund S. Morgan and Helen M. Morgan, *The Stamp Act Crisis: Prologue to Revolution* (Chapel Hill: University of North Carolina Press, 1953).

90. Jack P. Greene, "Society, Ideology, and Politics: An Analysis of the Political Culture of Mid-Eighteenth-Century Virginia," 267.

91. For Henry's place in Virginia's transitional politics of the 1780s, see Rhys Isaac, *The Transformation of Virginia, 1740–1790* (New York: W. W. Norton, 1982), 266–69 and *passim.*

92. Edmund Randolph to James Madison, 29 February 1788, *Documentary History,* 8: 437.

93. Hugh Blair Grigsby, *The History of the Virginia Federal Convention of 1788,* 1: 32, n. 36.

94. Henry Mayer, *A Son of Thunder: Patrick Henry and the American Republic,* 377.

95. Speeches of Patrick Henry and Edmund Pendleton, 4 June 1788, *Documentary History,* 9: 917.

96. James Madison to Edmund Randolph, 10 January 1788, *Ibid.,* 8: 290.

97. Speech of Patrick Henry, 24 June 1788, *Ibid.,* 10: 1,477.

98. Speech of Patrick Henry, 20 June 1788, *Ibid.,* 10: 1,425. Ironically, one might interpret Henry's comments as suggesting that Randolph had manipulated public opinion in the way he wanted Henry to do, only in the opposite direction.

99. Speech of Henry Lee, 4 June 1788, *Ibid.,* 9: 917.

100. For the conception of representation implicit in Lee's proposal, see Jack N. Rakove, *Original Meanings: Politics and Ideas in the Making of the Constitution,* 203–43.

101. Albert Beveridge, *The Life of John Marshall,* 1: 365.

102. These old modes of behavior did not prevail everywhere, though. George Anderson to Richard Claugh Anderson, 30 April 1788, *Documentary History,* 9: 579.

103. "Littleton Waller Tazewell: Sketches of His Own Family, 1823," *Ibid.,* 9: 623–26. The following account is from this source.

104. See Charles S. Sydnor, *Gentlemen Freeholders: Political Practices in Washington's Virginia* for a wonderful description of the procedures and social ambiance of Virginia elections.

105. James Madison, Sr. to James Madison, 30 January 1788, *Documentary History,* 9: 599.

106. Speech of Henry Lee, 4 June 1788, *Ibid.,* 9: 922.

107. Richard R. Beeman, "The Democratic Faith of Patrick Henry," *The Virginia Magazine of History and Biography* 95 (1987), 301–16, at 312–13. For Madison's attitudes concerning popular government, see Jeffrey L. Pasley, "'A Journeyman, Either in Law or Politics': John Beckley and the Social Origins of Political Campaigning," *Journal of the Early Republic* 16 (1996), 531–69; James Madison to Thomas Jefferson, 9 December 1787, *Documentary History,* 8: 227; James Madison to Archibald Stuart, 14 December 1787, *Ibid.,* 8: 238.

108. James Madison, *The Federalist* #10, Alexander Hamilton, James Madison, and John Jay, *The Federalist,* 56–65.

109. Jack P. Greene, "Society, Ideology, and Politics: An Analysis of the Political Culture of Mid-Eighteenth-Century Virginia," 263.

110. *Documentary History,* 8: 274.

111. He criticized Article 3, for example, in Speech of Edmund Randolph, 21 June 1788, *Ibid.,* 10: 1,452–53.

112. Speech of Edmund Randolph, 7 June 1788, *Ibid.,* 9: 1,045.

113. Two days after the Convention opened, an editorialist said the same thing in "The Impartial Examiner III," *Virginia Independent Chronicle*, 4 June 1788, *Ibid.*, 10: 1,577.

114. Speech of Patrick Henry, 9 June 1788, *Ibid.*, 9: 1,055.

115. Speech of Patrick Henry, 9 June 1788, *Ibid.*, 9: 1,064.

116. Speech of George Mason, 19 June 1788, *Ibid.*, 10: 1,408–9.

117. The editors of *The Documentary History of the Ratification of the Constitution* suggest that Mason may have been referring to the constitutional theorizing of John Adams, which was avowedly Anglophilic, but it also seems possible that Mason was referring to James Madison's *The Federalist* 10 or Alexander Hamilton's famous speech at the Philadelphia Convention. *Ibid.*, 9: 1,173, n. 8; Speech of Alexander Hamilton, 18 June 1787, *Notes of Debates in the Federal Convention, reported by James Madison*, 129–39; Alexander Hamilton, James Madison, and John Jay, *The Federalist*, 56–65. An attack on Madison certainly would have made the most rhetorical sense.

118. Richard R. Beeman, "The Democratic Faith of Patrick Henry," 313; James Madison to Thomas Jefferson, 9 December 1787, *Documentary History*, 8: 227.

119. "The State Soldier II," *Virginia Independent Chronicle*, 6 February 1788, *Ibid.*, 8: 349.

120. Jay Fliegelman, *Declaring Independence: Jefferson, Natural Language, & the Culture of Performance* (Stanford, Calif.: Stanford University Press, 1993), 94–107.

121. James Breckenridge to John Breckenridge, 13 June 1788, *Documentary History*, 10: 1,621. Gouverneur Morris, in Richmond as a coordinator of the interstate Federalist effort, called Henry "perfectly Master of 'Action Utterance and the Power of Speech to stir Men's Blood.[']" Gouverneur Morris to Alexander Hamilton, 13 June 1788, *Ibid.*, 10: 1,622. Another Federalist said of Henry's famous "thunderstorm" speech in the Richmond Convention that Henry had been "rising on the wings of the tempest, to seize upon the artillery of Heaven, and direct its fiercest thunders against the heads of his adversaries." Excerpt from William Wirt, *Sketches of the Life and Character of Patrick Henry*, *Ibid.*, 10: 1,511. Thomas Jefferson, often a Henry foe, resented Henry's prodigious persuasive powers. Jay Fliegelman, *Declaring Independence: Jefferson, Natural Language, & the Culture of Performance*, 94–95.

122. *Ibid.*, 95.

123. Speech of George Mason, 12 September 1787, *Notes of Debates in the Federal Convention, reported by James Madison*, 630.

124. Its first sentence reads "That all men are by nature equally free and independent and have certain inherent rights, of which, when they enter into a state of society, they cannot, by any compact, deprive or divest their posterity[.]" Robert A. Rutland, *George Mason: Reluctant Statesman*, 54. Rutland's discussion of the Declaration's drafting perhaps overemphasizes the Lockean influence. *Ibid.*, 44–63. For a summary of "the rights of Englishmen," see Forrest McDonald, *Novus Ordo Seclorum: The Intellectual Origins of the Constitution* (Lawrence: University Press of Kansas, 1985), 9–55.

125. "The Constitution of the United States," Article 3, Section 2; Speech of Patrick Henry, 16 June 1788, *Documentary History*, 10: 1330; Speech of Patrick Henry, 20 June 1788, *Ibid.*, 10: 1,421; "The Constitution of the United States," Article 3, Section 2; Speech of Patrick Henry, 20 June 1788, *Documentary History*, 10: 1,420; For example, Speech of Patrick Henry, 20 June 1788, *Ibid.*, 10: 1,421.

126. Speech of Edmund Randolph, 21 June 1788, *Ibid.*, 10: 1,453; Speech of Edmund Pendleton, 20 June 1788, *Ibid.*, 10: 1425; "An Independent Freeholder," *Winches-*

ter *Virginia Gazette, Ibid.*, 8: 312–13; Speech of Edmund Pendleton, 20 June 1788, *Ibid.*, 10: 1,428–29.

127. For American views concerning the importance of the right to jury trial, both for the accused and for the community, see Jack N. Rakove, *Original Meanings: Politics and Ideas in the Making of the Constitution*, 288–338. For Virginians' later use of the jury system to hedge in the federal government, see Thornton Miller, *Judges and Juries versus the Law: Virginia's Provincial Legal Perspective, 1783–1828* (Charlottesville: University Press of Virginia, 1994).

128. Speech of Patrick Henry, 5 June 1788, *Documentary History*, 9: 959; Speech of Patrick Henry, 9 June 1788, *Ibid.*, 9: 1,067.

129. Speech of Edmund Pendleton, 19 June 1788, *Ibid.*, 10: 1,400–1,401; Speech of Edmund Pendleton, 20 June 1788, *Ibid.*, 10: 1,426–27. Henry Lee made a similar argument in connection to Congress's power to regulate the time and place of federal elections. Speech of Henry Lee, 4 June 1788, *Ibid.*, 10: 919–20.

130. Speech of Edmund Randolph, 10 June 1788, *Ibid.*, 10: 1,096.

131. See, for example, James Madison to Thomas Jefferson, 24 October 1787, *The Papers of James Madison*, 10: 211–12, wherein Madison lamented the Philadelphia Convention's rejection of his proposal to give Congress a veto over all state laws.

132. Henry used the phrase repeatedly, including in Speech of Patrick Henry, 5 June 1788, *Documentary History*, 9: 1,046; and Speech of Patrick Henry, 7 June 1788, *Ibid.*, 9: 1,044.

133. Jack P. Greene, "The Happy Retreat of True Britons, 1720–1775."

134. See the Great Seal of the United States (for example, on the reverse of the one dollar bill).

135. Speech of Henry Lee, 9 June 1788, *Documentary History*, 9: 1,075.

136. Speech of Henry Lee, 9 June 1788, *Ibid.*, 9: 1,073–74.

137. Speech of William Grayson, 16 June 1788, *Ibid.*, 10: 1,306.

138. Edmund S. Morgan and Helen M. Morgan, *The Stamp Act Crisis: Prologue to Revolution*.

139. Speech of Green Clay, 14 June 1788, *Documentary History*, 10: 1,294.

140. Speech of George Mason, 14 June 1788, *Ibid.*, 10: 1,269.

141. Speech of Henry Lee, 9 June 1788, *Ibid.*, 9: 1,073–74. For a more accurate appraisal of the militia's performance than that provided by Lee, see *Ibid.*, 9: 1,090.

142. By the war's end, recognition of the militia's inadequacy for the task of fighting unaided by the Continental Army was widespread. Charles Royster, *A Revolutionary People at War: The Continental Army and American Character, 1775–1783* (New York and London: W. W. Norton, 1979), 320–27.

143. Speech of Henry Lee, 9 June 1788, *Documentary History*, 9: 1,074.

144. Speech of Edmund Pendleton, 5 June 1788, *Ibid.*, 9: 947.

145. United States Constitution, Article 1, section 2.

146. For example, Speech of Patrick Henry, 14 June 1788, *Documentary History*, 10: 1,284.

147. "Cato Uticensis," *Virginia Independent Chronicle*, 17 October 1787, *Ibid.*, 8: 73.

148. Speech of George Mason, 11 June 1788, *Ibid.*, 9: 1,161.

149. "Cato Uticensis," *Virginia Independent Chronicle*, 17 October 1787, *Ibid.*, 8: 75. The trepidation underlying this assessment had much in common with the paranoiac patriot fears of the 1770s.

150. Speech of George Mason, 11 June 1788, *Ibid.*, 9: 1,156.

151. Speech of William Grayson, 12 June 1788, *Ibid.*, 9: 1,185–86; Speech of George Mason, 4 June 1788, *Ibid.*, 9: 937.

152. Speech of Patrick Henry, 24 June 1788, *Ibid.*, 10: 1,476–77.

153. Republicans' argument here foreshadowed John C. Calhoun's theory of the "concurrent majority."

154. Speech of George Nicholas, 4 June 1788, *Ibid.*, 9: 923.

155. "Cato Uticensis," *Virginia Independent Chronicle*, 17 October 1787, *Documentary History*, 8: 73.

156. Speech of Henry Lee, 4 June 1788, *Ibid.*, 9: 923–24.

157. Speech of Henry Lee, 4 June 1788, *Ibid.*, 9: 927.

158. Speech of Patrick Henry, 24 June 1788, *Ibid.*, 10: 1,480.

159. Speech of Edmund Randolph, 13 June 1788, *Ibid.*, 10: 1,254.

160. Speech of Patrick Henry, 5 June 1788, *Ibid.*, 9: 955. His appraisal of Americans' wartime character apparently made Henry an exception. Charles Royster, *A Revolutionary People at War: The Continental Army and American Character, 1775–1783*.

161. Speech of Henry Lee, 9 June 1788, *Documentary History*, 9: 1,074. Also see Charles Royster, *A Revolutionary People at War: The Continental Army and American Character, 1775–1783*.

162. Speech of James Madison, 24 June 1788, *Documentary History*, 10: 1,499.

163. This may also help to explain the puzzle of Henry's conversion to Federalism in the 1790s, when the Republicans forthrightly threatened to break up the union.

164. *Ibid.*, 10: 1,560–62.

4

DEFENDING VIRGINIA'S REVOLUTION AGAINST THE FEDERALISTS

After a decade of political defeats, the Virginia Republicans found themselves faced in 1798 with the gravest scenario their ideology contemplated: the federal government, no longer headed by a Virginian Cincinnatus who had proven himself willing to relinquish power, stood on a war footing. Despite what Republicans understood as the nation's moral obligation and republican self-interest, the Federalists finally had taken sides in the European wars in opposition to republican France. This decision had led them also to expand the American army and augment the American navy. In addition, as Republican thought predicted, Federalists had taken drastic measures aimed at tamping down domestic dissent.

With the Alien and Sedition Acts, it seemed, the Federalist majority in Congress might guarantee itself a permanent domination—and thus permanently deprive predominantly Republican Virginia of any substantial say in the government. The Revolution, so far as leading Virginians were concerned, might be undone. The Federalists' Sedition Act prohibited all criticism of the Legislative branch and the Executive branches of the federal government (with the careful exception of negative views of Vice President Thomas Jefferson), while the Alien Friends Act subjected friendly foreigners to the president's arbitrary control. President John Adams, Jefferson's onetime revolutionary colleague, seemed a happy convert to the cause of "monarchism." Jefferson, recognized leader of the Republican opposition, decided to forego candid expression of his sentiments even in letters to bosom friends lest the Federalist postmasters, whom he suspected of rifling through his mail, expose him to prosecution.

At the end of its collective rope, the Republican high command lit upon a strategy: it would have the Virginia General Assembly and the legislature of a sympathetic state (Jefferson thought it should be North Carolina's, but the Nicholas family's influence in Kentucky meant that Kentucky's served the purpose in the end) adopt a statement of Republican constitutional principles. Americans at large would thus be offered an alternative political standard to which they could repair, and the Federalist government would receive a tacit dare to initiate sedition prosecutions against an unsympathetic state legislature.[1]

The Virginia and Kentucky Resolutions of 1798 should not be understood as the invention of distraught minds faced with extraordinary circumstances. Although the situation faced by the Virginia Republican high command at the end of the 1790s was urgent, the twin enunciations of the Republican constitutional position adopted by the Virginia and Kentucky legislatures corresponded closely to the explication of the federal Constitution offered by Virginia Federalists in the Richmond Ratification Convention of 1788. By the time matters came to a head in 1798, Virginians had insisted on holding the Federalists to their vows of 1788 for a full decade. The Revolutionary legacy depended on the federal arrangement ratified in 1788, not on the more centralized, militaristic one the Federalists in charge of the federal government touted in 1798.

From almost the minute they were promulgated, the Virginia and Kentucky Resolutions of 1798 came to be seen as the touchstone of Virginia's constitutionalism. When the identities of their main authors, James Madison and Thomas Jefferson, became known more than a decade after the fact, the resolutions took on additional luster, and particularists of north and south appealed to them up to 1861 and beyond. They were especially influential in Virginia, where they formed the bedrock of legal instruction both at the University of Virginia and at the College of William and Mary down through the Civil War (and well after).[2]

The standard accounts of the events of 1798 have Jefferson and Madison teaming to concoct a constitutional doctrine that might be useful in defense of civil liberties. According to these accounts, the two eminent Virginians directed their salvo against a seemingly endless string of Federalist victories in federal politics, what Jefferson called the "reign of witches," which finally drove many Republicans to desperation.[3]

Viewed solely from the perspective of Virginia, however, that standard account is simply mistaken. The decision to fall back on the state legislatures as on the last ditch, as Jefferson put it, may have been desperate from the point of view of national-minded Virginians like Jefferson, but all the elements of "the Virginia doctrine" of 1798 had been present in the Virginia political tradition for decades. For one leading Virginia Republican, sometime United States Senator John Taylor of Caroline, the convergence of his long-trumpeted views and those of his fellows in Virginia's Republican leadership marked the opportunity of a lifetime.[4] Taylor's views were not his alone. A growing number of Virginians agreed with him as the 1790s progressed, and he and Jefferson differed mainly in the timing of their respective conclusions that Virginia must respond to the reign of the Federalists with a reiteration of ultimate principles. Evidence of Jefferson's having long held views similar to those he had Kentucky adopt in 1798 can be found in his earliest political writings. Those writings in turn drew, as discussed in chapter one, upon a Virginia tradition first adumbrated by Richard Bland in the early days of the Imperial Crisis.

Among the views of other Virginians, those of Edmund Randolph concerning the relationship among the American republics would have momentous import in 1788.[5] As the leading Federalist speaker in the Richmond Ratification Convention,[6] Randolph engaged in a famous rhetorical duel with the continent's preeminent orator, Patrick Henry, the leader of the Anti-Federalist, or self-styled Republican, side. At the convention's close, Randolph, one of five members of the committee appointed to draft an instrument of ratification, found occasion to explain what that instrument meant.[7] Following one of Henry's many lengthy speeches warning that unspecified new federal powers would be inferred from the "necessary and proper" and "general welfare" clauses, Randolph denied that any such inference was justifiable. Pointing to the instrument of ratification, he said, "All rights are therein declared to be completely vested in the people, unless *expressly* given away. Can there be a more pointed or positive reservation?" Randolph's explanation reduced the significance of the proposed constitution from that of a national charter, in the conception and hopes of the most nationalist Federalists, to that of the latest in a long line of compacts between Virginia and what Virginians understood to be "federal" authority stretching back to the early seventeenth century. In fact, Randolph's use of the word "expressly" echoed Article II of the Articles of Confederation, the first American federal constitution, which famously limited the powers of the first federal government to those "expressly delegated" to it.[8]

Later that same day, George Nicholas, another member of the five-man committee that drafted the ratification instrument, assured the convention that the Constitution would be a contract and that Virginia was to be one of thirteen parties to it. Nicholas's explanation carried special weight because he was understood generally to speak for James Madison,[9] who was widely seen as the leading Federalist intellect in the convention. Nicholas's elaboration was totally unexceptionable as a matter of contract law. The ratification instrument, he said, would be binding in using the language to which Randolph had referred.

> For says he, these expressions will become a part of the contract. The Constitution cannot be binding on Virginia, but with these conditions. If thirteen individuals are about to make a contract, and one agrees to it, but at the same time declares that he understands its meaning, signification and intent, to be, what the words of the contract plainly and obviously denote; that it is not to be construed so as to impose any supplementary condition upon him, and that he is to be exonerated from it, whensoever any such imposition shall be attempted—I ask whether in this case, these conditions on which he assented to it, would not be binding on the other twelve? In like manner these conditions will be binding on Congress. They can exercise no power that is not *expressly* granted them.

In other words, despite ratifying the new constitution, leading Federalists said, Virginia was to retain the self-government for which it had contended in the Revolution. Ultimately, the federal government would exist only at the sufferance of Virginia. Thus reassured by two of the five men in a position to know that the Republicans' warnings were misplaced, and having obtained the further promise that radical amendments would be sought immediately, the Richmond Convention ratified the Constitution by a vote of eighty-nine to seventy-nine (or 52 percent to 48 percent).[10]

James Madison, a third of the five members of the committee to draft the instrument of ratification, also wrote much of *The Federalist*, including essay # 39. There, he observed that, "Each State in ratifying the Constitution, is considered as a sovereign body independent of all others, and only to be bound by its own voluntary act." While it seems that very few of the members of the Virginia ratifying convention of 1788 had read any of *The Federalist* by the time they voted on ratification, many at the top of the Virginia political pyramid certainly had read it by December 1798, when the Virginia Resolutions were adopted. To them, Madison's explanation was a truism.[11]

Virginia was at odds with the federal government virtually from the latter's inception. Republicans and reluctant Federalists detected "consolidation" from the start, and they viewed it as the chief prospect threatening the dissolution of the American union. Federalists in control of the federal government seemed determined to grasp at powers the Federalist leaders in Richmond in the summer of 1788 had insisted would be beyond Congress's reach. As early as 1789, Richard Henry Lee counseled "the friends of liberty to guard with perfect vigilance every right that belongs to the states, and to protest against every invasion of them." Leading Virginia Federalists of the 1787–1788 ratification struggle soon ruefully conceded the accuracy of Patrick Henry's gloomy prognostications by calling the Republican chieftain a "prophet," and almost none approved of Alexander Hamilton's program of social and financial consolidation. In 1790, Delegate Henry persuaded the General Assembly to apply its colonial method of remonstrance in a dispute with the general government by adopting a statement of Virginia's constitutional position. Henry's resolution, which he introduced in the House of Delegates on 3 November 1790, called Secretary Hamilton's act for federal assumption of all state debts "repugnant to the Constitution, as it goes to the exercise of power not *expressly* granted to the General Government." It passed the House that day, the Senate six weeks later. So far as Virginians were concerned, the Revolution had settled the extent of the General Assembly's rightful authority, and the Federalists' 1788 assurances formed the basis of construction of the federal Constitution.[12]

Seventeen days after Henry introduced his resolution, which he must have taken satisfaction in crafting to echo the language of Federalist spokesmen Edmund Randolph and George Nicholas's assurances in the Richmond Ratification Convention, a General Assembly committee reported an address on Washington Administration policy. That address lamented the Hamiltonian system's resemblance to the English fiscal system, which it blamed for corrupting both houses of the British Parliament, as well as the British courts, and thereby threatening liberty. Hamilton's policy, it claimed, threatened subordination of agriculture to other economic interests and "a change in the present form of the federal government." The states, it insisted in language echoing Randolph's and Nicholas's assurances in the Richmond Convention, were "contracting parties," their rights "sacred." Finally, it insisted that Virginia had ratified the Constitution of 1788 only on the understanding "that every power not granted was retained" by the states, and the power to service the states' debts certainly had not been granted. Nicholas and Randolph's explanation of the Constitution, and thus of the significance of Virginia's ratification, had come to be seen as completely authoritative by the overwhelming majority of Virginia's political leadership. As in the Imperial Crisis and the Confederation period, Virginians conceived of their interstate union as precisely a *federal* union, a union among parties that were somehow on an equal footing (as Nicholas had put it, thirteen contracting parties). Virginia, not America, remained the primary political unit, the United States Government a convenience. Virginian identity still trumped American identity. Home rule was the primary principle of Virginia politics.[13]

According to Edmund Randolph, then a member of George Washington's cabinet, a trip through Virginia in 1793 showed that planters at large had come under the influence of the brilliant Virginian pamphleteer John Taylor of Caroline. An Anti-Federalist in 1787–1788, Taylor was committed by his reading of history to a posture of hyper-vigilance in the new government's first years. If the fledgling government were allowed to lay down precedents antithetical to the contractual reading of the Constitution that Federalists had promised at Richmond, Taylor held, greater arrogations of the states' power would follow inevitably. If a new government be allowed to stray uninterruptedly, he wrote, "it will soon become too strong for correction, and instead of being a blessing, it will turn out a curse to its parents." "By sparing the rod, we may spoil the child." Taylor was therefore predisposed to make the 1790s, the new government's first, a contentious decade. Alexander Hamilton's love of Robert Walpole, the master of Parliamentary "corruption" through ingenious financial management, meant the localist Taylor had good reason for apprehension concerning the trajectory of federal policy.[14]

John Taylor's surviving private correspondence of the 1790s is filled with calls for his associates Thomas Jefferson, James Monroe, and James Madison to stir Virginia's state government into opposition via confrontation. His pamphlets of the 1790s were masterpieces of sometimes inspired, sometimes befuddled opposition to Federalism. In them, he argued that federal officeholders were using their control of the government to milk other Americans of money. In the end, he insisted again and again, they would convert the offices they held—those of senators and president—into lifetime fiefs in the former case, a hereditary one in the latter. (He claimed to have the testimony of then–Vice President John Adams as evidence of the Federalists' desire for a presidency for life.)[15]

Perhaps the most significant of Taylor's pamphlets was the one that he wrote in response to the institution of a federal carriage tax. Such a tax might seem to be a mere excise, one the owners of carriages (presumably, the wealthy) could pay without undue hardship. Yet, the carriage tax was highly sectional in its incidence. As Taylor noted, only two carriages were subject to the tax in the entire state of Connecticut, while carriage owners were concentrated in the South. He concluded by averring that "States which impose unequal taxes are masters; those which pay them, slaves." Thus, implicitly, Taylor was saying that the carriage tax reduced Virginians to the status of slaves by depriving them of control over their own property—that is, of self-government. Adoption of a policy of enslavement, he added, "dissolve[s]" the union. If the federal government could tax carriages, what other excise with a sectional bearing might it impose next? There was another type of property that was found almost exclusively in the South, he noted—and no one required clarification.[16]

Taylor's reference to unequal treatment of states (with its echo of Virginia's complaints during the Imperial Crisis) was not accidental, for he believed states to be the sole constituent element of the federal union: "The confederation is not a compact of individuals, it is a compact of states." From that predicate, Taylor logically derived Henry's and the General Assembly's 1790 postulate that it was the duty of the state legislatures to remain vigilant against overweening exercise of authority by the federal government. When the states detected federal overreaching, they should note it and oppose it. Americans must obey state and federal majorities "whilst legislating within the pale of the Constitution." If the federal government should violate that limitation, it would have "no controul over" the states, which would have the option of ignoring it.[17]

Taylor realized that this doctrine would be strange to some, but he reasoned that things must be as he described them. If only "those designed to be restrained" (for example, federal judges) could enforce the federal Constitution, "America possesses only the effigy of a Constitution." Constitutions would be violated, and someone must enforce them. It could not be up to the federal government to enforce the Constitution against itself in the last resort. In the American federal system, that must be up to the state legislators, the most representative officials of the constituent parties to the federal compact.[18]

In his earlier pamphlet, *An Enquiry into the Principles and Tendency of Certain Public Measures*, written in 1793, Taylor claimed that Article V of the federal Constitution recognized the state legislatures' status as "state conventions," for in it they were there granted a share of the amendment power. Since they were the ultimate representatives of the sovereign peoples of the individual states, it could not possibly be unconstitutional for them to protest, "to make known the public will." This they should do by expositing "explanations of the constitution, according with its spirit—its construction when adopted—its unstrained construction now—and with republican principles." Taylor's reasoning again led him to the hermeneutical method outlined by Randolph and Nicholas in Richmond in 1788.[19]

As far as Taylor was concerned, the problem Republicans faced in the 1790s lay not with Federalists themselves, but in the federal system. This was the great point of disagreement between him and the three eventual members of the Virginia Dynasty. Jefferson, on reading Taylor's apocalyptic letter to a third Virginian, wrote to Taylor to insist that the taxes to pay for the Federalists' new military establishment would cure the American people of their temporary infection with "the X.Y.Z. delusion." The Federalist reign, the vice president hoped, was ephemeral, and thus the tendency of the federal government to overstep its constitutional bounds would have a natural end.[20]

To Taylor's suggestion that Virginia and North Carolina should contemplate a separate existence, Jefferson responded that since human nature insured there must be parties in any free government, Virginia and North Carolina would soon be fighting each other if they formed a separate union, and even Virginia would be rent by division if it were independent alone. Jefferson preferred to retain the tie to New England, thus reserving Virginians' ire for the Yankees. Taylor's answer to Jefferson was to ask how, exactly, the predominance of a self-serving party such as the Federalist was unnatural if party division was natural. As he understood matters, what was needed was not simply a change of men, for a southern aristocracy oppressing the North would be equally as regrettable as a northern one oppressing the South. If a change of men brought amelioration of the problem, "It would be only like the lucid intervals of a madman." Taylor wanted a change of systems.[21]

The flaw in the federal system flowed, Taylor held, from the Hamiltonian fiscal structure. The Bank of the United States and the federal assumption of state debts had generated a large pool of money controlled by only a few, and those few dominated the federal government via corruption. Political power had been "transferred from the nation to a paper fabrick," yielding "a government of paper." Taylor's solution was the adoption of an amendment to the federal Constitution banning holders of federal debt and of bank stock from positions in Congress, along with another reducing senators' and presidents' terms in office to three years.[22]

John Taylor's vision of the proper form of government was the opposite of James Madison's. For Taylor, the most perfect embodiment of the people was the state legislature—and that was a good thing. Taylor believed that unlike the Congress, the Virginia General Assembly was in effect an annual convention of the people, its members chosen from small districts to short terms, thus sharing in their constituents' travails. Constitutional issues were properly decided by the state legislatures, Taylor told Jefferson in the wake of the Virginia Resolutions' adoption, and could be appealed from them to state conventions, as the Romans of the Roman Republic had in extreme circumstances appealed to dictators. The federal Constitution's flaw was that it offset power against power, which he told Jefferson he considered merely another way of saying that it offset party against party, faction against faction. Taylor would prefer that power be left in the people.[23]

Federal officeholders recognized that the state legislatures were the perfect republican organs, Taylor insisted, so they had persistently attempted to undermine those legislatures. Taylor understood the assumption of state debts, intended by Hamilton to tie the wealthy to the central government by tying their economic interests to it, as part of a calculated campaign to destroy the states' autonomy. As his uncle Edmund Pendleton put it in November 1798, "'the federal party' [stands for] absolute submission and non resistance to the administration of government, although it should be in direct violation of the constitution." Pendleton thought that a standing army, a sedition act, and patronage (all of which he, like Taylor, associated with the Federalists) would someday "subject America to executive despotism."[24]

At the decade's close, President John Adams and a Federalist Congress took several measures—expansion of the military establishment, abandonment of efforts to reach a modus vivendi with France, and adoption of the Alien and Sedition Acts—that struck Virginia Republicans as the capstones of a Federalist conspiracy to erect a monarchy. Taylor grew increasingly frustrated with Republican leaders', particularly Jefferson's, refusal to step up their opposition. He feared the approach of the time when the Constitution had been ignored so often that it was a dead letter. In short, he believed that Virginians' Revolution would be destroyed by Federalist officials.[25]

Republicans bemoaned "consolidation" in the 1790s as the road to despotism. When John Adams signed the Alien and Sedition Acts into law on Bastille Day, 14 July 1798, the last few wavering Virginia Republicans, the sanguine few, were finally prompted to act. Pride of place among those whom the events of 1798 persuaded that drastic measures were needed belonged to Vice President Thomas Jefferson.[26]

Jefferson wrote his famous letter to Taylor defending continued union with New England in June 1798. He was convinced, as he told several correspondents, that the taxation plank of the Federalist war program would drive the people into the Republican camp. By year's end, however, Jefferson had helped coordinate a campaign in the Virginia Republican leadership to have the General Assembly and some other state's legislature adopt resolutions setting out Virginia's position in the constitutional conflict with the Federalist administration. Those resolutions, penned by Jefferson and Madison and altered insignificantly in debate in the Virginia and Kentucky legislatures, floated like leaves on the stream of the Virginia constitutional tradition of Jefferson's *A Summary View of the Rights of British America*, Richard Bland's "An Inquiry Into the Rights of the British Colonies," John Taylor's pamphlets of the 1790s, and the Richmond Convention's instrument of ratification (as explicated by George Nicholas and Edmund Randolph). Their form and content were in the tradition of Patrick Henry's Stamp Act Resolves and his General Assembly Resolution of 1790.[27]

Thomas Jefferson had always been convinced that the general government of the United States should have power only regarding "foreign concerns" and that continental statesmen should "keep us distinct in Domestic ones." He wrote in that vein to Madison in 1786, then to two different correspondents while the

Philadelphia Convention sat in 1787, and his first inaugural address as president included a call for "the support of the state governments in all their rights, as the most competent administrators for our domestic concerns and the surest bulwarks against antirepublican tendencies." The formula of 1786–1787 is also approximately the same as the one Jefferson had used in his *Summary View* of 1774 to describe the relationship between the king and Virginia ("America"). This conception of the federal government's and Virginia's respective roles stuck in his mind ever after.[28]

Jefferson considered the Alien and Sedition Acts "merely an experiment on the American mind, to see how far it will bear an avowed violation of the constitution." For perhaps the sole time in his life, Jefferson feared lest the project of a hereditary king and lords, which "are in contemplation, I have no doubt," should succeed while his lethargic compatriots did nothing. He also saw the Alien and Sedition Acts as partisan attacks on himself and his fellow Republicans. The alien legislation, he told Madison in April, was aimed at Pennsylvania's leading Republican, Geneva-born Albert Gallatin, while the sedition bill was written to stifle "the whig presses. [Benjamin Franklin] Bache's [*Aurora*] has been particularly named." Although he was the incumbent vice president, Jefferson feared that he, too, would be targeted personally. Therefore, for example, he repeatedly implored James Madison during the period when the Sedition Act remained in effect to make sure that the seals on all of Jefferson's letters arrived unbroken.[29]

Jefferson thus felt the necessity of forceful measures in 1798, but he remained a Federalist of 1787–1788. Unlike Taylor, he was not convinced that the problem the Republicans faced grew naturally out of the form of the general government. He directed his efforts not at constitutional reform, but at persuasion—of his fellow public officials or, failing that, of the populace at large.

Jefferson's draft Kentucky Resolutions of 1798 bore the impress of his determination to defend the principle of home rule or, as he had put it in another situation a year earlier, "that the States retain as complete authority as possible over their own citizens." The first resolution declared simply that the states' adoption of the federal Constitution of 1788 did not constitute "unlimited submission," but was limited to certain "special purposes," the rest being reserved to the states. Here, Jefferson clearly followed Patrick Henry and the General Assembly of 1790 in elevating the Randolph-Nicholas explication of the ratification instrument to canonical status. When the federal government exceeded its mandate, Jefferson continued, its acts were "unauthoritative, void, and of no force"; in this, he followed George Nicholas's explanation of Virginia's contractual relationship to the other states under the federal Constitution. Each state was a party to the federal compact, Jefferson's first resolution concluded, with the other states forming, so far as it was concerned, the other party; this, too, was mere repetition of the argument made by Nicholas in the summer of 1788.[30]

The first half of the first resolution, which has seemed controversial to historians who have considered the Kentucky Resolutions in the past sixty years, was not controversial among Virginia Republicans in 1798. Jefferson himself had written in the *Notes*, complaining of the weak ground on which he thought Virginia's 1776 constitution stood, that, "It is not the name, but the authority which renders an act obligatory." He had gone on to claim that a constitutional convention in Virginia, followed by popular ratification, would "bind up the several branches of government by certain laws, which when they transgress their acts shall become nullities." The language of the first Kentucky Resolution of 1798 was axiomatic, in Jefferson's mind, given that the United States Constitution had been adopted by virtually the procedure he prescribed. In the *Notes*, the nullity of unconstitutional acts had been presented as a mechanism for averting rebellion—the proper resort of a republican people when its rights were infringed. In the period between Jefferson's authorship of the *Notes* and 1798, the idea that the federal Constitution established a simple compact among sovereign states had been clearly expounded by George Nicholas and Edmund Randolph in the Richmond Convention, and then it had been adopted as Virginia's official interpretation of the act of ratification with the promulgation of Henry's resolution in 1790.[31]

Jefferson's second draft Kentucky Resolution applied the first to the case of the Sedition Act. Finding no delegation to the federal government of a power to punish any such act as the Sedition Act undertook to criminalize, Jefferson held the Sedition Act ("and all their other acts which assume to create, define, or punish crimes, other than those so enumerated in the Constitution") to be "altogether void, and of no force." The third Kentucky Resolution applied the language of the First Amendment's speech and press clauses, along with the Tenth Amendment's reservation to the states or people of all powers not delegated to the federal government, to the case of the Sedition Act, which it found violative of both amendments. This resolution also said that if a violation of any part of the First Amendment were tolerated, the other enumerated rights (those regarding religion, assembly, and petitioning for redress of grievances) would be threatened, too. For that reason, too, the Sedition Act was "altogether void, and of no force."[32]

Jefferson's fourth resolution found the Alien Friends Act void on Tenth Amendment grounds, and the fifth pointed to the 1808 clause as explicitly leaving power over immigration matters to the states until 1808. The sixth resolution found the procedures established for enforcement of the Alien Acts to violate various procedural provisions of the federal Bill of Rights and of Article III of the federal Constitution.[33]

Jefferson's seventh draft Kentucky Resolution might be called the "John Taylor Resolution," for it encapsulated the Republican grievances expressed in Taylor's pamphlets of the 1790s. The officials of the "General Government" had constantly tended, Jefferson wrote, to construe the "general welfare" and "necessary and proper" clauses in such a way as to bring about "the destruction of all limits prescribed to their power by the Constitution." Those two clauses were meant to be "subsidiary only to the execution of limited powers," he claimed, not to wipe out the rest of the Constitution by themselves granting unlimited powers. Jefferson looked forward to "revisal and correction" of the General Government's tendency in this regard when the time was propitious, but the matters raised in earlier resolutions could not await that time. They demanded "immediate redress."[34]

Having stated his premise, and then found it applicable to the statutes at issue, Jefferson finally considered the question what action should be taken in response to the Alien and Sedition Acts in his eighth resolution. At over one-third the length of the whole draft, this was easily the most important of Jefferson's draft resolutions. A committee should be appointed, it began, to correspond with the other states regarding the resolutions. Kentucky must assure its sister states, its coparties to the federal Constitution in the Virginia Republican reading, that "this commonwealth continues in the same esteem of their friendship and union which it has manifested from that moment at which a common danger first suggested a common union." (Obviously, this section was not drafted with Kentucky in mind, for Kentucky did not exist as a separate entity when the Imperial Crisis began.) Kentucky, it continued (once again following George Nicholas's assurances concerning the Virginia instrument of ratification), viewed union "for specified national purposes, . . . those specified in the late federal compact" to be a good thing. It would uphold the Constitution establishing such a union "according to the plain intent and meaning in which it was understood and acceded to by the several parties."[35]

Consolidation of the states' powers in one general government "is not for the peace, happiness, or prosperity of these States," Jefferson insisted, and "therefore this commonwealth is determined . . . to submit to undelegated, and consequently unlimited powers in no man, or body of men on earth." (In other words, even the slightest transgression of the Constitution's limitations upon federal power was theoretically congruent to abolition of self-government, thus to despotism, and so it would be resisted.) Where delegated powers were abused, elections were the solution, but where undelegated powers were arrogated, "a nullification of the act is the rightful remedy," and every state had a right to nullify all such acts.[36]

Jefferson did not leave it at that, but would have had Kentucky call on other states to concur: "with them alone it is proper to communicate, they alone being parties to the compact, and solely authorized to judge the last resort of the powers exercised under it," unlike Congress, which was "merely the creature of the compact." If the Alien and Sedition Acts and the constitutional principles justifying them stood, the majority in the General Government could do as it liked to the minority, to state officials, and to citizens at large; self-government for the minority would be at an end, the Revolution thwarted. These acts therefore must be opposed "at the threshold," or revolution and the discrediting of republicanism worldwide would follow. "[F]ree government is founded in jealousy," Jefferson pontificated, and such jealousy led to constitutional limitations on power. The Alien and Sedition Acts showed that Americans' jealousy had been justified.

Congress had conferred and the president had accepted a tyranny, so "let no more be heard of confidence in man, but bind him down by the chains of the Constitution." Jefferson's statement that only the states were parties to the Constitution and that innovation must be met at the threshold matched the assertions Taylor had made in his pamphlets, thus capturing what Edmund Randolph in 1793 had called the common understanding of Virginia planters. This was not a doctrine concocted in 1798.[37]

Historians have claimed that Jefferson's reference to the right of resistance in cases not made federal as a "natural" right marked his doctrine as revolutionary, but a different reading seems more in line with his argument. Where the matter in question was beyond the General Government's authority, he said, its edicts thereon were null, and they might be treated as such. It was the General Government that was said by Jefferson to have been engaged in "seizing the rights of the States," so it was the General Government itself, and specifically the Federalists who had been administering it, who stood accused of engaging in revolution. The status quo had found the general and the state governments each in possession of its own rightful powers. Actions that Jefferson considered unlawful had brought the nation to the pass at which it found itself in 1798. When Virginia Republicans looked in the mirror, they did not see revolutionaries. As George Nicholas (of Richmond Convention fame) explained, the Republican leadership of 1798 contemplated merely "an appeal to the *real laws* of our country."[38]

James Madison's resolutions for Virginia were sponsored in the House of Delegates by John Taylor of Caroline. The leading figures in the party had agreed that the resolutions should be couched in language that would leave them room to push matters as far, or to do as little, as the situation required. (The exception was Taylor himself, who did not know of the plan to have Virginia and another state adopt such resolutions, and thus bring his decade's jeremiad to a partially successful close, until they had already been written. Ironically, state resolutions had long been Taylor's panacea.) Such careful calibration of their argument was necessitated by the tenuous position of Republicanism in the north, where talk of disunion might wreck both the political position of the small coterie of like-minded leaders and the prospects for continued union. The characteristically cautious Madison's version was vaguer than Jefferson's, but still clear enough (as he would later regret).[39]

Jefferson wrote Wilson Cary Nicholas, a rising politician who was to be a member of the General Assembly in 1798, to suggest a change in Madison's draft language. In keeping with the draft of Kentucky's resolutions, Virginia's should conclude by calling on the other states "to concur with this commonwealth in declaring, as it does hereby declare, that the said acts are, and were ab initio, null, void, and of no force, or effect." Nicholas obliged. Instead of consulting its sister states, Virginia would make a pronouncement and ask them to agree.[40]

Jefferson's Kentucky Resolutions gave later particularists a platform, but Jefferson was not in a localist mood. He still expected the Federalist program ultimately to lead to Federalism's downfall. Unlike John Taylor, who wanted to force the issue (which explains why he was kept out of the drafting process), Jefferson said he would simply have the two legislatures declare the Alien and Sedition Acts void, then bide his time. The effect of "the X.Y.Z. delusion" would pass when the weight of the Federalists' new war taxes began to be felt, and "our unanimity" would return. If he proved wrong, there would be time enough to jump from that bridge when they came to it.[41]

Thus chastened, Taylor carried the resolutions program into the Virginia General Assembly's preponderant lower house. The House of Delegates gave the Virginia Resolutions its approval by a vote of one hundred to sixty-three; the Virginia Senate concurred, fourteen to three, and the classic statement of state-rights dogma had Virginia's imprimatur.[42]

John Taylor introduced the Virginia Resolutions on 12 December 1798. In doing so, he offered several different rationales. First, he noted that English and British kings who had dared to attempt to exercise more power than they had a right to had been opposed by their fellow officers, whether lords, commons, or both groups in tandem. Surely Americans would be no less quick to defend their rights.[43]

Starting with the Alien Acts, Taylor played the stock Virginia rhetorical card. If aliens had rights, he said, the Constitution might defend them. If Congress could ignore or abridge aliens' rights, it could do the same to others'. He soon made the same point regarding the Sedition Act's abridgment of the freedom of speech. Turning to the question of opposition itself, Taylor characterized his position as a quandary: as a state representative, he had sworn "to oppose unconstitutional laws. What was he to do?"[44]

The United States Constitution, Taylor insisted in the language of Locke, was "nothing more than a deed of trust made by the people to the government." It could be interpreted (construed) as a contract or deed would be (just as George Nicholas had promised that it would be in Richmond in 1788). The ratifiers (whose opinions were the only ones that mattered, as they were the "signatories" to the compact) had never contemplated giving the federal government power to make sedition laws. If allowed to continue on its current path, Congress, controlling the dissemination of ideas, would soon detach the affections of "the people from the state governments, and attach them to the general government." Consolidation of this kind would lead to despotism, then to revolution (because the people insisted on local self-government).[45]

A Republican delegate noted that the inferential construction favored by Federalists differed in no essential way from the British mode of constitutional reasoning against which Americans had fought their war for independence. The entire experiment in writing state constitutions had at its root, he claimed, the desire to foreclose the possibility of such construction, and so did the decision to enumerate congressional powers explicitly.[46]

Another Republican added that the argument Federalists made would justify anything the general government might do. Then, "the nature of that Constitution was changed. It was not what the people and states understood it to be at the time of its ratification. Its powers were enlarged to a dangerous extent. It could no longer be considered as producing a confederation, but certainly established a consolidated government." If the nature of the Constitution were thus changed and the Sedition Act could prevent the people from learning of official malfeasance, "power would stand in the place of the Constitution" and American liberties would meet the same fate as other countries'.[47]

Virginian Republicans held that in adopting the proposed resolutions, Virginia would not be threatening violence, but would be attempting to persuade. Publius, they noted (in a reference to an essay penned by Hamilton, the Federalists' favorite), said such interstate coordination of opposition was perfectly desirable.[48]

A Republican delegate insisted that, "Implication would lead us into an endless discussion," so only constitutional exegesis founded upon the "plain sense and meaning of the Constitution" was acceptable. The ratification instrument of Virginia had binding legal effect, he thundered, including the section reserving to Virginia all powers not delegated. Once one understood this, the idea that the "necessary and proper" clause was a substantive grant of authority fell of its own weight.[49]

Republican James Barbour, who embarked in 1798 upon a political career that would include service as governor of Virginia and United States secretary of war, made a telling point that has often been ignored in considerations of the Virginia and Kentucky Resolutions: "If the alien and sedition laws are unconstitutional," he pointed out, "they are not law, and of course of no force." Usurpation of this type was "void." Virginia had always been in the forefront of the states when it came time to defend inherited rights, and he trusted it would be again. "[T]he sense of the American people, contemporaneous with the adoption of the general government, when the attributes and qualities of that government were best understood," was "that all powers not granted were retained." The Tenth Amendment underscored the point, and any other doctrine threatened despotism. To the Federalist argument that the Alien Act could not be unconstitutional because Virginia had enacted a similar statute in 1792, Barbour responded that a doctrine allowing the general government to do anything the state governments could do would allow it to do anything at all: the state governments were governments of general jurisdiction, while the federal government had, in Virginia's reading, only the powers it had been expressly delegated.[50]

A Federalist posited that even if the General Assembly adopted "Taylor's Resolutions," Virginians would still be bound to obey the Alien and Sedition Acts. The Acts' progenitor, Congress, possessed authority superior to that of the General Assembly, so the latter could not void the Acts. Congress was also due greater respect than the General Assembly because Virginia was more perfectly represented in Congress than in its own legislature (malapportioned, the argument went, as it was). The Virginia Resolutions struck Federalists as "dangerous," "improper," and "unnecessary," and the Kentucky version sounded "the tocsin of rebellion."[51]

A Republican instantly demanded to be told how congressmen from New Hampshire could be said to represent Virginia better than its own General Assembly. As all knew, "the eastern people in Congress" habitually called Virginians "disorganizers, jacobins, &c." A Republican then denied the applicability of the argument of Emmerich de Vattel, which Federalists had raised, about sovereigns' authority over aliens. Vattel assumed a unitary sovereign, but in America the federal government's want of the authority over aliens did not leave those aliens in limbo. Instead, the states retained authority over aliens. The constitutional reservation of control over immigration to the states at least until 1808 did *not* apply solely to slave imports, for the Tenth Amendment reservation of all matters not delegated to the federal government applied. The Virginia General Assembly had long understood itself to have power over immigration, or else it would never have passed the 1792 law regulating aliens to which Federalists had pointed.[52]

This Republican, too, borrowed the argument from Madison's "Memorial and Remonstrance" about uncontested violation of one right endangering all rights. Like his predecessors, he claimed that he saw a religious establishment in the offing. He also equated the Jeffersonian formula "null, void, and of no effect" with "unconstitutional." He would have no objection to removing the former if the latter were left, for the exact same meaning would still be conveyed.[53]

Federalist General Henry "Light-horse Harry" Lee argued that the states were not the only parties to the federal Constitution, despite the Resolutions' claim, but that the people somehow constituted a distinct party or parties. Republicans responded that the states had been the only ratifiers. "Should the words 'we the people,' then change the nature of the compact, contrary to the historical facts of the day?" Republicans "thought not." A Republican averred that the resolutions' specific phrasing did not matter, because "if they [the disputed federal acts] were unconstitutional, they, of course, were null and void."[54]

Having sat mute through several days' debate, John Taylor now made another appearance. For once echoing George Nicholas, he said that if all governments had powers of self-preservation, as a Federalist had claimed, then the states had the right to oppose "such unconstitutional laws of Congress, as may tend to their destruction." Neither a state nor the general government could be the ultimate judge of its own powers, Taylor reasoned, or the one with that power would swallow up the other.[55]

Some of the Federalists had said Taylor's resolutions were too strong, while some had taken the position that laws as egregious as Republicans said the Alien and Sedition Acts were should be met with military force. Taylor's thus became a "middle way," as he was quick to note. Back on the Montesquieu track that had come to be Republican dogma, Taylor insisted that consolidation would yield despotism, as no state as large as the United States could be both consolidated and free. Federalism with the small *f* was essential if freedom—self-government—was to endure in the United States.[56]

The notion, raised by Federalists, that the common law underlay the Sedition Act struck Taylor as a horrible threat to republicanism in Virginia. The ratifiers of the federal Constitution could never "have supposed that they were establishing a government which could at pleasure dip their hands into the inexhaustible treasuries of the common law and law of nations, and thence extract as much power as they pleased." (His doomsday scenario, predictably, involved an establishment of religion.) The federal government's power was limited on its face.[57]

Taylor denied that there was any "sovereignty" in the federal government at all. In Great Britain, sovereignty allowed the king, lords, and commons to legislate in any way that came to mind. The federal government was not sovereign, but was a creature of the American sovereigns—the state peoples. Yet, he feared that he detected the idea of a pact between the people and the government in Federalists' argument. From the idea of such a pact, which implied that the government existed independently of the peoples of the states, the distance to sovereignty in the federal government was short. Taylor held that the Constitution obliged the states to defend their rights as a way of averting the prospect of a sovereign (that is, all-powerful and theoretically uncontrollable) federal government.

On the last day of the debate, Federalists again asserted that the states were not, as the third resolution claimed, the only parties to the Constitution. Perhaps the states had been the instigators of the Philadelphia Convention, the Federalists conceded. However, the delegates to the Philadelphia Convention had ignored their writ, which was merely to recommend amendments to the Articles of Confederation. Then, the Philadelphia Convention had referred the proposed constitution to special conventions of the people for ratification. Nine states' ratification was required to insure that a majority of the people ratified. Only the people could have adopted the supremacy clause, which set the Constitution of the federal government above those of the states. (The General Assembly subsequently adopted the *Virginia Report* of 1799–1800 to explain the Virginia Resolutions. In that report, it defined "state" as the sovereign people of a state, thus answering this Federalist objection.) If the General Assembly could declare a federal statute void, as the seventh Virginia Resolution purported to do, so could any other state legislature. In that event, Federalists saw no hope for the federal union.[58]

William Branch Giles, who guided the Virginia Resolutions through the state Senate, held that the Sedition Act was not a means of dealing with any current crises, but was instead an end to which Federalism had long been pointing. Federalists in the General Assembly had criticized the Republicans for trying to convert the General Assembly into a judicial body. What was wrong with that?

Giles wanted to know. Had not the Delegates taken an oath to support the Constitution?[59]

Giles conceded (without explaining exactly what he meant) that the federal compact was not "only" among the states. Still, the last Congress had done what it could to usher in a monarchy (a consolidated government). Many in the House had called union desirable, but union to what end? "To abridge the freedom of the press." The language of the proposed resolutions had drawn criticism, but Giles doubted that the resolutions' critics would approve the wording of the Lord's Prayer. He, for his part, would be satisfied with a simple declaration of unconstitutionality. Anything less would be dereliction of duty.[60]

In the House of Delegates, John Taylor agreed to strike "alone" from the third resolution to bring it into line with Giles's concession that the states were not the sole parties to the Constitution—and thereby introduced an element of theoretical inconsistency into the document. He would also excise "but utterly null, void, and of no force or effect" from the same resolution, since several Federalists had objected to it and he agreed with the Republican speakers who had explained that it was a mere redundancy, anyway. At Wilson Cary Nicholas's urging, the House voted down Henry Lee's suggestion to omit the fourth resolution. As Nicholas (a Federalist in the Richmond Convention of 1788) put it, far more than the Alien and Sedition Acts was at issue. Virginia would disapprove of the entire Federalist regime of the 1790s.[61]

Despite the Resolutions' adoption, Taylor met the close of the debate with disappointment. He would have appealed the legality of the Federalist actions to a state convention as the Romans were wont to appeal to a dictator. In accepting a mere declaration, he had complied with Jefferson's wish for what Taylor considered a half-way measure instead.

Taylor need not have been so unhappy. He and his fellow delegates had laid down the marker, and the majority of Virginians would follow the path laid out in 1798 for decades to come. A General Assembly notable for the absence of the Revolutionary generation—of Richard Bland, George Mason, Patrick Henry, and their cohort—had dedicated itself to the constitutional faith of the fathers. Virginians rebelled "to have a Virginian government" in 1776, and their sons and grandsons would continue to insist upon local control of their government.[62]

As Jefferson, in Newtonian fashion, described it, many Virginians saw the federal union as an analogue of the solar system itself, dependent for its proper functioning on the "beautiful equilibrium" resulting from its parts' "respective weights and distances." Many others, however, would agree with John Taylor of Caroline, who at the high tide of Virginia Federalism had frankly avowed a theory of the sovereignty of the states (understood as distinct communities of people, not as governments). For the nonce, the Republicans could approve a federal government reflecting Judge St. George Tucker's dictum that the general government was founded "to be the organ through which the united republics communicate with foreign nations, and with each other." The Virginians had arrived at a consensus, too, that the federal Constitution should be interpreted, in Jefferson's words, "according to the true sense in which it was adopted by the States [read: Virginia], that in which it was advocated by its friends [such as Nicholas and Randolph].... I am for preserving to the States the powers not yielded by them to the Union."[63] As during the Imperial Crisis, so after the enactment of the federal Constitution, Virginians put their state first and the distant authority they had erected for their state's convenience—formerly in Great Britain, now in the federal capital—somewhere down the list. The question who should rule at home divided Virginians in 1798 as it had done before, but on the issue of home rule, they remained steadfast.

NOTES

1. Victor Dennis Golladay, "The Nicholas Family of Virginia, 1772–1820" (Ph.D. dissertation, University of Virginia, 1973).
2. Richard Henry Lee to Patrick Henry, 20 April 1776, *The Letters of Richard Henry Lee*, ed. James Curtis Ballagh (New York: Da Capo Press, 1970).
3. Adrienne Koch and Harry Ammon, "The Virginia and Kentucky Resolutions: An Episode in Jefferson's and Madison's Defense of Civil Liberties," *William and Mary Quarterly*, 3rd Series, 5 (April 1948), 147–76. Koch's and Ammon's account has been followed by many authors, including the two leading Jefferson biographers, Merrill D. Peterson, *Thomas Jefferson and the New Nation: A Biography* (New York: Oxford University Press, 1970), 609–16; and Dumas Malone, *Jefferson and His Time*, vol. 3: *Jefferson and the Ordeal of Liberty* (Boston: Little, Brown and Company, 1962), xix, 399–409, 509. Thomas Jefferson to John Taylor, June 1, 1798, in Paul Leicester Ford, ed., *The Works of Thomas Jefferson* (12 vols.; New York and London: G. P. Putnam's Sons, 1904–1905), 8: 430–33, at 432.
4. Norman Risjord, *The Old Republicans: Southern Conservatism in the Age of Jefferson* (New York and London: Columbia University Press, 1965), 11.
5. See Kevin R. C. Gutzman, "Edmund Randolph and Virginia Constitutionalism," *The Review of Politics* 66 (2004), 469–97.
6. While James Madison is often described as the great eminence of the convention, his feeble voice made him a poor floor leader. As a result, for example, he took no part in the debate concerning the report of the instrument of ratification, which the drafting committee's other members left largely to Randolph and to George Nicholas to defend. Nicholas's speeches throughout the convention echoed the letters of Publius, and, given the obvious discrepancy between Nicholas's and Madison's intellects, this cannot have been accidental. Madison's oratorical shortcomings were accentuated during the convention by a passing illness. John P. Kaminski and Gaspare J. Saladino, editors, *The Documentary History of the Ratification of the Constitution* (Madison: State Historical Society of Wisconsin, 1993), 9: 906.
7. *Ibid.*, n. at 10: 1,513.
8. Speech of Edmund Randolph, June 24, 1788, *ibid.*, 1483 (italics added); "The Articles of Confederation," *Colonies to Nation: A Documentary History of the American Revolution*, ed. Jack P. Greene (New York and London: Norton, 1975), 428–36 (Article 2 at 429).

9. See n. 5, *supra*.
10. Speech of George Nicholas, June 24, 1788, *The Documentary History of the Ratification of the Constitution*, 10: 1,506–7 (italics added).
11. Alexander Hamilton, James Madison, and John Jay, *The Federalist*, edited by Jacob E. Cooke (Middletown, Conn.: Wesleyan University Press, 1961), 250–57, at 254.
12. Richard Henry Lee to Patrick Henry, September 14, 1789, James Curtis Ballagh, ed., *The Letters of Richard Henry Lee* (New York: Da Capo Press, 1970), 2: 501–4, at 502; also see Richard Henry Lee to Patrick Henry, September 27, 1789, *ibid.*, 2: 504–7, at 506; Richard Henry Lee to Samuel Adams, April 25, 1789, *ibid.*, 2: 483–85, at 484; Richard Henry Lee to Samuel Adams, August 8, 1789, *ibid.*, 2: 495–97, at 495–96; Richard R. Beeman, *The Old Dominion and the New Nation, 1788–1801* (Lexington: University Press of Kentucky, 1972), 77; *Journal of the House of Delegates*, November 3, 1790; *Senate Journal*, December 21, 1790.
13. *Journal of the House of Delegates*, November 22, 1790, December 16, 1790; Richard Bland, "An Inquiry Into the Rights of the British Colonies" (1766) *Revolutionary Virginia: The Road to Independence*, ed. William J. Van Schreeven and Robert L. Scribner (Charlottesville: University Press of Virginia, 1973), 1: 28–44; Thomas Jefferson, "A Summary View of the Rights of British America," Julian Boyd, ed., *The Papers of Thomas Jefferson*, 1: 121–35. For the tendency among Republicans nationwide to see events of the 1790s through the prism of English history, see Lance Banning, *The Jeffersonian Persuasion: Evolution of a Party Ideology* (Ithaca, N.Y., and London: Cornell University Press, 1978).
14. Henry H. Simms, *Life of John Taylor: The Story of a Brilliant Leader in the Early Virginia State Rights School* (Richmond, Va.: The William Byrd Press, Inc., 1932), 58 (Taylor's influence); John Taylor, *An Enquiry into the Principles and Tendency of Certain Public Measures* (hereafter, *Enquiry*) (Philadelphia, 1794), 2, 82–83; also see *ibid.*, 46, and John Taylor, *A Definition of Parties, or the Political Effects of the Paper System Considered* (Philadelphia, 1794) (hereafter, *Definition*), 3. While Randolph's aristocratic prejudices led him to espy elite influence behind all commonly held beliefs, other Virginians did indeed share Taylor's notion that new limitations on the federal government's power must be added during the government's first years. Richard Henry Lee to John Jones, October 15, 1788, *The Letters of Richard Henry Lee*, 2: 478–79.
15. John Taylor to Daniel Carroll Brent, October 9, 1796, "Letters of John Taylor, of Caroline County, Virginia," William E. Dodd, ed., *The John P. Branch Historical Papers of Randolph-Macon College*, 2 (June 1908) (hereafter, "Letters of John Taylor"), 253–353, at 260–68 (Adams at 267). For an intimation of Taylor's "befuddled" opposition to Federalism, see *Enquiry*, 47, where he wrote, "And the want of simplicity in politics, is ever a badge of design."
16. It thus is incorrect to say that the Republicans, unlike later Democrats and Nullifiers, omitted fears of northern antislavery from their states'-rights edifice. John Taylor, *An Argument Respecting the Constitutionality of the Carriage Tax* (Richmond, Va., [1795]), 20, 33 n. 17; and James Roger Sharp, *American Politics in the Early Republic: The New Nation in Crisis* (New Haven, Conn., and London: Yale University Press, 1993), 206–7.
17. *An Argument Respecting the Constitutionality of the Carriage Tax*, 4, 28.
18. *Ibid.*, 3.
19. John Taylor, *Enquiry*, 64, 65.
20. Thomas Jefferson to John Taylor, June 1, 1798, Paul Leicester Ford, ed., *The Works of Thomas Jefferson*, (New York and London: G. P. Putnam's Sons, 1904) (here-

after, *Works*), 8: 430–33; Thomas Jefferson to John Taylor, November 26, 1798, *ibid.*, 8: 479–83, at 480.

21. John Taylor to James Monroe, March 25, 1798, Dodd, ed., "Letters of John Taylor," 268–70, at 269.

22. John Taylor, *Definition*, 5–6, 15.

23. John Taylor, *Enquiry*, 54–5; John Taylor to Thomas Jefferson, 1798, Dodd, ed., "Letters of John Taylor," 277–78 (dictator); John Taylor to Thomas Jefferson, June 25, 1798, *ibid.*, 271–76, at 272 ("What are checks and balances, but party and faction?" "Did the British people ever gain by a change of ministry?"); Taylor's partisanship for state legislatures was shared by most prominent Virginians. See (U.S. Rep.) Andrew Moore to Col. Robert Gamble, March 9, 1790, Claiborne Family Papers, Virginia Historical Society.

24. John Taylor, *Enquiry*, 47; John Taylor to Thomas Jefferson, June 25, 1798, Dodd, ed., "Letters of John Taylor," 271–76, at 274; John Taylor, *Enquiry*, 43; Edmund Pendleton, "Address to the Citizens of Caroline," November 1798, David John Mays, ed., *The Letters and Papers of Edmund Pendleton, 1734–1803*, (Charlottesville: University Press of Virginia, 1967), 2: 650–54, at 652; Edmund Pendleton, "An Address . . . on the Present State of Our Country," February 20, 1799, *ibid.*, 658–66, at 659; Lance Banning, *The Jeffersonian Persuasion: Evolution of a Party Ideology*, 263.

25. John Taylor, *Enquiry*, 54–55.

26. *The Virginia Report of 1799–1800 Touching the Alien and Sedition Laws, Together with the Virginia Resolutions of December 21, 1798, Including the Debate and Proceedings Thereon in the House of Delegates of Virginia* (1850; reprinted New York: Da Capo Press, 1970), xiii; Stanley Elkins and Eric McKitrick, *The Age of Federalism*, 724 ("sanguine").

27. Thomas Jefferson to John Taylor, June 1, 1798, *supra*, n. 19; Thomas Jefferson to Archibald Hamilton Rowan, September 26, 1798, Ford, ed., *Works*, 8: 447–48; Thomas Jefferson to James Lewis, Jr., May 9, 1798, Andrew A. Lipscomb, ed., *The Writings of Thomas Jefferson*, (Washington, D.C., 1905) (hereafter, *Writings*), 10: 36–38, at 37; Thomas Jefferson to John Tyler, November 26, 1798, Ford, ed., *Works*, 10: 479–83, at 480. For discussion of the Virginia constitutional tradition as it developed in the 1760s and 1770s, see chapter 1, above, and for its ongoing influence, K. R. Constantine Gutzman, "Jefferson's Draft Declaration of Independence, Richard Bland, and the Revolutionary Legacy: Giving Credit Where Credit Is Due," *The Journal of the Historical Society* 1 (2001), 137–54.

28. Thomas Jefferson to James Madison, December 16, 1796, *Works*, 5: 225–30, at 226; Jesse T. Carpenter, *The South as a Conscious Minority, 1789–1861* (1930; reprinted Columbia, S.C., 1990), 35 (Jefferson's first inaugural); Lee Cheek, *Calhoun and Popular Rule: The Political Theory of the "Disquisition" and the "Discourse"* (Columbia: University of Missouri Press, 2001); Thomas Jefferson to Destutt de Tracy, January 26, 1811, Ford, ed., *Works*, 11: 181–89; Thomas Jefferson to John Cartwright, June 5, 1824, Lipscomb, ed., *Writings*, 16: 42–52, at 43–44.

29. Thomas Jefferson to Stephens Thompson Mason [sic], October 11, 1798, Ford, ed., *Works*, 8: 449–51; Thomas Jefferson to James Madison, April 26, 1798, *ibid.*, 411–13, at 411–12; Thomas Jefferson to James Madison, April 5, 1798, *ibid.*, 397–99, at 397.

30. David N. Mayer, *The Constitutional Thought of Thomas Jefferson* (Charlottesville: University Press of Virginia, 1994), 199–200. Jefferson's draft of the Kentucky Resolutions of 1798 is at Ford, ed., *Works*, 8: 458–79.

31. Thomas Jefferson, *Notes on the State of Virginia*, ed. William Peden (Chapel Hill and London: University of North Carolina Press, 1954; 2d edition, 1982), "Query XIII: Constitution," 110–29, at 123–24, 129. Also see Kevin R. C. Gutzman, "Edmund Randolph and Virginia Constitutionalism," *The Review of Politics* 66 (2004), 469–97.

32. Thomas Jefferson, "Kentucky Resolutions" (draft), Ford, ed., *Works*, 8: 458–77, column 2 (second and third resolutions at 462–63, 463–65; quotations at 463, 465). Other than in the "Memorial and Remonstrance"—which is printed in William T. Hutchinson et al., eds., *The Papers of James Madison* (17 vols., Chicago and Charlottesville: University of Chicago Press and University Press of Virginia, 1973–), 8: 293–306—Madison made the same alarmist claim in James Madison to James Monroe, June 21, 1785, *ibid.*, 306–8, at 306.

33. Draft resolutions four, five, and six are at Ford, ed., *Works*, 8: 465–66, 466–67, 467–68.

34. The draft seventh resolution is at *ibid.*, 468–69, at 469.

35. The draft eighth resolution is at *ibid.*, 470–77, at 470.

36. *Ibid.*, at 470–71.

37. For Randolph in 1793, see the text at n. 13, *supra*.

38. Trevor Colbourn, *The Lamp of Experience: Whig History and the Intellectual Origins of the American Revolution* (2nd edition; Indianapolis: Liberty Fund, 1998), xix; James Roger Sharp, *American Politics in the Early Republic*, 201.

39. Adrienne Koch and Harry Ammon, "The Virginia and Kentucky Resolutions," 150, n. 12; Thomas Jefferson to James Madison, November 17, 1798, Ford, ed., *Works*, 8: 456–57; James Roger Sharp, *American Politics in the Early Republic*, 189; Kevin R. [C.] Gutzman, "A Troublesome Legacy: James Madison and 'The Principles of '98,'" *Journal of the Early Republic* 15 (1995): 569–89.

40. Thomas Jefferson to Wilson Cary Nicholas, November 29, 1798, Ford, ed., *Works*, 8: 483; James Roger Sharp, *American Politics in the Early Republic*, 197.

41. Thomas Jefferson to John Taylor, November 26, 1798, Ford, ed., *Works*, 8: 479–83; Thomas Jefferson to Samuel Smith, August 22, 1798, *ibid.*, 443–44. Jefferson was typical of Virginia's elite in thinking unanimity natural. Richard Henry Lee to Richard Bland Lee, February 5, 1794, Ballagh, ed., *The Letters of Richard Henry Lee*, (reprinted New York: Da Capo Press, 1970), 2: 563–75, at 564; Edmund Pendleton, "Address to the Citizens of Caroline," November 1798, *The Letters and Papers of Edmund Pendleton*, 2: 650–54, at 651.

42. *The Virginia Report of 1799–1800*, 157 (House vote), 158 (Senate vote).

43. This and the following two paragraphs are based on Speech of John Taylor, December 13, 1798, *ibid.*, 24–29.

44. *Ibid.*, at 25.

45. *Ibid.*, at 25, 27.

46. Speech of William Ruffin, December 14, 1798, *ibid.*, 38–39.

47. Speech of John Mercer, December 15, 1798, *ibid.*, at 40, 41.

48. Alexander Hamilton, James Madison, and John Jay, *The Federalist* 28, edited by Jacob E. Cooke, 176–80, at 179–80.

49. Speech of John Mercer, December 15, 1798, *The Virginia Report of 1799–1800*, 40–50, at 44.

50. Speech of James Barbour, December 17, 1798, *ibid.*, 54–70, at 55, 56, 57.

51. Speech of Edmund Brooke, December 18, 1798, *The Virginia Report of 1799–1800*, 79–81.

Chapter 4

52. Speech of John Pope, December 19, 1798, *ibid.*, 82–83, at 82; Speech of William Daniel, Jr., December 19, 1798, *ibid.*, 83–98.

53. Speech of William Daniel, Jr., December 19, 1798, *ibid.*, 83–98. (Contrast Adrienne Koch and Harry Ammon, "The Virginia and Kentucky Resolutions.")

54. Speech of Peter Johnston, December 20, 1798, *ibid.*, 109–111, at 109. (Contrast Adrienne Koch and Harry Ammon, "The Virginia and Kentucky Resolutions.")

55. Speech of John Taylor, December 20, 1798, *ibid.*, 111–22, at 112.

56. *Ibid.* (quotation at 114, Montesquieuan point at 115).

57. *Ibid.*, at 115–16.

58. "Report of 1800," *The Papers of James Madison*, 17: 307–50, at 308–9.

59. Speech of William Branch Giles, December 21, 1798, *The Virginia Report of 1799–1800*, 143–48, at 144.

60. *Ibid.*, 146–48, at 146.

61. Speech of John Taylor, December 21, 1798, *ibid.*, 148–50, at 150; Speech of Henry Lee, December 21, 1798, *ibid.*, 150; Speech of Wilson Cary Nicholas, December 21, 1798, *ibid.*, 150–51.

62. John Taylor to Thomas Jefferson, 1798, Dodd, ed., "Letters of John Taylor," 277–78, at 277.

63. Henry H. Simms, *Life of John Taylor*, 65; Thomas Jefferson to Peregrine Fitzhugh, February 23, 1798, Lipscomb, ed., *Writings*, 10: 1–4, at 3; Jesse T. Carpenter, *The South as a Conscious Minority, 1789–1801*, 36–7 (St. George Tucker); Thomas Jefferson to Elbridge Gerry, January 26, 1799, Lipscomb, ed., *Writings*, 10: 74–86, at 76–77.

5

"May All Your Dreams Come True"

Opposition to Federalism had yielded a new Virginia position, and the Virginia Federalist party would soon melt away, resulting in the "natural" elite consensus. At least, so it seemed in 1801. Within a short time, the expectation of consensus proved misplaced. Republicans in Virginia, once united in opposition to the Federalist administration of John Adams, soon fragmented. Both subparties found this phenomenon intensely disturbing.

Perhaps the Revolution of 1800—Republicans' victory in the federal elections of that year—had settled the question of the states' role in the federal system, and thus the contours of Virginia's right to self-government. Virginians had not decided, however, on the nature of politics within the Old Dominion itself, as a very public debate between John Taylor and *Richmond Enquirer* Editor Thomas Ritchie soon demonstrated. Ironically, Taylor took a position very similar to the one adopted by George Washington in his Farewell Address—that most political matters should be resolved by an elite behind closed doors—while newspaperman Ritchie predictably advocated wide dissemination of public information.

In addition, the status of slavery, once an issue no one bothered to raise, would be seriously debated in the first decades of the nineteenth century. Gabriel's Rebellion (1800) in Richmond brought it to the fore. Militia offices constituted one of the great troves of rewards for faithful service in the Republican Richmond "junto's" control, but in a period when the slaves seemed increasingly restive and the British threat was omnipresent, militia office was no sinecure. One alternative to heightened military preparedness, colonization of threatening blacks, appeared to be preferable, but it proved impracticable.

While elite politicians quarreled among themselves about the Jefferson administration's performance, many of them agreed that something had to be done to insure the continued availability of a pool of men fit to hold the Commonwealth's highest offices. "Proper" education might yield a cohort of such men uniformly devoted to "Virginia" principles. The abolition of primogeniture and entail in the decade of the Revolution, one of Jefferson's proudest achievements and once thought to be an unalloyed blessing, had proved problematic in practice; without the old landed aristocracy, who could fill the Commonwealth's high offices? Jefferson proposed a new elite educated in a republican manner. Some Virginians, however, doubting the consonance of Thomas Jefferson's education plan with the type of republican society the Revolutions of 1776 and 1800 had established, opposed it fiercely. While the Virginia Dynasty ruled Washington, the Jeffersonian suspicion of government that had brought it to power thwarted Jefferson's fondest hopes for republican reform in the Old Dominion itself.

As they fretted about the breakdown of the Republican consensus and their state's failure to replace the colonial landed aristocracy, political thinkers in Jeffersonian Virginia also had reason to be alarmed about the state of their economic mainstay, agriculture. Like the failure to produce a worthy republican ruling class, Virginians' economic plight threatened to make the Revolution futile. Virginians created a state-wide network of agricultural societies to counteract the decline in their economic fortunes, but this effort's success proved slight. James Madison perceptively blamed the opening of new farmland in the Gulf South for what everyone took to be Virginia's decline, but most Virginians followed John Taylor of Caroline in holding the federal government responsible. The political culture of republican Virginia, born in opposition to King George III and grown to maturity in the days of anti-Hamiltonian excess, proved ill-equipped to deal with the coincidence of stagnant-to-bad times and Virginia's own political preeminence. A great malaise, even a reconsideration of the Revolution itself, characterized the period. Old patriots, committed to the notion that problems had political remedies, cast about for solutions, but few attractive ones appeared. Self-government, surprisingly, had not brought on the republican millennium.

The Republicans of Virginia rejoiced in their victory in 1801. Their leaders never needed to act upon their determination to resist any Electoral College choice other than that of "the choice of the people," Thomas Jefferson.[1] Virginia likely would have taken violent measures to resist the election of Aaron Burr. Burr, the Republicans' candidate for vice president, had received as many electoral votes as Jefferson. In those pre–12th Amendment days, no distinction was made in Electoral College balloting between votes for president and those for vice president. Since all of the Republican electors voted for both of their party's candidates, the two of them stood deadlocked for president.[2]

Ballot after ballot passed, and Virginians, to borrow Patrick Henry's words from olden days, "smelt a rat." Republicans there as elsewhere believed they stood to suffer at the hands of secretive conspirators, those few aristocrats who held to poisonous Federalist principles. Finally, however, Jefferson was elected. A huge spasm of relief wracked the Virginian body politic, and a paroxysm of joy followed.

The reaction of the young aristocrats of the College of William and Mary was typical. As Joseph Carrington Cabell, who would one day be a state senator, canal company president, and prominent leader of the Virginia Democratic Party, wrote to Colonel Nicholas Cabell, jubilation marked the scene in Williamsburg. Virginia Federalists' reaction, he noted, augured a return to Virginia's wonted political unanimity. The wayward sheep would return to the fold. Federalists' insistence that Republican accounts of their national leaders' perfidy were overblown, young Cabell related, disappeared on receipt of incontrovertible proof. The machinations in the capital had made it "uncertain whether we should be a united or divided people," as Federalists now conceded.

After the House chose Jefferson, the students joined in an impromptu ceremony linking this "Revolution of 1800," as Jefferson would one day dub it, to the whole history of Virginia republicanism. They assembled in front of the Wren Building and, led by a musical band, marched down Williamsburg's main street "with triumphant joy." St. George Tucker, the prominent jurist, had them all in for a toast "to the health of the President elect." "We then continued our march as far as the old Capitol, where we shouted a number of republican sentiments . . . one particularly alluding to the famous speech of Mr. Henry which drew down the cry of Treason from every part of that venerable building. From thence we proceeded to the ruins of the Old Palace," where a flag was planted and all joined in shouting "May the banner of liberty thus for ever wave triumphantly over the ruins of despotism." The next evening, joined by a number of townsmen, they marched to the houses of prominent "aristocrats" to shout "Hurra for Jefferson." Supporters of self-determination (the Republicans) had won out over the scheming aristocrats (the Federalists).

Once, Virginians might have taken political satisfaction in the elevation of particular men. What made the tableau especially piquant for Joseph C. Cabell in 1801, by contrast, was the triumph of his and his compatriots' "principles." "Mr. Jefferson" was "perhaps the greatest man . . . in America," but his greatness lay not merely in his "talents & information." "The men who would make this country a scene of tyranny, & ruin" had been defeated by patriots determined "to administer our government upon the purest principles of republican liberty." These events combined to "cause the eye to swim in tears."

The Republican Party, or what some Federalists called the "Virginia Party," owed its genesis to a group of similarly situated ideologues. Their views concerning the vector of Federalist policy in the 1790s were similar because their education, economic interests, and ethnic inheritance were nearly identical. Joseph C. Cabell, of the generation just entering into public life in the first decade of the nineteenth century, was typical of them.

Cabell's political views captured the center of the Jeffersonian party perfectly. In 1808, in preparation for an electoral effort, he penned a long set of notes for a speech to the freeholders of Amherst County. In that speech, he perfectly adumbrated the principles whose victory in 1801 had brought tears to his eyes.[3] Cabell's version of Republicanism—his interpretation of the Revolution of 1800—rested on the principles of constitutional construction first laid out by George Nicholas and Edmund Randolph in the Richmond Convention of 1788.

First, Cabell noted, Federalists had been prone to assert the constitutionality of virtually any measure the federal government might take, while "Republicans contended that Government was limited to the means granted in the constitution." As Cabell told it, Federalists favored lodging power in the Executive, while Republicans sided with the Legislature. Federalists sought continually to strengthen the federal government, while Republicans strove to insure that the federal government and the state governments all remained free to exercise the powers the people had reposed in them. Perhaps most characteristically, "Federalists were friendly to a splendid and expensive government," while Republicans "dismissed useless agents, and lessened the impositions on the people." One threatening manifestation of Federalists' love of multiplying offices, as Cabell saw it, had been their establishment of "great navies, & standing armies in time of peace." Republicans, he insisted, were attached to the principle of maintaining no permanent military force beyond the needs of garrison duty, and they held that the largest naval force the United States could raise would be inadequate to the defense of the United States' trade, besides "expensive and ruinous." Federalist predilections would make naval engagements more likely, too, for while Republicans favored limiting "our connections with the powers of Europe," Federalists "were for spreading our ministers over the continent of Europe."

On the question of press freedom, Cabell asserted, the Republicans were convinced that "a suppression of falsehood, would be accompanied by a suppression of truth." Therefore, while Federalist officials had enacted the Sedition Act to protect themselves from censure, the Republicans had "left their administration open to the united, but fruitless rage of all the federal presses in the union." "In politics," young Cabell wrote, "I am an American—a decided republican—an ardent admirer of representative, popular governments." In this commitment to elective government, as in his notion that to be "American" was to agree with him, Cabell showed himself a typical Jeffersonian.[4]

President Jefferson's formulation of the Republican creed in his First Inaugural Address was, characteristically, more poetic. Still, he held virtually the same views as Cabell did. Like Edmund Randolph in the 1788 Richmond Convention, Jefferson believed that the run of men followed their betters closely, so that Federalists' repeated electoral victories did not need to be understood as the fruit of popular endorsement of their positions; thus, he could state that whatever ill intentions had driven their leaders to do, most Federalists were essentially "American" (that is, Republican). They should amalgamate with Republicanism, and those who did not could be left as monuments to the folly of error. "We are all republicans, we are all federalists," Jefferson held. "We have called by different names, brethren of the same principle."[5] By this, he seems to have meant not only that all Americans held fast to the representative form of government and the proper delineation of the division between federal and state authority. The "reign of witches" had passed; Americans would now be "consolidated in their ancient principles."[6] Given Americans' "benign religion" and "overruling providence," all that was needed was "a wise & frug[a]l gov[ern]m[en]t" that protected men from one another and generally left them alone for a millennium of mutual affection among all American citizens to dawn.[7]

Signs that this hope would be disappointed made their appearance almost instantly. While Jefferson struck a pose of magnanimity, the soldiers who had done the hard political fighting in the field expected their shares of the booty. William Branch Giles, an eminent congressman of the 1790s and Virginia Senate sponsor of the Virginia Resolutions, wrote early in 1801 to congratulate Jefferson on his recent electoral victory. On the question of patronage, this leading Republican captain told the new president that Republicans expected "a pretty general purgation of office." Jefferson should have few scruples, it seemed to Giles, because most Federalists were so vehement that "it would be hardly possible to err in exclusions."[8]

Virginia dominated American politics in 1801, and it would continue to do so through both of Jefferson's terms. Besides the president himself, the Republicans' first cabinet was headed by Jefferson's lieutenant and eventual successor, James Madison. In Congress, Jefferson's distant cousin, the prodigy John Randolph of Roanoke, rode the House majority—to hear the Federalists tell it—as if it were a docile, old nag. In the other chamber, Giles's dominance led John Quincy Adams to joke that if his appearance displeased the Virginian, he might easily be expelled.[9]

The *Connecticut Courant* editorialized in 1805 about the unbearable domination of Virginia.[10] Virtually anything the Virginians wanted, this Federalist organ lamented, Congress did. Surely Republicans must be mortified, too, that even the most picayune matters of parliamentary management were always entrusted to Virginians. Was there no one of abilities in any other state? In his "reign of witches" letter to John Taylor of 1 June 1798, Jefferson had conceded that Massachusetts and Connecticut rode Virginia "very hard"; now, the saddle was on a different back.

All things change, and a political or military body that is impregnable from without must eventually succumb to pressures from within. So it proved for the Virginia Republicans. Unhappiness in the ranks eventually degenerated into outright schism. The seeds of later troubles of great moment had already been planted when Jefferson replaced John Adams at the helm of the federal government. The General Assembly in 1801–1802 responded to an abortive slave insurrection in the environs of Richmond in 1800 by discussing the idea of "a penal colony for rebellious slaves and free Negro criminals." The resulting correspondence between Governor Monroe and President Jefferson illuminated

Virginia Republicans' racial views—and exposed some of the latent tensions underlying Virginia republicanism (and Republicanism).[11]

Governor Monroe was quite unhappy with the idea of executing all of the many slaves convicted of participating in the conspiracy. After the first round of hangings, he wrote Jefferson to ask whether the federal government could not locate lands appropriate for the colonization of felonious bondsmen. The new president promised he would endeavor to secure the backing of Congress for Monroe's scheme.

Jefferson soon ran into difficulty. It would be extremely expensive, he noted, for Virginia to buy the lands it wanted in the Northwest, inconvenient for all the states to erect a state populated and governed by ex slaves into a member of the union, and surprising if Great Britain, France, or Spain allowed the settlement of freedmen and black convicts in their nearby lands. The one promising possibility was settlement of Virginia's unwanted blacks in the West Indies. (Black rebels might not appear criminal to the black ruler of St. Domingo.) As a last resort, the Africa option could be kept in reserve.[12] Jefferson rationalized his scheme through the idea that Virginians were doing black deportees a favor.[13] His efforts proved unavailing.[14]

Jefferson hoped, he always insisted, that the young generation would have attitudes about slavery similar to his.[15] St. George Tucker, successor to Jefferson's mentor George Wythe as professor of law at William and Mary, published a "Virginia" edition of Blackstone's *Commentaries on the Laws of England* in 1803. Essentially, that text was Blackstone's work with the addition of a group of appendices "correcting" the English Whig positions taken in the text's main body. Among them was one on slavery in Virginia from which three generations of Tucker's students, who came to dominate the Virginia legal profession, were indoctrinated with Jefferson's abolition proposal from the 1780s' *Notes on the State of Virginia*. In the end, however, even Tucker rejected even Jefferson's tepid abolitionism.[16] The problem of slavery would fester, ever at the back of Virginians' minds, until it burst upon their consciousness again in the guise of Nat Turner's Rebellion at the end of the Jeffersonian period.

The alternative to abolition was racial control, primarily through the militia. From their earliest appearance, militia units also filled an important social function. Everyone knew who "Col. Mason" and "Col. Taylor" (not "Senator Taylor") were; militia ranks were significant social markers, and military service would continue to play a significant role in elite Virginians' view of themselves. After Thomas Jefferson's death, for example, one of his devoted followers attempted to institute compulsory military training at the new University of Virginia—purportedly in compliance with Jefferson's express wish.[17]

Predictably, the Republican ascendancy brought removal of Federalists from many militia positions, as the Virginia gentry purged the militia's ranks of Federalist "aristocrats." Giles's, not the public Jefferson's, attitude predominated here. Some units even took on partisan names, such as "Richmond Republican Blues."[18] Captain Robert Anderson of Williamsburg, a Federalist, found himself unable to obtain an officer's position in the state military.[19] Finally, he learned that another resident of the area had circulated an account of Anderson's having asserted that in case of war with England, Federalists would know who their friends were. A Federalist could not be a good Virginian, so far as Republicans were concerned. Soon, this attitude would be brought to bear on Republican dissenters, too. Republicans had envisioned a community of like-minded men similar to the one that had governed colonial Virginia, but their ascension engendered a climate of political retribution.

John Taylor of Caroline spoke for a minority faction of Republicans when he urged Jefferson to more extreme measures in 1798, but he was not a solitary figure. After only a few months of what would prove to be a twenty-four-year-long Virginia Republican ascendancy in the federal government, complaints echoing Taylor's resounded in Virginia politics. As Edmund Randolph had lamented to George Washington a decade earlier,[20] Taylor's views had wide currency.

Taylor was orphaned early in childhood. On the other hand, he was fortunate to have as a maternal uncle the prominent politician and judge Edmund Pendleton, President of the Revolutionary Committee of Safety, the Virginia Convention of 1776, and the Virginia Ratification Convention of 1788. Pendleton was persuaded to support ratification in Richmond, recall, only by the assurances of Edmund Randolph and George Nicholas that the new union was to be one of strictly limited powers, those that were "expressly" granted.

Those assurances, as we have seen, soon proved controversial. Alexander Hamilton, for one, certainly did not feel bound by them. Like Taylor, Pendleton concluded in the 1790s that amendments to the federal charter were necessary. The amendments Pendleton desired, under the title "The Danger Not Over," made their appearance in 1801. Posing as a statesman too old to be motivated by ambition, Pendleton urged his compatriots to make the proper use of their recent victory, which otherwise would amount to naught.[21]

Virginians must not be lulled into complacency by Jefferson's evident trustworthiness, Pendleton counseled, for the national charter itself was in need of accurate reinterpretation in some regards, of amendment in others. "The rare event of such a character at the head of a nation," Pendleton wrote, "imposes on Us the sacred duty of seizing the propitious opportunity, to do all in our power to perpetuate that happiness: as to that species of confidence, which would extinguish free enquiry and popular watchfulness, it is never desired by *patriotism*, nor ought to be yielded by *freeman*." Jefferson, and thus all the Virginians in the new government, were on notice: Virginians would remain vigilant in sniffing out incipient tyranny.

After recapitulating many of the Republican complaints of the 1790s, particularly that the line between federal and state power had not been drawn with adequate clarity, Pendleton noted that "Many of these objections were foreseen, when the constitution was ratified, by those who voted for its adoption; but waved [sic] then, because of the vast importance of the union, which a rejection might have placed in hazard." (This had been Edmund Randolph's position in the summer of 1788.) It had been hoped, Pendleton added, that the constitution would be amended as its faults became evident, but the 1790s showed that bad administrators could exploit its shortcomings to bad ends, "and that even the most valuable parts of the constitution may be evaded or violated."

Pendleton would have barred presidents from serving consecutive terms and given their power to appoint judges, as in the Virginia constitution, to the Legislative Branch. He would have reassigned the Senate's executive powers and either shortened senators' terms or subjected them to recall. Judges would have been removable by petition of both legislative houses, as in England, and both they and congressmen would have been made ineligible for appointment to new offices for some set period after they left office.

Pendleton held the abuse of public credit to be one of the leading problems of the 1790s, and he suggested that this problem must be addressed. Also directly in response to one of the controversies of the Federalist era, Pendleton would have required approval by both houses of Congress for any treaty regarding war and peace or expenditure of money. A further response to Federalist "abuses" could be found in Pendleton's proposed amendment requiring clearer specification of Congress's powers, declaring that the English common law was no part of the federal law, and prohibiting subterfuges such as circumvention of the constitution's tight restriction on treason law via use of words such as "sedition." Pendleton also proposed "marking out with more precision, the distinct powers of the *General* and *State* Governments."

"The Danger Not Over" displays collaboration, or at least very close sympathy of political thought, between Pendleton and Taylor. The amendments Pendleton suggested would have incorporated into the federal charter precisely the types of changes Taylor had urged on Jefferson during the Federalist era. All the Federalist measures Taylor had vociferated against as laden with consolidationist danger to Virginia republicanism would have been rendered nugatory by amendments on Pendleton's wish list.

Omission to act on these and related concerns led many of the ablest Republicans to desert their old chieftain. In the end, disgruntled "Old Republicans" waged what they knew would be fruitless political warfare for principle's sake on Thomas Jefferson's hand-picked successor, the supposed Republican (who seemed suspiciously sympathetic to Federalism) James Madison. Taylor essentially approved of the breakaway "Tertium Quids'" schism, if not of their tactics.[22]

The factors precipitating the so-called "Quid Schism" in Congress have been adequately described elsewhere. Suffice it to say here that disagreements between Republicans led by Jefferson's House floor leader, John Randolph of Roanoke, on one hand and the Jefferson administration (particularly, the Quids suspected, Madison), on the other, led the Tertium Quids to bolt the party they had recently helped lead. The Tertium Quids' was a backward-looking schism predicated on the notion that the Republican Party in power should act as the

Republican Party in opposition had. Within a short time, Randolph's inveterate opposition to Jefferson struck many even of his sympathizers as simply a personal spat, and his influence in Congress dwindled. Matters were different in Virginia. Unlike Randolph, most of the disaffected in the Old Dominion remained devoted to the notions that Virginia Republicans ought to be of one mind and that such consensus was attainable. John Taylor certainly did.

In his theoretical writings of the 1790s, particularly in *A Definition of Parties*, Taylor placed blame for the divisions in American political life on selfish plutocrats heedless of the common good. Taylor believed that all wealth came from the soil. Banks were no more than private taxation for the good of a few, their shareholders' profits direct transfers from the public, and the only good money was specie; bank paper smacked of favoritism, of government-granted monopoly and the legal privileges enjoyed by the English aristocracy.[23]

During a political career that today would strike us as bizarre, Taylor served three stints in the House of Delegates and three in the United States Senate, from which he always voluntarily beat a hasty retreat. He truly believed that the life of a farmer was superior to that of a politician. In an account of the life and career of his late father-in-law and fellow Caroline County native, onetime congressman John Penn, Taylor laid encomia at an "arator's" feet.[24] Penn, he said, came to his country's defense in time of war. Despite the cost to his estate, he did all he could in the cause of the Revolution, though he loved his farm the best. Penn never took advantage of his public station to put the public's money into his own pockets. Such men as Penn might be less beloved than others, Taylor noted, but that did not make them less useful.[25]

With such a belief in the primacy of agrarian life and its clear moral supremacy, Taylor easily arrived at the conclusion that right-minded men should share similar, if not identical, political views. Disagreement was a sign that something was amiss in American politics. (Taylor's books dealt almost exclusively with American politics, but, in the manner of Jefferson in *A Summary View of the Rights of British America*, he seems to have seen America as simply Virginia writ large. While expressing no sectional antipathy, even the opposite of it, Taylor flattened America out conceptually into a large terrain dotted by well-cultivated fields tended by capable slave owners living lives of well-regulated equality. Each freeman was a productive member of society: a farmer.[26]) The developing cleavage in Virginia's Republican elite played on Taylor's mind. In a remarkable exchange of letters with Wilson Cary Nicholas, who remained inside the Jeffersonian tent, Taylor made clear what his worries were and what he hoped Virginia, both within its borders and in control of the general government, would be.[27] The Taylor-Nicholas correspondence began, ominously enough, with Taylor granting the chronically indebted Nicholas's request for more time to make a loan payment. Then, Taylor launched right into a reiteration of Pendleton's arguments in "The Danger Not Over."[28]

Taylor, who knew that Nicholas had Jefferson's ear, noted the rumors that Jefferson was considering serving only two terms as president. Jefferson evidently hoped that such a self-limitation, in combination with Washington's example, would "set an useful fashion of rotation." Taylor found this thesis completely untenable. No "fashion" would bind a usurper, he insisted. Only a good president like Thomas Jefferson would follow a precedent of self-abnegation. Jefferson, Taylor insisted, must seek a constitutional amendment limiting presidents to two terms. Taylor regarded it as a great failing on the Republicans' part that they had not pursued the course Pendleton had prescribed. Jefferson's intention to retire from office before a term limitation was added to the constitution seemed a blithe frittering away of the opportunity provided by the Revolution of 1800.

Taylor claimed to find the upcoming succession contest between James Madison and James Monroe distasteful. In early 1806, he wrote Nicholas, "Plots, intrigues, and combinations are spoken of." Joint efforts between Federalists and Republicans abounded. (Madison, some Republicans lamented, had kept Federalists in some of the top State Department offices, while Monroe evidently intended to pursue Federalist backing. The type of Quid-Federalist alliance Monroe supposedly sought had already led to the election in 1805 of a governor, William H. Cabell, who was not a mainline Jeffersonian.) "As to politics," Taylor wrote, "I believe I have done with them." This "spectacle of my friends, or republicans, dividing among themselves" had disabused him of the notion that the contest concerned "principles and not men."[29]

Two months later, evidently spurred by the many negative reports he had heard of Madison's principles,[30] Taylor's reevaluation of the situation had commenced. "I begin to think that Mr. Madison's political opinions and my own, are hostile to each other." Taylor did not deign to set his own opinion above Madison's, however. He held that all Republicans usually should agree, and the one who disagreed ought to seek correction in the well-considered positions of other right-minded men. Having pursued that course, Taylor concluded that James Madison differed from "the great body of republicans." "It is in the whole party," he assured Nicholas, "and not in myself, that I have more confidence than I have in Mr. Madison."

Not only had Madison shown himself to be at best neutral between Federalists and Republicans in hiring Alexander Hamilton's former private secretary to serve him in the same capacity in the State Department, but Taylor blamed "Madison's system of doing nothing" for the omission to amend the constitution. "I really believe it is owing to him, that all Mr. Jefferson's great principles not to be found in our policy, are to die with him, and perhaps to be thus lost for ever." Taylor held that the amendments he desired had been the true goal of the Revolution of 1800 and that their adoption would amount to "the attainment of Mr. Jefferson's principles."

Soon enough, Taylor became completely convinced that Madison was a traitor in the Republicans' midst.[31] "I am at this time reading the book called the federalist," he informed Nicholas, "and really several passages occur, of which I should be glad to hear an explanation." His reading of *The Federalist*, necessarily without the aid of a list of the numbers written by each of the three authors (thus without any sure way of distinguishing the essays written by Madison from those written by Alexander Hamilton and John Jay), seemed to make clear why Madison opposed the amendments Taylor, Pendleton, and, as Taylor well knew, the majority in the Richmond Ratifying Convention held necessary: he had a view of the federal government's proper role and structure different from the Republican norm.

Taylor claimed to admire James Madison as a man, but in response to Nicholas's efforts to dissuade him, he disclosed that the prospect of defeat would not prevent him from doing his republican duty by opposing Madison's presidential aspirations. Such opposition was "the duty of a free citizen," and "even an unsuccessful opposition, may operate as a check or an alarm." Madison was too much the Federalist, he said, adding that, "By federalism, I mean the reverse of what the word implies." Real "federalism is an union of distinct states, with a portion of power reserved, sufficient to restrain the power conceded to the union."

Besides this point of theory, Taylor believed that Madison's generalized opposition to constitutional amendments was mistaken, too. Taylor said

> that changes in constitutions, are the only means of keeping a government unchanged. The human mind is unable to foresee its own devices, or to provide against future evasion. A code of laws to restrain these, never to be amended or augmented, would presently insuffice for civil order. Can it then be possible for a constitution to preserve political order, without amendment or augmentation? If the wisest legislature is unable to provide against the devices and evasions of an ignorant individual, whose means are narrow, for a single year, can it foresee & provide against the devices & evasions of a skilful government, whose means are spacious, forever?

Taylor went on to list the various Federalist policies of the 1790s to which the Republicans had objected so strenuously, then asked whether such policies might not do permanent damage to the regime. If not, he asked, why had the Republicans complained of them? If so, "why no amendments?" James Monroe agreed with Taylor, and that was why Monroe had Taylor's support for president. Taylor would happily submit to attempts to change his impression of Madison. Nearly any step to prevent Republican schism was appropriate, as Taylor saw it.[32]

Nicholas's answer to these ruminations displayed a certain blindness to the stultifying nature of the Republican political and social dominance in Virginia, which in the first third of the nineteenth century included control of economic plums such as bank presidencies and canal companies, as well as traditional political patronage.[33] He had long suspected that the minority's motives were other than laudable, Nicholas confided. (When Nicholas used the word "minority," he referred to the schismatic Republicans, not to Virginia's few Federalists.) While Taylor believed that unanimity of views could be achieved only after adoption of constitutional reforms, Nicholas understood the situation differently. "I have no idea that an administration, or that an individual is to be denounced because of a variance of opinion upon questions of mere policy." Madison, he implied, differed from his schismatic brethren only on such questions, not on the basic issues dividing Republicans from Federalists. "I have long seen & lamented a spirit of intolerance that prevails in this country [Virginia]. It will I fear be our ruin." The Republican minority's grievances were evanescent, Nicholas implied, and it was the minority, not the Republican majority, that was politically vengeful.

By the time of the election, Taylor had become completely exasperated with Madison's influence over Jefferson. Like the Russian peasants who went to the Gulag insisting that all would be well "if only Stalin knew," Taylor remained a devoted follower of Thomas Jefferson by blaming every untoward act of the federal administration on the secretary of state. In a letter to Madison, Taylor asked, "Does Thomas Jefferson think an army of 32,000 men, less dangerous than an English invasion [?] Does he think our carrying trade, beneficial to a few capitalists only, a sufficient recompense for ingrafting a perpetual funding system in our policy?" Taylor believed the answers to these questions to be "no," and Madison, the supposed formulator of Jefferson's military policy, bore the brunt of his frustration.[34]

While Taylor interpreted coziness with Federalists, or insufficient shunning of them coupled with adoption or perpetuation of Federalist measures, as Federalism itself, ex-Federalist Nicholas was prone to accept a broader array of policy options as legitimately Republican. Taylor took strong exception to Nicholas's argument. The chief source of the Republican schism, Taylor insisted, was that good Republicans had discerned Madison's Federalist leanings. To divide the Republican party by driving out the Quids, then "replac[e] them with monarchists," struck Taylor as "dream and theory."

Nicholas confided to Taylor that he, too, favored several amendments.[35] Nicholas must have been familiar with "The Danger Not Over," for his program resembled Pendleton's. He agreed with Taylor that faction was a very serious problem, but then went so far as to say that "war, armies, and debt, are not more deadly foes to liberty than factions." Taylor certainly disagreed. Yet, Nicholas's desperate desire to eliminate the Monroe coterie's challenge to Madison in 1808 mirrored Taylor's own yearning. Unlike Nicholas, however, Taylor saw systemic causes at work. Before the end of 1810, Taylor wrote Monroe to complain about Madison's, thus Jefferson's, compromise with Federalism. "It was this project which divided the republican party by changing its principles from real to nominal," he insisted.[36]

Taylor also held that while factions were desirable in despotic states, where they often conduced to liberty, they should be avoided in republics, where their tendency was to "slavery." Still, the fact that factions could have ill effects did not indicate to Taylor that they need always be suppressed.[37] New York's De Witt Clinton, then a popular party leader, was not the cause of faction in that state; if he lived in Virginia, he could not raise a faction, while his passing from the scene would not end factionalism in New York. The baubles of office, plentiful in New York, led to party contests. Dissension had a moral cause: "find it—remove it—the effect ceases." Virginia's state politics had very little of faction about them, Taylor noted, and the cause of Virginia's placidity lay in its well-constructed government. "Scattering patronage as in Virginia" would eliminate faction in New York; similar systemic remedies would still roiling divisions over federal matters, as well. Taylor offered to mediate between the main party and the schismatics. He solicited arguments from Nicholas "to persuade Monroe to desist." Taylor would try to dissuade him from running for president.[38]

Taylor wound up his three years' correspondence with Nicholas with a lecture on the corruption of the main body of Republicans. Nicholas, as Taylor understood matters, had fallen prey to temptation: he had given some of the content of one of Taylor's private letters to Thomas Ritchie, editor of the *Richmond Enquirer*. "Two politicians," Taylor wrote, "can seldom remain friends, if either is very zealous about the disposition of civil benifice, and the other happens to disagree with him, any more than two religious sects, if either wants church livings. And he that has least zeal, will commonly meet with most persecution." Since Nicholas had chosen to ignore their friendship, Taylor demanded immediate repayment of his loan. Where once their letters had been filled with amity, he signed off, "Yr. obt. Sert. John Taylor."[39]

Nicholas, as Taylor understood matters, had violated the Virginia code. One did not sic a toady on one's fellow members of the Republican elite, even obliquely. The analogy of Nicholas's behavior to that of a parson hoping for state support was truly a grievous insult in the context of Republican ideology. To cap matters, Taylor effectively put himself in the category of the victims of the Inquisition, and the demand that Nicholas repay his loan reminded the latter that he actually was in the position of one seeking to make a living by holding office. Taylor implied that Nicholas and his allies were persecuting him from unrepublican motives. The serpent in the garden had spoken sweetly to the mainline Republicans, not to the schismatics.

Taylor responded to Ritchie's criticism of him in what was to be the first of several letters rebuking the newspaperman and further developing Taylor's view of the proper comportment of the Virginia Republican. In his exchange with Nicholas, Taylor had undertaken to justify a conscientious Republican's temporary refusal to participate in politics; in his letters to Ritchie, he elaborated his beliefs about the proper tone of a republican polity.[40]

In ancient Rome, Taylor instructed Ritchie, attachment to individuals in place of principles foreshadowed the end of the republic.[41] In Virginia, a similar trend was reinforced by newspapers. "An adherence to men, is often disloyalty to principles," Taylor taught, "and the ambuscades of revolution, are constantly laid behind professions of patriotism." As Taylor pointed out, Rome only fell into tyranny when popular opposition to government measures became impossible. Ritchie's failure to understand this argument might be explained by the fact that "a man's interest often . . . blinds him to the public good, as in the cases of office holders, office hunters, and whippers in of party for pay."[42]

Taylor knew that the reference to Roman history would carry powerful persuasive force among other members of the Virginia elite, who were steeped in Greek and, particularly, Roman history almost from the cradle.[43] Dislike of party organization, suspicion of it as inherently antipatriotic and unprincipled, also formed a staple of Virginians' thinking in the nineteenth century's first decade. Taylor's argument with Ritchie was intended, then, both to underscore the social implications of the difference between his politics and Ritchie's and to remind other prominent Virginians that principle must come before men in the Old Dominion.

For Taylor, "Little of principle; much of party; adulation and invective, are the means which transform a genuine loyalty for liberty, into a spurious loyalty for men; and the degradation by which the human mind descends from a capacity for freedom, to a fitness for slavery." Ritchie's attempt to attach "odium to an honest difference of opinion," to besmirch Taylor simply because he happened to disagree with Madison, ignored the importance of principle. Taylor preferred a more reflective, philosophical politics; Ritchie's rhetoric was mere invective, intended more to inflame unthinking (common) Virginians against one another than to rouse the educated to love of principle. Ritchie was to be the master of a new, more democratic day in Virginia, at the head of a newspaper whose political influence was only beginning to be established. His political influence would reach its apex only in the days after Virginia identity was overwhelmed (largely in accord with Ritchie's wishes) by the imperatives of federal politics.[44]

Taylor's reading of the Roman classics, shapers of his political and economic views, dominated his social and moral positions, as well. In his mind, he was the perfect exemplar of the revolutionary Virginia aristocrat, and the Virginia of his imagination teemed with disinterested patriots possessed of finely honed intellects. Republican history, he instructed Ritchie, showed that social currents could exercise powerful control over men's characters. If party flattery prevailed, men whose capacities might make them able, selfless, republican leaders tended to become demagogues. Reservation of social rewards for those who acted in pursuit of "the public good" might make the same men patriots. Indiscriminate castigation of opponents, then, threatened republicanism. Those who acted self-interestedly should be castigated, but not men who arrived patriotically at conclusions different from one's own.

Taylor saw devious plotting in the general government's omissions as readily as in its acts. After Madison secured election in 1808, defeating the Federalists easily in the country at large and Monroe easily in Virginia, Taylor perceived threats to liberty in the new president's inaugural address. To Ritchie, Taylor wrote that then-Rep. Madison's advocacy of protectionism in Congress in 1793 had been his worst act, his recantation of the principle in the General Assembly's Report of 1800 a hopeful indicator.[45] Now, Taylor saw that Madison proposed "*authorized* encouragements to agriculture, manufactures, and education," and he noted that this implied either that Madison had concocted a novel way of reading the Constitution or that he advocated a new, "dangerous" delegation of power to the federal government. As Madison had asserted in 1800, using tariffs to fund such schemes must lead to "consolidation and monarchy."

Taylor held that Virginia's very essence was threatened by Madison's project. Protective tariffs reallocated labor from its current occupations to those government deemed more desirable. The author of *Arator* ("Farmer") could not abide the notion that Virginia husbandmen should be shuffled off their farms and into other occupations. He could not believe that the states, fonts of all federal power in his conception, had ever meant to delegate authority to undertake such projects to the general government.

For Taylor, the Republican/Federalist distinction was one between a theory of divided power (the Republican) and a theory of checks and balances (the Federalist). Giving government power to decide what economic activities citizens should pursue was directly contrary to the "principle of dividing power" by giving only limited parcels to particular officers and levels of government and holding most authority to be retained by the people. In other words, since it did not reflect the Republican version of constitutionalism, Madison's proposal smacked of Federalism. (Taylor contrasted Madison to Hamilton, who at least had endeavored to spread the tax burden evenly across the whole society.) True "federalism," Taylor's "divided power," could not long survive measures such as Madison advocated.[46]

According to Taylor, Ritchie's failure to see that Madison's proposal was the most dangerous type of threat to republicanism in America was unsurprising, for men tended to rationalize the misdeeds of their own parties. A "succession of such precedents" by a string of parties, whether those parties were bent on subversion or simply confident in their leaders, "will destroy our liberty and happiness 'by the destruction of all the limits prescribed to the power of the general government by the constitution.'" In Taylor's understanding, republicanism, "founded in moral rectitude," entailed opposition even of the most politically self-destructive kind to phenomena such as the Madison ascendancy.[47]

"May all your dreams come true," the Chinese curse says, and Taylor's political dreams had come true with the Revolution of 1800. By 1809, feeling the lash of the Republican press and pining for the adoption of his favorite measures, Taylor must certainly have understood that success could be surprisingly unsatisfying. His arguments may have been cogent, but they did not win the sympathy of Virginia's leading Republican newspaper. He had to publish his responses to Ritchie's scathing attacks in a competing paper with far inferior circulation.

Madison's supporters hoped that their victory in 1808 would stifle dissent within the Republican camp, but it did not. Rumors flew, men took offense, political campaigns were waged, and the *Enquirer* attacked the dissidents. All was not peaceful in Jefferson's polity, despite Jefferson's, Taylor's, Cabell's, and other Republicans' fond expectations.[48]

Perhaps consensus politics were impossible in Jeffersonian Virginia. After all, the harmonious old House of Burgesses had never found itself divided by serious religious, ethnic, or economic cleavages, let alone foreign policy differences resulting from the Napoleonic Wars. Early republican Virginians' formative experience lay largely in the Revolution and in the old conditions of colonial and Revolutionary politics. They kept the template of the old politics in the backs of their minds, and when they could, Virginia politicians of the Virginia Dynasty years tried to replicate old conditions; John Taylor was not alone in preferring an aristocratic political culture, as our discussion of the Richmond Ratification Convention demonstrated. Virginians' economic views also reinforced the notion that consensus was natural. All recognized, however, that the main element of the old politics, a landed aristocracy, was missing. Much of the reform impulse's energy in Virginia politics in the years after 1801 was devoted to replicating that old aristocracy, whose foundation had been primogeniture and entail, in republican guise. Unfortunately for the reformers, their fellow Virginians had no intention of forsaking their long-standing hostility to taxation in the name of reconstituting an elite. Low levels of taxation beckoned them far more alluringly than did harmonious politics.

Following the decision to dissolve the landed aristocracy, many leading Virginians soon realized that its old functions must be performed by a new ruling elite, perforce of a new type. John Tyler, Sr. and Jefferson both came to the conclusion that the political functions performed by the old aristocracy could be performed by a new one culled from Virginia's male citizens at large. This required establishment of a system of public schools. Tyler became an ardent, influential proponent of the idea, which Jefferson had first put forward as part of the revision of Virginia's laws undertaken during the Revolutionary decade.[49]

In 1807, the future president John Tyler, Jr. told John Tyler, Sr. that he was to give a Fourth of July address to his fellow students in the College of William and Mary. Soon-to-be-Governor Tyler responded, "Education is a good subject. Ignorance is the mother of superstition, whose offspring is slavery, which begets a tyranny in the end. See how Athens flourished in her literary age; also Rome. When the sciences were neglected, see in turn how degraded was the human character." Turning from ancient to modern history, Tyler repeated the standard Whig argument that the promulgation of laws in a language, Latin, that was not commonly spoken had aided the Normans in enslaving the Britons. General, popular understanding of the law was essential to the maintenance of a free state, the older Tyler insisted. Yet, Virginia stood in a poor position in the matter of education, "behind all the sister States."[50]

We do not know what Tyler, Jr.'s fellows thought of his presentation, but his father did not let the education issue die. He soon wrote to Governor William H. Cabell in the same vein. Nothing, he lamented, was being done in relation "to diffusion of knowledge on easy terms throughout the State." The cause of the Commonwealth's paralysis, Tyler guessed, was the "eternal war declared against Arts and Sciences," which grew out of "a determination to pay nothing by way of Taxes to ye support and encouragement of Education, the true and solid foundation of free government."[51]

On 4 December 1809, Governor John Tyler, Sr. carried his argument for state efforts in support of common schooling to the General Assembly. Keying his argument to his audience, Tyler resorted to the Jeffersonian argument that young men must be educated to lead their "country." Thirty years after independence was declared, he fumed, Virginia had not even a single new public school to show for itself. As a result, only the wealthy could afford to educate even one son "to serve his country, either in the field or in its councils."[52]

The matter of public education was of foremost importance, Governor Tyler cajoled the assemblymen, for only education could ensure the republican constitution's permanence. Yet, even the schools founded before independence received wholly inadequate funding. "In a rude and ignorant state of mind," he lectured a room full of men familiar with the history of Rome and Greece, the few dominated. Virtue must under gird free government. Government itself must inculcate virtue. Knowing that Virginians were congenitally opposed to taxation, Tyler reassured their representatives that an educated people would appreciate its principled rulers. Rather than leaving the state for instruction, only to return with "manners not congenial with republican simplicity," young men could be drawn to a reformed College of William and Mary.[53]

Soon after Thomas Jefferson retired from the Presidency, he received a letter in which Governor Tyler explained the rationale behind his education initiative.[54] Tyler said he understood why Jefferson found the prospect of retirement from public life appealing; after all, malice and party spirit abounded. Yet, "I could not help indulging a wish of seeing you once more on the floor of the Virginia Assembly." Drawing Jefferson's memory back to the days when they both admired the participants in the pre-Revolutionary government, Tyler lamented that there was "nothing now like the order and decorum" that had marked the old elite's dominance of the General Assembly. More men now had "knowledge of government," but none approached "the great men of our Revolution." "Now, there are more streams, but then there were more great rivers, and"—the main point—"this arises from the bad mode of education which prevails."

Virginia's governor was disenchanted with the entire harvest of the republican orchard. He saw one promising possibility, however: the adoption of an education program along the lines of that proposed, three decades earlier, by Jefferson. Power's tendency to abuse, the governor reminded Jefferson, had made Tyler an opponent of ratification in the Richmond Convention of 1788. Subsequent events had borne out his dire prognostications. Strong government had yielded "less political happiness." Virginia was distinguished in the old days, Tyler recalled wistfully, by "friendship and hospitality" not to be found anywhere else. Now, he saw "[t]he peace of society broken up." Tyler had expected better from the Revolution. He entertained doubts that it had been worthwhile. He hoped Jefferson would forward an education blueprint for him to propose, even though the skinflints in the General Assembly would surely reject it.

In his final annual address, Tyler told the legislature that commerce made men "citizens of the world—the worst citizens in the world." It begat contempt for American products and foreign interference in America's domestic policy. Fortunately, Tyler held, an easy solution to the moral problem of commerce suggested itself: interruption of foreign trade. Fourteen years before Henry Clay introduced his "American System," Tyler proposed that the Old Dominion develop its domestic market with the aim of reducing its foreign dependence. To undertake such a system of public policy would require a general diffusion of knowledge among, and high statesmanship from, officeholders. Since Virginia no longer had "a *breed* of such great men as have filled the chair of state," such a breed must be cultivated. Infusion of resources into government schooling was the way. Tyler's efforts resulted in the creation of the Literary Fund in February 1810. Despite whatever hopes the Fund's creators may have had, it proved inadequate to any purpose. John Tyler left the governorship in January 1811, and his interest in spurring the Commonwealth to new governmental exertions in the field of education went with him. However, when Jefferson's friend, neighbor, and one-time political lieutenant (not to mention John Taylor's former correspondent) Wilson Cary Nicholas became governor in 1814, an education plan once again formed a component of the leading Virginia politician's vision.[55]

In his second term as president, Jefferson had advocated a coordinated economic effort including educational and infrastructure measures.[56] His preconditions, a budgetary surplus and a constitutional amendment authorizing such initiatives, were not issues in Virginia, where the state constitution of 1776 gave the General Assembly general legislative power. If Jefferson had failed to obtain his desires from Congress, Jeffersonians might succeed in Richmond.

Writing to Joseph C. Cabell, who would be instrumental in the enactment of part of Jefferson's program, Jefferson said in 1815 that the public education system's purpose was to prepare the "natural aristocracy . . . for the care of the public concerns." He believed, along with John Tyler, Sr., that some way must be found to approximate, consistently with republicanism, the colonial aristocracy. Instead of birth and classical education, Jefferson would found his "natural" aristocracy of quasi-plebeian origins on the type of cultivation he judged appropriate. Not birth, but scholastic success, would identify the Virginia elite.[57]

Nicholas concurred. As governor from December 1814 to December 1816, he was in a position to exploit the glow of triumph following the War of 1812. (Whether the war was actually an American victory affected political events far less than the perception of it as a triumph.) Governor Nicholas's program was an integrated initiative to restore Virginia's economic prosperity. With the interest on Virginia's wartime loans to the federal government, Nicholas would pursue very ambitious goals. First, he wanted Jeffersonian education reform. The reform of agriculture via widespread adoption of scientific methods beckoned as a second potential practical application of improved education. Besides making efforts in those areas, Nicholas hoped for Virginia to enjoy the benefits of vastly improved road and canal transportation and the economic impetus of an improved, expanded banking system.[58]

Like Tyler's before it, Nicholas's effort failed, but he, John H. Cocke, and state senator Joseph C. Cabell did succeed in putting the state government's support behind Central College in Albemarle County. Nicholas's reiteration of Jefferson's three-tiered scheme withered on the vine much as the original version had in the 1780s. The Literary Fund's directors claimed to have dedicated Virginia to the "great cause of literature and science," but the General Assembly, perhaps out of self-interest, inverted Nicholas's and the Literary Fund directors' priorities by deciding to concentrate on postsecondary, rather than on primary and secondary, education.

The explanation given by reformers in his day for the decidedly mixed success of Jefferson's education proposal was that of John Tyler, Sr.: the typical Virginia voter was simply too averse to taxation to support it. Other factors were at work, too. John Randolph of Roanoke, who footed the bills for several impoverished wards, was joined by western reformer Charles Mercer and College of William and Mary President John Augustine Smith in calling government schooling unjust. Those who could afford it already paid for their own children's schooling, Randolph argued; if one man's property could be expropriated for another man's good, the form of private property might remain, but the substance had been abolished.[59]

Mercer, a leading Western education proponent, may perhaps have spoken "with forked tongue." He presented an education bill of his own in the General Assembly in January 1817, but although it passed the House, the Senate rejected it. A second attempt met the same fate, despite great Western enthusiasm. Mercer and his Western allies blamed his bill's defeat on the apportionment of the Senate, in which the West was underrepresented. Mercer's complaints about Eastern and Piedmont proposals must have been impelled by objections that the West was not to receive all the attention it deserved, not by generalized objection to public education.[60]

After Mercer's defeats, Jefferson had friends submit another proposal. In September and December 1817, it met with rejection. Sectional interests—notably, Tidewater defensiveness about the future of the College of William and Mary—combined with sectarian considerations (William and Mary, like the Tidewater generally, was dominated by Episcopalians, while Jefferson's planned inland university presumably would not be). When the bill to create the University of Virginia passed, Mercer, who had wanted it to be located in the West and divorced from the influence of Thomas Jefferson, held his loss on those points unfortunate and the decision to stress advanced rather than elementary education unwise. Besides leaving the University of Virginia within the Jeffersonian ambit, the General Assembly washed its hands of regulations regarding teachers, students, and facilities.[61]

Chapter 5

Beginning on 1 January 1818, the *Richmond Enquirer* published what was alternately a sarcastic and a hysterical, a myopic and an incisive criticism of Jefferson's education proposal written by "A Constituent," Jefferson's onetime close political associate, William Branch Giles. In seven closely packed editorials, each covering between three and five newspaper columns in the *Richmond Enquirer*'s standard microscopic type, Giles leveled every conceivable criticism against Jefferson's scheme. While Jefferson, Tyler, Nicholas, and Cabell looked to their education plan to ensure that the republican society created in Virginia by the revolutionary generation would endure, Giles warned that the education plan and the tactics and attitudes of its supporters were grave threats to republicanism.

In response to a recently publicized letter from President James Monroe expressing support for Jefferson's scheme, Giles noted that faith in its advocates outweighed consideration of the education plan's merits in the minds of many.[62] Monroe admitted that he had never read the bill in its entirety, yet the knowledge that Jefferson endorsed it induced him to do so, too. Giles asked whether Virginians at large ought not to draw the opposite inference: that if Jefferson supported such a plan, it likely was impractical. Was not Jefferson's plan exactly the kind of dreamy project on which a philosopher whose life was abstracted from practical considerations would be likely to launch? Giles admitted that to dare to say such a thing was to court conviction of "the sins of heresy & schism, and the consequent excommunication, from the only true, catholic, and apostolic church of fashionable politics." His comparison of the Jeffersonians' faith to the Nicene Creed underscored Giles's assertion that republicans should abandon faith in men in favor of calm reason.

Giles objected to the idea that the people should be consulted before a measure such as Jefferson's education proposal was considered in the legislature. Here was the nub of Giles's disagreement with Jefferson: Giles assumed the essential impossibility that the people at large could be so well informed as to deserve deference from their representatives. In that sense, his views by 1818 were rather closer to those propounded by Edmund Burke in the 1790s than to those of George Mason in the 1770s.[63]

"A Constituent" rattled off a lengthy list of the Jefferson plan's "defects."[64] Perhaps most importantly in Giles's estimation, the new education scheme would convert private education rights and duties into public ones. Not only did advocates of the Jefferson scheme expect the people's elected representatives to yield up their judgement in the face of gaudy names, and not only did they hope to whip up popular sentiment (a tactic, in Giles's telling, that recalled the inauspicious example of direct democracy provided by classical Athens), but they hoped that men would yield up their duty to instruct their sons in the name of ... what?

Giles lamented the enormous discretion the Jefferson bill proposed to lodge in a new-fangled state "board of public instruction." Love of power was "the most universal, the most insinuating, the most uncontrollable, and the most mischievous" passion. Why, then, give this appointed board control of "the religious, moral, mathematical, literary, military, agricultural, mechanical, gymnastic, musical, and diversional instruction of the whole commonwealth?"

Turning to an area of concern that often marked his political reasoning, Giles considered the new education plan's unequal incidence. The governor wanted "to make the genius of youth *public property*, that it may be a *national benefit*." Yet, only the children of those not financially able to educate their children as they saw fit would see their sons thus conscripted.

To a Republican who had come to the political fore in the 1790s, as Giles had, the profusion of government offices contemplated by Jefferson's plan was one of its most galling elements.[65] A state board of education, local boards, regional academies, and so on amounted to over two thousand new "demi-corporations." Only the state board was to be responsible. Given the wide ambit of the educators' authority, their organization, and their dispersion across the Commonwealth, they must soon have great influence in the General Assembly.

Giles found much to deplore in the bill's provision for election of the various education officials by householders—people in mere possession of land. Freeholders—substantial owners of land—had always exercised the suffrage exclusively in Virginia, colonial and republican. Agitation against the Virginia constitution of 1776 had centered on the West's demands for Jeffersonian apportionment and suffrage changes, and Giles, the representative of a heavily planter-dominated county, opposed what he saw as an effort to insinuate householders into the governmental process. Once the most numerous cadre of government officials ("an hierarchy of incorporated pedagogues") was dominated by householders, the householders must come to dominate Virginia politics. How could two hundred state legislators resist the blandishments of ten thousand corporate functionaries? (In Giles's account of British history, householders there had always formed the Crown's party, while the wealthier freeholders had supported liberty.)

While he was on the constitutional point, Giles noted that the people and their constitution had never given the General Assembly power to transfer authority to a board of education. In fact, the people had never given the General Assembly itself such power. Echoing John Randolph of Roanoke, Giles demanded a justification of the plan to transfer some people's property to other people in the name of education; the next thing one knew, he predicted, property would be transferred from the rich more directly for the purpose of making the poor rich. The constitutional hermeneutic Jefferson (and Giles) had used against the Federalists in the 1790s now struck back at Jefferson's own dearest program with a vengeance. Giles did not notice that the Virginia constitution of 1776, unlike the federal Constitution of 1788, endowed the legislature with a general legislative power.

Giles also insisted that the Jefferson plan threatened a resuscitation of the colonial religious establishment.[66] Privatization of religion marked the outstanding innovation of the American Revolution, and Giles shuddered to think what must happen if, as he judged inevitable, the Board of Public Instruction came to be dominated by "religious men." Soon, its first qualification in hiring would be "conformity in religion." Since the same men who did the hiring would be in charge of devising curricula, human nature—the love of power—would complete the task. Sectarian strife's spirit had not been killed, Giles held, it only lay at rest. Giles pointed to the advances made by "camp meetings" and the "wild phrenzy which is often offered up as the worship of God" as bad omens. If the principle of disestablishment were overthrown, a brand of Protestantism objectionable to educated republicans might gain government's favor.

The budding education establishment's control over religious thought merely represented, in Giles's mind, the general phenomenon of its complete control over all that its charges thought, said, and did. Giles's was a Republican nightmare version of Plato's *Republic*, with young minds eagerly soaking in the indoctrination, malevolent or benevolent, of irresponsible functionaries. "A celebrated English politician has observed," he wrote, "that if the government would give him the exclusive privilege of dictating all the songs, which should be sung in any nation, he could overturn its government."[67] Such sway paled in comparison to the proposal to give a small board control of young Virginians' instruction in "religion, politics, philosophy, morals, and all the military, agricultural and mechanical arts."

Giles imagined that since all young men were to receive three years of schooling, the best few of those were to receive three additional years, and the best of those were to go to college for three years, Virginia's poor families would soon face a horrible situation. Boys with three years' education would be "half-made gentlemen," unfitted to be mechanics and yet not truly educated. "[A]ll the dunces and the vicious are to be returned to poor parents" after three years, and those parents would receive no compensation for the "irreparable loss" of three years' labor per son. What a boy could learn in three years, a smattering of "reading, writing and figures," was useless, and he would certainly be stripped of his disposition to labor, his sole support in life. His parents, on the other hand, must be pained at their inability to satisfy his newfound taste for learning, besides the new necessity to pay for his room and board during his three-year reprieve from productive work. A man with six boys, under the reformers' plan, would lose at least eighteen years' productive labor, and his compensation would be six idle ex-schoolboys.

Besides aristocratic assumptions about the potential of average Virginians, concern for the perpetuation of slavery also played a role in Giles's opposition to education reform. He blamed slavery for whites' growing aversion to labor. In the mechanical arts, the slaves' and free blacks' increasing prominence left whites increasingly unwilling to work. Conversion of all whites to "philosophers," Giles sneered, would only exacerbate the problem. Rather than this inducement to sloth, he preferred to offer poor whites what labor unions later provided: exclusion of black laborers from their trades.

Giles's opposition to Jefferson's scheme drew criticism. Thomas Ritchie, the editor of the *Richmond Enquirer*, took pains to note that the "A Constituent" series ran against the political views of his paper and that its publication was a courtesy to a distinguished Virginian. A letter to the editor accompanying the last number pointed out that a Petersburg paper had identified the author, and it castigated Giles for his acerbic commentary on the "philosopher" of Monticello. Yet, in Virginia's political class at large, the arguments about the sweep of government, the suffrage, and the potential establishment of religion must have been persuasive. The taxation question and the threat of a completely sedentary lower class of whites, backed by a warning about the potential economic clout of black mechanics, were probably convincing. The traditional subordination of most whites and an even greater proportion of blacks would not be jeopardized by adoption of expensive education reforms. Never in the Jeffersonian era did Virginia adopt an education scheme like Jefferson's; ironically, reconfigured versions of Jefferson's own antigovernment sensibilities carried the day instead.

Jefferson *did* live to see the establishment of his University of Virginia, but without the other two legs of his education tripod, it served mainly as a bulwark of the old gentry. The university represented only a partial vindication of the effort Jefferson had initiated a half-century before, but attainment of a greater portion of his goal proved simply impossible. Jefferson's personal influence, carefully husbanded through a lifetime of political activity, was spent in the difficult struggle to establish a secular republican university.[68]

The first half of the Virginia Dynasty period disappointed the leading avatars of Virginia Republicanism. The unhappiness these Virginians felt over the course of Virginia's republican experiment resulted in part from their utopian expectations. If a monarchical society was to be remade along republican lines, we may now conclude, disgruntlement was sure to set in along the way. Virginia Republicans' victory in 1800 did not produce the one-party consensus the vast majority had expected. Education reform efforts failed to restore the wonted social cohesion and substitute for the colonial ruling elite—partly because some judged Jefferson's education proposals un-Jeffersonian. If virtually every leading figure in Virginia's political life found the state of things unacceptable by 1815, most of them would be more discontented two decades later.

Notes

1. Philip Norborne Nicholas to Archibald Stuart, 17 February 1801, Archibald Stuart Papers, Virginia Historical Society.

2. For likely Virginia reaction to a Burr victory, *Ibid.*; for that and the scene in Williamsburg, Joseph Carrington Cabell to Colonel Nicholas Cabell, 5 March 1801, Cabell Family Papers, University of Virginia.

3. The following account is based on Joseph Carrington Cabell, "First thoughts of a speech delivered to the people of Amherst," March 1808, Cabell Family Papers, University of Virginia.

4. John Tyler, Sr., called the 1799 gubernatorial victory of Republican James Monroe that of "Truth over falsehood" and linked it to the victory of "Democracy over Tyranny all over the World." John Tyler to James Monroe, 27 December 1799, *The Letters and Times of the Tylers*, ed. Lyon G. Tyler (3 vols., 1884–1896; reprinted New York: Da Capo Press, 1970), 3: 13–14. William Branch Giles congratulated Jefferson on his 1801 election "to reestablish American principles." William Branch Giles to Thomas Jefferson, 16 March 1801, in Dice Robins Anderson, *William Branch Giles: A Study in the Politics of Virginia and the Nation from 1790 to 1830* (1914; reprinted Gloucester, Mass.: Peter Smith, 1965), 75–77, at 75.

5. Thomas Jefferson, First Inaugural Address, 4 March 1801, *The Works of Thomas Jefferson*, ed. Paul Leicester Ford (New York: G. P. Putnam's Sons, 1892–1899), 9: 193–200, at 195.

6. Thomas Jefferson to Benjamin Hawkins, 18 February 1803, *Ibid.*, 9: 445–49, at 446. Also see Thomas Jefferson to John Dickinson, 6 March 1801, *Ibid.*, 9: 201–2; Thomas Jefferson to James Monroe, 7 March 1801, *Ibid.*, 9: 202–205, at 203.

7. For the Rousseauean Jefferson, see Andrew Burstein, *The Inner Jefferson: Portrait of a Grieving Optimist* (Charlottesville and London: University Press of Virginia, 1995); and Richard K. Matthews, *The Radical Politics of Thomas Jefferson* (Lawrence: University Press of Kansas, 1984).

8. Mary A. Giunta, "The Public Life of William Branch Giles, Republican, 1790–1815" (Ph.D. dissertation, Catholic University of America, 1980), 43; Benjamin Watkins Leigh to [Joseph Carrington Cabell?], 7 August 1801, Cabell Family Papers, University of Virginia.

9. Mary A. Giunta, "The Public Life of William Branch Giles," 54–55.

10. *The Connecticut Courant*, 20 February 1805.

11. P. J. Staudenraus, *The African Colonization Movement, 1816–1865* (New York: Farrar, Straus and Giroux, 1980), 4; Douglas R. Egerton, *Gabriel's Rebellion: The Virginia Slave Conspiracies of 1800 & 1802* (Chapel Hill and London: University of North Carolina Press, 1993); Kevin R. C. Gutzman, "Lincoln as Jeffersonian: The Colonization Chimera," in *Lincoln Emancipated: The President and the Politics of Race*, ed. Brian Dirck (Northern Illinois University Press, 2006) (forthcoming).

12. For Jefferson's thought on blacks' place in America, see Peter Onuf, "'To Declare Them a Free and Independent People': Race, Slavery, and National Identity in Jefferson's Thought," *Journal of the Early Republic* 18 (1998): 1–46; and Kevin R. C. Gutzman, "Lincoln as Jeffersonian: The Colonization Chimera."

13. Thomas Jefferson to Rufus King, 13 July 1802, *The Works of Thomas Jefferson*, 9: 383–87; Thomas Jefferson to James Monroe, 24 November 1801, *Ibid.*, 9: 315–19.

14. Thomas Jefferson to James Madison, 2 June 1802, *Ibid.*, 9: 373–75.

15. Thomas Jefferson to Edward Coles, 25 August 1814, *Ibid.*, 11: 416–20, at 417, 419.

16. Philip Hamilton, "Revolutionary Principles and Family Loyalties: Slavery's Transformation in the St. George Tucker Household of Early National Virginia," *The William and Mary Quarterly*, 3d series, vol. 55 (1998), 531–56.

17. "Speech of Mr. [William Cabell] Rives, of Virginia, on Retrenchment and Reform: Delivered in the House of Representatives of the United States, on the 5th February, 1828." (Washington: Green and Jarvis, 1828), 18–19.

18. Muster Roll, Richmond Republican Blues, 31 October 1809, Ambler Family Papers, Virginia Historical Society.

19. Letterbooks of Robert Anderson, 1804–1807 and 1807–1813, Virginia Historical Society.

20. See chapter 4.

21. Edmund Pendleton, "The Danger Not Over," 5 October 1801, *The Letters and Papers of Edmund Pendleton*, ed. David John Mays (Charlottesville: University Press of Virginia, 1967), 2: 695–99.

22. Norman K. Risjord, *The Old Republicans: Southern Conservatism in the Age of Jefferson* (New York: Columbia University Press, 1965); Arthur M. Schlesinger, Jr., *The Age of Jackson* (Boston: Little, Brown, 1953), 18–29.

23. John Taylor, *A Definition of Parties: Or the Political Effects of the Paper System* (Philadelphia, 1794); John Taylor, *Tyranny Unmasked*, ed. F. Thornton Miller (1822; reprinted Indianapolis: Liberty Fund, 1992); John Taylor to ———, 25 November 1803, University of Virginia; John Taylor to Lucy P. Taylor, 2 February 1823, Virginia Historical Society.

24. John Taylor, "The Life of John Penn," University of Virginia.

25. Taylor's views were not typical of all schismatic Republicans. See the criticism of Taylor in John Randolph to John Taylor, 11 September 1807, John Randolph of Roanoke Papers, University of Virginia.

26. For lack of sectional antipathy, see John Taylor to Lucy P. Taylor, 22 February 1823, Virginia Historical Society; John Taylor, *Arator; Being a Series of Agricultural Essays, Practical and Political: In Sixty-Four Numbers*, ed. M. E. Bradford (1818; reprinted Indianapolis: Liberty Fund, 1977).

27. Virtually all of the Taylor-Nicholas letters are in the Randolph Family Papers ("Edgehill-Randolph Papers"), the Carter-Smith Papers, or the Wilson Cary Nicholas Papers at the University of Virginia. The correspondence is collected in David Nicholas Mayer, "Of Principles and Men: The Correspondence of John Taylor of Caroline with Wilson Cary Nicholas, 1804–1809" (M.A. thesis, University of Virginia, 1982).

28. John Taylor to Wilson Cary Nicholas, 4 April 1805, Edgehill-Randolph Papers, University of Virginia.

29. John Taylor to Wilson Cary Nicholas, 19 March 1806, Wilson Cary Nicholas Papers, University of Virginia. This became a theme of John Randolph's correspondence, too. John Randolph to Edward Booker, 10 January 1808, John Randolph Papers, University of Virginia; John Randolph to Micajah Woods, 5 June 1812, John Randolph Papers, University of Virginia.

30. John Taylor to Wilson Cary Nicholas, 19 March 1806, Wilson Cary Nicholas Papers, University of Virginia.

31. John Taylor to Wilson Cary Nicholas, 10 June 1806, Edgehill-Randolph Papers, University of Virginia. Taylor was not alone in doubting that a coauthor of *The Federalist* could be a good Jeffersonian at heart. "Conon to James Madison," *The [Richmond] Enquirer*, 18 March 1808. However, many Virginia Republicans doubtless agreed

with "Publicola" that support for Monroe was criticism of Jefferson. *Ibid.*, 11 March 1808.

32. John Taylor to Wilson Cary Nicholas, 22 August 1807, Edgehill-Randolph Papers, University of Virginia.

33. Wilson Cary Nicholas to John Taylor, 7 October 1807, Edgehill-Randolph Papers, University of Virginia; George Hay to Peter Carr, 25 June 1804, Virginia Historical Society.

34. John Taylor to James Madison, 15 January 1808, University of Virginia.

35. Wilson Cary Nicholas to John Taylor, 19 November 1807, Carter-Smith Papers, University of Virginia.

36. John Taylor to James Monroe, 26 October 1810, "Letters of John Taylor, of Caroline County, Virginia," ed. Wm. E. Dodd, *The John P. Branch Historical Papers of Randolph-Macon College* 2 (1908), 253–353, at 309–13.

37. John Taylor to Wilson Cary Nicholas, 5 February 1808, Edgehill-Randolph Papers, University of Virginia.

38. Taylor had thought a few months earlier that Monroe would not be run. Joseph Carrington Cabell to Isaac A. Coles, 16 November 1807, Cabell Family Papers, University of Virginia.

39. John Taylor to Wilson Cary Nicholas, 16 June 1809, Edgehill-Randolph Papers, University of Virginia. (Mayer mistranscribed this letter.) When Nicholas's death left his widow and children in very difficult financial straits, Taylor anonymously forwarded them a large monetary gift. John Taylor to Thomas Jefferson, 3 February 1821, "Letters of John Taylor of Caroline," ed. Hans Hammond, *Virginia Magazine of History and Biography* 52 (1944): 1–14, 121–34, at 131; John Taylor to Thomas Jefferson, 24 July 1821, *Ibid.* at 133–34.

40. John Taylor "A Pamphlet Containing a Series of Letters, Written by Colonel John Taylor, of Caroline, to Thomas Ritchie, Editor of the 'Enquirer'" (Richmond, 1809).

41. John Taylor to Thomas Ritchie, 24 March 1809, *Ibid.*, 12–15.

42. John Taylor to Thomas Ritchie, 7 April 1809, *Ibid.*, 32–38, at 33; John Taylor to Thomas Ritchie, 11 April 1809, *Ibid.*, 38–44.

43. Even elite Virginians who gained little else from their formal schooling generally left it with a firm grasp of Latin. John Randolph to Francis Walker Gilmer, 2 July 1825, John Randolph Papers, University of Virginia.

44. Charles H. Ambler, *Thomas Ritchie: A Study in Virginia Politics* (Richmond: Bell Book & Stationery, 1913); William G. Shade, *Democratizing the Old Dominion: Virginia and the Second Party System, 1824–1861* (Charlottesville and London: University Press of Virginia, 1996).

45. John Taylor to Thomas Ritchie, 30 March 1809, "A Pamphlet," 21–26.

46. *Ibid.* For divided power, see John Taylor to Thomas Ritchie, 27 March 1809, *Ibid.*, 26–31. Also see Andrew Lenner, "John Taylor and the Origins of American Federalism," *Journal of the Early Republic* 17 (1997), 399–423 (regarding Taylor's conception of federalism, not the origin of the American theory of federalism—for which see chapters 3 and 4 above, as well as Kevin R. C. Gutzman, "Edmund Randolph and Virginia Constitutionalism," *The Review of Politics* 66 (2004): 469–97). John Taylor to Thomas Ritchie, 30 March 1809, "A Pamphlet," 21–26.

47. John Taylor to Thomas Ritchie, 14 April 1809, *Ibid.*, 44–50.

48. Creed Taylor to William Murray, 22 February 1805, Creed Taylor Papers, University of Virginia; Peyton Randolph to Wilson Cary Nicholas, 13 November 1808, Edgehill-Randolph Papers, University of Virginia (hope that 1808 marked the termina-

tion of the Quid Schism); Creed Taylor to Benjamin Botts, 24 November 1812, Creed Taylor Papers, University of Virginia (concerning the need to find a Monroe man to contest the upcoming gubernatorial election against the Madison candidate because Madison men always stuck together); John Randolph to Charles Goldsborough, 7 August 1813, John Randolph Papers, University of Virginia ("seven years' unremitting calumny of my motives and character"); John Randolph to Charles Harris, 23 February 1814, John Randolph Papers, University of Virginia; John Randolph to Charles Harris, 23 February 1814, John Randolph Papers, University of Virginia (the *Richmond Enquirer*'s partisan stance).

49. It is somewhat ironic that Tyler, a devout opponent of the proposed federal constitution in the Richmond Ratification Convention, should a quarter-century later have come to agree with James Madison's appraisal of Virginia's post-1776 political leadership.

50. John Tyler, Jr., to John Tyler, Sr., 1 March 1807, *The Letters and Times of the Tylers*, 1: 202–203, at 203. For common acceptance of Tyler's idea that the law should be understood by all, see Gary L. McDowell, "The Language of Law and the Foundations of American Constitutionalism," *The William and Mary Quarterly*, 3d series, vol. 55 (1998), 375–98.

51. John Tyler to William H. Cabell, 10 February 1808, *The Letters and Times of the Tylers*, 3: 19–20.

52. Governor John Tyler, Education Address, 4 December 1809, *Ibid.*, 1: 237–41.

53. Tyler and Jefferson were not alone in believing that William and Mary should be reformed or abolished. Joseph Carrington Cabell to Isaac A. Coles, 16 March 1807, Cabell Family Papers, University of Virginia.

54. John Tyler to Thomas Jefferson, 12 May 1810, *The Letters and Times of the Tylers*, 1: 244–47.

55. Governor John Tyler, Annual Address, 3 December 1810, *Ibid.*, 1: 250–53. Tyler's views of commerce closely resembled the teachings of the ancients. *Cf.* Paul Rahe, *Republics, Ancient & Modern: Classical Republicanism and the American Revolution* (Chapel Hill and London: University of North Carolina Press, 1992), 80–104; Robert O. Woodburn, "An Historical Investigation of the Opposition to Jefferson's Educational Proposals in the Commonwealth of Virginia" (Ph.D. dissertation, American University, 1974), 91, 94.

56. Thomas Jefferson, Sixth Annual Message, 2 December 1806, *The Works of Thomas Jefferson*, 10: 302–20, at 317–18; Thomas Jefferson to Joel Barlow, 10 December 1807, *The Writings of Thomas Jefferson*, ed. Andrew A. Lipscomb (Washington: The Thomas Jefferson Memorial Association, 1905), 11: 400–401.

57. Thomas Jefferson to Joseph Carrington Cabell, 5 January 1815, *Ibid.*, 11: 446–50. Also see Douglas L. Wilson, "Jefferson and the Republic of Letters," in *Jeffersonian Legacies*, ed. Peter S. Onuf (Charlottesville: University Press of Virginia, 1993), 50–76.

58. Elinor Janet Weeder, "Wilson Cary Nicholas, Jefferson's Lieutenant" (M.A. thesis, University of Virginia, 1946), 105–6, 110, 112–15.

59. Robert O. Woodburn, "An Historical Investigation of the Opposition to Jefferson's Educational Proposals in the Commonwealth of Virginia," 117–19.

60. *Ibid.*, 97–101.

61. *Ibid.*, 102–3; for Tidewater defensiveness concerning William and Mary, see William Waller to George Blow, 2 February 1820, Blow Family Papers, Virginia Historical Society; Robert O. Woodburn, "An Historical Investigation of the Opposition to Jefferson's Educational Proposals in the Commonwealth of Virginia," 103. Mercer would

have been more unhappy if he had known that Jefferson and his acolytes intended to include indoctrination in their party's politics in the new University's curriculum. James Madison to Thomas Jefferson, 8 February 1825, *The Writings of James Madison*, ed. Gaillard Hunt (New York: G. P. Putnam's Sons, 1910), 9: 218–21.

62. "A Constituent," *Richmond Enquirer*, 1 January 1818.

63. See chapter 1. Giles's movement toward Burke reflected the trajectory of many Virginians at this date. William Halyburton to William Branch Giles, 25 May 1824, Virginia Historical Society.

64. "A Constituent," *Richmond Enquirer*, 3 January 1818.

65. "A Constituent," *Ibid.*, 8 January 1818.

66. "A Constituent," *Ibid.*, 22 January 1818.

67. "A Constituent," *Ibid.*, 31 January 1818.

68. Thomas Jefferson Randolph to Alexander Smyth, 5 February 1830, Edgehill-Randolph Papers, University of Virginia.

6

"LIKE DUST AND ASHES"

The period between 1815 and 1830 saw the further breakdown of the old Virginia political and social system. The victory of anti-Revolutionary monarchs in Europe left the leading partner in the anti-French coalition, Great Britain, free to transfer its military resources westward, which meant that the War of 1812 might easily have become a complete American debacle. When American negotiators unexpectedly secured a return to the prewar state of things from their British opposite numbers, far-reaching plans for economic and social reform gained a hearing in Richmond. Soon enough, however, economic dislocation brought by the abdication of Napoleon in 1814 left Virginia's small economy reeling.

While suffering economic pains as a result of these events beyond its control, Virginia also experienced severe internal political stresses. The West, tired of seeing its needs ignored in Richmond, began seriously to question the justice of Virginia's constitution. The growing tension between the two great sections of Virginia was rendered far more difficult to resolve by the United States Supreme Court. While James Monroe served as president, Chief Justice John Marshall and his colleagues handed down several nationalizing opinions contrary to the Virginia Republicans' understanding of the federal constitution. Virginia's highest court, egged on by former president Thomas Jefferson, confronted Marshall, and John Taylor of Caroline produced a series of books decrying developments in Washington; Jefferson endorsed them all.

Virginia's leading Republicans were sure not only that the behavior of the federal government was unconstitutional, but that it was hurting Virginia. James Madison, who found himself shunted aside in Virginia Republican leadership, saw ineluctable forces at work in the ongoing impoverishment of Virginia, but most Republicans traced the source of the Old Dominion's woes to the federal tariff, the national bank, or some other federal initiative. Some well-placed observers saw the decline of Virginia's aristocracy as a result of pure folly, of prodigal spending habits; for others, notably Jefferson, that explanation hit a little too close to home. Besides, their revolutionary ideology left Virginians unwilling to believe that there were problems politics could not solve.

The Missouri Crisis beginning in 1819 highlighted the decay of Virginia's place in the American union. Federalists, many Virginians believed, had concocted a means of uniting the majority North in opposition to the ruling South, and the prospect of things getting better appeared remote. Conservative eastern Virginia responded to Missouri by holding more tightly to the status quo, including by refusing to knuckle under to the booming West's demands; the sectional rift within Virginia, like that among the United States, grew ever deeper.

In the end, Virginia's West won its call for a reform convention. The East, after insuring that the convention to decide on apportionment reform would be apportioned in the old way, elected a group of conservative delegates who delighted in telling the West's men that they opposed democracy. "Change is not reform," John Randolph's summary of his stance, became the East's slogan. While the reform delegates shared the East's political culture in many respects, a notable difference between them raised its head that summer. Virginia's last great constituent assembly yielded only partial reform. Pressure for further change would last until the secession of West Virginia, and the reactionary impulse that became dominant in this period would endure a little longer.

Like most states, Virginia suffered severe economic and social dislocation during Jefferson's Embargo and the War of 1812. Virginians' response to these problems of their own making, however, differed markedly from that of their compatriots in New England. For the most part, they bore up under them, and news of Andrew Jackson's victory at New Orleans touched off a wave of excitement and jingoistic chest-thumping.

James Madison's elections as president in 1808 and 1812 came on much closer margins than Jefferson's reelection in 1804, and the foreign policy fiasco of his friend and mentor's second term must shoulder part of the responsibility. To some of Virginia's more committed Republicans, advantages could be found in this hardship. Joseph Carrington Cabell, for example, was a kinsman of the governor of Virginia in early 1808 when he wrote to a friend about matters foreign and domestic. "You will perceive that our old friend H[enry] T[ucker] is taking his [half-]brother J[ohn] R[andolph] as his model in politics," he sneered. "[H]e also is opposed to the embargo. What think you of his early appeal to the avarice of the people?" Typically of elite Virginians who expected consensus among the elite on political questions, young Cabell held that any argument against the Embargo was an "appeal to avarice," while stoic compliance with Republican policy, come Hell or high water, was *ipso facto* patriotic, a sign of virtue.[1]

The War of 1812 cemented the divisions in Virginia's political elite. Dissident Republicans saw the Madison policy as foolhardy and contrary to American interests. As John Taylor understood things, Virginia's long-run interest lay in a stable trading relationship with the United Kingdom, while it had little to gain via ties to France. If there must be a war, he told Monroe, it should be with France. Yet, John Randolph wrote of the mainline Republicans that Francophilia so dominated their thinking that if the French bombarded New York into rubble, most congressmen would oppose declaring war on Napoleon.[2]

A more positive reading would hold that the Napoleonic Wars served as a sort of tonic, tamping down the embers of division between Virginia's growing West (roughly, what is now West Virginia) and its conservative East. The Louisiana Purchase and the European demand for wheat, the West's staple crop, made Eastern rule in Washington popular and the West prosperous.[3] The East had reason to complain, then, when the West proved hesitant to contribute its fair share to the common defense in the War of 1812. Western delegates to the General Assembly opposed improvements to coastal towns' defenses, and they earned a reputation second only to that of New England Federalists for opposition to martial measures.[4]

At war's end, a committee under the direction of Gov. Wilson Cary Nicholas concluded that the sparseness of population in some areas of Virginia resulted from transportation difficulties. Nicholas therefore proposed that the General Assembly sink substantial resources into a program to tie the East and the West more firmly together. This plan received same-day approval from the legislature, and an issue that was to cause intersectional friction within Virginia through the rest of its days as a unified state seemed about to be addressed.[5]

The West never would be placated on the question of public works. The Tidewater representatives in the General Assembly never supported expenditures for these purposes on the scale that the West preferred. Explanations for Tidewater opposition to internal improvements are not difficult to find, since that region stood to benefit directly very little, if at all, from them.

Tidewater Virginia was settled first along the major waterways from which it took its name, as far as the falls of each of the great rivers (most famously at Alexandria and at Richmond).[6] Trade and other communications among the great families of the James and Virginia's other major rivers ran along those very rivers. As can still be seen at the homes of leading colonial families, riverfront acreage gave easy access to trading vessels come to take the latest crop to Europe. The East's leading men had no need of substantial public transportation projects.

With the westward migration of the late colonial and early republican period came desire for internal improvements. The tobacco price went through the roof in 1815, at the end of the Napoleonic Wars, and Virginia's rulers responded with an optimistic project. Gov. Wilson Cary Nicholas's internal improvements message of 1815 made clear that the state would open trade routes in areas that lacked capital. The Trans-Allegheny was to be a special beneficiary, but Nicholas, ever a pragmatist, included sops to the state's other regions in his plan.[7] Finally, in 1816, the Old Dominion became the first state to launch a public works program. George Washington's vision of the 1780s and 1790s, when he had hoped that public transportation projects would help Virginia capture the inland trade, was slated to come into effect. However, the West seldom could raise the money it needed to incorporate road and navigation companies; therefore, state matching funds did not often find their way to the West.[8]

Virginia sank much of its money into the James River Canal, in which many prominent politicians (such as eventual James River Canal Company President Joseph Carrington Cabell) had personal stakes. The state took over the James River Canal in 1820, when it also acquired the Kanawha Road (in what is now West Virginia). These seemed likely to be the first steps in the development of a Trans-Allegheny communications network. Yet, it would be eleven years before Virginia added to this foundation. In the meantime, possible state involvement in railroad projects, in other canals, and in Western roads was preempted by the costly James River Canal ("JRC") fiasco, to the detriment of East-West relations.[9]

Virginia's eastern governors of the 1820s were chagrined that the JRC absorbed all of Virginia's internal improvements efforts. The JRC could not even cover interest on its loans, let alone begin to pay down the principal. Claudius Crozet was hired to perform geographical surveys in the West to lay the groundwork for internal improvements, and neutral observers thought him quite slow. When the surveys were completed, however, Virginia was ready to undertake construction of a major road from the Valley to the Ohio. It was years in the making, but it fared better than other such projects; a more typical one, the Chesterfield Railroad linking Midlothian's coal deposits to the East, received no more state support than a Crozet survey.[10]

The West was always the only Federalist region in the Virginia, and the advent of the Virginia Dynasty in Washington promised to thwart the slim Western hopes for federally sponsored economic development. By the time James Madison left office, the West was thoroughly alienated. Dissidents in the East, such as Monroe, Taylor, and Randolph, may have thought Madison a tepid Republican, but from the West, he seemed fully fanatical enough. The center of the West's grievance was Madison's Bonus Bill Veto of 1817, which dashed the project to enact an extensive program of federally financed internal improvements. (The veto followed the East's opposition to the bill, based more on pragmatic than on constitutional grounds, in Congress. Most Virginia representatives calculated that since Virginia already had an internal improvements program, a federal one would not benefit it.)[11]

The concept of a federal program of internal improvements had been floated by President Thomas Jefferson years earlier, and James Madison repeated requests for such a program in his annual messages. Each year, however, Madison took care to say that if Congress decided it lacked constitutional authority for such a program, it might remedy that shortcoming via the mode the constitution prescribed.[12] Why Madison did not simply say, "I think that you should amend the constitution, and then enact a system of internal improvements" is unclear, but congressional leaders were stunned by Madison's decision to veto the Bonus

Bill. Madison, Jefferson, and others thought an internal improvements amendment might easily be secured, but none ever was, and federal internal improvements programs were considered unconstitutional by virtually all Democrats and the most significant Virginia Whigs for generations thereafter.[13]

In his veto message, Madison laid out a constitutional reading inconsistent with his own conduct as president, but consistent with the main line of Virginia Republican thinking—and with the understanding of their Commonwealth's place in the federal union to which most of the Virginia elite had subscribed since the Richmond Convention of 1788.[14] He said that the bill did not come within any of the constitution's grants of power to Congress. To say that it fell within Congress's power "to regulate commerce among the several States" was impossible, Madison noted, "without a latitude of construction departing from the ordinary." If he reasoned that this legislation was permissible under the "general welfare" clause, he would thereby approve the notion that Congress might do virtually anything it liked; he would also disable the Supreme Court from policing the line separating federal from state authority, which would seriously weaken that institution. In sum, Madison instructed, only an amendment could empower Congress to fund internal improvements. He hoped for an amendment empowering Congress to adopt the Bonus Bill, but for now, he had to veto it.

Madison's Bonus Bill Veto pleased leading Virginia Republicans. Jefferson, for example, lamented that the question whether the federal government's powers were limited seemed to have come into doubt. That question was "almost the only landmark which now divides the federalists from the republicans," and Jefferson was glad to see the principle stated by Madison so starkly. He had no doubt that the requisite amendment would follow.[15] Western Virginia, on the other hand, read Madison's message as another reason to be unhappy with the East. Not only did the East reject the state-sponsored internal improvements the undeveloped West desired, but the East's domination of the federal government effectively had blocked federal assistance in construction of Western roads, canals, and bridges.

The public philosophy of the Tidewater and Piedmont increasingly came to resemble that of John Taylor of Caroline, the avatar of 1790s Republicanism who had found himself at odds with Madison and the Republican establishment in the 1800s and 1810s. Underlying his view of federal-state relations were two ideas: first that the federal constitution of 1788 represented only a parsimonious delegation of state authority to the federal government; and second, that checks-and-balances theories such as those of the authors of *The Federalist* had proven ineffective guarantors of liberty in practice. The program that grew out of the combination of the Taylor ideology and the interests of Eastern Virginia consisted essentially of telling the federal government "no." After 1798, several prominent politicians—Governors William Branch Giles and Littleton Waller Tazewell, most notably—repeated the account of Virginia that underlay the Virginia Resolutions.[16] The most important spokesman for the Jeffersonian Virginian version of federalism in the period, however, was Judge Spencer Roane.

Not only was Roane responsible for the establishment of the South's, perhaps the country's, most important newspaper, the *Richmond Enquirer*, under the editorship of his cousin, Thomas Ritchie, but as judge of the Virginia Court of Appeals, Roane also was in a position to wage jurisprudential war on the United States Supreme Court. By quirk of circumstance, some of the most important cases in American history were decided in this period by a Virginia Federalist and his colleagues in opposition to the Jeffersonian stated dogma of Virginia's Republican Party. Seemingly at every opportunity, Marshall flouted Republican political principle. Jefferson, for one, believed Marshall's sway over the court and his "abuse" of his position constituted nothing less than an attempted *coup de régime*, a full-scale assault by the irresponsible branch of the federal government on the express will of the people (represented, in Jefferson's understanding, by the Republicans).

The ire of the Virginia courts was first roused by the Marshall Court's decision in *Martin v. Hunter's Lessee*. The issue on appeal in *Martin* was whether the Supreme Court was empowered to hear appeals from decisions of Virginia's highest court, and the Supreme Court ruled that it did.[17] The word "firestorm" describes the Virginians' response to this decision. The *Enquirer* lambasted the opinion by Justice Joseph Story, which many thought to have been secretly written by Marshall. The gravest outpouring of anger against the federal government since 1798 rocked Virginia's political elite. Seemingly all of Virginia's political class fell behind Roane's opinion, which the federal court had purported to overturn on appeal. Having cleared his opinion with Jefferson beforehand, Roane stood on solid ground in Virginia.[18]

Roane's opinion reiterated the view of the federal constitution Jefferson had laid out in 1798, taking for granted that the Federalists of 1788 had represented the constitution accurately in the Richmond Convention when they said that Virginia was one of thirteen parties to it, not, as the Supreme Court claimed, one of thirteen parts of one party. Roane's opinion fairly crackled with the electricity of his anger at what he considered bald-faced usurpation, an attempt to rouse Hamiltonian Federalism from its well-deserved slumber.[19]

In response to Story, Roane began his opinion for the leading state's highest court by saying that there existed in American federal politics centripetal, as well as centrifugal, forces. The questions at issue, he said, were whether the section of the Judiciary Act of 1789 giving the Supreme Court power to hear appeals of this type was constitutional, whether this case fell under that section, and whether the Court of Appeals had power to answer the first two questions "no." Roane would not rely, he said, on *The Federalist* for instruction, for everyone knew that it had originated as a mere newspaper series and that its chief author was a rank consolidationist. *The Federalist* was a purely partisan document, born in the heat of battle, and even its authors said that the opinions of the Philadelphia Convention did not determine the federal charter's meaning.

Turning to Section 25 of the Judiciary Act, which purportedly granted the Supreme Court appellate power over his court, Roane began by noting that—as all Republicans believed, and as Story claimed to concede—the states retained all the powers they had not surrendered. This, Roane noted, was the meaning of the term "federal republic" laid out by the preeminent authority on international law, Emmerich de Vattel; both Article II of the Articles of Confederation and the Tenth Amendment to the constitution of 1788 clearly incorporated this idea.

In response to the Federalist tendency to point to the Preamble of the United States Constitution as a substantive grant of power, Roane explicitly followed the Report of 1800[20] in noting that preambles never had been understood to convey any authority on their own. One could find additional evidence for this assertion in the case of the U.S. Constitution in the Articles of Confederation, because the language from the Preamble that was at issue had been copied directly from the Articles, where its effect was understood to be nugatory.

To Roane's way of seeing, the idea of appeals from state to federal courts, besides the fact that it clashed with the people's purposes, was simply nonsensical. What would be the point of requiring state judges to take an oath recognizing the supremacy of the federal Constitution and laws if the state courts' decisions could be appealed anyway? As he understood the federal system's allocation of powers, federal and state functions were "neither dependent on, nor intermingled with" each other. The federal Supreme Court's appellate jurisdiction, then, rightly extended only to cases originally instituted in federal courts. The Supreme Court's demand for records of the Court of Appeals' proceedings in the *Hunter* case threatened that court's power to regulate its own proceedings—as the federal government had no right to do. Story said that its incidental consideration of some question of federal law converted the Virginia Court of Appeals into a federal court, Roane fulminated, and the same technique might easily be used to federalize the courts of Calcutta.

In conclusion, Roane pointed out that in the recent case of *Commonwealth v. Cobbett*, the highest court in Pennsylvania had averred that each state was a party to the federal constitution with the other states. As a result, it said, there was no final arbiter among them; each must decide for itself "the extent of the powers vested by the Constitution" in the federal government. Thus, in Roane's account, the United States Supreme Court had no power to review the Court of Appeals' opinion, Section 25 of the Judiciary Act of 1789 did not apply, and the Court of Appeals would enforce its own decree, whatever the federal courts might say.

Roane's Virginia Court of Appeals colleague Francis T. Brooke put the matter in a slightly different way.[21] Since state courts did not come under Article III of the federal constitution, Judge Brooke reasoned, they had no part of the federal judicial power. The state governments are "the guardians of the people's and their own rights," bound, as the Virginia Resolutions asserted, to resist "general government" infractions of the federal constitution. Like Roane, Brooke used Jefferson's trope of the foreignness of the federal government. The

Virginia Republicans of the 1810s, like those of the 1790s and, before that, the 1770s, regarded the Old Dominion as their "country," the "imperial" government as one of limited function. For a brief time, Roane's personal popularity blossomed. The East applauded him for his principled stand against that inveterate bastion of "monarchy," the United States Supreme Court; the West, characteristically less concerned with the theoretical than with the practical, rejoiced that the litigation had been decided in favor of Westerners' land claims.[22]

If Virginia reacted with energy and anger to the Supreme Court's rebuke in *Martin v. Hunter's Lessee*, an actual crisis atmosphere was engendered by the epochal decision, three years later, in *McCulloch v. Maryland*.[23] The Supreme Court again traced the line between state and federal authority, but this time Virginia could not effectively countermand its opinion.

McCulloch v. Maryland marked the first time the Supreme Court had taken up the federal-state issue in a contest between federal and state legislatures. A Maryland statute undertook to retaliate against the Bank of the United States for "causing" the Panic of 1819 by taxing its branch office. In response to Maryland counsel Luther Martin's assertion that the United States Constitution, as a compact, should be read strictly, Marshall leveled a resounding blow to Virginia strict construction dogma—and thus to Virginians' notion that theirs was a constituent republic in a "federal republic" of the Vattel type. Echoing Story in *Martin*, Marshall said that the United States Constitution was the act of one people, and that it was not the states that had delegated its powers to it, but that one people. One could not expect that all its powers would be enumerated, for "it is *a constitution* we are expounding."

What means were permissible to the federal government's ends? In Marshall's and the court's opinion, any means that seemed convenient to Congress. The United States constituted a dual sovereignty, partly national, partly state, and the question which of the two antedated the other was immaterial. Turning to one of the favorite arguments of the Virginian Republicans, Marshall insisted that the necessary and proper clause was a substantive grant of authority to the federal Congress; logically, it had been included in Article I, Section 8, the site of the main enumeration of congressional powers. However, despite the niggardly quibbling of the counsel for Maryland (Luther Martin, a participant in the Philadelphia Convention who knew whereof he spoke[24]), "necessary" did not really *mean* necessary, it only meant "useful." Since 1819, appropriate means are those the Congress judges to be "plainly adapted" to a "legitimate," "constitutional," and "not prohibited" end. Congress has some economic powers, and since it might judge chartering a bank useful in their exercise, the bank was constitutional.

The other chief question was whether the state of Maryland might tax its branch of the bank. It could not, according to Marshall, for "the power to tax involves the power to destroy," and no state could be allowed to destroy an appropriate instrumentality of the federal government. Congress, Marshall noted in an *obiter dictum*, might tax a state instrumentality, because the federal government stood for the whole, while the state was only a part.

Virginia's response to this ringing rejection of all its most beloved constitutional principles was swift and resounding. Hezekiah Niles wrote against *McCulloch v. Maryland* in the 13 March 1819 issue of the national *Niles' Weekly Register*, and Ritchie's *Enquirer* called ten days later for "firm Republicans of the Old School" to "rally round the banners of the constitution, defending the rights of the states against federal usurpation." "This opinion," Ritchie insisted, "must be controverted and exposed. Virginia has proved herself the uniform friend of state rights—again, she is called to come forth!"[25] Virginia hearkened back to the Report of 1800 in clearly expounding the Republican view regarding sovereignty. John Taylor of Caroline, who was once again to become Virginia's favorite thinker in the last decade of his life, penned his topical book, *Construction Construed, and Constitutions Vindicated*, in response to *McCulloch*.[26] In that 1820 tome, he demolished the idea that either the federal government or the state governments had any sovereignty at all.

Sovereignty, the unreviewable power to make final decisions, lay neither in the federal government nor in the state governments, in the Virginia reading Taylor recapitulated, nor even in the people. In the end, only God could be sovereign. The people of each state had ratified the federal constitution, so each state's people was a party to the federal compact. Those peoples therefore were sovereign insofar as federal constitutionalism was concerned. When the Virginia and Kentucky Resolutions pointed to the rights of the states, they contemplated—according to the gloss of 1800—the rights of the people of each state.

Marshall had scored rhetorical points by noting that the people's intention in delegating powers to the federal government must not be thwarted by a crimped interpretation of the scope of those powers. Taylor conceded the point, but he noted that, "If a delegation of powers implies an unrestrained choice of the means for the execution of those powers," the state governments' argument had twice the claim to respect that the federal government's did, for the state governments' powers had all first been delegated by the people, and then those not granted to the federal government had been reserved to the states by the Tenth Amendment.[27]

The gravamen of Taylor's argument was that *McCulloch v. Maryland* stood for the destruction of the Revolutionary legacy. The United States Constitution would stand for naught, he said, in a reprise of his arguments of the 1790s, if the general government were converted into an unlimited government. If Congress could do anything it judged convenient for the "common defense and general welfare," the general government would be an unlimited one. *Construction Construed* found in Marshall's *McCulloch* opinion an attempt by the federal government to arrogate the high station of the people of each state to itself. Vehement as was Taylor's presentation, however, it was temperate next to the expositions of the *McCulloch* opinion penned for the *Richmond Enquirer* by two leading Virginia judges.

Marshall, back home in Richmond, heard rumblings of unhappiness with his handiwork. To Story, he wrote, "Our opinion in the bank case has roused the sleeping spirit of Virginia—if indeed it ever sleeps. It will I understand be attacked in the papers with some asperity; as those who favor it never write for the publick it will remain undefended & of course be considered as *damnably heretical*." A few days later, Marshall wrote the second most sympathetic member of his court, Bushrod Washington, in a similar vein. As Marshall soon told Story, "The opinion in the Bank case has brought into operation the whole antifederal spirit of Virginia. Some latent feelings which have been working ever since the decision of Martin & Hunter have found vent."[28]

The first notable newspaper attack on Marshall's opinion came from "Amphictyon," alias Judge William Brockenbrough, on 30 March 1819.[29] This member of the Richmond Junto, Virginia Republicans' supposed coordinating committee, analyzed *McCulloch* in a relatively dispassionate way. Marshall's opinion perfectly summarized the position of his (Federalist) party, Brockenbrough asserted, and the Supreme Court's two leading principles posed a threat to "the very existence of state rights." To Marshall's first principle, that the federal government's powers had not been delegated by the states, Brockenbrough replied that the Philadelphia Convention had represented the states, that the states' sovereigns—the people in convention assembled—had ratified the Constitution, and that the Constitution was only effective in those states that had ratified (as North Carolina's several months and Rhode Island's years outside the federal union proved). Each state, he insisted (reminding his readers of the myth of Virginia history they first had learned from Richard Bland, Thomas Jefferson et al.), "was an independent political society" when it ratified the Constitution, and he had thought that the contrary doctrine, the Federalists' doctrine of the 1790s,[30] had suffered a permanent refutation.

In his second installment as Amphictyon, Brockenbrough picked up on Marshall's other arguments, saying in response to his weakest one that if "the framers of the constitution" had meant "*useful,* or *convenient,* or *conducive* to the effectual execution of the foregoing powers," they would not have used the word "necessary" in the "necessary and proper" clause.[31] Invoking the stock Virginia bogeyman, Brockenbrough next noted that under Marshall's reading, the Constitution empowered Congress to do almost anything, even pay "those ministers of the gospel, whose tenets may in their opinion best advance the general welfare."

Brockenbrough's performance exposed the weakness of Marshall's reasoning without engaging in splenetics. That mode of argumentation was to be reserved for Judge Spencer Roane. In a 2 April 1819 letter to the *Enquirer*, Roane carried the disputation over *McCulloch* as far as an essayist could: he counseled that Virginia should nullify unconstitutional federal actions, using armed force if necessary.[32] Before he did, however, Marshall's unhappiness at seeing his handiwork attacked without response led the chief justice to write in favor of his court himself. "A Friend of the Union" could find no publisher in the Old Dominion, so it appeared only in the distant Philadelphia *Union*.[33] There, among other things, Marshall said that the constitutional preamble's use of the phrase "We the people" was dispositive on the question who ratified the constitution.

He also insisted that the Supreme Court could not begin by assuming that a state challenging Congress's authority was right, for the people had as much interest in seeing Congress's duties performed as they did in ensuring that it not overstep its bounds.

No one knew until 1969 that "A Friend of the Union" was John Marshall, so his arguments went unanswered in Virginia. "Hampden" (Roane) and friends, however, found quite enough grist for their mills in Marshall's official pronouncements. In his second "Hampden" essay, Roane, adopting a method Marshall never used, considered the record of the Richmond Ratification Convention of 1788. There, Roane noted, Madison had said that the general government's powers under the new Constitution were enumerated and limited to those that were enumerated; he added that Marshall, Edmund Randolph, and George Nicholas (the three Federalists who carried the bulk of the argument on their side) had repeated Madison's assurance. Roane next called attention to the fact that "Publius," one of Marshall's favorite sources of constitutional exegesis, had written that the word "necessary" in Article I, Section 8 was to have its usual signification.

Roane's correspondence in this period included an exchange with James Madison, whom John Taylor already considered a "heretic and Apostate" but whom Roane, along with the majority of Virginia Republicans, thought an ornament to his Commonwealth.[34] Madison had an extremely harsh opinion of the Supreme Court's course, and specifically of *McCulloch v. Maryland*. He decried the Supreme Court's decision for giving Congress latitude as to means "to which no practical limit can be assigned" (thus, he might have added, effectively rejecting the teaching of Madison's Bonus Bill Veto Message). The court was abandoning its task of policing the limits of congressional authority; Congress had to be the judge of expediency, and now the justices equated expediency with constitutionality. "It . . . was foreseen at the birth of the Constitution" that the federal/state line would be vague, but people had expected it to be enforced, and "the avowal of such a rule [as Marshall's in *McCulloch*] would . . . have prevented [the federal Constitution's] ratification." Any new power the federal government needed should be granted by formal amendment; "constructive assumption of powers never meant to be granted" was simply a betrayal: grants of power *could* be limited, Madison insisted.

Thomas Jefferson's endorsed Roane's efforts with rather more brio.[35] "I have read in the Enquirer, and with great approbation, the pieces signed Hampden," the avatar of Republicanism wrote. "I subscribe to every tittle of them. They contain the true principles of the revolution of 1800, for that was as real a revolution in the principles of our government as that of 1776 was in its form." Jefferson's only quibble was that he would go further than Roane in paring the federal judiciary down to size: he denied its right to interpret the constitution dispositively even for the other two branches of the federal government.

Marshall, too, thought highly of the "Hampden" essays. As he wrote to Justice Washington: "The storm which has been for some time threatening the

Judges has at length burst o[n] their heads & a most serious hurricane it is." According to Marshall, all knew Roane to be the author, and on the basis of the essays' quality and of their author's identity, "It is worth your while to read them." Richmond, where Federalists maintained considerable social sway, bore few signs of Roane's influence. In the countryside, however, where virtually all Virginians lived, Roane's doctrines suffused political disputation.[36]

The furor over *McCulloch* had not subsided two years later when the Supreme Court handed down its opinion in *Cohens v. Virginia* (1821). Once again, Virginia's leading politicians thought that the federal government claimed a right to flout the laws of a sovereign state, and unlike the McCulloch matter, the Cohens' case arose out of a transgression of the laws of Virginia itself. The Cohen brothers were convicted of selling District of Columbia lottery tickets in Norfolk in violation of Virginia law.[37] When they appealed the case to Marshall's court, the Commonwealth responded to the federal summons angrily. The Supreme Court lacked jurisdiction, Virginia averred, because the case had originated in a state court and Supreme Court jurisdiction (as Roane had held in *Hunter v. Martin*) did not extend to appeals from state courts. In sum, "a sovereign and independent State is not liable to the suit of any individual, nor amenable to any judicial power, without its own consent." Virginia would not stoop to argue any point other than the jurisdictional one before the Supreme Court.

The General Assembly adopted a series of resolutions setting out its response to the Supreme Court's recent behavior. First, obviously in answer to *Martin v. Hunter's Lessee*, it denied the Supreme Court's authority to hear appeals from state courts. Relying on the Eleventh Amendment, the Virginia legislature reiterated the idea that a state could not be made a party defendant in a case such as *Cohens*; while on the subject of *Cohens*, it added that congressional legislation for the District of Columbia had no more effect outside the district than did the legislation of a state outside the boundaries of that state.[38] The General Assembly's resolutions foreshadowed Virginia's argument before the Supreme Court.

Marshall, for a unanimous Supreme Court, reiterated *Martin* and *McCulloch*, concluding that the federal courts did have jurisdiction because the Article III federal question ("arising under") jurisdiction should be read broadly. The United States, Marshall insisted, was a permanent union to which the states were necessarily subordinated. The Eleventh Amendment's limitation on suits against states in federal courts, as Marshall strictly interpreted it, did not apply. Unlike the Virginian officials, the Supreme Court paid no attention to the ratifiers' understanding of the Constitution, but it used the old English technique of reasoning from the four corners of the document and, where that did not suffice, from abstract principles. Having asserted his court's jurisdiction, Marshall found that the Cohens' convictions were proper. Once again, Virginia's Republican elite was left with no way to respond.[39]

Thomas Jefferson mused in private correspondence that the *Cohens* decision was merely the latest manifestation of the fact that the Supreme Court was the "instrument which, working like gravity, without intermission, is to press us at last into one consolidated mass." Ritchie filled his *Enquirer* with the anti-*Cohens* opinions of "Somers" and "Fletcher of Saltoun." Roane responded to the Supreme Court's latest anti-Virginia Doctrines pronouncement with five more anonymous essays. Where formerly he had adopted the name "Hampden," he would now be "Algernon Sydney." Roane's first "Algernon Sydney" essay may be taken as typical of the series. *Cohens*, he fumed, stood for the simple proposition that the United States were not "sovereign and independent States." "That is no federal republic," he insisted, "in which one of the parties to the compact, claims the exclusive right to pass finally upon the chartered rights of another." The Supreme Court's decision should be understood as a change to the Constitution.[40]

Marshall's uncharacteristic strict construction of the Eleventh Amendment also elicited Roane's ire. Although its terms applied only to suits in which states were defendants,[41] Roane insisted that the amendment demonstrated the states' and the people's generalized opposition to the possibility of states being hailed into federal court without their consent. Besides that, Article III of the federal Constitution listed grounds of federal court jurisdiction over states, and *Cohens v. Virginia* came under none of them, so Roane reasoned that under the Tenth Amendment the federal courts should be held not to have the power the Cohen brothers were asking them to exercise.

Roane took all of this to be common sense. John Marshall surely understood the arguments Roane found dispositive in the same way Roane did; after all, to be Virginian was to understand things in the Republican way. "Love of power" alone explained the Supreme Court's assertion of authority in an area clearly off limits to it. As so often before, Virginia's leading Republicans saw corruption in their opponents' steps to undercut their state's hallowed self-determination. The Supreme Court and the federal government generally stood to gain the most, for *Cohens* "destroy[s] the state governments altogether and establish[es] on their ruins, one great, national, and consolidated government." Roane insisted that Virginians had fought the Revolution to secure control of their government, and then set up a new government on the sanction of the people. Yet, the Supreme Court in *Cohens* claimed power to destroy the federal compact by making it "whatever it pleases to make it." Like Parliament in olden days, "it starts upon the principle, that itself is never in the wrong." Not bound by the people's power, the court set itself above the sovereign people by nullifying their acts, and the only rule it recognized came from its own precedents.

In response to Marshall's notion about state courts' inferiority to federal ones, Roane again invoked the authority of Emmerich de Vattel, who taught that states joining federal republics retained their sovereignty. Only the delegated powers lay in the federal governments, so the constituent parts' governments were not inferior, just separate. Otherwise, they would not retain their sovereignty, and the federal republic would become a different type of government.

As in the case of his anti-*McCulloch* essays, Roane's efforts drew great acclaim within Virginia. Jefferson wrote with thanks, noting that he "had read

[them] with great approbation successively."[42] The Sage of Monticello was only disappointed that Ritchie had not printed them in pamphlet form, too, so they could be circulated outside Virginia. He gave Roane a signed letter for circulation calling the federal government "coordinate" with, not superior to, the states' and prescribing appeal to the people when the two levels of government disagreed.[43]

James Madison's opinion, however, had begun to change. Now insulated from political imperatives within Virginia and the Republican Party, Madison began once again to move toward the line he had followed as "Publius" thirty years earlier. In response to Roane's solicitation of approval for the "Algernon Sydney" essays, he gave a response far different from the one he had given "Hampden."[44] After thanking Roane for his gift of the essays, Madison wrote that when federal and state claims of authority came into conflict, "the sounder policy would yield to the claims of the former." To add insult to injury, Madison also averred that federal-state clashes would probably decrease in frequency as the quality of the state governments improved.

The crux of Madison's divergence from the mainline Virginia position lay in his approach to constitutional interpretation. As he explained at the end of 1821, the Constitution's meaning was to be found in the understanding of *"the nation* at the time of its ratification."[45] Other Virginians found this idea perplexing, for the states had ratified in individual conventions; "the nation" had never been consulted. John Taylor, commenting on Madison's statement in The Federalist #39 that *"the assent and ratification of the people of America"* was that of "the *people of each distinct and independent state*," noted that it could not logically be both.[46]

Since "the nation" had not been polled in 1787–1790 on the meaning of the constitution, Madison could draw eclectically from the record of the Philadelphia Convention, The Federalist, the records of the state conventions, other nations' practices,[47] and his own impressions in disputing Virginia Republicans' assertions about the Constitution's meaning. As the debates in the Richmond Convention of 1788 and the General Assembly of 1798 had shown, Virginia Republicans generally believed that state ratification left the states (however defined) as the contracting parties, the government a federation. Madison's insistence that the notion "that the States have never parted with an atom of their sovereignty" was new-fangled and congruent to the Nullifiers' doctrine was the opposite of Virginians' experience and contrary to the explanations offered them in 1788 and 1798.[48] Given the events of the Richmond Convention's closing days, his description of The Federalist as "the most authentic exposition of the text of the federal constitution," as understood by the drafters and the ratifiers, was simply wishful thinking.[49] A party to a federal compact giveth, and it can retrieve; it entereth into a union, and—Jefferson and the vast majority of Virginia Republicans believed—it can exit from that union.[50] From Roane's point of view, Madison's position was a moving target.

Madison wrote to Thomas Ritchie late in 1825 to clarify his position concerning the proper response to federal arrogations. Ritchie, like Roane, apparently had broached the idea of a scheme remarkably like John C. Calhoun's later doctrine of Nullification.[51] No, Madison said, Virginia should not protest the federal government's latest internal improvements scheme while standing ready to acquiesce in the event three-fourths of the states disagreed, for that would strip the majority of its "rights . . . in expounding the Constitution." He obviously did not share Ritchie's and other leading Republicans' (including Jefferson's) view that Virginia was one of several states united in a classic federal republic. In time, he held Republicans who had such views equivalent to Satan in the Garden, "the serpent creeping into Paradise."[52] For his part, Roane lamented that Jefferson and Madison did not enter the lists with swords drawn against the dragon of Hamiltonian construction. Rather than resting on their couches, they should take as their example the French writer whose dying breath was spent on a defense of proper French. Roane's suggestions came to naught.

Virginians' response to the Supreme Court's nationalizing decisions may well have been exacerbated by the economic hardship then gripping the Old Dominion. As early as 1808, Taylor's *Arator* lamented at length the sorry state of Virginia agriculture. This leading thinker of Virginia Republicanism believed that the basic problem facing agriculture was the carryover from the days when Hamilton and his "money men" and "stockjobbers" had carved out neo-feudal rents for their friends from the federal tax revenue. The vast preponderance of the burden of such rents, Taylor held, had to be paid by agriculture, the majority's economic endeavor.[53]

Whether they agreed with Taylor's analysis or not, by the time *McCulloch v. Maryland* was handed down a decade later, Virginians certainly felt the sting of recession, if not already of depression. As Madison noted in his eighth and final state of the union message, some of the American manufacturing sector came out of the War of 1812 in a severely impaired state.[54] Although the "bank mania" of the immediate postwar period masked some of the long-term dislocations associated with the war, the interlude of economic growth soon ended.[55] In 1819, the year of the *McCulloch* decision, business activity in Richmond hit a virtual standstill.[56]

Virginians' skepticism about the likelihood that the "bank mania" would endure rested on an accurate perception of the state of Virginia's economy.[57] The War of 1812's end sparked an economic contraction, and soon the Bank of the United States began to call in loans. State banks, which had borrowed money from the Bank of the United States, had to follow suit in order to repay their loans to the national institution, and the contraction accelerated. Bankruptcies ballooned across the United States, especially outside New England, and prices of "the great export staples" led a marked deflation. American exports fell by 25 percent between 1818 and 1820; imports, the fruits of Virginia farmers' labors, fell even more.[58]

The Bank of the United States, target of Virginians' ideological opposition, loomed as an apparent (though it was not the actual) cause of their economic troubles.[59] As Thomas Jefferson told rising political star William Cabell Rives, "the flood, then . . . the ebb of bank paper" caused "The distresses of our country."[60] Those "distresses" consisted not merely of temporary economic discomfiture, but of a "revolution of property, which without more wisdom than we possess, will be much greater than were produced by the revolutionary paper," and to no good end. "We have been truly sowing the wind, and are now reaping the whirlwind."[61]

The Virginia General Assembly, true to Jeffersonian constitutionalism even when the Jeffersonians running the federal government were not, had protested the idea of recharter of the first United States Bank in 1811 with assertions that recharter would be "not only unconstitutional, but a dangerous encroachment on the sovereignty of the States."[62] In short, it would dilute Virginians' control of their state's economy. Virginia Republicans leapt at the first opportunity to blame this "unconstitutional" institution they did not control for their troubles. Jefferson, mired in debt, happily led the way. He described the process by which the sudden calling of bank loans was impoverishing the rich and making their landed (including slave) fortunes available to a new breed of men of mainly plebeian origins at cut-rate prices. First, bad loans went unpaid. Then, a sufficient number of defaults led to bank failure, resulting in calling of loans. Indebted landowners often saw their estates sold at sheriffs' auctions at ridiculously low prices, sometimes as low as "one year's rent" for land, $100 for slaves, and one-third the normal price for produce.[63] Typically of Virginia's master class, Jefferson blamed "the banking system" for problems in his own and other Virginia planters' economic lives. He lamented that the average voter lacked the "knolege [sic] of Political economy" requisite to his diagnosis.[64]

James Madison's divergence from the Republican view of the Supreme Court's behavior may owe something to his more nuanced evaluation of the Commonwealth's economic problems.[65] Late in 1820, he wrote to the former marquis de la Fayette with a prediction: time would heal Virginia's economic wounds. Those wounds, according to Madison, owed their genesis to the European peace, with the resulting elimination of America's profitable role as neutral trader with both sides. When America ceased to be the sole neutral, and when the combatants' economies reverted to their peacetime patterns, America suddenly found itself in the unaccustomed position of rival to European enterprises. Predictably, some American businesses and farmers could not compete with the "inundation of foreign merchandizes" or cope with the declines in wheat and tobacco prices. (Madison's evaluation of Virginia's economic situation in the last decade of his life stood in marked contrast to his rejection of Richard Henry Lee's, and other Virginia Republicans', similar evaluation of Virginia's situation in the late 1780s.)

Virginia's economic distress was very severe. As one well-placed attorney described the capital city in early 1820, "Things here grow worse & worse—the merchants all failed—the town ruined—the banks broke—the Treasury empty—commerce gone, confidence gone, character gone—well a day—But the people of the country think the Legislature will cure all by a 'stay law.' It would do no good if passed—but it will not pass."[66]

Looking back on his life through the intervening Reconstruction years, and recalling the sorry financial condition in which his grandfather had ended his, Thomas Jefferson Randolph asserted that, "The collapse of 1819 the most terrible which we have ever known lasted 10 years."[67] Jefferson's land had to be sold to pay his enormous debts, and the auction apparently closely resembled the fire sales he had described only a few years before.

An "arator" like Taylor or a filiopietist such as Thomas Jefferson Randolph may have ascribed the blame for their class's circumstances to "bank mania," and Madison may have attributed Virginia's decline to international factors, but some of their contemporaries saw another force at work: profligacy. John Randolph of Roanoke lamented that, "A young man, who has inherited nothing from his father but a taste for expensive living, thinks himself justified in indulging in the same style of expense, so that all the land-marks of morality are removed, and the distinction between *meum* and *tuum* almost lost sight of."[68]

Another contemporary who blamed the free-spending ways of the Virginia moneyed class for its financial problems was Francis Walker Gilmer. The son of a friend of Jefferson's, Dr. George Gilmer, Francis was one of a notable clan. One Gilmer would rise to the positions of governor of Virginia and United States secretary of the navy, and another would serve as governor of Georgia, but all recognized Francis as the smartest of the bunch. Jefferson pleaded with Gilmer for years to take the position as first law professor at the University of Virginia, and he appears to have stuck to that insistence despite fellow visitors' misgivings.[69] Jefferson's solicitude and his frequent access to the sanctum sanctorum on Monticello mark Gilmer as an especially useful source of reflections on the Virginia elite's ways.

The Gilmers decried the close tie between money and influence in Virginia.[70] A poor performance by the brothers' guardian had left them to shift for themselves, and each appears to have resented the necessity to climb the Old Dominion's social and political ladders from a very low rung.[71] Francis Walker Gilmer noted to his brother, Peachy Gilmer, that if Thomas Jefferson had died young and George Gilmer and two of his friends had spent several terms as president, George Gilmer likely would have been of far more help to the surviving Jeffersons than the Virginia dynasts had been to the Gilmers.

Apparently, Peachy Gilmer would have liked to become a federal judge, and the brothers' evaluation of other contestants for the spot their man wanted left no room to doubt that money and connections, not merit, had left Peachy Gilmer on the outside. They were even more scathing in their evaluations of Jefferson's successors. James Monroe, Francis Walker Gilmer noted on several occasions, was an idiot, after whom no man of reasonable ability should doubt his own fitness to be president. At Monticello one day, Francis Gilmer reported, he heard Monroe admit his incapacity for the presidency. Besides that, Monroe's positions on internal improvements and on the Missouri Crisis did not gibe with the Virginia consensus. Gilmer could barely stand to be in the presence of those at the top of Virginia's political hierarchy.[72]

Leading Jeffersonian reformer John H. Cocke, a devoté of colonization, the University of Virginia, agricultural societies, and other enlightened causes, experienced great difficulty in this period paying the costs of his compulsive remodeling of his home. Gilmer judged him quite foolish in this regard. James Madison had to scrape up a loan from Nicholas Biddle to keep himself in the style of living to which he had grown accustomed. The worst of all in Gilmer's estimation, however, was Jefferson, whose octagonal buildings would scar the Virginia landscape for generations to come and whose debt at his death resulted in part from his high living. (Luckily for Gilmer, he did not live to see James Barbour's Jeffersonian villa at Barboursville burned to a bare, octagonal shell—which remains a Virginia landmark to this day.) Francis Walker Gilmer told Peachy that in light of the Virginia elite's prodigality, it was no wonder they were all broke. (Never once did he mention the pestilential bankers, whose sin seems to have consisted in loaning Jefferson and friends the money they asked to borrow at the rates they agreed to pay.) If he had been born to money, Gilmer repeatedly aped Shakespeare's Timon of Athens, he would have exposed the Virginia aristocracy for the fools they were.[73]

The end of the nineteenth century's second decade was a supercharged period in Virginia's politics for a reason other than the economy and the Supreme Court's decisions, too. In 1819, the Missouri Crisis, Jefferson's "fire bell in the night," convinced many, perhaps most, Virginians that the Federalist schemers had contrived to indict slavery for purely political reasons, and Virginians did not appreciate the supposed cabal's daring stroke one bit.[74] Virtually no one who mattered glimpsed the least possibility of good for Virginia in the Missouri Crisis. Francis W. Gilmer was not alone in holding the Missouri instigators' goal to be "that we are to be taxed to support the Yankees & make [Sen. Rufus] King President or have our throats cut."[75]

Slavery was a non-issue in Virginia. True, Gabriel's Rebellion raised a ruckus at the end of John Adams's presidential administration, but stepped up security measures seem to have been accepted by all as the proper response. Virtually no one complained about the racial clamp-down in the wake of Gabriel's escapade. John Taylor of Caroline captured his countrymen's views perfectly in *Arator*, where he called slavery a misfortune with which white Virginians simply had to live. Virginians probably accepted, too, Taylor's negative judgement on Jefferson's idea from Query XVIII of *Notes on the State of Virginia* that slavery negatively affected masters' character and made them unfit for republicanism. Total sway over black men was no harder on a republican's character, Taylor wrote, than total sway over a horse, for slaves, like horses, were too far below the status of their masters to excite furious passions.[76]

The Missouri Crisis seemed obviously a trumped-up controversy. Northern Republicans joined with former Federalists in refusing to admit Missouri (which contained a large colony of Virginia expatriates[77]) into the federal union. Before it would be admitted, they said, it must accept a ban on slavery within its limits.

The debate took two years, eventuating in the admission of Missouri on certain conditions, joined to the admission of a new northern state, Maine. For most political Virginians, as for many other southerners, the imbroglio signaled a new day when they would be treated as special pariahs by their northern ex-brethren. This change in status came unwelcome in the ill economic times surrounding the year 1820. Linking the Panic of 1819 to debates in Congress, one Virginian surmised that Virginia must henceforth be "tributary to northern shoe makers, Irish potato, pumpkin, and Ruta-baga men." They were everywhere, "overrunning the country . . . and our legislature will soon be filled with them." Others responded even more harshly, describing the Missouri Compromise line as a "cordon" around the South and drawing glum conclusions about Yankees' "tender mercies."[78]

For Jefferson, the Missouri Compromise's principle of geographic demarcation called into question "the hope that man can ever enjoy the two blessings of peace and self-government." The Missouri debates led him to reinvigorate his dedication to the University of Virginia, which he viewed as the one hope of educating Virginians in Virginia's principles concerning matters such as the Missouri question. Madison agreed. The party system had always been based on divisions within each of the states, he noted, and he doubted that the union could long survive with divisions "founded on geographical boundaries and other Physical & permanent distinctions." If such divisions came into being, there would be nothing to avert clashes between "those great repulsive Masses."[79]

Madison also rejected the idea that Congress had authority to mandate constitutional provisions to new states. The Louisiana Purchase, through which the United States had acquired Missouri, could not allow Congress to enact discriminations between new and old states, he thought, any more than among the latter group. Here, Madison read the constitution as a compact among sovereigns. The unstated predicate for him, as for other Virginians, was that if northern majorities could work their arbitrary, unconstitutional will on Missouri, they could work it on Virginia. The General Assembly adopted resolutions stating this position in 1820, and Madison suggested that the admission of Missouri to the union be delayed until all conditions were retracted.[80]

Virginians' constitutional scruples, powerful when Virginia owned a commanding height in American politics, showed no signs of weakening as Virginia's relative position declined. When the "American System," an interlocking set of proposals including protective tariffs and internal improvements, made its appearance in the wake of the Missouri mess, Virginians fell back upon the argument made by President Madison in his Bonus Bill Veto Message: internal improvements rested on no constitutional authorization, and they therefore must be opposed as unconstitutional; if the proposed tariffs' brunt fell largely on the South, so much the worse.[81]

The first notable exposition of this view came in 1821 in John Taylor's topical tome, *Tyranny Unmasked*.[82] With the aim of starting a permanent opposition party, Taylor flayed the banking and tariffs system as nothing but a large web of favoritism based on the wealth of American farmers.[83] Since the opportune moment for explicitly banning it via constitutional amendment, Jefferson's victory in 1800, had been allowed to slip away, the only remaining option was opposition.

By decade's end, Henry Clay had made his famous "American System" speech of 1824, and William Branch Giles—driven from the federal senate a decade earlier by his refusal to toe the General Assembly's line—dusted off his old skill for polemics.[84] In doing so, he had the blessing of Thomas Jefferson, who responded to the adoption of the tariff of 1824 by lamenting the error of some "younger recruits who, having nothing in them of the feelings or principles of '76, now look to a single and splendid government of an aristocracy, founded on banking institutions, and moneyed corporations."[85] Politicians throughout the Old Dominion echoed Jefferson and revivified the Principles of '98. Gov. John Tyler's son, named for his father, succeeded him in the governor's chair in the middle of the 1820s, and the future president proved even more of a stickler for republican propriety than his father. At the tail of a three-year antitariff, antifederal internal improvements campaign in the *Richmond Enquirer*, Giles shepherded a strong set of resolutions supporting his position through the state legislature. Within a short time, an appreciative General Assembly elected Tyler the younger to the United States Senate ("If Virginia has changed her representative," he promised, "her principles remain unaltered"[86]) and Giles to the governorship. Another set of antitariff resolutions soon followed.[87]

From his position as governor, Giles endeavored to unite the southern states in a new league of countervailing tariffs. If the South erected tariffs on northern manufactures, Giles reasoned, the federal tariffs of 1824 and 1828 might be repealed.[88] His idea failed, despite the efforts of Senator Littleton Waller Tazewell (who would one day succeed Giles as governor). One important result *did* come from Giles's efforts, however: the West became increasingly convinced that its ties to the East redounded to its detriment. While the ossified East, beneficiary of Virginia's extensive network of rivers and streams, stifled nearly all state and federal initiatives tending to improve the trans-Allegheny's transportation facilities, the West increasingly resented the East's efforts. For the East, the failure of its agriculture now could be traced to an obvious "cause," the "American System," which replaced the banks as the leading scapegoat of troubled Old Virginia; for the West, the problem was the East's obstruction of the same "American System."[89]

From his Piedmont plantation, James Madison took a subtler view.[90] Writing to Nicholas Trist, Madison averred that, "The fall in the price of land particularly in Virginia may be attributed to several causes. (1) to the uncertainty & low prices of the crops. (2) to the quantity of land thrown into market by debtors.... But the (3) and main cause is the low price at which fertile lands in the Western market are available." People moved West, he summarized, because for less work they could reap greater profits. The trend hurt manufacturing, not to mention the general agricultural economy of the seaboard. In a sense, Madison's opponents on the question of tariffs retained more of the Revolution's optimism than he; they still believed, despite their protestations to the contrary, that if a problem beset Virginia, if Virginia's traditions were threatened, the proper solution lay in some rearrangement of government institutions. Madison, unlike John Taylor in decades past and the tariff's opponents c. 1830, imagined a changed Virginia. He believed it inevitable that manufactures would grow up, that agricultural products would diversify. In his eighties, he looked on it all with equanimity.[91]

Madison was not the only one to notice that a concomitant of the economic troubles besetting the Old Dominion was the emigration of a mass of Virginia's most promising young men to western states. Wealth might be difficult to accrue in the Commonwealth, but tales of rapidly amassed fortunes in Alabama traveled with dizzying speed. "Alabama is at present the loadstone of attraction," wrote John Randolph disapprovingly, "cotton, money, whiskey, and the means of obtaining all these blessings—*Slaves*. The road is thronged with droves of these wretches & the human carcase butchers who drive them on the *hoof*."[92]

Westward movement of population caused renewed focus on what once had been essentially a philosophical issue. When the state constitution of 1776 was adopted, Thomas Jefferson raised some theoretical objections to it. Over time, the West's interest, covered with the Jeffersonian contentions' abstract appeal, pushed many of the immigrant families of the West to support the Jeffersonian arguments concerning the Virginia constitution. The main problem Jefferson and the West saw in George Mason's handiwork was the apportionment of representation, which disfavored the West markedly.

The apportionment problem grew worse as sectional division regarding internal improvements intensified, for the West's white population was growing rapidly through the Jeffersonian period, while the East's remained stagnant. Since the 1776 constitution provided for neither periodic reapportionment nor amendment, the West agitated for a constitutional convention. Legislative efforts in the first decade of the nineteenth century, although unsuccessful, roused interest in the West. The James River Canal Company's near-monopoly of state internal improvements funds angered the West, and Easterners' vociferous opposition to, and occasional success in defusing, federal internal improvements programs reinforced the West's sense that it was ill served by Eastern domination.

As early as 1796, the General Assembly resolved that the people should "instruct their Representatives to the next session of the General Assembly, upon the propriety of calling a" constitutional convention.[93] The first petition to the General Assembly for a constitutional convention arrived from the West in 1802, and it elicited no response. The second was rejected by the 1805 House of Delegates by a vote of ninety-eight to fifty-eight. In 1807, the House of Delegates approved a convention, but the Senate balked. Each of the following three years saw the House of Delegates defeat the notion; in 1810, even though the Eastern Shore county of Accomack supported the Western campaign, the House of Delegates voted it down, eighty-two to seventy-nine. When next the issue was brought to a vote, in 1815, it lost once again, this time by ninety to eighty-seven.[94]

In 1816, reformers organized meetings in various western towns to demand suffrage and apportionment reform. The largest such gathering assembled for a grand constituent convention in the Augusta County seat, Staunton. Thirty-eight counties sent delegates to the five-day event. Conservatives were quick to note the questionable nature of the reformers' claim to speak for the areas from which they hailed, for few people had taken part in choosing the delegates to the Staunton Convention and other gatherings; they also noted that some of the counties represented in the Staunton gathering ended up voting against the measure the majority adopted.

Perhaps the classic expression of anti-Staunton sentiment is to be found in a set of resolutions adopted on 15 September 1825 by a meeting of freeholders in Charles City County, the Tidewater epicenter of the old landed elite.[95] The resolutions, reputedly drafted by John Tyler, Jr., covered the whole field of opposition to constitutional reform. First, the meeting accused the Staunton Convention of attempting to undermine the proper, filial respect of Virginians for their constitution, which sounded in the Charles City men's words vaguely like an accusation of impiety. The Charles City meeting saw no reason to revise the constitution of 1776. While it was "in the nature of things that the work of man should be imperfect," the constitution of 1776 served its function well:

> under its happy auspices justice has ever been administered in mercy, & government scarcely known except by its blessings— . . . while none is so high as to escape punishment for well ascertained offences, neither is any so low as not to be secure in his person and protected in his property— . . . we esteem these to be the essentials of good government; and possessing these, we cannot yield them to theory or experiment.

Tyler's resolutions pointed to the three-fifths clause of the federal constitution, which counted slaves as three-fifths of a person for purposes of legislative (thus also of Electoral College) apportionment. Virginia was a slave-holding state, and any implication that damaged slave-holders' position in the federal councils would harm Virginia. Virginians should not adopt the principle of white apportionment, for the implication would be obvious. Similarly, the resolutions defended the exclusive freehold suffrage as giving "the permanent inhabitants of the state" and fathers control of Virginia politics. Virginia's apportionment might well be unfair, the residents of this small, sparsely populated county conceded, but the solution had not changed in recent years. Each county had two representatives in the House of Delegates, and Virginians could divide counties anytime; Charles City County's delegates would support such efforts in the General Assembly. The Charles City County men disliked the idea of making the governor the creature of direct elections by the people (thus, perhaps, of the increasingly populous West). Other "communities" had suffered for doing that, they averred. The "peaceful and quiet state which we now enjoy" would yield, if the governorship were made the object of political striving, to contests of party.

Obviously, John Tyler and his neighbors spoke for a static conception of Virginia, one in which very little changed and very little should. Filial affection for inherited institutions and perception of a "peaceful and quiet state" of society were not the rage among the immigrant Virginians west of Monticello. John Tyler's Virginia was the Virginia in which he and his father and his father before him had grown up, and he did not want change. Within weeks of his resolutions' adoption, John Tyler was rewarded for his forthright defense of his birthright with elevation to the gubernatorial chair.

Notwithstanding such arguments, the West provided the impetus for a reapportionment of the Virginia Senate. Where formerly the West had had four of twenty-four senators, it would henceforth have nine of twenty-four. It was not white apportionment, but it was closer to that ideal. The West was temporarily placated, but soon the old grievances stirred the old resentments.[96]

Thomas Jefferson supported the West's reform efforts in spirit (and in private). To Samuel Kerchival, one of the reformist leaders, he wrote a long epistle recapitulating some of *Notes on the State of Virginia*.[97] As in the 1780s, so now, Jefferson wanted equal apportionment on the basis of white population. Unlike reform's opponents, Jefferson would never have adopted "Mason of '76" as a pen name. While the East stood for a tradition of which Mason's constitution of 1776 was an important element, Jefferson felt no such bonds. When Virginians wrote their constitution in 1776, he told his young ally, their minds remained clouded by "the abuses of monarchy," and "our first constitutions had really no leading principles in them." (He would later remark that it was no surprise Virginia's constitution was imperfect, for it had been the world's first. Other states, in his opinion, had improved on Virginia's example.[98] The Enlightenment faith in progress manifested here prevented Jefferson from fearing alteration of the constitution in the way others did.) Experience had reinforced Jefferson's devotion to the principle of white apportionment.

Virginia's institutions, Jefferson lamented, were very unrepublican in their bases. His advice: "Only lay down true principles, and adhere to them inflexibly." It was an impractical prescription, one that in the end led to the division first of the American union, then of the Old Dominion itself. He would carry it to every citadel of the East's cherished constitution, and he would prefer to see reforms more far-reaching than he had advocated in *Notes on the State of Virginia*. First, he held, judges should be removable by the Executive on the appeal of both houses of the Legislative, as in England (if not more easily). Suffrage and apportionment should be liberalized and equalized, the governor elected directly. Perhaps most radically, Jefferson would have made judges responsible, had county officials elected (instead of appointed by county courts), and inserted an amendment provision into the constitution.

Jefferson did not believe in amendment as a daily habit, but he opposed reverence he considered to be misplaced. He would prefer to see his countrymen agree that they should "avail ourselves of our reason and experience." Therefore, he thought there should be a new constitution every nineteen years. The living majority had a right to make its own constitution.

In another letter to Kerchival at the end of that summer, Jefferson considered the impact on Virginia's stance in federal politics of adoption within the Old Dominion of white manhood suffrage.[99] Some held that Virginia must discontinue its support of the federal three-fifths clause in order to maintain its reputed devotion to principle, he said. Yet, this was a red herring, for the internal organization of "any country is a matter of municipal arrangement." Jefferson was sure that the limited, contractual nature of the federal government left Virginia perfectly free to do whatever it wanted internally without the slightest commentary from other states. His views had changed markedly since the days of his *A Summary View of the Rights of British America* and draft Declaration of Independence, which both looked to outsiders for moral support.

Thomas Ritchie's *Richmond Enquirer* supported constitutional reform in the 1820s because demographic trends indicated that if the East waited until after the 1830 census, the reapportionment would have to be more severe than one conducted before 1830. Other conservatives in the East, however, objected to the reformers' ad hoc conventions as revolutionary. If the constitution of 1776 did not provide for such a mechanism, they insisted, that mechanism could not be justified under the law.[100]

Reformers attempted to base their support for white apportionment on the Virginia constitution's statement that government is instituted for the common benefit, which they read as a statement about equality. Benjamin Watkins Leigh, a representative leader from the East, noted that the government was instituted for women's and children's benefit, too, and then asked whether even they had to be allowed to participate in public affairs.

Leigh, for one, agreed with George Washington's 1790s argument against the "self-created societies" that sprang up in support of the French Revolution, which Washington made most forcefully in his Farewell Address. The people had the right to create their own government, and any attempt to overawe the legally constituted government in the mode of the Staunton Convention was destructive of that right because it elevated a small, well-organized faction over the entire people. In all, the organizers of reform meetings (and their supporters, including Thomas Jefferson) struck Leigh as "inciters to anarchy and disunion."[101] For Leigh, there was "no way for man to judge of the future but from the past." For that reason, he would "continue to defend the institutions which have so long preserved my country free, tranquil and happy." Anyone who had read Leigh's nom de plume, the name of the main author of Virginia's founding documents, would have realized that.

The Staunton Convention of 1825, easily the most important reform convention, angered conservatives on other grounds, too. First, the Convention responded to the class-based constitutional and social thought of the East in kind. Following Jefferson's reasoning in *Notes on the State of Virginia* and elsewhere, reformers demanded white apportionment and white, male suffrage to replace the freehold requirement. They made reference to an "odious landed aristocracy who ruled the true majority through a violation of true principles of a free republic." Such a reform, conservatives noted, could only injure Virginia and the South in the federal arena.[102] One of the most pro-Southern provisions of the federal constitution provided that each slave count as three-fifths of a person for purposes of House of Representatives apportionment; how could the South refuse to accept reform of that provision, conservatives asked, if the East yielded to the West in the Virginia constitution? In Congress, conservatives used the argument that Jefferson found convincing: that this was an internal matter for each state. In state politics, however, they warned of reform's repercussions.

In the end, Ritchie's argument won the day, and the General Assembly called a referendum on a constitutional convention—with discussions of the West's secession from Virginia as a backdrop.[103] Virginians voted in 1829 to hold a convention by a margin of approximately 5,000 out of 38,500 votes cast. At the insistence of the East, which dominated the General Assembly, the new constitution would be drawn by a body apportioned in the same manner as the General Assembly. William Branch Giles, Benjamin Watkins Leigh, and John Randolph of Roanoke would have their way, more or less, in the end. The fix was in.[104]

Despite the ground rules, the Convention of 1829–1830 provided the best opportunity in two generations for Virginians to debate the future of their Commonwealth. All of Virginia's great men, including former Presidents Madison and Monroe and Chief Justice Marshall, future President Tyler, John Randolph of Roanoke, and Governor Giles, participated. Indeed, all of those luminaries of Virginia's past greatness played leading roles, as did newcomers (and future senators) Benjamin Watkins Leigh and John Y. Mason.

Former Presidents Monroe and Madison entered the Convention with the intention of bridging the gap between the West's demands and the East's opposition to innovation. As Monroe put it, republics' record for longevity did not inspire confidence.[105] Only "contentment" between the traditionalist East and the rapidly expanding West could maximize the Virginia republic's chances of success in supporting its "great principles." He wanted to secure "such amendments as will correspond with the great principles" reformers had in mind, but his constituents knew him to be a stolid, plodding man, certainly not a radical. This kind of moderation, which mixed a notion of Virginia as experimental republic with characteristic Eastern conservatism, would be in short supply in the Convention.

To the consternation, even shock, of the West, delegates from the East often took forthrightly aristocratic positions.[106] Where once republicanism had seemed revolutionary, now it smacked of reaction. Littleton Waller Tazewell, the future governor and United States senator (and son of a United States senator) from Norfolk, told the convention that as blacks voting would merely reflect the opinions of their masters and women voting would simply echo their fathers or husbands, they should not vote. Only educated, white men should vote, "and education can only be acquired by the fruits of property. So there should be a property qualification." The East rejected the West's demands for suffrage liberalization.[107]

The East's attitude toward reformers was crystallized in an exchange in the convention's legislative committee. When one of the reformers, pointing to the Jeffersonian formulations of natural rights on which the reform effort rested, pleaded with the members from the East to put self-interest aside and behave as statesmen, Benjamin Watkins Leigh responded, "I choose (looking closely at Cooke) to follow the example of the gentleman than his precept. (A laugh)" The reformers' "litany of Jeffersonian phrases" had little effect on their opponents, who found it odd that so many long-time Federalists had suddenly embraced Jefferson.[108]

In place of the utopian spirit that pervaded politics in the wake of Jefferson's 1801 presidential victory, the East stood now for distrust of the populace at large. To Delegate Charles Francis Mercer of Loudoun County, who offered to include guarantees that the new constitution would be interpreted as promised in that constitution itself, Leigh said, "I have no confidence in guarantees—none whatever; and least of all do I believe they would be observed by gentlemen who construed the plainest, simplest words in the world opposite to their plain and palpable meaning. (An allusion to Mr. Mercer's federal politics. Another laugh from the committee and from the lobby.)"[109]

A reformer from the West told the Convention that "every principle for which we contend is supported by the deliberate opinions of Mr. Jefferson," and he was right—for all the good it did him. The conservatives in the Convention of 1829–1830 had no time for democratic sentiments. They preferred old ways and established hierarchy—that is, the continued dominance of their own section and class—to individual striving, and the ties between generations seemed more compelling to them than the prospect of individual opportunity.[110]

The most galling thing about the reform scheme, from the point of view of the East, was precisely that it threatened to take control of the Old Dominion, *their* Old Dominion, and give it to the "potboilers and mechanics," not to mention "the peasantry of the west." It threatened to democratize Virginia's culture and its economy along with its politics. Randolph and Leigh had no intention of surrendering their society to any such people. Just as conservatives believed only a man with no sons could have initiated Jefferson's campaign to eliminate entails, so they surely thought that only a man in that situation would have wiped out the last of the old aristocratic society that already seemed to be slipping away from the East's besieged conservatives.[111]

As the incumbent governor, William Branch Giles was given the position of chairman of the convention's committee on the executive branch. He inaugurated that committee's activities with a speech calling on his fellow delegates to recognize exactly what it was that they had inherited.[112] Not only was the governorship of Virginia, unlike its United States analogue, characterized by "an actual, efficacious" responsibility, but the constitution of 1776 was one of the great achievements in the history of the world.

Giles could not conceive, he said, what had led the people of Virginia to yield the preference for commemoration to the 4th of July, instead of the 29th of June (the day their constitution was adopted). Perhaps their acquiescence in this decision had grown out of "their noble, generous self-denial, for which they have been so justly celebrated on other occasions, in being willing to share the honour and glory of this great political discovery with the people of their sister States." The Declaration of Independence, after all, was "a mere act of diplomacy," while "the Virginia Constitution is a written social compact, the first ever entered into by man," a "model" unto "the whole human race." (In later speeches, Giles referred to Virginia's as "the best Constitution that was ever presented to any people under the sun" and called 29 June "the greatest day in the political calendar."[113])

Giles went on to defend the system of indirect election by which Virginians had chosen their governors throughout the republican half-century. In the mode of the Eastern aristocrats, he predicted that if the popular elections favored by the reformers were instituted, a populace ignorant of the candidates' characters would be left at the mercy of electioneers. Indirect elections insured more informed choice. It also explained why Virginia had no experience with political hucksters, according to Giles, unlike its sister states.

The Virginia constitution's freehold suffrage provision placed power in the hands of a "middling class," not in those of either the very rich or the very poor. Both Great Britain's haughty nobility and Kentucky's debtor relief laws cautioned against putting the preponderance of political power in the hands of one extreme of society. Virginia's constitution wisely avoided that mistake.

Perhaps the most forceful reform position was taken by Norfolk's Robert B. Taylor, one of the small number of reformers from the East.[114] Virginia was "our country" to him, yet he insisted that the position of the extreme conservatives who wanted no change at all was indefensible. Whenever some citizens had rights others did not have, he insisted, the Declaration of Rights was violated. The General Assembly's unequal apportionment seemed to be the classic instance.

Taylor explored the clash between equality of suffrage and defense of property in suffrage, and he finally concluded that the two principles were incompatible. If property owners continued to enjoy the favor from which they had benefited in the past, the people would doubt their institutions' justice. The resulting failure of the political system would endanger property far more than the equal apportionment the West demanded. He supported a perfect representation, which "must throw back such an image [a perfect image] of the *people represented.*" (Here he adopted George Mason's formula.)

In response, Leigh proclaimed that he hoped that those who desired apportionment on the basis of white population, without taking heed of the situation of Virginia society, had better reasons than that "such principles were unknown to our English ancestors, from whom we have derived our institutions; better than the rights of man as held in the French school; better than that they were calculated in their nature to lead to rapine, anarchy and bloodshed, and in the end, to military despotism" (an allusion to the French and Haitian Revolutions). He wanted no "arithmetical and mathematical reasons; no mere abstractions."[115]

John R. Cooke, with whom Leigh had jousted in the committee on the legislature, was up like a shot.[116] Mr. Leigh, he said, had dared to blast Revolutionary truths based on the thought of "Locke, and Sidney, and Milton," and he apparently approved of "the *privilege* of the *Noble*." Majority rule and the sovereignty of the people, he intoned, were not "metaphysical subtleties," but practical principles. "[N]ature itself . . . pronounced, on women and children, a sentence of incapacity to exercise political power," so equality of liberty in the Virginia constitution had nothing to do with some imaginary situation in which women were admitted to equality with men. The Declaration of Rights's equality principle meant that all adults "and free agents by situation" (not children, wives, spinsters, or slaves) had equal rights to "political power." Cooke closed his demand for democratic reform by warning that the majority would only submit temporarily to a government organized on different principles.

Leigh's and the other conservatives' frequent references to the Revolutionary generation annoyed Cooke. As he understood it, the county-based apportionment of the General Assembly to which reformers objected did not date to 1776, but to a General Assembly decision of 1661—when only the Tidewater region was settled. Freehold suffrage, similarly, dated to a royal governor's instruction in 1677. The Revolutionary generation left these matters unchanged out of military necessity, but Thomas Jefferson, for one, objected to the constitution of 1776 on these bases as early as 1781.

Leigh and others insisted that without constitutional protection, property would succumb to the mob. (His characterization of average Virginians echoed Federalist Edmund Randolph's use of the phrase "the herd" in the 1788 Richmond Convention.) Cooke rejoined that Virginia should not base its lonely abstention from the American trend to white, manhood suffrage on this assertion, for it was simply mistaken; man was "an *affectionate*, a *social*, a *patriotic*, a *conscientious* and a *religious* creature," "philanthropic" by nature, and—despite Leigh's aspersions—men were governed by their consciences. A slaveholding minority need not fear a non-slaveholding majority.

Judge John W. Green of Piedmont Culpeper restricted the Declaration of Rights's statement that all men were equal when they entered into society to "natural," not political, rights.[117] The majority did not acquire a right to govern as a result of its mere force; where all men had the same interest, yes, the majority had a right to govern, because more people could be assumed to have more interest. Where society was divided among interests, however, interests must be protected systemically. Green pointed out that the East already bore a disproportionate share of the tax burden, a higher rate of land tax per acre. Otherwise, he noted, the West would not object to apportionment that took property holdings into account. The West wanted to tax the East for its own benefit, to use the East's money to build roads and canals in the West. Green wanted the West simply to admit it.

Northern reformer Charles F. Mercer had a ready answer to Green's complaints about the tax burden imposed on the wealthy East: it was not the West's responsibility.[118] The West did not control the General Assembly, so it could not be blamed for the taxation system. In any event, this veteran of decades' agitation for constitutional reform held that no injustice inhered in taxing profitable property, so long as the taxes were laid proportionately. Still, he would support inclusion in the constitution of guarantees to mollify the East on this score.

Mercer had a complaint about the East's rhetorical tack, however.[119] He wished the men on the stand-pat side of the question would infuse their speeches with a bit more public-spiritedness. Delegates had been told, he complained, that the money of the wealthy was to be used to educate the poor. He was ashamed that such an argument should be made in Virginia. Education for the poor was a republican necessity. Was the need sectional? "Who are the people of the West? Are they not our fellow-citizens, our friends and brothers? Whence did they spring? From the East? Have they forgot their common origin?" He believed Virginia's experience in the War of 1812 showed the West to be perfectly loyal to Virginia.

Another conservative delegate, Eastern Shore Accomack County's young Abel P. Upshur, denied that a majority had a right to rule in any case.[120] If there were seven men in a community, he asked, what gave four the right to govern the other three? The Virginia constitution recognized no such right, and neither did compact law. In fact, if majorities alone were to govern, he did not understand why women and blacks should not participate equally. He wanted to know where the majority had ever governed. Man is only known in society, and from the first—when Eve was subordinated to Adam ("Here then was no equality")—the reformers' favorite principle never formed the basis of any government. The only equality Upshur recognized lay in the lack of any right to rule anyone else. "[T]here are no original principles of Government at all," the future United States secretary of state insisted. The rule of the majority was a convenient device where common interests pervaded a society, but where that condition did not obtain, majority rule was unjustifiable. Virginians' interests differed in 1829 when it came to property, so property should be considered in devising a system of government. "Persons *and property*," this non-slaveholding delegate from a slaveholding region held, are "the constituent elements of society."

The Revolution, according to Upshur, had begun over taxpayers' insistence that they alone should lay taxes upon themselves. This remained the East's view in 1829. If taxation depended upon ability to pay, so should apportionment. He also put a new twist on the hackneyed argument concerning the three-fifths clause: it would be impossible to defend that federal provision if the East accepted the West's preferred amendments, he said, but to incorporate representation for property into the Virginia constitution would stamp Virginia once again as the most consistently principled of states, because that would make Virginia's constitution perfectly consistent with the three-fifths clause.

Upshur and his fellows did not say property should be represented everywhere, he noted. They spoke only about conditions in Virginia, for "*our* property, so far as slaves are concerned, is *peculiar*." Western hostility to slavery meant the two sections would never homogenize. The proximity of free states to the West and the difference between the West's and the East's agricultural products added further obstacles to Virginia's internal harmony—and to majority rule. Constitutional provisions protecting property were inadequate where the majority claimed a theoretical right to rule, Upshur insisted. Yet, the West need not be so concerned: "For fifty-four years, the taxing power has been with us, and who can say it has ever been abused?" If the East had never abused its position, no one could say it should be divested of it.

Upshur's performance in the convention—forthrightly supporting the conservatives on apportionment but voting to liberalize the suffrage—is elucidated by a letter he wrote years before the convention assembled.[121] After summarizing the West's complaints, he admitted the constitution of 1776 to be "extremely defective." If he were a Western man, he confided, he undoubtedly would side with the West on apportionment; since he was from the East, he opposed it. This opposition gained force from his suspicion that leading reformers aimed to eliminate Virginia slavery. Although he claimed to "abhor slavery," Upshur held to the view that its abolition should come about as a result of a necessarily "slow operation of moral causes," not a constitutional ban. Too great an alteration of the constitution might accustom the people to change, and no one knew where that might end. (It certainly was not the kind of development that an aristocrat could be expected to favor.) His correspondent agreed.[122]

Thomas R. Joynes, also of Accomack County, underscored Upshur's un-Jeffersonian opinion: "One of the greatest errors which can be committed in the science of Government, it appears to me, is to lay down certain general fundamental principles, and, like the bed of Procrustes, compel every community to conform to them, without regard to circumstances. A Constitution, to be of any value, must be adapted to the particular circumstances and situation of the country for which it is intended. The Government which would be best for one country might be worst for another. Every man in this Convention; nay, every man, I am sure, in America, would unite in saying, that a Republican form of Government was best adapted to the situation of the people of the United States and to the individual States: but he would be an unwise politician indeed, who would attempt at this day to establish a Republic in Russia or Turkey; and humanity has had to mourn over the unsuccessful efforts to establish a Republic in France; and, from recent indications, we have too much reason to apprehend that a Republican Government is not suited to the late Spanish possessions on this continent."[123]

The West's Philip Doddridge, on the other hand, responded to Upshur's bravura defense of the status quo with an equally forceful espousal of Jeffersonian discontent.[124] The constitution under which Virginia lived, he parroted Jefferson, was adopted by a body that assumed power to adopt a new charter. That body "did little more than to continue the existing state of things." The House of

Delegates represented a mere continuation of the old House of Burgesses, the Council was perpetuated, and little thought was given to either. Apportionment and suffrage, the great sticking points, must be addressed. Of course children, the insane, and women should not be allowed to vote, for they simply were not up to it; however, contrary to the East's arguments, the rich should pay the most, not weigh the most in the Old Dominion's councils.

Doddridge upbraided his interlocutors for their inconsistency: At one minute, the Declaration of Rights received lavish praise; at the next, the Declaration's principles were branded "metaphysical abstractions," even "visionary theories, which appear very well on paper, but are wholly unfit for practical application." The East's argument portended "perpetual slavery" for the West, for when the day came that the West was ten times as populous as the East, the Eastern arguments against reapportionment would apply with even more force than they did in 1829. Eastern slaveholders' dominance made Doddridge, as a man of the West, "a slave." So much for "our Constitution the best on earth, and ourselves the most fortunate of men."[125]

Philip P. Barbour of Orange County had had about all of Doddridge's brand of politics he could take.[126] Echoing the argument made by Robert Carter Nicholas in the May Convention of 1776, Barbour bluntly asserted that if Virginians took the Declaration of Rights's statement that *"all men are by nature, equally free"* literally, Virginia would recapitulate the bloody Haitian Revolution. Anyway, rights dependent on the existence of government (such as the right to participate in government) could not be based on a condition existing only in government's absence (for example, equality of all men). When Doddridge based nonparticipation of women on their inherent weakness, said Barbour, he might as easily exclude weak men from participation in government. Doddridge's argument was not based on nature at all.

Calling to mind Virginia planters' proverbial conservatism, Barbour opined, "There is not a farmer in your State, who will try an experiment, that is suggested to him, till he finds out that somebody else has tried it before him. Shall we trust to an authority like this, in laying the foundation of our Commonwealth?" Despite the West's protestations, he suggested, it might be called absence of liberty for residents solely of one place to tax those solely of another. In response to the notion that the East should simply rely on the West's good will, Barbour showed that he, too, could marshal Jeffersonian arguments. Faith is the ground of religion, he asserted, but its opposite is the ground of free government. "[N]o nation is free, unless they possess *political* liberty, by which I understand the power to secure their own freedom." Therefore, the East would never yield its control over its own taxation.[127]

A leading reformer, Augusta County's Briscoe G. Baldwin, answered Barbour with a more far-sighted view of things.[128] "The only effect of the proposed amendment would be, to give permanency to any hostile sectional feelings which may now exist in this Commonwealth, and by exasperating those feelings, perhaps bring about that very insecurity of property which it is the object of its advocates to guard against." The two sections' interests need not always jar on the question of internal improvements, but might be joined in a pan-Virginian water transportation network. Arguments that Virginia had "hostile and irreconcileable [sic] sectional interests" militated in favor of a division of the Commonwealth. They were also untrue.

Having adopted the rhetorical strategy of protecting the Old Dominion against the newly "disunionist" East, reformers followed up with a "defense" of the Virginia citizenry against the imputed charge that it was unfit for freedom. Frederick County's Alfred H. Powell insisted that if any people was fit for liberty, Virginia's ("a virtuous, an honest, an intelligent people") was. They had proved it in 1776, and "are the people of Virginia the degenerate sons of such fathers? I think not. A similar occasion would produce similar evidences of virtue at the present day. The demoralizing principle has not here had the inviting channels which have been opened to it in some other States of the Union. We have no large cities in Virginia, to present an inviting refuge for the vicious, the profligate, and the convicts of foreign countries." The Declaration of Rights' statements that the people was sovereign and that the majority was to rule supported the white basis. The proposed admixture of property apportionment would deny the majority its right to institute a constitution—and thus depart from Virginia tradition.

Reformers insisted that the only guarantee of property in a republic was the virtue of the people and that republicanism required reapportionment and broadened suffrage,[129] while conservatives answered that so long as they had the preponderance of authority in their hands, they had all the guarantee they needed; to them, appeals to republican principle seemed starry-eyed, "French," a return to the status quo ante bellum, unacceptable.[130]

Another reform delegate insisted that if there had never been a state of nature, there were no first principles to form a basis for political reasoning, so he had to take the state of nature for granted. Many seem to have been unpersuaded by this argument.[131] He asked why some men clung so tightly to a state of things under which Virginia had prospered so little. "Virginia has been long in a state of decline, which time she has been strictly confined to a certain course of political regimen, but still she is sinking more and more. Is it not time to change it?" Since Virginia had natural advantages over states that were outstripping it, slavery and the constitution—the two most obvious factors distinguishing Virginia from other states—must be the causes.

Richard H. Henderson, of Loudoun County in what is now the northern section of Virginia, picked up on this theme.[132] "What is the general condition of the Commonwealth? A commerce far inferior to that of the little State of Rhode Island, an agriculture languishing, the mechanic arts in a state of depression and thriftlessness, and provision made for the education of about one-eighth of the children annually educated by the small State of Connecticut. Yes, Sir, and they are not half so well educated." The constitution was to blame.

Leigh had a ready response.[133] Gentlemen asked why Virginia had fallen from first to third among the states in both population and wealth, and the answer was obvious: it ceded Kentucky. Freehold suffrage had nothing to do with it. Picking up a thread of argumentation James Madison had used in defense of the internal improvements program, Leigh said that so long as free, fertile land beckoned the young to emigrate, coastal states' populations would stagnate. Still, Virginia's character, principles, and morality were unparalleled.

One enraged reform delegate noted that Thomas Jefferson's name, that of "the great Apostle of liberty," had not been invoked once in the weeks he had sat in the close, stuffy room in the Richmond capitol.[134] What a change had befallen Virginia.

> There was a time when it was honorable to profess the faith of these great fathers of the church, when it was perilous to be a sceptic, when the name of Fox was venerated, and the principles of Burke abhorred. . . . Then, the authority of the Sage of Monticello would have stood against the world; now, there are "none so poor as to do him reverence." Then, was Burke regarded as the enemy of human rights and the firmest defender of aristocracy and monarchy—but now, Burke, Filmer, and Hobbes, judging from their arguments, have become the text books of our statesmen.

As few were overt atheists, so everyone was avowedly republican, but he would judge a tree by its fruit, a Christian by his works, and a "professor of republicanism by his practice."

The allusion to Shakespeare's "Julius Caesar" (and tacit comparison of the conservatives to Brutus), the references to Burke (to whose arguments the East's were indeed similar), Filmer (against whom Sidney argued in his *Discourses Concerning Government*[135]), and Hobbes (like the reference to Filmer, evidently calculated to insult the East), and the paraphrase of the Book of St. Matthew (12: 33) marked this reformer as a traditionalist member of the Virginia elite in much the same mode as his opponents. Through the Shakespearean comparison of Thomas Jefferson to the dead Julius Caesar, he showed himself as well educated a man as they; ticking off a list of the Revolutionaries' favorite political writers, even without grasping their teachings fully, demonstrated his political *bona fides*; and the quotation from the Evangelist's account of Christ's life was at once a slam of the conservatives and a way of asserting his own fidelity to the Truth. This speech said much about the fidelity to one strand of Revolutionary thinking that lay behind reform's appeal. Despite the Easterners' assumptions, the men of the West were Virginian, too.

President Monroe noted at this point that slavery was the cause of the sectional division in the convention.[136] He prognosticated that the elimination of slavery would loose four hundred thousand destitute poor upon the land, and he guessed they would soon turn to crime for subsistence. Virginia could not colonize them without federal help. Although Virginia had followed its thwarted colonial efforts with a ban on slave imports "among the first acts, of State sovereignty," it was stuck with the problem. Thus, each of the two sections had just claims, and compromise was necessary.

Monroe's reference to his long-held view that the United States would have to help Virginia if the Old Dominion hoped ever to eliminate slavery troubled other Eastern delegates. No idea, according to Governor Giles, was so pregnant with "the annihilation of all state rights—the destruction of the State Governments—and more, the amalgamation of a great mass of power in the Federal Government."[137] Despotism would result from concentration of power in hands beyond Virginia's influence. This, Giles returned to his old theme, would be the opposite of the current situation. Virginia's constitution was literally "a Godsend." "So happy have we been under it . . . as almost to forget that there was any government. Government may be said to approach perfection, when man does not know that he is governed at all."

Leigh insisted that the West's sole goal was to hitch Virginia to the United States internal improvements train, which only Virginia had been able to brake.[138] Western men had told him so repeatedly. Once again, considerations of federal politics intruded into Virginians' theoretically self-contained debate, stunting Virginia's hopes for itself.

In time, various apportionment compromises—one house on one basis, one on the other, the federal basis in both houses, etc.—were proposed, and the conservatives took heart. When the issue moved forthrightly from principle to power, they had had their way.[139] Republicanism rested, in the conservatives' old understanding, on limitation of power, not on symmetry of constitutions. (Here they echoed John Taylor's distinction, in his correspondence with Wilson Cary Nicholas, between *The Federalist*'s checks and balances and federalism's division of power.) The men of the East could feel justified in maintaining control of *both* houses once those of the West surrendered the "high" ground. John Randolph noted that he and his fellows had vested rights, "and we'll not yield them."[140] The East's representatives would have their way on the apportionment issue, and maintain their section's predominance, yet a while.

Other questions the more ideologically oriented men from the West found interesting, such as the structure of the executive branch and the fate of the county courts, were more easily resolved. The East did not insist so rigidly on maintaining the old structure of the executive branch as it had insisted on winning the apportionment contest, and the West cared far less about the county courts—linchpin of the county oligarchies—than did the East.

In the end, some of the conservatives, such as Abel P. Upshur, broke ranks on the suffrage question, and as a result, housekeepers and leaseholders received the suffrage. About one-third of white men still remained voteless. Virginia's governor would have a three-year term, but the General Assembly still elected him, and the Council was not abolished. Local government, which conservatives held to have assumed its aristocratic form many centuries earlier, was entirely unchanged. Randolph of Roanoke succeeded in arguing down the idea of an amendment provision, and democratic ratification suffered a similar fate. (Randolph said he would as soon see the people of Japan ratify the document.) In short, a long-term conflict between the Jeffersonian decentralizers and the

Jeffersonian natural rights–popular sovereignty advocates materialized in Richmond that winter.[141]

The West remained unsatisfied. In opposing ratification, Western reformer Philip Doddridge called the proposed constitution a "political compact for the slavery of us and our children."[142] The 3 December 1830 issue of the *Winchester Republican* warned that if Virginia did not begin to spend an "adequate" amount of money on internal improvements there, the West would secede from Virginia. Indeed, if the northwest were allowed to secede and the southwest were given increased internal improvements spending, all would be well. (That paper also calculated that the north of Virginia looked to future unification with either Pennsylvania or Maryland.) In short, the notion of "Virginia" no longer had any purchase at all on the minds of many Westerners.[143]

At decade's end, then, Virginia stood at a crossroads. During the quarter-century of its political dominance, the seeds of Old Virginia's destruction had been sown. The East's response to the United States Supreme Court's attacks on its fondest conception of Virginia was the adoption of a Burkean localism. The East's political philosophy, dusted off in the middle of the 1810s as if the preceding two decades had never occurred, led it to blame the federal government for its economic plight. Leading Easterners determined to defend their aristocratic privileges to the bitter end. One of the results of the Eastern aristocrats' newfound self-centeredness, opposition to federal internal improvements, banks, and other schemes for economic development, drove a wedge between the Old Dominion of Carters, Harrisons, Lees, and Randolphs and the new society of immigrant Virginians beyond the Blue Ridge. Residents of the newly settled areas in what is now West Virginia decided that Jeffersonianism, and particularly reform of the state constitution, was for them.

Yet, the West's Jeffersonianism, like the East's, was not free of alloy. Jefferson never coupled his desire for reform of the state constitution with constitutional latitudinarianism in the federal realm, and his acceptance of economic change was only grudging. He always remained a Virginian, if an uncharacteristically optimistic one, at heart. Thus, neither the East nor the West could be said to be thoroughly Jeffersonian at the end of the "Age of Jefferson." Virginia was riven by the ethnocultural and slave-free cleavages that would rend the Old Dominion—and the American union—in the decades to come.[144]

NOTES

1. Joseph Carrington Cabell to Isaac A. Coles, 22 January 1808, Cabell Family Papers, University of Virginia.
2. John Taylor to James Monroe, 2 January 1812, "Letters of John Taylor, of Caroline County, Virginia," ed. Wm. E. Dodd, *The John P. Branch Historical Papers of Randolph-Macon College* 2 (1908), 253–353, at 327–32; John Randolph to Benjamin Watkins Leigh, 6 March 1812, Virginia Historical Society.

3. Charles Henry Ambler, *Sectionalism in Virginia from 1776 to 1861* (1910; reprint New York: Russell & Russell, 1964), 81.

4. *Ibid.*, 92–93.

5. Elinor Janet Weeder, "Wilson Cary Nicholas, Jefferson's Lieutenant" (M.A. thesis, University of Virginia, 1946), 101, 116–17.

6. Rhys Isaac, *The Transformation of Virginia, 1740–1790* (New York and London: W. W. Norton, 1982).

7. Philip Morrison Rice, "Internal Improvements in Virginia, 1775–1860," 133–34, 138, 136.

8. *Ibid.*, 1, 163.

9. *Ibid.*, 301–3, 385.

10. *Ibid.*, 158–59, 386–87, 298–99.

11. For the Bonus Bill controversy, John Lauritz Larson, "'Bind the Nation Together': The National Union and the Struggle for a System of Internal Improvements," *The Journal of American History* 74 (1987): 363–87. For Virginians' calculations, Philip Rice Morrison, "Internal Improvements in Virginia, 1775–1860," 168–70.

12. Thomas Jefferson, "Sixth Annual Message," 2 December 1806, *The Works of Thomas Jefferson*, ed. Paul Leicester Ford (New York and London: G. P. Putnam's Sons, 1892–1899), 10: 302–20, at 317–18; James Madison, "Seventh Annual Message," 5 December 1815, *The Writings of James Madison*, ed. Gaillard Hunt (New York: G. P. Putnam's Sons, 1900–1910), 8: 335–44, at 341–42.

13. James Madison to James Monroe, 29 November 1817, *Ibid.*, 8: 397–98; Thomas Jefferson to George Ticknor, May 1817, *The Works of Thomas Jefferson*, 12: 58–61, at 59.

14. James Madison, "Veto Message," 3 March 1817, *The Writings of James Madison*, 8: 386–88; Kevin R. C. Gutzman, "Edmund Randolph and Virginia Constitutionalism," *The Review of Politics* 66 (2004): 469–97; K[evin] R. Constantine Gutzman, "The Virginia and Kentucky Resolutions Reconsidered: 'An Appeal to the *Real Laws* of Our Country,'" *The Journal of Southern History* 66 (2000): 473–96.

15. Thomas Jefferson to Albert Gallatin, 16 June 1817, *The Works of Thomas Jefferson*, 12: 70–74, at 72.

16. Littleton Waller Tazewell, *A Review of the Proclamation of President Jackson of the 10th of December, 1832, in a Series of Numbers Originally Published in the "Norfolk and Portsmouth Herald," under the Signature of "A Virginian"* (Norfolk: J. D. Ghiselin, 1888).

17. The best discussion of the litigation is F. Thornton Miller, *Juries and Judges versus the Law: Virginia's Provincial Legal Perspective, 1783–1828* (Charlottesville: University Press of Virginia, 1994), 74–86; also see *The Papers of John Marshall*, ed. Charles F. Hobson et al. (Chapel Hill: University of North Carolina Press, 1995), 7: 108–19.

18. Albert J. Beveridge, *The Life of John Marshall* (New York and Boston: Houghton Mifflin, 1919), 4: 160. Roane described himself as "gratified to find, that I have not erred, in the great principles at least, on which the question seems to turn." Spencer Roane to Thomas Jefferson, 28 October 1815, "Roane Correspondence," ed. Wm. E. Dodd, *The John P. Branch Historical Papers of Randolph-Macon College* 2 (1905), 123–42, at 131–32.

19. *Hunter v. Martin*, Judge Roane's opinion, *Richmond Enquirer*, 1 February 1816. For the Federalists' explication of the Constitution in the Richmond Convention, Kevin R. C. Gutzman, "Edmund Randolph and Virginia Constitutionalism," *The Review of Politics* 66 (2004): 469–97.

20. *The Papers of James Madison*, ed. William T. Hutchinson et al. (Chicago and Charlottesville: University of Chicago Press and University Press of Virginia, 1962–), 17: 307–50.
21. *Hunter v. Martin*, Judge Brooke's opinion, *Richmond Enquirer*, 30 January 1816.
22. Charles Henry Ambler, *Sectionalism in Virginia From 1776 to 1861* (1910; reprint New York: Russell & Russell, 1964), 103.
23. *McCulloch v. Maryland* (1819), Chief Justice John Marshall for the court, *The Papers of John Marshall*, 8: 259–79.
24. Albert J. Beveridge, *The Life of John Marshall*, 4: 286.
25. Editor's note, *The Papers of John Marshall*, 8: 282.
26. John Taylor, *Construction Construed, and Constitutions Vindicated* (Richmond: Shepherd and Pollard, 1820).
27. *Ibid.*, 83.
28. John Marshall to Joseph Story, 24 March 1819, *The Papers of John Marshall*, 8: 280; John Marshall to Bushrod Washington, 27 March 1819, *Ibid.*, 8: 281; John Marshall to Joseph Story, 28 April 1819, *Ibid.*, 8: 309–10; John Marshall to Joseph Story, 27 May 1819, *Ibid.*, 8: 313–14.
29. "Amphictyon," *Richmond Enquirer*, 30 March 1819, in *John Marshall's Defense of McCulloch v. Maryland*, ed. Gerald Gunther (Stanford: Calif.: Stanford University Press, 1969), 52–64.
30. Marshall's opinion echoed the arguments made by Federalists in the 1790s debates over congressional power. *Cf.* "Jefferson versus Hamilton on the Bank of the United States 1791," *American Legal History: Cases and Materials*, eds. Kermit Hall et al., 105–7.
31. "Amphictyon," *Richmond Enquirer*, 2 April 1819, *Ibid.*, 64–77. Marshall borrowed this argument from Hamilton. "Jefferson versus Hamilton on the Bank of the United States 1791," 107. "Amphictyon's" came from Jefferson. *Ibid.*, 106.
32. Rex Beach, "Judge Spencer Roane: A Champion of States Rights," 95.
33. John Marshall, "A Friend of the Union," [Philadelphia] *Union*, 24 April 1819, in *John Marshall's Defense of McCulloch v. Maryland*, 78–91; John Marshall, "A Friend of the Union," [Philadelphia] *Union*, 30 June 1819, *Ibid.*, 155–61.
34. James Madison to Spencer Roane, 2 September 1819, *The Writings of James Madison*, 8: 447–53.
35. Thomas Jefferson to Spencer Roane, 6 September 1819, *The Works of Thomas Jefferson*, 12: 135–40, at 135–37.
36. John Marshall to Bushrod Washington, 17 June 1819, *The Papers of John Marshall*, 8: 316–17; John Marshall to Bushrod Washington, 28 June 1819, *Ibid.*, 8: 317.
37. The following account relies on Francis N. Stites, *John Marshall: Defender of the Constitution* (Boston and Toronto: Little, Brown, 1981), 134–36; and Charles F. Hobson, *The Great Chief Justice: John Marshall and the Rule of Law* (Lawrence: University Press of Kansas, 1996), 127–32. Also see Albert J. Beveridge, *The Life of John Marshall*, 4: 342–70.
38. The resolutions are at *State Documents on Federal Relations: The States and the United States*, ed. Herman V. Ames (New York: Da Capo Press, 1970), 104; for the *Cohens* case as a setup, see Editorial Note, *The Papers of John Marshall*, 9: 106–12.
39. The Supreme Court's opinion is at *Ibid.*, 9: 113–41. Marshall's hermeneutical approach and exposition of some of the inconsistencies in his *Cohens* opinion can be found at *Ibid.*, 9: 108–10. Marshall's general approach to law is captured in Jean Edward

Smith, *John Marshall: Definer of a Nation* (New York: Henry Holt and Company, 1996), 425–26.

40. Algernon Sidney wrote *Discourses on Government*, against Sir Robert Filmer's defense of divine right monarchy, *Patriarcha*, so the nom de plume "Algernon Sidney" carried powerful implications about Marshall's position. Spencer Roane, "Algernon Sidney," 25 May 1821, *Richmond Enquirer*, in "Algernon Sidney" essays, ed. Wm. E. Dodd, *The John P. Branch Historical Papers of Randolph-Macon College* 2 (1906), 78–183, at 78–90.

41. The Eleventh Amendment reads, "The judicial power of the United States shall not be construed to extend to any suit in law or equity, commenced or prosecuted against one of the United States by citizens of another state, or by citizens or subjects of any foreign state."

42. Thomas Jefferson to Spencer Roane, 25 June 1821, "Roane Correspondence," 123–42, at 138–39.

43. Thomas Jefferson to Spencer Roane, 27 June 1821, *The Works of Thomas Jefferson*, 12: 202–3, at 203.

44. James Madison to Spencer Roane, 29 June 1821, *The Writings of James Madison*, 9: 65–68. Madison doubted the general government could long transgress the states' authority. James Madison to Spencer Roane, 6 May 1821, *Ibid.*, 9: 55–63, at 58.

45. James Madison to John G. Jackson, 27 December 1821, *Ibid.*, 9: 70–77.

46. John Taylor, *New Views of the Constitution of the United States* (1823; reprint New York: Da Capo Press, 1971), 87.

47. James Madison to Joseph C. Cabell, 18 September 1828, *The Writings of James Madison*, 9: 316–40, at 328–30; James Madison to Joseph C. Cabell, 22 March 1827, *Ibid.*, 9: 284–87, at 285.

48. James Madison to William Cabell Rives, 12 March 1833, *Ibid.*, 9: 511–14; Kevin R. C. Gutzman, "Edmund Randolph and Virginia Constitutionalism"; K[evin] R. Constantine Gutzman, "The Virginia and Kentucky Resolutions Reconsidered: 'An Appeal to the *Real Laws* of Our Country.'"

49. James Madison to Thomas Jefferson, 8 February 1825, *Ibid.*, 9: 218–21.

50. Thomas Jefferson to William Branch Giles, 26 December 1825, *The Works of Thomas Jefferson*, 12: 424–28, at 426.

51. Some have interpreted the Old Dominion's silence in the wake of Kentucky's defeat in *Green v. Biddle*, 21 U.S. (8 Wheat.) 1 (1823), as a surrender of the "Principles of '98," but the subsequent behavior of Ritchie and other leading Virginians demonstrated that they clearly had not understood it thus.

52. Drew McCoy, *The Last of the Fathers: James Madison & the Republican Legacy* (New York: Cambridge University Press, 1989). Also see James Madison to M. L. Hurlbert, May 1830, *The Writings of James Madison*, 9: 370, *et seq.*; James Madison to Robert S. Garnett, 11 February 1824, *Ibid.*, 9: 176–77; James Madison to Thomas Ritchie, 18 December 1825, *Ibid.*, 9: 231–36; Thomas Jefferson to Edward Everett, 8 April 1826, *The Works of Thomas Jefferson*, 12: 469; James Madison, "Advice to My Country," *The Writings of James Madison*, photographs following 9: 610.

53. John Taylor, *Arator, Being a Series of Agricultural Essays, Practical and Political: In Sixty-Four Numbers*.

54. James Madison, "Eighth Annual Message," 3 December 1816, *The Writings of James Madison*, 8: 375–85, at 376.

55. Lyon G. Tyler, *The Letters and Times of the Tylers* (3 vols., 1884–1896; reprinted New York: Da Capo Press, 1970), 1: 302.

56. John Marshall to Bushrod Washington, 27 March 1819, *The Papers of John Marshall*, 8: 281.

57. James Madison to Clarkson Crolius, December 1819, *The Writings of James Madison*, 9: 15–20, at 16.

58. Murray N. Rothbard, *The Panic of 1819: Reactions and Policies* (New York and London: Columbia University Press, 1962), 12–13.

59. Leading Republicans privately confessed ignorance of banking. Thomas Ritchie to Thomas Jefferson Randolph, n.d., Edgehill-Randolph Papers, University of Virginia; Littleton Waller Tazewell to John Ambler, 10 February 1844, Ambler Family Papers, Virginia Historical Society. What was blamed on banks seems actually to have been the fault of the Republican Department of the Treasury, where Secretary William Crawford intentionally hid his department's responsibility for contraction of the money supply behind the Bank's façade. Richard H. Timberlake, Jr., *The Origins of Central Banking in the United States* (Cambridge, Mass., and London: Harvard University Press, 1978), 21–26.

60. Thomas Jefferson to William Cabell Rives, 28 November 1819, *The Works of Thomas Jefferson*, 12: 149–50.

61. Thomas Jefferson to Richard Rush, 22 June 1819, *The Works of Thomas Jefferson*, 12: 126–29.

62. Mary A. Giunta, "The Public Life of William Branch Giles, Republican, 1790–1815" (Ph.D. dissertation, Catholic University of America, 1980), 126–27.

63. Thomas Jefferson to Hugh Nelson, 12 March 1820, *The Works of Thomas Jefferson*, n. 1 at 12: 157–58. Also see John Randolph to Harmanus Bleecker, 6 September 1812, John Randolph Papers, University of Virginia.

64. For Jefferson's problems, see Bernard Peyton to Thomas Jefferson Randolph, 9 September 1819, *Edgehill-Randolph Papers*, University of Virginia. John Taylor of Caroline taught that agriculture could only fail in a place suitable to it if government caused its failure. Without the Bank of the United States, he and his students would have had to find some other federal instrumentality to blame. John Taylor, *Arator, Being a Series of Agricultural Essays, Practical and Political: In Sixty-Four Numbers*, 73 and *passim*. For an analysis of the causes of the Panic of 1819 similar to Jefferson's, see Murray N. Rothbard, *The Panic of 1819: Reactions and Policies*, 14.

65. James Madison to [former] marquis de la Fayette, 25 November 1820, *The Writings of James Madison*, 9: 35, *et seq*. Also see Francis Walker Gilmer to Peachy R. Gilmer, 16 January 1820, Peachy Ridgway Gilmer Papers, Virginia Historical Society; Francis Walker Gilmer to Peachy R. Gilmer, 30 May 1822, *Ibid*.

66. Francis Walker Gilmer to Peachy R. Gilmer, 16 January 1820, *Ibid*.

67. "Memoirs of Thomas Jefferson Randolph," c. 1874, typescript, University of Virginia, 52.

68. John Randolph to Peter Browne, 21 January 1833, John Randolph Papers, University of Virginia.

69. Joseph Carrington Cabell to St. George Tucker, 9 January 1825, Joseph Carrington Cabell Letters, University of Virginia.

70. Harmer Gilmer to Francis Walker Gilmer, 29 January 1809, Gilmer Letterbooks, University of Virginia; Francis Walker Gilmer to Peter Minor, 23 January 1812, *Ibid*.; Francis Walker Gilmer to Peter Minor, 3 August 1820, *Ibid*.

71. See the account of elite Virginians' treatment of the Gilmers in Francis Walker Gilmer to Peachy R. Gilmer, 9 June 1819, Peachy Ridgway Gilmer Papers, Virginia Historical Society.

72. Francis Walker Gilmer to Peachy Ridgway Gilmer, 7 August 1822, *Ibid.*; Francis Walker Gilmer to Peachy R. Gilmer, 30 March 1823, *Ibid.*; Francis Walker Gilmer to Peter Minor, 3 August 1820, Gilmer Letterbooks, University of Virginia; Francis Walker Gilmer to Peachy R. Gilmer, 6 October 1821, Peachy Ridgway Gilmer Papers, Virginia Historical Society; Francis Walker Gilmer to Peter Minor, 7 March 1823, *Ibid.*; and especially, on F. W. Gilmer's attitude toward the Virginia elite, Francis Walker Gilmer to Peachy R. Gilmer, 29 June 1819, *Ibid.* Others also judged Monroe an apostate from Virginia principles. Lyon G. Tyler, *The Letters and Times of the Tylers*, 1: 372–73; Rex Beach, "Judge Spencer Roane: A Champion of States Rights," 98–99.

73. James Madison to Nicholas Biddle, 16 April 1825, *The Writings of James Madison*, 9: 221–22.

74. Thomas Jefferson to John Holmes, 22 April 1820, *The Works of Thomas Jefferson*, 12: 158–60, at 159; for the spread of the conspiracy explanation, James Madison to James Monroe, 10 February 1820, *The Writings of James Madison*, 9: 21–23. Some historians agree with the Virginians' appraisal of the Missouri instigators' motives. William H. Riker, *Liberalism Against Populism: A Confrontation between the Theory of Democracy and the Theory of Social Choice* (San Francisco: W. H. Freeman, 1982), 215–19; Michael F. Holt, "Coming of the Civil War" lectures delivered at the University of Virginia, 1992.

75. Francis Walker Gilmer to Peter Minor, 22 February 1820, Gilmer Letterbooks, University of Virginia.

76. John Taylor, *Arator; Being a Series of Agricultural Essays, Practical and Political: In Sixty-Four Numbers*, 115, 123.

77. Robert J. Brugger, *Beverley Tucker: Heart over Head in the Old South* (Baltimore and London: Johns Hopkins University Press, 1978).

78. Francis Walker Gilmer to Peter Minor, 25 March 1821, Gilmer Letterbooks, University of Virginia; Dabney Carr to John Coalter, 18 February 1820, University of Virginia.

79. James Madison to Robert Walsh, 27 November 1819, *The Writings of James Madison*, 9: 1–13, at 12.

80. Dice Robins Anderson, *William Branch Giles: A Study in the Politics of Virginia and the Nation from 1790 to 1830* (1914; reprint Gloucester, Mass.: Peter Smith, 1965), 209; James Madison to James Monroe, 19 November 1820, *The Writings of James Madison*, 9: 30, *et seq.*

81. James Madison to Henry Clay, April 1824, *Ibid.*, 9: 183–87; Lyon G. Tyler, *The Letters and Times of the Tylers*, 3: 70.

82. John Taylor, *Tyranny Unmasked*, ed. F. Thornton Miller (1821; reprint Indianapolis: Liberty Fund, 1992).

83. For Taylor's party-building goal, John Taylor to Spencer Roane, 29 November 1821, Harrison Family Papers, Virginia Historical Society.

84. Kevin R. [C.] Gutzman, "Preserving the Patrimony: William Branch Giles and Virginia versus the Federal Tariff," *The Virginia Magazine of History and Biography* 104 (1996): 341–72.

85. Charles Henry Ambler, *Sectionalism in Virginia from 1776 to 1861*, 120–21.

86. John Tyler to the General Assembly Committee, 18 January 1827, Gooch Family Papers, Virginia Historical Society.

87. *The Writings of James Madison*, 9: 344–45, n. 1.

88. Littleton Waller Tazewell to William Branch Giles, 26 June 1828, University of Virginia.

89. See generally William Branch Giles, *Political Miscellanies* (Richmond, 1830). Governor John Tyler, Giles's immediate predecessor in that office, agreed with Giles regarding the tariff. John Tyler to Dr. Henry Curtis, 18 March 1828, in Lyon G. Tyler, *The Letters and Times of the Tylers*, 1: 383–86. The West's sentiment toward Giles is found in ? to William Cabell Rives, 5 December 1828, Papers of William Cabell Rives, University of Virginia.

90. James Madison to Nicholas P. Trist, 26 January 1828, *The Writings of James Madison*, 9: 301–5; also see James Madison to Reynolds Chapman, 6 January 1831, *Ibid.*, 9: 429–37.

91. See generally Richard K. Matthews, *If Men Were Angels: James Madison & the Heartless Empire of Reason* (Lawrence: University Press of Kansas, 1995); James Madison to ?, 1833, *The Writings of James Madison*, 9: 520–28, at 523–26.

92. John Randolph to Harmanus Bleecker, 10 October 1818, John Randolph Papers, University of Virginia; also see John R. Clay to John Randolph, 23 December 1827, *Ibid.* Among aspiring emigrants was Francis Walker Gilmer. Francis Walker Gilmer to Peachy R. Gilmer, 7 August 1822, Peachy Ridgway Gilmer Papers, Virginia Historical Society.

93. "Order from the Virginia House of Delegates," 13 December 1796, Edgehill-Randolph Papers, University of Virginia.

94. Robert P. Sutton, *Revolution to Secession: Constitution Making in the Old Dominion* (Charlottesville: University Press of Virginia, 1989), 61–62.

95. The resolutions are published in a newspaper clipping included in Philip Norborne Nicholas to Joseph Carrington Cabell, 20 September 1825, Cabell Family Papers, University of Virginia.

96. *Democracy, Liberty, and Property: The State Constitutional Conventions of the 1820s*, ed. Merrill D. Peterson (Indianapolis: Bobbs-Merrill, 1966), 273–74; Robert P. Sutton, *Revolution to Secession: Constitution Making in the Old Dominion*, 62; "A Citizen" [Joseph Carrington Cabell], *Richmond Enquirer*, 5 July 1825; Analysis of Philip Norborne Nicholas's Letter to A. Garrett, 20 September 1825, Cabell Family Papers, University of Virginia; Archibald Stuart, Jr., to ?, 25 August 1816, A.G. Robertson Papers, Virginia Historical Society.

97. Robert P. Sutton, *Revolution to Secession: Constitution Making in the Old Dominion*, 63; Thomas Jefferson to Samuel Kerchival, 12 July 1816, *The Works of Thomas Jefferson*, 12: 3–15.

98. Thomas Jefferson to John Hampden Pleasants, 19 April 1824, *Ibid.*, 12: 351–55, at 352.

99. Thomas Jefferson to Samuel Kerchival, 5 September 1816, *Ibid.*, 12: 15–17.

100. Robert P. Sutton, *Revolution to Secession: Constitution Making in the Old Dominion*, 69. For criticism of the reform movement, see "Mason of '76" [Benjamin Watkins Leigh], 21 June 1825, 28 June 1825, *Richmond Enquirer*, which are the sources of the following discussion of Leigh's position. The census of 1830 indeed showed the East to be in steady decline. Robert P. Sutton, *Revolution to Secession: Constitution Making in the Old Dominion*, 53.

101. Also see *Ibid.*, 66–67.

102. *Ibid.*; Philip Norborne Nicholas to Joseph Carrington Cabell, 20 September 1825, Cabell Family Papers, University of Virginia.

103. Dickson D. Bruce, Jr., *The Rhetoric of Conservatism: The Virginia Convention of 1829–1830 and the Conservative Tradition in the South* (San Marino, Calif.: Huntington Library, 1982), 25–26. Western secession was floated at least as early as 1802. John

Randolph to Creed Taylor, 31 January 1802, Creed Taylor Papers, University of Virginia; William H. Cabell to Joseph Carrington Cabell, 16 December 1802, Cabell Family Papers, University of Virginia.

104. *Democracy, Liberty, and Property: The State Constitutional Conventions of the 1820s*, 273–74.

105. James Monroe to S. M. Edwards, 6 April 1829, *The Writings of James Monroe*, 7: 194–95.

106. Peachy Harrison to Gessner Harrison, 4 November 1829, Gessner Harrison Papers, University of Virginia.

107. Alden Griswold Bigelow, "Hugh Blair Grigsby: Historian and Antiquarian" (Ph.D. dissertation, University of Virginia, 1957), 23–24. Easterners had long guessed that broader suffrage would yield more pronounced plutocracy. Francis Walker Gilmer to Peter Minor, 24 June 1816, Gilmer Letterbooks, University of Virginia.

108. *Democracy, Liberty, and Property: The State Constitutional Conventions of the 1820s*, 281; Merrill D. Peterson, *The Jefferson Image in the American Mind* (New York: Oxford University Press, 1960), 42.

109. Hugh Blair Grigsby, *The Virginia Convention of 1829–1830*, 86.

110. *Democracy, Liberty, and Property: The State Constitutional Conventions of the 1820s*, 273; Dickson D. Bruce, Jr., *The Rhetoric of Conservatism: The Virginia Convention of 1829–1830 and the Conservative Tradition in the South*, xvi–xvii and *passim*.

111. Merrill D. Peterson, *The Jefferson Image in the American Mind*, 43.

112. William Branch Giles, Address to the Executive Committee, 17 October 1829, *Proceedings and Debates of the Virginia State Convention, of 1829–1830*, 905–13.

113. Speech of William B. Giles, 9 November 1829, *Ibid.*, 235–46, at 236; Speech of William Branch Giles, 10 November 1829, *Ibid.*, 256. In *Political Miscellanies*, Giles had suggested that young Virginians be instructed in the preeminent glories of their state's political tradition, and here, he suggested that all the niches in the capitol be filled with busts of republican Virginia's founders.

114. Speech of Robert B. Taylor, 27 October 1829, *Ibid.*, 46–53.

115. Speech of Benjamin Watkins Leigh, 27 October 1830, *Ibid.*, 53.

116. Speech of John R. Cooke, 27 October 1829, *Ibid.*, 54–62.

117. Speech of John W. Green, 27 October 1829, *Ibid.*, 62–64.

118. Speech of Charles F. Mercer, 5 November 1829, *Ibid.*, 199.

119. Speech of Charles F. Mercer, 5 November 1829, *Ibid.*, 202.

120. Speech of Abel P. Upshur, 27 October 1829, *Ibid.*, 67–71; Speech of Abel P. Upshur, 28 October 1829, *Ibid.*, 72–79.

121. Abel P. Upshur to Francis Walker Gilmer, 7 July 1825, Gilmer Letterbooks, University of Virginia.

122. Francis Walker Gilmer to Peachy R. Gilmer, 28 April 1824, Peachy Ridgway Gilmer Papers, Virginia Historical Society. Opponents of suffrage reform had supporters in the West. Archibald Stuart, Jr., to ?, 25 August 1816, A.G. Robertson Papers, Virginia Historical Society.

123. Speech of Thomas R. Joynes, 5 November 1829, *Proceedings and Debates of the Virginia State Convention, of 182–1830*, 206.

124. Speech of Philip Doddridge, 28 October 1829, *Ibid.*, 80–89.

125. The slavery metaphor, popular among Westerners, found an odd accompaniment in one reform delegate's correspondence during the convention. While complaining about his "enslavement," he repeatedly pestered his son to buy him a "girl." Peachy Harrison to Gessner Harrison, 5 December 1829, Gessner Harrison Papers, University of Virginia; Peachy Harrison to Gessner Harrison, 17 December 1829, *Ibid.*

126. Speech of Philip P. Barbour, 29 October 1829, *Proceedings and Debates of the Virginia State Convention, of 1829–1830*, 91–97.

127. Barbour here echoed Giles's and other Southerners' view concerning the federal tariff. Kevin R. [C.] Gutzman, "Preserving the Patrimony: William Branch Giles and Virginia versus the Federal Tariff." The same argument underlay the American Revolution. John Phillip Reid, *Constitutional History of the American Revolution* (abridged edition; Madison: University Press of Wisconsin, 1995).

128. Speech of Briscoe G. Baldwin, 29 October 1829, *Proceedings and Debates of the Virginia State Convention, of 1829–1830*, 100–102.

129. As in Speech of Alexander Campbell, 31 October 1829, *Ibid.*, 118–20.

130. See Speech of Richard Morris, 30 October 1829, *Ibid.*, 113–15.

131. Speech of William Naylor, 31 October 1829, *Ibid.*, 129, 133.

132. Speech of Richard H. Henderson, 18 November 1829, *Ibid.*, 359.

133. Speech of Benjamin W. Leigh, 20 November 1829, *Ibid.*, 405.

134. Speech of Lucas P. Thompson, 21 November 1829, *Ibid.*, 411.

135. Algernon Sidney, *Discourses Concerning Government* (1698; reprint Indianapolis: Liberty Fund, 1996).

136. Speech of James Monroe, 2 November 1829, *Proceedings and Debates of the Virginia State Convention, of 1829–1830*, 148–50.

137. Speech of William B. Giles, 9 November 1829, *Ibid.*, 235–46.

138. Speech of Benjamin W. Leigh, 3 November 1829, *Ibid.*, 154–64. Randolph echoed this theme. Speech of John Randolph, 14 November 1829, *Ibid.*, 315.

139. Speech of John S. Barbour, 2 November 1829, *Ibid.*, 135.

140. Speech of John Randolph, 14 November 1829, *Ibid.*, 318, 321.

141. *Democracy, Liberty, and Property: The State Constitutional Conventions of the 1820s*, 281, 284–85; for a reform delegate's hopes concerning the Council's abolition, see Peachy Harrison to Gessner Harrison, 14 October 1829, Gessner Harrison Papers, University of Virginia.

142. Alison Goodyear Freehling, *Drift Toward Dissolution: The Virginia Slavery Debate of 1831–1832* (Baton Rouge and London: Louisiana State University Press, 1982), 79.

143. Charles Henry Ambler, *Sectionalism in Virginia From 1776 to 1861*, 174.

144. William G. Shade, *Democratizing the Old Dominion: Virginia and the Second Party System, 1824–1861* (Charlottesville and London: University Press of Virginia, 1996).

CONCLUSION:

THE ROAD FROM SOUTHAMPTON

Writing to a friend in those events' immediate wake, the reformer John Hartwell Cocke referred to the "Southampton Tragedy" of August 1831 as "the most unaccountably short sighted affair I ever heard of involving the sheding of blood." What shocked this sympathizer with enslaved Africans was the fact that Nat Turner's band must have known how their rampage would turn out. After all, they had acted against "the denunciations of God & man."[1]

The Southampton slave rebellion shook Virginia's political class, indeed its white populace at large, vigorously. Accustomed to seeing themselves as the masters of their own lives, Virginians suddenly faced a striking reminder that their black subjects could not be controlled completely. Cocke concluded that if only the whites gave their slaves greater opportunity to understand their place, he hinted through formal education, the events of Southampton would not recur. Others thought differently.

Thomas Jefferson Randolph, the late president's favorite grandchild, dusted off his namesake's favorite "French" project: abolition. In response to a fellow delegate's proposal that all petitions for reform of the slave system be rejected, Randolph submitted Jefferson's old bill for post-nativity emancipation to the House of Delegates.[2] The ensuing debate divided Virginians into two camps similar to those that had formed in the recently concluded constitutional convention. This time, however, no reform resulted. Although the House of Delegates appropriated a substantial sum for colonization, the bill died in the Senate. College of William and Mary Professor Thomas R. Dew's article in *The American Quarterly Review* persuaded even some committed colonizationists that theirs was a hopeless cause, as it offered convincing new arguments respecting that program's impracticability. A temporary rush of pro-colonization feeling died down, and vowing someday to take up the issue of emancipation again, the General Assembly decided to do nothing on that score, either—effectively setting the Old Dominion's commitment to slavery in stone. With the presence of a substantial free black population in their state slavery's only practical alternative, Virginians resolved not to discuss the issue further. In thirty years, forced to choose, the Lees and Randolphs, Henrys and Masons would be wearing Confederate gray.[3]

John Tyler, Jr., then a United States senator and a firm devoté of the fathers' politics, wrote in 1839 that nine of ten men in Tidewater Virginia placed their political faith in what had come to be called "states' rights" (a Jacksonian name for what the Jeffersonian era had known as the "Principles of '98," which Andrew Jackson called simply "the Virginia Doctrine"). The West, on the other hand, permanently came down in opposition to the East's position in federal politics, and to its devotion to Old Virginia, during the Nullification Crisis.[4] By the time James Madison died in 1836, the Tidewater, Piedmont, and Southside regions were committed to all of the political and social, historical and constitutional positions whose fruit would be secession—first of Virginia from the United States, then of West Virginia from Virginia. There would be no slavery reform, no significant network of state-financed internal improvements in the western counties, and no program of public primary and secondary education so long as the East's aristocracy dominated Virginia politics. Most significantly, for several more decades to come, Virginians would remain committed to the revolutionary ideology that put their Old Dominion above the United States in its sons' affections. Like George III's empire, Abraham Lincoln's federal union would run aground on the shoal of Virginia's insistence upon self-determination. It was only a matter of time.

NOTES

1. John H. Cocke, Sr. to Randolph Harrison, Sr., 11 September 1831, Harrison Family Papers, Virginia Historical Society.

2. Alison Goodyear Freehling, *Drift Toward Dissolution: The Virginia Slavery Debate of 1831–1832* (Baton Rouge and London: Louisiana State University Press, 1982).

3. Charles Henry Ambler, *Sectionalism in Virginia From 1776 to 1861* (1910; reprinted New York: Russell & Russell, 1964), 191–92; Thomas R. Dew, "Debate in the Virginia Legislature of '31 '32, on the Abolition of Slavery," *The Pro-Slavery Argument; as Maintained by the Most Distinguished Writers of the Southern States* (1852; reprinted 1968, New York: Negro Universities Press), 277, *et seq.*; P. J. Staudenraus, *The African Colonization Movement, 1816–1865* (New York: Farrar, Straus and Giroux, 1980), 180–82, 106–7.

4. John Tyler to W. F. Pendleton, 27 October 1836, in Lyon G. Tyler, *The Letters and Times of the Tylers* (3 vols., 1884–1896; reprinted New York: Da Capo Press, 1970), 3:67–69; John Tyler to Henry Clay, 18 September 1839, *Ibid.*, 3: 75–76.

BIBLIOGRAPHY

PRIMARY SOURCES

Books including collections

"Address of Joseph C. Cabell to the citizens of Richmond, on the 10th Dec. 1834, on the expediency of a liberal subscription to the stock of the James River and Kanawha Company." Richmond: T. W. White, 1835.

"Algernon Sidney" essays. Edited by Wm. E. Dodd. *The John P. Branch Historical Papers of Randolph-Macon College.* 2d vol. 1906, 78–183.

American Archives, Fifth Series. Edited by Peter Force. 9 vols. Washington, 1836–1853.

Cabell, Joseph Carrington. "Letter and Accompanying Documents Relative to the Literary Institutions of the State: Addressed to his Constituents by Joseph C. Cabell." Richmond: John Warrock, 1825.

———. "Speech on the Anti-tariff resolutions Passed at the Session of the Legislature of Virginia, 1828–9." Richmond: T. W. White, 1831.

Colonies to Nation, 1763–1789. Edited by Jack P. Greene. New York and London: W. W. Norton, 1975.

"Controversy between Caius Gracchus and Opimius, in Reference to the American Society for Colonizing the Free People of Colour of the United States. First published in the Richmond Enquirer." Georgetown, D.C.: James C. Dunn, 1827.

Curtius [pseud.]. "A Defence of the Measures of the Administration of Thomas Jefferson." Providence: William Olney, 1805.

Democracy, Liberty, and Property: The State Constitutional Conventions of the 1820s. Edited by Merrill D. Peterson. Indianapolis: Bobbs-Merrill, 1966.

de Montesquieu, Charles Secondat, Baron. *The Spirit of the Laws.* New York and London: Hafner, 1966.

Dew, Thomas R. "Debate in the Virginia Legislature of '31 '32, on the Abolition of Slavery." *The Pro-Slavery Argument; as Maintained by the Most Distinguished Writers of the Southern States.* New York: Negro Universities Press, 1852; reprinted 1968, 287 *et seq.*

The Diary of Landon Carter of Sabine Hall, 1752–1778. Edited by Jack P. Greene. 2d ed. Richmond: The Virginia Historical Society, 1987.

Documentary History of the Ratification of the Constitution. Edited by John P. Kaminski and Gaspare J. Saladino. Virginia volumes: Madison: State Historical Society of Wisconsin, 1988–1993.

Documentary History of the Struggle for Religious Liberty in Virginia. Edited by Charles F. James. 1900. Reprinted New York: Da Capo Press, 1971.

The Eighteenth-Century Constitution, 1688–1815: Documents and Commentary. Edited by E. Neville Williams. Cambridge: Cambridge University Press, 1960.

Garrison, William Lloyd. *Thoughts on African Colonization.* 1832; reprinted New York: Arno Press and the New York Times, 1968.

Giles, William Branch Giles. *Political Miscellanies.* Richmond, 1830.

Grigsby, Hugh Blair Grigsby. *The Virginia Convention of 1829–30.* 1854; reprinted New York: Da Capo Press, 1969.

Hamilton, Alexander, James Madison, and John Jay.*The Federalist.* Edited by Jacob E. Cooke. Middletown, Conn.: Wesleyan University Press, 1961.

Henry, William Wirt. *Patrick Henry: Life, Correspondence, and Speeches.* 3 vols. Reprinted Harrisonburg, Va.: Sprinkle Publications, 1993.

Jefferson, Thomas. *Notes on the State of Virginia.* Edited by William Peden. Chapel Hill and London: University of North Carolina Press, 1954; 2d ed. 1982.

John Marshall's Defense of McCulloch v. Maryland. Edited by Gerald Gunther. Stanford: Stanford University Press, 1969.

Journal of the House of Delegates of the Commonwealth of Virginia, 1777–1778. Richmond, Va.: Thomas W. White.

Leigh, Benjamin Watkins. "The Letter of Appomatix [sic] to the People of Virginia: Exhibiting a Connected View of the Recent Proceedings in the House of Delegates, on the Subject of the Abolition of Slavery; and a Succinct Account of the Doctrines Broached by the Friends of Abolition, in Debate: and the Mischievous Tendency of Those Proceedings and Doctrines." Richmond: Thomas W. White, 1832.

The Letters and Papers of Edmund Pendleton, 1734–1803. Edited by David John Mays. Charlottesville: University Press of Virginia, 1967.

Letters of Delegates to Congress, 1774–1789. Edited by Paul H. Smith. Washington, D.C.: Library of Congress, 1976–1996.

"Letters of John Taylor of Caroline." ed. Hans Hammond, *Virginia Magazine of History and Biography* 52 1944, 1–14, 121–34.

"Letters of John Taylor, of Caroline County, Virginia." Edited by William E. Dodd. *The John P. Branch Historical Papers of Randolph-Macon College*, vol. II, nos. 3 and 4. 1908, 253–353.

Letters of Members of the Continental Congress. Edited by Edmund C. Burnett. 1921; reprinted Gloucester, Mass.: Peter Smith, 1963.

The Letters of Richard Henry Lee. Edited by James Curtis Ballagh. 1911–1914; reprinted New York: Da Capo Press, 1970.

Madison, James. *An Address Delivered before the Agricultural Society of Albemarle, on Tuesday, May 12, 1818.* Richmond: Shepherd and Pollard, 1818.

Nicholas, Wilson Cary Nicholas. "An Address from Wilson C. Nicholas, A Representative in Congress From Virginia, To His Constituents. Together with a Speech." Richmond, 1809.

———. "To the Electors of the Congressional District Composed of the Counties of Amherst, Albemarle and Fluvanna." 1809.

Notes of Debates in the Federal Convention, Reported by James Madison. Edited by Adrienne Koch. 1966; reprinted New York: W. W. Norton, 1987.

Official Letters of the Governors of the State of Virginia. Edited by H. R. McIlwaine. 3 vols. Richmond: Virginia State Library, 1926–1929.
"A Pamphlet Containing a Series of Letters, Written by Colonel John Taylor, of Caroline, to Thomas Ritchie, Editor of the 'Enquirer.'" Richmond, 1809.
The Papers of George Mason, 1725–1792. Edited by Robert A. Rutland Chapel Hill: University of North Carolina Press, 1970.
The Papers of James Madison. Edited by William T. Hutchinson et al. Chicago and Charlottesville: University of Chicago Press and University Press of Virginia, 1962– .
The Papers of John Marshall. Edited by Herbert A. Johnson et al.Williamsburg: University of North Carolina Press, 1974– .
The Papers of Thomas Jefferson. Edited by Julian P. Boyd et al.Princeton: Princeton University Press, 1950– .
The Portable Thomas Jefferson. Edited by Merrill D. Peterson. New York: Penguin, 1975.
Proceedings and Debates of the Virginia State Convention, 1829–1830. 1830; reprinted in 2 vols., New York: Da Capo Press, 1971.
"Proceedings at a Public Dinner in Albemarle County, Virginia, Given to Mr. William C. Rives, Late a Senator of the United States from That State." N.p., 1834.
Randolph, Edmund. *History of Virginia.* Edited by Arthur H. Shaffer. Charlottesville: University Press of Virginia, 1970.
"Remarks of William C. Rives, of Virginia, On Resigning His Seat in the Senate of the United States. In Senate, Saturday February 22, 1834." Washington, 1834.
Revolutionary Virginia: The Road to Independence: A Documentary Record. Edited by Brent Tarter et al. Charlottesville: University Press of Virginia, 1973–1983.
"Roane Correspondence." Edited by Wm. E. Dodd. *The John P. Branch Historical Papers of Randolph-Macon College* 2. 1905, 123–42.
Rowland, A. Kate Mason. *The Life of George Mason, 1725–1792.* New York: G. P. Putnam's Sons, 1892.
Sidney, Algernon. *Discourses Concerning Government.* 1698; reprinted Indianapolis: Liberty Fund, 1996.
"Speech of Mr. Rives, of Virginia, on Retrenchment and Reform: Delivered in the House of Representatives of the United States, on the 5th February, 1828." Washington, D.C.: Green and Jarvis, 1828.
State Documents on Federal Relations: The States and the United States. Edited by Herman V. Ames. New York: Da Capo Press, 1970.
The Statutes at Large; Being a Collection of All the Laws of Virginia, from the First Session of the Legislature, in the Year 1619. Edited by William Waller Hening. 12 vos. Richmond: 1819–1823; reprinted 1969.
Swem, Earl G., and John W. Williams. *A Register of the General Assembly of Virginia, 1776–1918.* Richmond, 1918.
Taylor, John. *A Definition of Parties: Or the Political Effects of the Paper System.* Philadelphia, 1794.
———. *An Argument Respecting the Constitutionality of the Carriage Tax.* Richmond, 1795.
———. *An Enquiry into the Principles and Tendency of Certain Public Measures.* Philadelphia, 1794.
———. *An Inquiry into the Principles and Policy of the Government of the United States.* 1814; reprinted New Haven, Conn.: Yale University Press, 1950.

———. *Arator; Being a Series of Agricultural Essays, Practical and Political: In Sixty-Four Numbers*. Edited by M. E. Bradford. 1818; reprinted Indianapolis: Liberty Fund, 1977.

———. "A Pamphlet Containing a Series of Letters, Written by Colonel John Taylor, of Caroline, to Thomas Ritchie, Editor of the 'Enquirer.'" Richmond, 1809.

———. *Construction Construed, and Constitutions Vindicated*. Richmond: Shepherd and Pollard, 1820.

———. *New Views of the Constitution of the United States*. 1823; reprinted New York: Da Capo Press, 1971.

———. *Tyranny Unmasked*. Edited by F. Thornton Miller. 1821; reprinted Indianapolis: Liberty Fund, 1992.

Tazewell, Littleton Waller. *A Review of the Proclamation of President Jackson of the 10th of December, 1832, in a Series of Numbers Originally Published in the "Norfolk and Portsmouth Herald," under the Signature of "A Virginian."* Norfolk: J. D. Ghiselin, 1888.

Tyler, Lyon G. *The Letters and Times of the Tylers*. 3 vols. 1884–1896; reprinted New York: Da Capo Press, 1970.

The Virginia Report of 1799–1800, Touching the Alien and Sed. Laws; Together with the Virginia Resolutions of December 21, 1798, the Debate and Proceedings Thereon in the House of Delegates of Virginia, and Several Other Documents Illustrative of the Report and Resolutions. 1850; reprinted New York: Da Capo Press, 1970.

Voltaire, François Marie Arouet de. *Letters on England*. New York: Penguin Books, 1980.

The Works of Thomas Jefferson. Edited by Paul Leicester Ford. New York and London: G. P. Putnam's Sons, 1892–1904.

The Writings of James Madison. Edited by Gaillard Hunt. New York: G. P. Putnam's Sons, 1908–1910.

The Writings of James Monroe. Edited by Stanislaus M. Hamilton. 7 vols. 1898–1903; reprinted, New York: AMS Press, 1969.

The Writings of Thomas Jefferson. Edited by Andrew A. Lipscomb. Washington: The Thomas Jefferson Memorial Association, 1904–1905.

Manuscripts

University of Virginia:
    Lewis M. Allen Donation
    Elizabeth Barbour Ambler Collection
    Argosy Collection
    Roger Atkinson Letterbook
    Barbour Family Papers
    John Beckley Letter
    Berkeley Family Papers
    Launcelot Minor Blackford Correspondence
    Allen Caperton Braxton Papers
    William M. Burwell Papers
    Cabell Family Papers
    Joseph Carrington Cabell Letters
    Carter-Smith Papers

John Coalter Papers
William Branch Giles Papers
Francis Walker Gilmer Correspondence
Gilmer Letterbooks
Hugh Blair Grigsby Papers
Gessner Harrison Papers
George Harrison Sanford King Letters
"Memoirs of Thomas Jefferson Randolph," c. 1874
Papers of James Minor
Wilson Cary Nicholas Papers
John Henry Purviance Letters
John Randolph Cartoon
Randolph Family "Edgehill-Randolph" Papers
John Randolph to Mr. Carrington
John Randolph of Roanoke Papers
Thomas Jefferson Randolph Letters
Thomas Ritchie Letter
Rives Family Papers
William Cabell Rives Papers
Samuel Smith Letter
Stuart-Baldwin Family Papers
Creed Taylor Papers
John Taylor, "The Life of John Penn"
John Taylor Letter
John Taylor Papers
Littleton Waller Tazewell Letters
Transactions of the Agricultural Society of Albemarle [County, Virginia], *1817–1828* photocopy of the original in the Virginia Historical Society
Virginia Documents Miscellany

Virginia Historical Society:
- Adams Family Papers
- Allen Family Papers
- Ambler Family Papers
- Robert Anderson Papers
- Archer Family Papers
- Aylett Family Papers
- Ayres Family Papers
- Bagby Family Papers
- Henry Banks Papers
- Barbour Family Papers
- William Wilfrid Bayne Letter
- Robert Carter Berkeley Diary
- Berryman Family Papers
- Bland Family Papers
- Blow Family Papers
- Bolling Family Papers
- Benjamin Brand Papers
- Breckenridge Family Papers
- James Breckenridge Papers

Robert Alonzo Brock Papers
Brodnax Family Papers
Byrd Family Papers
William Cabell Commonplace Book
Peter Carr Papers
Archibald Cary Papers
Pablo Chacon Letterbook
W. G. Chisolm Papers
Thomas Chrystie Papers
Claiborne Family Papers
John Coalter Papers
John Cropper Papers
William Branch Giles Papers
Peachy Ridgway Gilmer Papers
Gooch Family Papers
Hugh Blair Grigsby Papers;
Grinnan Family Papers
John C. Grinnan manuscripts
Harrison Family Papers
Henry Heth Papers
Henry Family Papers
Holladay Family Papers
Hopkins Family Papers
James Ambler Johnston Papers
Benjamin Watkins Leigh Papers
Letterbooks of Robert Anderson, 1804–1807 and 1807–1813
Thomas Massie Papers
Memorandum of Benjamin Watkins Leigh re William Branch Giles and John Randolph of Roanoke, 4 August 1807
Mercer Family Papers
Minor Family Papers
Wilson Cary Nicholas Papers
Samuel P. Parsons Papers
John Randolph of Roanoke Papers
Martha Randolph Letter
Thomas Jefferson Randolph Papers
A. G. Robertson Papers
Stuart Family Papers
Alexander H.H. Stuart Letter
Archibald Stuart Papers
John Taylor Papers
Todd Family Papers
St. George Tucker Coalter–Tucker Papers
John Tyler Letter, Virginia Historical Society
George Wythe, "The Late Chancellor Wythe's opinion respecting Religions, delivered by Himself"

Legal Texts and Opinions

Black's Law Dictionary. 5th ed., St. Paul: West Publishing Co., 1979.
Blackstone, William. *Commentaries on the Laws of England.* Edited by St. George Tucker. Philadelphia: William Young Birch and Abraham Small, 1803.
Corbin, A. *Contracts.* 2d ed. 1960.
Green v. Biddle. 21 U.S. 8 Wheat. 1.
Howard, A. E. Dick. *Commentaries on the Constitution of Virginia.* Charlottesville: University Press of Virginia, 1974.
Kamper v. Hawkins. 1 Va. Cases 20 1793.
Raffles v. Wichelhaus. 159 Eng. Rep. 375 1864.
Restatement Second of Contracts.
4 S. Williston. *Contracts* 3d ed. 1961.

Newspapers

American Farmer
The Connecticut Courant
The Richmond Enquirer
The Virginia Gazette and Weekly Advertizer

Secondary Works

Books

Adams, Willi Paul. *The First American Constitutions: Republican Ideology and the Making of the State Constitutions in the Revolutionary Era.* Chapel Hill: University of North Carolina Press, 1980.
Albion's Fatal Tree: Crime and Society in Eighteenth-Century England. Edited by Douglas Hay. London: Allen Lane, 1975.
Alden, John Richard Alden. *The South in the Revolution, 1763–1789.* Baton Rouge: Louisiana State University Press, 1957.
Ambler, Charles Henry. *Sectionalism in Virginia From 1776 to 1861.* 1910; reprinted New York: Russell and Russell, 1964.
———. *Thomas Ritchie: A Study in Virginia Politics.* Richmond: Bell Book and Stationery, 1913.
Ammon, Harry. *James Monroe: The Quest for National Identity.* 1971; reprinted Charlottesville: University Press of Virginia, 1990.
Anderson, Benedict. *Imagined Communities: Reflections on the Origin and Spread of Nationalism.* revised ed.; London and New York: Verso, 1991.
Anderson, Dice Robins. *William Branch Giles: A Study in the Politics of Virginia and the Nation from 1790 to 1830.* 1914; reprinted Gloucester, Mass.: Peter Smith, 1965.
Bailyn, Bernard. *The Ideological Origins of the American Revolution.* 2d ed.; London and Cambridge: Harvard University Press, 1992.

Banning, Lance. *The Jeffersonian Persuasion: Evolution of a Party Ideology.* Ithaca, N.Y., and London: Cornell University Press, 1978.
———. *The Sacred Fire of Liberty: James Madison and the Federal Republic.* Ithaca, N.Y., and London: Cornell University Press, 1995.
Beeman, Richard R. *The Old Dominion and the New Nation, 1788–1801.* Lexington: University Press of Kentucky, 1972.
———. *Patrick Henry: A Biography.* New York: McGraw-Hill, 1974.
Beveridge, Albert J. *The Life of John Marshal.l* New York and Boston: Houghton Mifflin, 1919.
Bradford, M. E. *A Better Guide than Reason: Federalists & Anti-Federalists.* 1979; reprinted New Brunswick, N.J.: Transaction Publishers, 1994.
———. *Founding Fathers: Brief Lives of the Framers of the United States Constitution.* 2d ed.; Lawrence: University Press of Kansas, 1994.
———. *Original Intentions: On the Making and Ratification of the United States Constitution.* Athens and London: University of Georgia Press, 1993.
Brant, Irving. *James Madison: The Virginia Revolutionist.* Indianapolis and New York: The Bobbs-Merrill Company, 1941.
Breen, T. H. *Tobacco Culture: The Mentality of the Great Tidewater Planters on the Eve of Revolution.* Princeton: Princeton University Press, 1985.
Brown, Robert E., and B. Katherine Brown. *Virginia 1705–1786: Democracy or Aristocracy?* East Lansing: Michigan State University, 1964.
Bruce, Dickson D., Jr. *The Rhetoric of Conservatism: The Virginia Convention of 1829–1830 and the Conservative Tradition in the South.* San Marino, Calif.: Huntington Library, 1982.
Brugger, Robert J. *Beverley Tucker: Heart over Head in the Old South.* Baltimore and London: The Johns Hopkins University Press, 1978.
Burstein, Andrew. *The Inner Jefferson: Portrait of a Grieving Optimist.* Charlottesville: University Press of Virginia, 1995.
Carpenter, Jesse T. *The South as a Conscious Minority, 1789–1861.* 1930; reprinted Columbia: University of South Carolina Press, 1990.
Chitwood, Oliver Perry. *Richard Henry Lee: Statesman of the Revolution.* Morgantown: West Virginia University Library, 1967.
Clark, J. C. D. *The Language of Liberty, 1660–1832: Political Discourse and Social Dynamics in the Anglo-American* World. Cambridge: Cambridge University Press, 1994.
Colbourn, H. Trevor. *The Lamp of Experience: Whig History and the Intellectual Origins of the American Revolution.* Chapel Hill: University of North Carolina Press, 1965.
———. *The Lamp of Experience: Whig History and the Intellectual Origins of the American Revolution.* 2d ed. Indianapolis: Liberty Fund, 1998.
The Constitution and the States: The Role of the Original Thirteen in the Framing and Adoption of the Federal Constitution. Edited by Patrick T. Conley and John P. Kaminski. Madison: Madison House, 1988.
Craven, Avery O. *Edmund Ruffin, Southerner: A Study in Secession.* Baton Rouge: Louisiana State University Press, 1966.
Dabney, Virginius. *Virginia, The New Dominion: A History From 1607 to the Present.* Charlottesville: University Press of Virginia, 1971.
Davis, David Brion. *The Problem of Slavery in the Age of Revolution, 1770–1823.* Ithaca, N.Y., and London: Cornell University Press, 1975.

Douglas, Elisha P. *Rebels and Democrats: The Struggle for Equal Political Rights and Majority Rule during the American Revolution*. Chapel Hill: University of North Carolina Press, 1955.

Eckenrode, Hamilton J. *The Revolution in Virginia*. Boston and New York: Houghton Mifflin, 1916.

Egerton, Douglas R. *Gabriel's Rebellion: The Virginia Slave Conspiracies of 1800 & 1802*. Chapel Hill and London: University of North Carolina Press, 1993.

Elkins, Stanley, and Eric McKitrick. *The Age of Federalism*. New York: Oxford University Press, 1993.

Fliegelman, Jay. *Declaring Independence: Jefferson, Natural Language, & the Culture of Performance*. Stanford, Calif.: Stanford University Press, 1993.

Flippin, Percy Scott. *The Royal Government in Virginia, 1624–1775*. New York: Columbia University, 1919.

Fox, Early Lee. *The American Colonization Society 1817–1840*. 1919; reprinted New York: AMS Press, 1970.

Freehling, Alison Goodyear. *Drift toward Dissolution: The Virginia Slavery Debate of 1831–1832*. Baton Rouge and London: Louisiana State University Press, 1982.

Frey, Sylvia. *Water from the Rock: Black Resistance in a Revolutionary Age*. Princeton: Princeton University Press, 1991.

Green, Fletcher M. *Constitutional Development in the South Atlantic States, 1776–1860: A Study in the Evolution of Democracy*. Chapel Hill: University of North Carolina Press, 1930.

Greene, Evarts Boutell. *The Provincial Governor in the English Colonies of North America*. Cambridge: Harvard University Press, 1898.

Greene, Jack P. *Landon Carter: An Inquiry into the Personal Values and Social Imperatives of the Eighteenth-Century Virginia Gentry*. Charlottesville: University Press of Virginia, 1967.

———. *Peripheries and Center: Constitutional Development in the Extended Polities of the British Empire and the United States, 1607–1788*. New York and London: W. W. Norton and Company, 1986.

———. *Pursuits of Happiness: The Social Development of Early Modern British Culture and the Formation of American Culture*. Chapel Hill: University of North Carolina Press, 1988.

———. *The Quest for Power: The Lower Houses of Assembly in the Southern Royal Colonies, 1689–1776*. Chapel Hill: University of North Carolina Press, 1963.

Grigsby, Hugh Blair. *Discourse on the Life and Character of the Hon. Littleton Waller Tazewell*. Norfolk, 1860.

———. *The History of the Virginia Federal Convention of 1788*. 2 vols. 1890; reprinted as 2 vols. bound in 1. New York: Da Capo Press, 1969.

———. *The Virginia Convention of 1776*. 1855; reprinted New York: Da Capo Press, 1969.

Hartz, Louis. *The Liberal Tradition in America*. New York: Harcourt, Brace, 1955.

Hill, C. William, Jr. *The Political Theory of John Taylor of Caroline*. Cranbury, N.J.: Associated University Presses, 1977.

Hilliard, Sam Bowers. *Atlas of Antebellum Southern Agriculture*. Baton Rouge and London: Louisiana State University Press, 1984.

Hobson, Charles F. *The Great Chief Justice: John Marshall and the Rule of Law*. Lawrence: University Press of Kansas, 1996.

Holt, Michael F. "Coming of the Civil War." Lectures delivered at the University of Virginia, 1992.
Isaac, Rhys. *The Transformation of Virginia, 1740–1790*. New York and London: W. W. Norton, 1982.
Jaffa, Harry V. *Original Intent and the Framers of the Constitution: A Disputed Question*. Washington: Regnery Gateway, 1993.
Ketcham, Ralph. *James Madison: A Biography*. 1971; reprinted. Charlottesville and London: University Press of Virginia, 1990.
———. *Presidents above Party: The First American Presidency, 1789–1829*. Chapel Hill: University of North Carolina Press, 1984.
Klein, Rachel N. *Unification of a Slave State: The Rise of the Planter Class in the South Carolina Backcountry, 1760–1808*. Chapel Hill and London: University of North Carolina Press, 1990.
Kramnick, Isaac. *Bolingbroke and His Circle: The Politics of Nostalgia in the Age of Walpole*. Cambridge, Mass.: Harvard University Press, 1968.
Kruman, Marc W. *Between Authority & Liberty: State Constitution Making in Revolutionary America*. Chapel Hill: University of North Carolina Press, 1997.
Lingley, Charles Ramsdell. *The Transition in Virginia From Colony to Commonwealth*. New York: Columbia University, 1910.
Maier, Pauline. *American Scripture: Making the Declaration of Independence*. New York: Alfred A. Knopf, 1997.
Malone, Dumas. *Jefferson and His Time, Volume One: Jefferson the Virginian*. Boston: Little, Brown and Company, 1948.
———. *Jefferson and His Time, Volume Three: Jefferson and the Ordeal of Liberty*. Boston: Little, Brown and Company, 1962.
———. *Jefferson and His Time, Volume Six: The Sage of Monticello*. Boston: Little, Brown and Company, 1981.
Mathew, William M. *Edmund Ruffin and the Crisis of Slavery in the Old South: The Failure of Agricultural Reform*. Athens and London: University of Georgia Press, 1988.
Matthews, Richard K. *If Men Were Angels: James Madison & the Heartless Empire of Reason*. Lawrence: University Press of Kansas, 1995.
———. *The Radical Politics of Thomas Jefferson: A Revisionist View*. Lawrence: University Press of Kansas, 1984.
Mayer, David N. *The Constitutional Thought of Thomas Jefferson*. Charlottesville and London: University Press of Virginia, 1994.
Mays, David John. *Edmund Pendleton, 1721–1803: A Biography*. Cambridge: Harvard University Press, 1952.
McColley, Robert. *Slavery and Jeffersonian Virginia*. Urbana: University of Illinois Press, 1964.
McCoy, Drew R. *The Elusive Republic: Political Economy in Jeffersonian America*. New York and London: W. W. Norton, 1980.
———. *The Last of the Fathers: James Madison & the Republican Legacy*. Cambridge and New York: Cambridge University Press, 1989.
McDonald, Forrest. *Novus Ordo Seclorum: The Intellectual Origins of the Constitution*. Lawrence: University Press of Kansas, 1985.
Miller, F. Thornton. *Juries and Judges versus the Law: Virginia's Provincial Legal Perspective, 1783–1828*. Charlottesville and London: University Press of Virginia, 1994.

Miller, Perry. *Orthodoxy in Massachusetts, 1630–1650*. New York, Evanston, and London: Harper and Row, 1961.
Morgan, Edmund S., and Helen M. Morgan, *The Stamp Act Crisis: Prologue to Revolution*. Chapel Hill: University of North Carolina Press, 1953.
Newmyer, R. Kent. *Supreme Court Justice Joseph Story: Statesman of the Old Republic*. Chapel Hill and London: University of North Carolina Press, 1985.
O'Brien, Conor Cruise. *The Great Melody: A Thematic Biography of Edmund Burke*. Chicago: University of Chicago Press, 1992.
Onuf, Peter S. *The Origins of the Federal Republic: Jurisdictional Controversies in the United States, 1775–1787*. Philadelphia: University of Pennsylvania Press, 1983.
———. *Statehood and Union: A History of the Northwest Ordinance*. Bloomington and Indianapolis: Indiana University Press, 1987.
Perkins, Edwin J. *American Public Finance and Financial Services, 1700–1815*. Columbus: Ohio State University Press, 1994.
Peterson, Merrill D. *The Jefferson Image in the American Mind*. New York: Oxford University Press, 1960.
———. *Thomas Jefferson and the New Nation: A Biography*. New York: Oxford University Press, 1970.
Porter, Albert Ogden. *County Government in Virginia: A Legislative History, 1607–1904*. New York: Columbia University Press, 1947.
Pulliam, David L. *The Constitutional Conventions of Virginia from the Foundation of the Commonwealth to the Present Time*. Richmond: John T. West, 1901.
Ragsdale, Bruce A. *A Planters' Republic: The Search for Economic Independence in Revolutionary Virginia*. Madison, Wisc.: Madison House, 1996.
Rahe, Paul A. *Republics Ancient & Modern: Classical Republicanism and the American Revolution*. Chapel Hill and London: University of North Carolina Press, 1992.
Rakove, Jack N. *The Beginnings of National Politics*. New York: Alfred A. Knopf, 1979.
———. *Original Meanings: Politics and Ideas in the Making of the Constitution*. New York: Alfred A. Knopf, 1996.
Reardon, Jack J. *Edmund Randolph: A Biography*. New York: Macmillan, 1974.
Reid, John Phillip. *Constitutional History of the American Revolution*. Abridged ed. Madison: University Press of Wisconsin, 1995.
Riker, William H. *Liberalism against Populism: A Confrontation between the Theory of Democracy and the Theory of Social Choice*. San Francisco: W. H. Freeman, 1982.
Risjord, Norman K. *The Old Republicans: Southern Conservatism in the Age of Jefferson*. New York: Columbia University Press, 1965.
Rodick, Burleigh Cushing. *American Constitutional Custom: A Forgotten Factor in the Founding*. New York: Philosophical Library, 1953.
Roeber, A. G. *Faithful Magistrates and Republican Lawyers: Creators of Virginia Legal Culture, 1680–1810*. Chapel Hill: University of North Carolina Press, 1981.
Rothbard, Murray N. *The Panic of 1819: Reactions and Policies*. New York and London: Columbia University Press, 1962.
Royster, Charles. *The Destructive War: William Tecumseh Sherman, Stonewall Jackson, and the Americans*. New York: Alfred A. Knopf, 1991.
———. *A Revolutionary People at War: The Continental Army and American Character, 1775–1783*. New York and London: W. W. Norton, 1979.
Rutland, Robert A. *George Mason: Reluctant Statesman*. Baton Rouge and London: Louisiana State University Press, 1961.

———. *The Ordeal of the Constitution: The Antifederalists and the Ratification Struggle of 1787–1788.* 1966; reprinted Boston: Northeastern University Press, 1983.

Shade, William G. *Democratizing the Old Dominion: Virginia and the Second Party System, 1824–1861.* Charlottesville and London: University Press of Virginia, 1996.

Shalhope, Robert E. *John Taylor of Caroline: Pastoral Republican.* Columbia: University of South Carolina Press, 1980.

Sharp, James Roger. *American Politics in the Early Republic: The New Nation in Crisis.* New Haven and London: Yale University Press, 1993.

Simms, Henry H. *Life of John Taylor: The Story of a Brilliant Leader in the Early Virginia State Rights School.* Richmond: The William Byrd Press, 1932.

Smith, Jean Edward. *John Marshall: Definer of a Nation.* New York: Henry Holt and Company, 1996.

Smith, Margaret Vowell. *A Few Notes Upon the History of the Constitution or Form of Government of Virginia from the Foundation of the Colony to the Present Time.* Glens Falls, N.Y.: Glens Falls Publishing Co., 1901.

Speed, John Gilmer. *The Gilmers in America.* New York, 1897.

Staudenraus, P. J. *The African Colonization Movement, 1816–1865.* New York: Farrar, Straus and Giroux, 1980.

Stites, Francis N. *John Marshall: Defender of the Constitution.* Boston and Toronto: Little, Brown, 1981.

Storing, Herbert J. *What the Antifederalists Were For.* Chicago and London: University of Chicago Press, 1981.

Sutton, Robert P. *Revolution to Secession: Constitution Making in the Old Dominion.* Charlottesville: University Press of Virginia, 1989.

Sydnor, Charles S. *Gentlemen Freeholders: Political Practices in Washington's Virginia.* Chapel Hill: University of North Carolina Press, 1952. Reprinted as *American Revolutionaries in the Making: Political Practices in Washington's Virginia.* New York: Collier Books, 1962.

Taylor, William R. *Cavalier & Yankee: The Old South and American National Character.* 1957; reprinted New York and Oxford: Oxford University Press, 1993.

Timberlake, Richard H., Jr., *The Origins of Central Banking in the United States.* Cambridge, Mass., and London: Harvard University Press, 1978.

Tucker Robert W., and David C. Hendrickson. *Empire of Liberty: The Statecraft of Thomas Jefferson.* New York and Oxford: Oxford University Press, 1990.

Van Schreeven, William J. *The Conventions and Constitutions of Virginia, 1776–1966.* Richmond: The Virginia State Library, 1967.

Vile, M. J. C. *Constitutionalism and the Separation of Powers.* Oxford: Clarendon Press, 1967.

The Virginia Statute for Religious Freedom: Its Evolution and Consequences in American History. Edited by Merrill D. Peterson and Robert C. Vaughan. Cambridge: Cambridge University Press, 1988.

Washington, H[enry] A[ugustine]. *The Virginia Constitution of 1776: A Discourse Delivered before the Virginia Historical Society, at Their Annual Meeting, January 17th, 1852.* Richmond: Macfarlane and Ferguson, 1852.

Williamson, Chilton. *American Suffrage: From Property to Democracy, 1760–1860.* Princeton: Princeton University Press, 1960.

Wiltse,Charles. *The Jeffersonian Tradition in American Democracy.* New York: Hill and Wang, 1960.

Wood, Gordon S. *The Creation of the American Republic, 1776–1787.* 1969; reprinted New York and London: W. W. Norton, 1972.
———. *The Radicalism of the American Revolution.* New York: Alfred A. Knopf, 1992.
Wormuth, Francis D. *The Origins of Modern Constitutionalism.* New York: Harper and Brothers, 1949.
Wright, Benjamin Fletcher. *Consensus and Continuity, 1776–1787.* New York: W. W. Norton, 1958.

Articles and chapters

Anderson, Dice R. "Jefferson and the Virginia Constitution." *American Historical Review* 21 (1915–1916): 750–54.
Appleby, Joyce. "Introduction: Jefferson and His Complex Legacy." *Jeffersonian Legacies.* Edited by Peter Onuf. Charlottesville: University Press of Virginia, 1993, 1–16.
Adair, Douglas. "'That Politics May Be Reduced to a Science': David Hume, James Madison, and the Tenth *Federalist*." *Huntington Library Quarterly* 20 (1957): 343–60.
Banning, Lance. "James Madison, the Statute for Religious Freedom, and the Crisis of Republican Convictions." *The Virginia Statute for Religious Freedom: Its Evolution and Consequences in American History.* Edited by Merrill Peterson and Robert C. Vaughan. Cambridge: Cambridge University Press, 1988, 109–38.
———. "Virginia: Sectionalism and the General Good." *Ratifying the Constitution: Ideas and Interests in the Several American States.* Edited by Michael Allen Gillespie and Michael Lienesch. Lawrence: University Press of Kansas, 1989.
Beeman, Richard R. "The Democratic Faith of Patrick Henry." *The Virginia Magazine of History and Biography* 95 (1987): 301–16.
Bjork, Gordon C. "The Weaning of the American Economy: Independence, Market Changes, and Economic Development." *Journal of Economic History* 24 (1964): 541–60.
Brewer, Holly. "Entailing Aristocracy in Colonial Virginia: 'Ancient Feudal Restraints' and Revolutionary Reform." *William and Mary Quarterly*, 3d series, 54 (1997): 307–46.
Conkin, Paul K. "The Religious Pilgrimage of Thomas Jefferson." *Jeffersonian Legacies.* Edited by Peter Onuf. Charlottesville: University Press of Virginia, 1993, 19–49.
Dunn, Richard S. "Black Society in the Chesapeake, 1776–1810." In *Slavery and Freedom in the Age of the American Revolution.* Edited by Ira Berlin and Ronald Hoffman. Charlottesville: University Press of Virginia, 1983, 49–82.
Editors' note introducing Adrienne Koch and Harry Ammon. "The Virginia and Kentucky Resolutions." *William and Mary Quarterly*, 3d series, 5 (1948): 145–46.
Greene, Jack P. "The Happy Retreat of True Britons, 1720–1775." *Douglas Southall Freeman Historical Review* Spring (1996): 72–101.
———. "The Hopefullest Plantation, 1584–1660." *Douglas Southall Freeman Historical Review* Spring (1996): 3–36.
———. "The Intellectual Reconstruction of Virginia in the Age of Jefferson." *Jeffersonian Legacies.* Edited by Peter Onuf. Charlottesville: University Press of Virginia, 1993, 225–53.
———. "Society, Ideology, and Politics: An Analysis of the Political Culture of Mid-Eighteenth-Century Virginia." In *Negotiated Authorities: Essays in Colonial Politi-*

cal and Constitutional History. Charlottesville and London: University Press of Virginia, 1994, 259–318.
———. "Unjustly Neglected by Its Own Inhabitants, 1660–1720." *Douglas Southall Freeman Historical Review* Spring (1996): 37–71.
Gutzman, K[evin] R. Constantine. "Edmund Randolph and Virginia Constitutionalism." *The Review of Politics* 66 (2004): 469–97.
———. "Jefferson's Draft Declaration of Independence, Richard Bland, and the Revolutionary Legacy: Giving Credit Where Credit Is Due." *The Journal of the Historical Society* 1 (2001): 137–54.
———. "Lincoln as Jeffersonian: The Colonization Chimera." In *Lincoln Emancipated: The President and the Politics of Race.* Edited by Brian Dirck. DeKalb: Northern Illinois University Press, 2007, 46–72
———. "'Oh, What a Tangled Web We Weave': James Madison and the Compound Republic." *Continuity* 22 (1998): 19–29.
———. "Preserving the Patrimony: William Branch Giles and Virginia versus the Federal Tariff." *The Virginia Magazine of History and Biography* 104 (1996): 341–72.
———. Review of Isaac Kramnick and R. Laurence Moore, *The Godless Constitution: The Case against Religious Correctness* (New York and London: W. W. Norton, 1996). In *Humanitas* 9 (1996): 85–90.
———. "A Troublesome Legacy: James Madison and 'The Principles of '98.'" *Journal of the Early Republic* 15 (1995): 569–89.
———. "The Virginia and Kentucky Resolutions Reconsidered: 'An Appeal to the *Real Laws* of Our Country.'" *The Journal of Southern History* 66 (2000): 473–96.
———. "William Grayson." *American National Biography.* Edited by John A. Garraty and Mark C. Carnes. New York: Oxford University Press, 1999, 9: 456–57.
Hamilton, Philip. "Revolutionary Principles and Family Loyalties: Slavery's Transformation in the St. George Tucker Household of Early National Virginia." *The William and Mary Quarterly*, 3d series, 55 (1998): 531–56.
Holton, Woody. "Rebel against Rebel: Enslaved Virginians and the Coming of the American Revolution." *Virginia Magazine of History and Biography* 105 (1997): 157–92.
Hutson, James H. "Country, Court, and Constitution: Antifederalism and the Historians." *The William and Mary Quarterly*, 3d series, 38 (1981): 337–68.
Isaac, Rhys. "The First Monticello." *Jeffersonian Legacies.* Edited by Peter Onuf. Charlottesville: University Press of Virginia, 1993, 77–108.
Johnston, F. Claiborne, Jr., "Federalist, Doubtful, and Antifederalist: A Note on the Virginia Convention of 1788." *The Virginia Magazine of History and Biography* 96 (1988): 333–44.
Kenyon, Cecilia M. "Men of Little Faith: The Anti-Federalists on the Nature of Representative Government." *William and Mary Quarterly*, 3d series, 12 (1955): 3–43.
Koch Adrienne, and Harry Ammon, "The Virginia and Kentucky Resolutions: An Episode in Jefferson's and Madison's Defense of Civil Liberties." *William and Mary Quarterly*, 3d series, 5 (1948): 147–76.
Kukla, John. "A Spectrum of Sentiments: Virginia's Federalists, Antifederalists, and 'Federalists Who Are For Amendments,' 1787–1788." *The Virginia Magazine of History and Biography* 96 (1988): 277–96.
Larson, John Lauritz. "'Bind the Nation Together': The National Union and the Struggle for a System of Internal Improvements." *The Journal of American History* 74 (1987): 363–87.

Lenner, Andrew. "John Taylor and the Origins of American Federalism." *Journal of the Early Republic* 17 (1997): 399–423.
Matthews, Albert. "Notes on the Proposed Abolition of Slavery in Virginia in 1785." Colonial Society of Massachusetts. *Publications* 6 (1904): 370–80.
McDowell, Gary L. "The Language of Law and the Foundations of American Constitutionalism." *The William and Mary Quarterly*, 3d series, 55 (1998): 375–98.
Oakeshott, Michael. "Rationalism in politics." In *Rationalism in Politics and Other Essays*. Indianapolis: Liberty Fund, 1991, 5–42.
O'Brien, Michael. Introduction to "The Social System of Virginia." In *All Clever Men, Who Make Their Way*. Edited by Michael O'Brien. Athens: University of Georgia Press, 1992, 228–30.
Onuf, Peter S. "'Empire for Liberty': Center and Peripheries in Post-Colonial America." Unpublished manuscript in author's possession.
———. "Federalism, Republicanism, and the Origins of American Sectionalism." In Edward L. Ayers et al. *All Over the Map: Rethinking American Regions*. Baltimore: Johns Hopkins University Press, 1996, 11–37.
———. "'To Declare Them a Free and Independent People': Race, Slavery, and National Identity in Jefferson's Thought." *Journal of the Early Republic* 18 (1998), 1–46.
Pasley, Jeffrey L. "'A Journeyman, Either in Law or Politics': John Beckley and the Social Origins of Political Campaigning." *Journal of the Early Republic* 16 (1996): 531–69.
Pole, J. R. "Representation and Authority in Virginia from the Revolution to Reform." *The Journal of Southern History* 24 (1958): 16–50.
Risjord, Norman K. "Virginians and the Constitution: A Multivariant Analysis." *The William and Mary Quarterly*, 3d series, 31 (1974): 613–32.
Schlesinger, Arthur M., Jr., "Keepers of the Jeffersonian Conscience." In *The Age of Jackson*. Boston: Little, Brown, 1953, 18–29.
Selby, John E. "Richard Henry Lee, John Adams, and the Virginia Constitution of 1776." *The Virginia Magazine of History and Biography* 84 (1976): 387–400.
Sloan, Herbert, and Peter Onuf. "Politics, Culture, and the Revolution in Virginia." *The Virginia Magazine of History and Biography* 91 (1983): 259–84.
"A Stately Duel in Virginia." *Life* 10 (1987): 66–74.
Tarter, Brent. "George Mason and the Conservation of Liberty." *The Virginia Magazine of History and Biography* 99 (1991): 279–304.
Tate, Thad W. "The Coming of the Revolution in Virginia: Britain's Challenge to Virginia's Ruling Class, 1763–1776." *William & Mary Quarterly*, 3d series, 19 (1962): 323–43.
Thomas, Robert E. "The Virginia Convention of 1788: A Criticism of Beard's *An Economic Interpretation of the Constitution*." *Journal of Southern History* 19 (1953): 63–72.
Turner, Charles W. "Virginia State Agricultural Societies[,] 1811–1860." *Agricultural History* 38 (1964): 167–177.
Washburn, Wilcomb E. "Law and Authority in Colonial Virginia." *Law and Authority in Colonial America*. Edited by George Athan Billias. Barre, Mass.: Barre Publishers, 1965, 116–35.
Wilson, Douglas L. "Jefferson and the Republic of Letters." *Jeffersonian Legacies*. Edited by Peter Onuf. Charlottesville: University Press of Virginia, 1993, 50–76.

Wren, J. Thomas. "The Ideology of Court and Country in the Virginia Ratifying Convention of 1788." *The Virginia Magazine of History and Biography* 93 (1985): 389–408.

Wright, Benjamin F., Jr., "The Early History of Written Constitutions in America." In *Essays in History and Political Theory in Honor of Charles McIlwain*. Cambridge: Harvard University Press, 1936, 344–71.

Theses and dissertations

Anderson, James LaVerne. "The Governors' Councils of Colonial America, A Study of Pennsylvania and Virginia, 1660–1776." Ph.D. dissertation. University of Virginia, 1967.

Beach, Rex. "Judge Spencer Roane: A Champion of States' Rights." M.A. thesis. University of Virginia, 1941.

Bigelow, Alden Griswold. "Hugh Blair Grigsby: Historian and Antiquarian." Ph.D. dissertation. University of Virginia, 1957.

Buckley, Thomas Edwin. "Church and State in Virginia, 1776–1787." Ph.D. dissertation. University of California, Santa Barbara, 1974.

Cheek, Lee. "Calhoun and Popular Rule: The Political Theory of the *Disquisition* and the *Discourse*." Ph.D. dissertation. Catholic University of America, 1999.

Daetweiler, Robert Chester. "Richard Bland, Conservator of Self-Government in Eighteenth-Century Virginia." Ph.D. dissertation. University of Washington, 1968.

Gage, Thomas Edgar. "The Established Church in Colonial Virginia, 1689–1785." Ph.D. dissertation. University of Missouri, 1974.

Giunta, Mary A. "The Public Life of William Branch Giles, Republican, 1790–1815." Ph.D. dissertation. Catholic University of America, 1980.

Golladay, Victor Dennis. "The Nicholas Family of Virginia, 1722–1820." Ph.D. dissertation. University of Virginia, 1973.

Hege, Elma Josephine. "Benjamin Harrison and the American Revolution." M.A. thesis. University of Virginia, 1939.

Hilldrup, Robert Leroy. "The Virginia Convention of 1776: A Study in Revolutionary Politics." Ph.D. dissertation. University of Virginia, 1935.

Hochman, Steven Harold. "Republicanism in Virginia and the Constitution of 1776." M.A. thesis. University of Virginia, 1970.

Lohrenz, Otto. "The Virginia Clergy and the American Revolution, 1774–1799." Ph.D. dissertation. University of Kansas, 1970.

Matthews, John Carter. "Richard Henry Lee and the American Revolution." Ph.D. dissertation. University of Virginia, 1939.

Mayer, David Nicholas. "Of Principles and Men: The Correspondence of John Taylor of Caroline with Wilson Cary Nicholas, 1804–1809." M.A. thesis. University of Virginia, 1982.

Rice, Philip Morrison. "Internal Improvements in Virginia, 1775–1860." Ph.D. dissertation. University of North Carolina, 1948.

Smith, Glenn Curtis. "Pamphleteers and the American Revolution in Virginia, 1752–1776." Ph.D. dissertation. University of Virginia, 1937.

Weeder, Elinor Janet. "Wilson Cary Nicholas, Jefferson's Lieutenant." M.A. thesis. University of Virginia, 1946.

Woodburn, Robert O. "An Historical Investigation of the Opposition to Jefferson's Educational Proposals in the Commonwealth of Virginia." Ph.D. dissertation. American University, 1974.

INDEX

Adams, John, 23, 25, 26, 33, 113, 117, 120, 135, 139, 180
Adams, John Quincy, 139
Adams, Samuel, 12, 22
Adams, Thomas, 47
Africa, 140
agricultural societies, 136, 180
Alabama, 183
"Algernon Sydney," 175, 176
Alien and Sedition Acts, 113, 120, 121, 123, 125, 126, 127, 129
Ambler, Jacquelin, 48
amendments (U.S. constitutional), 85
The American Quarterly Review, 207
"American System," 4, 152, 181–82
Anglican (Episcopal) Church/Establishment, 9, 15, 28, 34, 53, 54, 55, 69, 153, 156
Antifederalists/Republicans, 3, 83, 84, 85, 86, 87, 90, 94, 95, 98, 99, 100, 101, 102, 113, 114, 116, 118
apportionment, 11, 183, 184, 185, 186, 187, 189, 190, 191, 192, 193, 194, 196
Arator, 143, 149, 177, 179, 180
Article I, § 8 (U.S. Constitution), 170, 173
Article II (Articles of Confederation), 169
Article III (U.S. Constitution), 169, 174, 175
Article V (U.S. Constitution), 118
Articles of Confederation, 49, 50, 51, 61, 63, 64, 70, 89, 95, 115, 128
assumption of state debts, 61

Athens, 150, 154
Aurora, 121

Bache, Benjamin Franklin, 121
Baldwin, Briscoe G., 193
Bank of the United States, 119, 163, 170, 171, 172, 177, 178
Barbour, James, 126, 180
Barbour, Philip P., 193–94
Battle of Guilford Courthouse, 99
Biddle, Nicholas, 180
Bill of Rights, 86, 98, 122
Blackstone, Sir William, 140
Blair, John, 96
Bland, Richard, 2, 8, 16, 17, 18, 19, 20, 21, 23, 29, 33, 34, 46, 50, 54, 69, 114, 120, 129, 172
Board of Public Instruction, 154, 156
Bonus Bill, 167
Bonus Bill Veto, 166–67, 173, 181
Boston, 21
Boston Port Act, 12, 19, 21
Botetourt, Norborne Berkeley, Lord, 9–10
Braxton, Carter, 10, 25, 26, 27
Briton, 150
Brockenbrough, William ("Amphictyon"), 172
Brooke, Francis T., 169–70
Buffon, Georges-Louis Leclerc, comte de, 67
Burke, Edmund, 154, 195, 197
Burr, Aaron, 136
Byrd, William III, 46

Cabell, Joseph C., 137–38, 149, 152, 153, 154, 164, 166
Cabell, William H., 144, 150, 177–78
Caesar, Julius, 195
Calhoun, John C., ix, 176–77
carriage tax, 117–18
Carter, Landon, 11, 16, 17, 20, 26
Central College, 153
Charles I, 12
Charles II, 9, 18
Charles City County Resolutions, 184
Chesterfield Railroad, 166
church-state relations, 4
Christ, 195
Clay, Henry, 4, 152, 182
Clinton, De Witt, 146–47
Cocke, John H., 153, 180, 207
Coercive Acts, 19
Cohens v. Virginia, 174–75
Coke, Edward, 11
College of William and Mary, 26–27, 114, 137, 150, 151, 153
colonization, 180, 207
Commentaries on the Laws of England, 140
Committee of Safety, 10, 27
common law, 11, 18, 29
Common Sense, 10, 26
Commonwealth v. Cobbett, 169
compact theory of the U.S. Constitution, 87, 121–23, 129, 143, 170, 171, 175, 176, 181, 189, 197
Confederation, 49, 50, 60, 61, 61–62, 63, 64, 65, 69–70, 84, 88, 89, 90, 91, 92, 101, 117, 118, 126
Congress (Continental/Confederation), 8, 10, 12, 13, 20, 22–23, 32, 46, 49–50, 60–63, 84, 88, 91, 92, 100
Congress (federal), 97, 100, 113, 119, 124, 126, 129, 139, 142, 143, 152, 166, 167, 170, 171, 172, 173, 181, 187
Connecticut, 118, 139, 194
Connecticut Courant, 139
Constitution (British), 8, 10, 27, 30, 96, 97
Constitution (U.S.), ix, x, 1, 2, 3, 4, 83, 84–88, 90, 92, 94, 95, 96–97, 98, 99, 100, 101, 113–30, 144, 158, 163, 166–67, 168, 169–70, 171, 172, 173, 174, 175, 176, 177, 181

Construction Construed, and Constitutions Vindicated, 171
Cooke, John R., 190
Corbin, Francis, 89
Council, 11, 13–15, 17, 26, 32, 33–34, 46, 49, 59, 67, 184, 193, 196
county courts, 7, 14–15, 23, 31, 32–34, 52, 59, 185, 196
"crisis of republican government," 88–91, 100, 102
Cromwell, Oliver, 20
Crown (British), 10, 13, 17, 18, 25, 29, 31, 34, 50, 65, 155
Crozet, Claudius, 166

"The Danger Not Over" (by Edmund Pendleton), 141, 142, 143, 146
Dawson, John, 93–94
Declaration of Independence, 9, 24, 25, 186, 189
"A Definition of Parties" (John Taylor of Caroline), 143
Democratic Party, 137
Democrats, 167
Dew, Thomas R., 207
Dinwiddie, Robert, 16–17
divided power, 149
Doddridge, Philip, 192–93, 197
Dunmore, John Murray, Lord, 14, 22, 27, 31, 50, 59
Dutch, 91

East, 164–67, 70, 182–83, 185–97
education, public, 4, 60, 135–36, 150–57, 191, 194
elections (federal), 98
Electoral College, 136
Eleventh Amendment, 174, 175
embargo, 164
emigration right, 19, 20, 21, 22, 27–28, 31
English Civil War, 13
English Commonwealth, 18
Enlightenment, 60, 67–68
Enquirer, 135, 147, 149, 154, 157, 168, 171, 172, 173, 175, 182, 186
"An Enquiry into the Principles and Tendency of Certain Public Measures" (by John Taylor of Caroline), 118

faction, 141, 146–47
Farewell Address of George Washington, 135, 186
Federalism, 117, 125, 128, 129, 135, 142. 145, 146, 149, 168
The Federalist, 3, 116, 144–45, 167, 168, 176, 196
The Federalist #10, 89
The Federalist #39, 116, 176
Federalist Party, 135, 172
Federalists, 3, 83–90, 92, 94–102, 113–20, 124–29, 137–39, 140–41, 144, 145, 145, 148, 155, 164, 165, 168, 172, 173, 174, 180, 188
Filmer, Sir Robert, 195
First Amendment, 122
First Inaugural Address (Thomas Jefferson's), 121, 138
Fleming, William, 26
Fourth of July, 189
Fox, Charles James, 195
France, 24, 33, 113, 120, 140, 165, 192
French and Indian (Seven Years') War, 9, 12, 13, 17, 89
French Revolution, 186
"A Friend of the Union" (John Marshall), 172–73

Gabriel's Rebellion, 135, 140, 180
Gallatin, Albert, 121
General Assembly, 7, 13, 17–18, 21, 31, 32–33, 46–47, 48, 49, 52, 53, 54, 55, 56, 58, 59, 63, 64, 66, 67, 69, 89, 95, 97, 100–101, 102, 113, 116, 118, 119, 120, 121, 124, 125, 126–27, 128, 129, 139, 148, 151–52, 153, 155, 165, 174, 176, 178, 181, 182, 184, 187, 189, 190, 191, 196
General Assessment, 53–56
"General Welfare Clause," 167
George III, 11, 13, 18, 19, 20, 21, 22, 28, 30, 31, 45, 50, 136, 208
Germania (by Tacitus), 16
Giles, William Branch, 4, 139, 140, 154–57, 167, 182, 187, 188, 189, 196
Gilmer, Francis Walker, 4, 179, 180
Gilmer, George, 179
Gilmer, Peachy, 179–80

Glorious Revolution (1688), 8, 9, 13, 21, 25, 28
God, 17, 19, 20, 22, 171
Grayson, William, 84, 91, 94
Green, John W., 190–91
Grigsby, Hugh Blair, 94

Haitian Revolution, 190, 193
Hamilton, Alexander, 116, 117, 119, 120, 126, 136, 141, 144, 145, 149, 168, 177
Hamiltonian policy, 119
"Hampden" (Spencer Roane), 173–74, 175, 176
Hampden-Sydney College, 84
Harrison, Benjamin, 48, 62, 66, 67, 92, 95
Harvie, John, 63
Henderson, Richard H., 194
Henry VIII, 18
Henry, Patrick, 3, 8, 23, 25, 26, 45, 46, 47, 49, 50, 51, 53, 55, 56, 62, 63, 69, 84, 89, 90, 90–91, 93, 94, 97, 101, 102, 115, 116, 120, 121, 129, 136, 137
Henry's (1790) Resolution, 116, 118, 120, 122
Henrys, 208
Hobbes, Thomas, 195
House of Burgesses, 9–10, 11, 13–15, 17, 18, 20, 23, 24, 25, 30, 33, 34, 46, 47, 49, 54, 89, 94, 150, 193
House of Commons, 101
House of Delegates, 7, 23, 29, 31, 32, 33, 34, 47, 48, 49, 53, 54, 55, 56, 58, 59, 62, 24, 29, 70, 116, 124, 125, 129, 143, 183, 184, 193, 207
House of Hanover, 68
House of Representatives, 138
Hunter v. Martin, 174

immigration act (1792), 126, 127
Imperial Crisis, 4, 7, 8, 9, 10, 11, 13, 20, 54, 65, 117, 117, 118, 123, 130
Indians, 16, 31, 33, 51
inherited rights. *See* Rights of Englishmen
Inquisition, 56, 147
instrument of ratification, 87, 115

Jackson, Andrew, 164

James I, 10, 11, 18, 33
James River Canal Company, 166, 183
Jamestown, 26
Japanese, 196
Jay, John, 62–63, 145
Jay-Gardoqui Affair, 62
Jefferson, Thomas, ix, 1, 2, 3, 4, 8, 9, 10, 11, 12, 14, 19, 20–22, 24, 25, 26, 27, 28, 30, 31, 33, 34, 45, 47, 48, 49, 51, 53, 54, 55, 56–60, 62, 63, 64, 66, 67, 68–69, 113, 114, 117, 119, 120–25, 127, 129, 135, 136–37, 138–41, 142–44, 146, 149–50, 151–55, 157, 163, 164, 166–67, 168, 172, 173, 174, 175–76, 177–78, 179–80, 181–82, 183, 185–87, 188, 190, 192, 193, 195, 196–97, 207, 208
Jefferson Administration, 3
Joynes, Thomas R., 192
Judiciary Act of 1789, 168–69
"Julius Caesar" (by William Shakespeare), 195

Kanawha Road, 166
Kentucky, 49, 50, 51, 52, 63, 84, 123, 189, 195
Kentucky Legislature, 114, 120
Kerchival, Samuel, 185, 186
King, Rufus, 180

La Fayette, Marie Joseph Paul Yves Roch Gilbert du Motier, marquis de, 178
land tenures, 3, 53, 57, 69, 136, 150, 188–89
Latin, 150
Lee, Arthur, 12, 49
Lee, Henry, 63, 99, 127, 129
Lee, Richard Henry, 8, 11, 12, 22, 23, 25, 26, 48, 49, 50, 53, 54, 61, 62, 66, 67, 87, 88, 90, 91, 93, 95, 116, 178
Lee, Thomas Ludwell, 25, 26
Lees, 208
Leigh, Benjamin Watkins, 186–87, 188, 189, 190, 194–95, 196
Lincoln, Abraham, 208
Literary Fund, 152, 153
Locke, John, 98, 125
Lord's Prayer, 129

Louis XVI, 68
Louisiana Purchase, 165, 181
Loyalists, 67
Lycurgus of Sparta, 70

Madison, James, ix, x, 1, 3, 28, 30, 47, 48–49, 53, 54–57, 61–64, 65–66, 67, 68, 69–70, 84, 85, 86–87, 88–90, 91, 94–95, 96, 97, 98, 102, 114, 115, 116, 117, 119, 120–21, 124, 127, 136, 139, 142, 144–46, 148–49, 163, 164–65, 166–67, 173, 176–77, 178, 179, 180, 181, 182–83, 187, 193
Magna Carta, 21
Maier, Pauline, 10
Maine, 180
Marshall, John, ix, 4, 51, 63, 95, 97, 163, 168, 170–75, 187
Martin, Luther, 170
Martin v. Hunter's Lessee, 168, 170, 172, 174
Maryland, 50, 51, 170, 171, 173, 197
Mason, George, 8, 19, 24, 25, 26, 27, 28, 29, 30, 31, 47, 52, 53, 62, 66, 68, 85, 86, 87, 88, 89–90, 92, 94, 95, 96, 97, 98, 100, 102, 129, 140, 154, 183, 185, 189, 208
Mason, John Y., 187
Mason, Thomson, 13, 16, 19–20
Mason-Dixon Line, 50–51
Masons, 208
Massachusetts, 2, 9, 12, 22, 27, 90, 139
Matthew, Book of, 195
May 15, 1776 Resolutions, 1, 8, 23, 24
McCulloch v. Maryland, 170–71, 172, 173, 174, 175, 177
"Memorial and Remonstrance against Religious Assessments," 55, 127
Mercer, Charles, 153
Mercer, Charles Francis, 188, 191
Mercer, John Francis, 62
migration, 61
militia, 14–15, 29, 30, 32, 99–100, 135, 140
Mississippi River, 51–52, 62–63
Missouri Crisis, 164, 179, 180
Monroe, James, 61, 63, 90, 117, 139–40, 144, 145, 146–47, 148, 154, 163, 165, 166, 179, 187, 195, 196

Montesquieu, Charles Louis Secondat, baron de, 127–28
Monticello, 176, 179, 185, 195
Mount Vernon, 51

Napoleon, 163, 165
Napoleonic Wars, 150, 165
Nat Turner's Rebellion, 140, 207
Necessary and Proper Clause, 170, 172
New England, 9, 29, 84, 87, 92, 119, 120, 164, 165, 177
New Orleans, 164
New York, 146–47
Nicene Creed, 154
Nicholas, Anne Cary, 47
Nicholas, George, 4, 86, 102, 115, 116, 117, 118, 120, 121, 122, 123, 124, 125, 127, 130, 138, 141, 173
Nicholas, Robert Carter, 24, 27–28, 53, 193
Nicholas, Wilson Cary, 124, 129, 143–47, 152–54, 165, 196
Nicholas Family, 113
Niles, Hezekiah, 171
Niles' Weekly Register, 171
Norman Conquest, 11, 18
Normans, 150
North, 164
North Carolina, 113, 119, 172
North Carolina Legislature, 113
Northwest Territory, 91
Notes on the State of Virginia, 12, 57, 67, 122, 140, 180, 185, 186
Nullification, 177
Nullification Crisis, 208
Nullifiers, 176

Old Republicans, 142
Onuf, Peter S., ix

Page, John, 22, 25, 54
Panic of 1819, 170, 181
paper money, 89–90, 91
Parliament, 7, 9, 10, 12, 13, 16, 17, 18, 19, 20, 21, 22, 29, 31, 116, 117
Parsons' Cause, 17, 54
Pendleton, Edmund, 10, 23, 24–25, 46, 49, 53, 63, 67, 68, 92, 93, 94, 120, 141–43, 144, 145, 146
Penn, John, 143
Pennsylvania, 169, 197

Philadelphia Convention, 45, 51, 61, 63, 70, 83, 85, 86, 87, 88–89, 90, 95, 98, 120–21, 128, 168, 170, 172, 176
Piedmont, 167, 182, 190
Pistole Fee Controversy, 16
Ports Bill, 67
Portugal, 20
Powell, Alfred H., 194
press freedom, 29, 138
"Principles of '98," ix, 116, 176, 182, 208
Publius, 97, 126, 173, 176

Quid Schism, 142–43
quitrents, 60

Randolph, Edmund, 24, 25, 27, 28, 57–58, 61, 64, 67, 85–88, 95–97, 115, 116, 117, 118, 120, 121, 122, 124, 130, 138, 141, 142–43, 173, 190
Randolph, John, of Roanoke, 4, 139, 153, 155, 164, 165, 166, 183, 187, 188, 196–97
Randolph, Sir John, 11
Randolph, Peyton, 15, 46
Randolph, Thomas Jefferson, 179, 207
Randolphs, 46, 197, 208
Reconstruction, 179
religious liberty, 30
Report of 1800, 128, 148, 169, 171
representation, 98, 100, 101
The Republic (by Plato), 156
republicanism, 138, 140, 157, 167, 173, 177, 180, 187, 194, 195, 196
Republican Party, 137, 140, 142–43, 146, 168, 176
Republicans, 2, 3, 98–102, 113, 114, 116, 118, 120, 121, 124, 126, 127, 128, 129, 135, 136–37, 138–40, 141, 142–43, 144–47, 149, 157, 163, 164–65, 167, 168, 169, 170–71, 172, 173, 175, 176–77, 178, 180
reserved rights, 86
Revision of the Laws, 59–60, 69
"Revolution of 1800," 135, 137, 138, 144, 149, 150, 151, 157, 173, 181–82
Rhode Island, 172, 194
Richmond Junto, 135, 172

Rights of Englishmen (inherited rights), 9, 10–12, 18, 19, 20, 21, 22, 28, 29, 303, 98, 189–90
Ritchie, Thomas, 4, 135, 147–49, 157, 168, 171, 175, 176–77, 186, 187
Rives, William Cabell, 177–78
Roane, Spencer, 4, 168–70, 172–74, 175–77
Roman Catholicism, 68
Roman Republic, 92, 119, 129, 147–48, 150, 151
rotation in office, 29

Saxons, 14, 18, 20, 32, 33, 54
Senate (U.S.), 143
separation of powers, 11, 12–13, 14, 31
Shays's Rebellion, 91
slavery, 11, 14, 16, 18, 19, 20, 21, 27, 28, 53, 54, 57–59, 64, 92, 100, 118, 127, 135, 139–40, 143, 146, 148, 150, 156, 178, 180, 183, 184, 187, 190, 191–93, 194, 195–96, 197, 207, 208
Smith, John Augustine, 153
Smith, Meriwether, 24, 66
social compact, 4
Solon of Athens, 70
South, 84, 87, 88, 92, 100, 118, 119, 164, 168, 181, 182, 187
sovereignty, 3, 20, 28, 50, 56, 63, 70, 116, 118, 122, 127, 128, 129, 170, 171, 172, 174, 175, 176, 178, 181, 190, 194, 195, 197
Spain, 52, 60, 62, 63, 68, 140
Stalin, 146
Stamp Act, 10–11
Stamp Act Resolutions (Stamp Act Resolves) (Virginia), 10, 94, 120
states' rights, 3
Staunton Convention, 184, 186
Story, Joseph, 168–69, 170, 171–72
strict construction, 49–50
Stuart, Archibald, 47
suffrage requirements, 7, 11, 18, 25–26, 27, 28, 29, 33, 155–57, 184, 185, 186–87, 188, 189, 190, 192, 193, 194–95, 196
A Summary View of the Rights of British America, 10, 14, 19, 20, 21, 28, 30, 69, 120, 121, 143, 186

Supreme Court of the United States, 163, 167, 168–70, 172, 173, 174–75, 177, 178, 180, 197

tariffs (protective), 149, 163, 181–83
taxation, 10, 11, 16–17, 18, 29, 31, 48, 63, 64, 70, 100, 101, 150–51, 157, 170, 177, 180, 190–92
Taylor, John, of Caroline, 4, 114, 117–20, 121, 122, 124–25, 126, 127–28, 129–30, 135, 136, 139, 140–41, 142–50, 152, 163, 165, 166, 167, 171, 173, 176, 177, 179, 180, 181, 183, 189, 196
Taylor, Robert B., 189
Tazewell, Littleton Waller, 167–68, 182, 187
Tenth Amendment, 122, 126, 127, 169, 171, 175
Three-fifths Clause, 184, 186, 191, 192
Tidewater, 53, 57, 153, 165, 167, 184, 190, 208
Timon of Athens, 180
tobacco, 65–66, 165, 178
Townshend (Revenue) Act, 12
Treaty of Paris, 89
trial by jury, 11, 29
Tucker, Henry, 164
Tucker, St. George, 129, 137, 140
Twelfth Amendment, 136
Twenty-ninth of June, 189
Two-Penny Acts, 17–18
Tyler, John, Jr., 150–51, 182, 184, 185, 187, 208
Tyler, John, Sr., 3, 4, 150–51, 152–53
Tyranny Unmasked, 181

Union, ix
University of Virginia, 68, 114, 140, 153, 159, 179, 180, 181
Upshur, Abel P., 191–92, 196
U.S. Government, 117, 124

Vattel, Emmerich de, 127, 169, 175
vestries, 14–15
Virginia and Kentucky Resolutions of 1798, 3, 114, 116, 119, 121–22, 123–30, 139, 171, 173
Virginia Capitol, 66 ,67–68
Virginia charters, 10, 11, 17

Virginia colonial Constitution, 12, 15–16, 24, 87–88
Virginia Constitutional Convention of 1829–1830, 164, 186, 187–88
Virginia Constitution of 1776, 2, 7, 8, 13, 14, 15, 24, 25, 28, 30, 31, 32, 33–34, 45, 46, 64, 69, 97, 152–55, 183–92
Viriginia (May) Convention of 1776, 1, 4, 7, 8, 11, 16, 22, 23–24, 25, 27–29, 30, 32, 33, 54, 93, 141, 193
Virginia Court of Appeals, 168, 169
Virginia Declaration of Rights, 2, 7, 8, 11, 23, 24, 25, 27–28, 30, 33, 33–34, 53, 54, 55, 56, 57, 98, 190, 193, 194
Virginia Dynasty, 119, 136, 150, 157, 166, 179
Virginia Plan, 64, 85
Virginia Ratification Convention, x, 61, 70, 83, 85, 86, 87, 88, 89, 90, 91, 92, 93, 94, 95, 97, 98, 114, 115, 116, 117, 118, 119, 120, 121, 122, 124, 128, 129, 138, 141, 145, 151, 167, 168–69, 170, 172, 173, 76, 187, 188, 190, 192
Virginia Senate, 32, 33, 46, 68, 139, 185
Virginia Statute for Religious Freedom, 53, 68, 69–70, 97

viva voce voting, 7

Washington, D.C., 163, 165, 166
Washington, Bushrod, 172, 173–74
Washington, George, ix, 4, 45, 46, 51–52, 61–62, 69, 70
Washington, Henry Augustine, 9
Washington administration, 3

Walpole, Robert, 117
War of 1812, 152, 163, 164, 165, 177, 191
West, 163, 164, 165, 166, 167, 170, 182, 183, 184, 185, 187, 188, 189, 190, 191, 192, 193, 195, 196, 197
Western lands, 49–50, 51, 52
West Indies, 140
Westmoreland Association, 11
West Virginia, 49, 50, 52, 63, 84, 164, 165, 166, 197, 208
William III, 16–17, 28
Winchester Republican, 197
Wren Building, 137
Wythe, George, 64, 96, 140

Yankees, 180, 181
Yorktown, 58, 67

ABOUT THE AUTHOR

Kevin R. C. Gutzman is associate professor of American history at Western Connecticut State University. He received his Master of Public Affairs (1990) from the Lyndon B. Johnson School of Public Affairs at the University of Texas, his J.D. (1990) from the University of Texas School of Law, and his M.A. (1994) and Ph.D. (1999) in American history from the University of Virginia. Dr. Gutzman is author of *The Politically Incorrect Guide to the Constitution* (2007) and of "Lincoln as Jeffersonian: The Colonization Chimera," in *Lincoln Emancipated: The President and the Politics of Race*, ed. Brian Dirck (2007), 46–72; editor of John Taylor of Caroline, *Tyranny Unmasked* (forthcoming 2007) and *New Views of the Constitution of the United States* (forthcoming 2007); author of articles in *The Journal of Southern History*, *The Journal of the Early Republic*, *The Review of Politics*, *The Journal of the Historical Society*, *The Virginia Magazine of History and Biography*, and several other journals; writer of over seventy encyclopedia articles; and author of scholarly reviews of over eighty books, films, and exhibitions in all the leading history journals—as well as of numerous essays in popular publications. He was a featured expert in the documentary film *John Marshall: Citizen, Statesman, and Jurist*.